LIKE DEW BEFORE THE SUN

Life and Language in Northamptonshire

LIKE DEW
BEFORE THE SUN

Life and Language
in Northamptonshire

by Dorothy A Grimes

Reprinted with minor revisions January 1992
and September 1992 with map added
Reprinted December 1993

ISBN 0 9518496 0 3

Film set in Garamond, printed and bound by
Stanley L Hunt (Printers) Ltd, Midland Road
Rushden, Northamptonshire

Published privately by Mrs Dorothy A Grimes
27 Winchester Road, Delapre, Northampton NN4 8AZ
from whom copies may be obtained

Front cover illustration:
Abington Street, Northampton in 1906

Back cover illustration:
A village street in Benefield in the 1920s,
with sheep and straying lambs

Frontispiece:
Lovell and Eliza Eyles with their children:
Alfred, Rose, Mabel, Jim, Arthur and Albert,
in about 1887. Lovell Eyles was a small holder
and lived in Far Cotton, Northampton

'I want to say to you
the ancient things
as are done away with now'
William Burt, shepherd, of Harpole

To my husband and all the friends
who helped make this book

CONTENTS

FOREWORD

Northamptonshire is central in England, and as such shares features of life with north and south, east and west. It remains an agricultural county, it carries the spine road of the first modern motorway, it contained the largest part of a leading industry, the boot and shoe trade, it suffered some of the greatest depression in both industry and agriculture. In speech it varies widely from north to south. In the north you might just still hear the northern short vowel in 'pass', but for the most part it lengthens the vowel. In 'thunder' you can hear both the northern 'u' like the vowel in 'pull' and the southern vowel as in 'come', in 'furrow' the main vowel comes in three varieties across the county, and the vitality of the people perhaps stems from the variety of speech and activity within the county. Struggle and hardship always seems to promote a great deal of philosophy, strength of character, wisdom, and also humour in those people who have to suffer. Northamptonshire has had its share of these, and from the troublesome times has come a great body of remembered tales, some of them told in later life by the people who suffered them earlier, others retained by those who remember the older folk, and a great many collected and stored by Dorothy Grimes who here gives us a fascinating cross-section of her material.

It can be said at once that the matter of this book represents only a part of the richness that has come into Mrs Grimes' total collection. It is probably true, too, that new material put before the readers will call forth in many of them memories that Mrs Grimes has not yet heard. It is perhaps one of the most joyous results of reading a collection such as this that we have our minds stirred to think of things we know and have lost in our minds for years. For others, the tales of such a recent past may be an absolute astonishment. Modern living has quite blotted out a good deal of the daily toughness that used to be taken for granted.

The two watersheds of the twentieth century must be the two world wars of 1914–18 and 1939–45. At one time it seemed that the 1914–18 war was the root cause of all the social changes that convulsed the country after the placidity of the Victorian era. Mrs Grimes' informants can tell us that the latter war was equally important in propelling life forward into a new way. As we get further away from it, the second war can be seen in perspective as bringing about undreamed-of alterations to rural and working class life.

We have in this volume the distillation of direct reporting, memory and also of some of the written records that illuminate the bygone way of life in the county. The idea of what makes history has so changed in the past few years that the views and lifestyle of the ordinary people are thought to be the real foundation of modern living, not really related to the political lists of parliamentary decisions and political change until they are put beside the effects at the lowest level.

This is only in part true, for what has been settled in battles and in parliament has in most cases been the cause of change at some time later for the ordinary people. What Mrs Grimes is doing here is putting before us the scene, and we can then see how this change was often the result of government decisions. One of the great effects upon life of the 1870 Education Act and the ones that followed it was upon the use of child labour and the continual broadening of horizons under the education system for the children of illiterates. Short term effects for some families were disaster, for others there were long term benefits, but the old style historical points of importance are what often brought about the new style local historical points of emphasis. Changes in the Poor Law, the Corn Laws, the Education Acts, are heightened in importance when we can know their effects upon the lives of the people who suffered daily experience of the changes. There is lots of memory here to relate activities in the towns and villages to those central events.

Love and care in collection, insight, and sympathy in the sifting, are the skills that are important when amassing this kind of material, so as to take a broad view of the life of the people in a whole county. Under her separate topics Mrs Grimes has skilfully sorted the strands that have been woven over lifetimes.

Most of those who know any of these storytellers or their contemporaries will want to recall their own tales of similar sort. My own work in Northamptonshire over thirty years ago was to meet and talk to these very people, culling some of the same tales, and I have often told sufferers from warts of the cure *I* heard in Warmington; take a black snail, rub it on the warts and pierce the snail with a living thorn, leaving the snail on the bush to wither and die along with the wart.

One typical aspect of Northamptonshire life is to put behind you the sadness and trouble, and remember the joy and triumph, and there is plenty of that too.

Northamptonshire has had its mixed agriculture, and then its own speciality in industry, the leather trade. Northampton people survived by feet, other people's feet. The processes of the leather trade in boots and shoes are themselves full of fascination and give rise to tales of their own. Mrs Grimes has not let these escape and we have a full picture of these activities.

The life of the people in church and chapel, their seasonal activities, their children's games, all provoked stories well worth the preserving, and are nicely sorted for us here. The people speak for themselves through Mrs Grimes.

Enormously valuable is the glossary of the County's words that appears here. So satisfying too is the research Mrs Grimes has done from her *English Dialect Dictionary* and the *Oxford English Dictionary*. It is useful to have some sort of continuing picture of the local vocabulary. 'Does a word still exist that was common in Victorian times?'–the answer is often here. Once again, readers will produce their own favourites that they heard in the past or still use today that do not appear (mine was *'gilt'*–a young sow– the common word in south Northants, but which I know in the north of the County used to be *'yeld'*–a Scandinavian word). The patchwork of words that makes up a county's wordhoard has so many influences, some coming in from each direction. Mrs Grimes has not failed to find the Scandinavian influence that came in from the north a thousand years ago, leaving the strong mark of its boundary against King Alfred's Saxons in the placenames and vocabulary [the boundary of the Viking Danelaw]. This book unites parts of so many subjects that made up the life of the ordinary people; it should whet the appetite of the reader to look more widely at other records of the County.

The story of Northamptonshire's past is incomplete without a reference to sad, mad John Clare, the brilliant poet who hardly came to the fore for many a decade because he wrote so much of the local speech into his poems. Mrs Grimes' chapter on Clare, quoting from the *Shepherd's Calendar* and his other works, summarises beautifully his life and the background in which he lived. The fens were not far from his home, but his poetry recalls so much of the rolling middle landscape of England, and Clare deserves to be given a section to himself in any work on the County.

A comprehensive selection such as this puts together a wonderful memory of the preceding age which could not envisage the television and the video. We have some memories of the first radios and the magic of that particular box. The wave of technology washes into the homes that were rather dark and lacking in power until the great rural electrification of the nineteen-fifties. This is the newer-yet revolution, that will be seen in the future, no doubt, as evolution.

I have seen this work grow from early days; Mrs Grimes and I have corresponded over it and she and her family have, I know, worked and worried over its shape and presentation. A book such as this is not the effort of only one person, and I know how she is grateful for the backing and loyalty of a host of friends, many of whom, long dead, appear in her text. None of this would have been any use without her personal determination and devotion, which I for one admire enormously.

STANLEY ELLIS
University of Leeds
1986

Acknowledgments

I gratefully acknowledge the help given in turn by the following people.

Miss M Arnold, Local History Librarian, Northamptonshire Studies Collection, and other staff, Central Library, Northampton; Mr T Cooper, Hardingstone; Mr S Ellis, Honorary Fellow, formerly Senior Lecturer in English Language and Staff member, The Institute of Dialect and Folk-life Studies, University of Leeds; Mr A Fookes, Great Billing; Mr R G Foulkes, Warden, The University

Centre, Northampton; Mrs M Hamer, Bedford; Mrs H Hammond, Publications Assistant, Northamptonshire Libraries; Mr V A Hatley, Northampton; Miss J Hodgkinson, Keeper of Social History, Abington Park Museum, Northampton; Mr B Lewis, formerly Midlands Development Officer, English Folk Dance and Song Society (EFDSS); Mr J Munro, former County Leisure and Libraries Officer, and Editor, Northamptonshire Libraries Publications; Dr K C Phillipps, Senior Lecturer in English, University of Leicester; Dr I Russell, University of Sheffield, academic adviser to EFDSS; Mr S F Sanderson, The Harold Orton Fellow, formerly Senior Lecturer and Director, The Institute of Dialect and Folk-life Studies, University of Leeds; Mr J Stafford, former Editor, Northamptonshire Libraries Publications; Stanley L Hunt (Printers) Ltd, Midland Road, Rushden especially to Mr David Hunt for his invaluable guidance; Miss J Swann, formerly Keeper, Shoe Collection, Central Museum, Northampton; Mrs V L Taylor, County Librarian; Mr R Thomson, Oundle; The late Mr J Thornton, formerly Head of the Boot and Shoe Department, College of Technology, Northampton; Dr R Whittaker, Shoe and Allied Trades Research Association, Kettering; Dr P Wright, Honorary Senior Lecturer and Fellow in English Dialect Studies, University of Salford.

Editors of the following newspapers: *The Chronicle and Echo,* Northampton; *The Northants Post; The Northamptonshire Evening Telegraph; The Harborough Mail; The Banbury Guardian; The Bedfordshire Journal; The Milton Keynes Express; The Daventry Express; The Stamford Mercury.*

BBC Radio Northampton; Hereward Radio; Radio Nene Valley; BBC Radio 4.

The late Mr R Wykes of Spratton, who knew well over a hundred dialect words, and Mrs Wykes; the late Mr J Davis, Northampton; Audrey Smith, Grendon; Miss B Adkins, Banbury; Mrs L Smith who still works in her native Little Houghton. All these friends helped me over a number of years.

I must also thank Miss Deacon, Little Houghton; Mr R Eady, Moulton; Mr D Flower, Wellingborough; Mrs S Glenister, Australia formerly of Banbury; Mrs M Hamp, Northampton; the late Mr R and Mrs Key, Newnham; Mrs B March, Kettering; Miss M Nash, Northampton; Mrs J Palmer, Earls Barton; Mr D Parker, Wolverton; Pury End Historical Society; Mr Rowlett, Broughton; Mr H Saunders, Eastcote; Mr R Shillman, Rushden; Mrs B Slack, Pury End; Mr M Tebbutt, Northampton; Mrs G White, Northampton; Mr F White, Northampton; Lt-Col Yates,

Guildford; the late Miss K Coales and also Mr C Howlett, Market Harborough and the late Mr H Grimes of Stamford. Many others will find something of their own in the book, often with their names, and to all of them I am very grateful. A more complete list of contributors is on pages 346 and 347.

Our whole family, especially our son Alan, was called upon at one time or another, to help me come to decisions in the shaping of the text, and my husband compiled the index and had to live with the book for a very long time. Uncomplainingly he gave me time to myself and transported me and my tape-recorder the length and breadth of the south-east Midlands. I was grateful for his technical skills with tape-recorder and camera, and his wide knowledge of the town and the countryside that we and all who have helped us love so much.

Lovely old photographs bring the text to life. I gladly acknowledge the help of a number of friends and by Northamptonshire Libraries, who let me choose freely from their large collection.

I have tried to trace all copyright owners of photographs taken from Northamptonshire Libraries Local Studies Collection. I acknowledge the copyright of any which I have been unable to trace.

So many people helped me in my research that it is impossible to name them all. I hope they will accept my grateful thanks.

Dorothy Grimes

Introduction

One of my earliest memories is of a day when I was three years old, playing in the narrow *jitty* at the back of Euston Road, Far Cotton, Northampton and suddenly seeing my father coming home from work, though it was neither dinner-time nor tea-time. He had been called out on strike. The year was 1926.

He did not come out willingly. He had seen far harder times in his twenty-eight years of life–poverty, the trenches, unemployment. Now, like many other Far Cotton men, he worked 'down the Shed' –the LMS engine sheds. He never really enjoyed his work in the office, but he stayed where he was and kept us properly fed and clothed and housed during the Depression and the war and for long after that. Our meals were sometimes frugal, our clothes had to be worn as long as possible and our house was icy cold on winter mornings until the fire burnt up, and by then, as I well remember, it was time for my father to go to work and for me to set off for school.

Yet most of us who were children at that time would say we had a good childhood. It was a safe time. We played in the streets and *jitties* or out in the fields, and our careful mothers had no cause to fear for us. I was an only child, but both my grandmothers and my grandfather lived nearby and so did a good number of rather elderly aunts and uncles, who all loved and admonished me in the old working-class way, their speech full of sayings and dialect words. I grew up knowing about the past fifty years and more as they talked about their childhood in Victorian times and their own grandparents, who nearly all lived in the country.

People talked together far more than we do now and sang together as well, so we children were rich in the oral tradition, whatever else we lacked.

It surprises me that in this conservation-conscious age so little has been done to preserve this part of our heritage. Most people are more than willing to talk, especially about themselves, as if they are starved of the opportunity by the television, the car and pop-music. What they have to say is usually interesting, especially if they talk about the things they know best–their homes and families, their work or their past life. How they speak is interesting as well. Here in Northampton and the County, as elsewhere, the *sound* of local speech survives, but dialect words and phrases and most of the old sayings are disappearing *like dew before the sun*.

A good few are recorded in this book, in which people from town and county talk about their own lives in their own words. They first responded with enthusiasm to my letters in newspapers throughout Northamptonshire and in bordering counties. Readers will notice that the response from some places was very good, from others less so. I hope that this book may encourage some of them to record their own memories. But hurry–time is running out.

PEOPLE AT HOME

Courtship and Marriage

'In wreath and fall'

Courtship rituals were pleasant, the boy and girl standing and talking, then walking decorously home together from work or choir practice or the *Bunny Run*–Abington Street, Northampton. After a time there would be an invitation to tea and then an unhurried series of welcoming signals between the families. 'Rushing into things' was not encouraged, except in wartime, but if the couple continued 'going steady', the time came when the young man had to prepare himself to speak to the girl's parents and perhaps have to answer some important questions before they agreed and she agreed.

Now that they were engaged they were happily aware of a new standing in the community. They were *chap and gal,* preparing for a marriage that would be loving and life-long.

Chastity before the wedding and fidelity within it was expected, though there was often little open discussion about this within the family. One just learned by what from time to time was said. One thing that was said was *'She's about as much good as a*

Caption: This poignant photograph from Peterborough was taken from a glass slide. NRO

cracked pancheon'. Most homes had one of these large earthenware vessels for making wine or preserving eggs. A cracked one was no good at all. Sometimes an unlucky girl was *'left hanging in bellropes'* by a young man who delayed the wedding even after the banns had been called.

The outward symbol of purity was the bride's white dress and *wreath and fall*, the head-dress of flowers and the veil. In general no girl who had fallen from grace or who was marrying for a second time would dream of wearing white. It was often a very simple celebration, with little money to spare for luxuries. My grandmother's wedding in 1905 was a notable exception. She was a single girl, living in poverty with her little son, but it seems, from the elegant photograph below on facing page that the family wanted to put a bold face on it. The reception was often at home, the flowers grown in the garden. There was often no honeymoon, especially in wartime, and no home of their own till later.

'We inherited a four-poster bed. The base was wood slats with straw palliasses on top. There was a feather bed (mattress) made by baking fowls' feathers in the oven in paper bags, stripping the quills of down and putting the feathers in a large bag—very warm and comfy.'   *Mrs E Wood*, Weedon Lois.

Childbirth

'They bring love with them'

When a woman *fell* [became pregnant], a number of old beliefs came to the fore.

She's carrying all round so it'll be a boy.

Our gal's overdue and all in front so I expect it's another girl.

Caption above left: Abington Street, Northampton in 1906. In the cobbled road are a tram, a hansom cab, a horse-drawn cart and a delivery boy's handcart. NL Below left: The wedding of Annie Rainbow of Far Cotton, Northampton and Dick Littlemore, a Boer War veteran from London, in 1905. AC

You're eating for two, my duck, so have anything you fancy, else when the *bab's* born, he'll cry till he gets it.

Don't look at anybody *dibby,* else the bab'll be *dibby* as well.

Babies were nearly all delivered at home by the local midwife. Betty Vincent (1801–1878) of Finedon used to declaim the following when the birth was over.

> Here's to the cock that treads the hen,
> Here's to the cock that treads her again,
> Here's to the hen that never refuses,
> And lets the cock tread her whenever he chooses.
>
> From *Finedon Revealed*
> by *Councillor John L H Bailey*, Finedon.

There is no record of what any of the mothers said.

My grandmother used to tell us about her aunt, Comfort Cox of Malting Yard, Hardingstone, who had her family in the 1870s and 80s.

> 'She had a lot of children and after each one was born she used to sit up in bed and ask for a *haunch* of bread and cheese and half a pint of ale.' *Mrs Rose Pearce*, Northampton.

> 'The day I was born at Great Billing, September 28th 1891, so my mother told me, my grandmother left her alone all day with half a pint of porter and some bread and cheese by the bed and went off to the gleaning field.'
> *Mrs. Lucy Linnett (née Tipler)*, Great Billing.

When Mrs. Pearce's own daughter gave birth, forty years on, it was a different story.

> 'I would have given anything for a cup of tea, but Nurse Adnitt would only let me have bread and milk. I had to stay in bed for ten days with my legs tied together in case I haemorrhaged.' It was a normal delivery. *Mrs Alice Rainbow*, Northampton.

A little publicised belief, whispered from mother to daughter, was that the most virile men tended to have daughters. The father of a baby boy born in the 1950s was told that he had not *proved his manhood.* There was general approval for a *pigeon pair,* a boy and girl. There would then be no need to *fill the house with boys, trying for a girl.*

Some of the old words, sayings and beliefs survive to this day. He *features* his father. Is she *about* some teeth? She's got a bit of cradle-cap [scurf, now more usually dandruff]. *When they're little they're arm-ache, but when they're older they're heart-ache.* Loveliest of all–*They bring love with them.*

The outlook was bleak for a baby *come by the light of the moon* [illegitimate] and his mother, unless, as often happened, the family would look after them.

'A girl said *"There's forgiveness for the first,* but I had to go in the workhouse for the second".'

Mrs Dorothy Warren, Yardley Gobion.

Within living memory, stillborn babies were buried with almost secret ritual.

'She never lost a mother, but if the baby was stillborn she left it in the house till twilight, whatever time of year it was. Then she came back, wearing a long black cloak, and went with the sexton to bury the baby in unconsecrated ground.

Mrs Bedford, Cogenhoe, talking of a midwife at Brafield.

I want to say to you the ancient things as are done away with now. In that time [between the wars] if there was a stillborn baby, I used to have to bury that little infant after ten o'clock at night. The midwife had to bring the little casket to the churchyard gates, and I felt sorry for them old ladies and I said 'This is going to stop. I shall fetch that little infant and take this out of your hands.'

Mr William Burt, village man [sexton], Harpole.

Stillborn babies were buried at dusk in a corner of the churchyard with only the sexton and the midwife in a black shawl present. The older girls, about twelve to fourteen, used to carry the little white coffin, and afterwards went to the bereaved parents' house, where they were each given a little bag containing a penny and some sweets. Their mothers told them not to refuse this as it would give offence. Described to *Mrs L Firth* of Market Harborough by her aunt from Naseby.

A *kell* [caul] covering the head of a newborn baby was thought to be lucky and to protect anyone who possessed it from drowning. An egg was also thought to bring luck.

'When a newborn baby was brought into a house for the first time, it was always given an egg for luck. The contents of the shell were blown out and the shell itself painted, blue for a boy, pink for a girl, and tied round with ribbon.'

Mr Roy Payler, Kislingbury.

Lowbelling

'You're not going to watch that kind of thing'

Inevitably some marriages ran into trouble. Kindly souls would try to help the couple and their children, but others were unforgiving, and from time to time there occurred a frightening demonstration of public censure. In Northampton it was known as *tin-canning* or *tin-kettling* and was carried out up to 1936 and perhaps later. It was called *banging-out* at Piddington and *lew-belling* in the south and south-west of the county. The word is *lowbelling*—both elements of the word mean 'make a loud noise'.

The Northampton Mercury of May 24, 1895 reported a *tin-kettling* at Blisworth in censure of the conduct of an unmarried couple. Two hundred demonstrators were put to flight by two police officers and fled, throwing their cans and kettles over a hedge and leaving two effigies lying in the road.

Mr George Freeston, Blisworth.

'While I lived at Middleton Cheney I saw one of the last performances of *lewbelling*. An effigy of the guilty person was carried at the head of a procession, followed by a crowd of people beating washing-*trays* [tubs] saucepans, old tins— anything to make a noise, plus, of course, the shouting. After being paraded round the village the effigy would be burnt on the green. This was in 1909. The custom died out in the first world war.'

Mr Arthur Seckington, Greatworth.

'This was done when a couple were caught in a compromising situation. The young bloods of the village used to make an effigy and parade round the village banging tin trays, cans and buckets and stop outside the culprit's house and give a concert. Yes, I've seen that done. I should think the last time I saw that done I should be about eight or nine.' [Before WW1].

Mr Percy Foster, Pury End.

'It was frightening. Our mother used to keep us in and lock the

door, otherwise they would push these brooms into the house. She used to say "You're not going to watch that kind of thing".'
Mrs Rose Foster, Pury End.

The attack was organised secretly and on the first night the 'marked house' was surrounded by the *tin-kettlers.* If the noise they made failed to evict the offender they came again, and if this failed, the third night was the 'big bang'. A fire was lit and frenzied dancing continued into the night. By the next day the culprit had usually fled.

I well remember an incident in Stoke Road in the 1920s. My parents forbade me to go, but I went, and still remember the woman's frightened face lit up by the flames, peeping through the curtains.

In 1936 there was another confrontation between the tin-kettlers and the police. This time the mob scrambled up a bank and over a hedge. *Mr George Freeston,* Blisworth.

At Newnham the French wife of one of the villagers was lowbelled because she was unpopular. (Information from *Mr Robert Key,* Newnham.)

A Rushden lady told of an incident 'just over the border in Huntingdonshire' in which tin-kettling took place at the funeral of a much-disliked old man. Pans and trays were thrown on the coffin. The ritual more often took place at night and the wretched couple then had to live through the next day in the knowledge that it would begin again as darkness fell, and yet again for a third night. After this the effigies were sometimes ritually drowned or burnt. It was not uncommon for one or both of the victims to leave the village.

THE TIN-CANNERS OF BROUGHTON

I don't know how the custom started. Perhaps it was once a way of driving gypsies away. Only men took part and no one was allowed to move until the church clock struck midnight. Then we could all look out of our windows and watch these muffled figures banging tin cans. They would stop outside the fishmongers for example and shout insults – 'How much rotten fish have you sold today?' and so on at different places round the village. The council tried to stop it once – said it was just a stupid custom. The police were waiting but all they did was walk along with the men, laughing. They had to take names and addresses, though and all these people were summoned and fined. But they held a dance and that raised enough money to pay all the fines and there was enough left over to provide a day out for all the old people. The tin-canning went on. They couldn't stop it.

Mrs Rose Clark, Barton Seagrave.

Children

'. . . and there was the smell of the scrubbed table and hot toast with home-made lard on it'

'Our mother had eleven children–there was always two as couldn't walk. She never went out, never had time, only to Chapel on Sundays and take all the children with her. After we'd had *weer* [our] dinner, we all had to sit quiet round the table so Mam and Dad could have forty winks. If anybody moved or giggled, our Dad'd clout the one as sat next to him, whether it was that one or not. We had to go to bed at six o'clock at night, so our Mam and Dad could make *weer* clothes with us out the road [out of the way].

I could never learn much at school. Sometimes Dad'd come to the school house door and say to the governess, 'Can Rose come and catch the pony?' Nobody else could catch it when it was loose in the field. Mabel (her sister) was cleverer than me. She could sing and she wanted to learn to play the harmonium like we had at chapel. She kep on about it till our Dad got one for her. He had been born at Moulton, and every so often, Mam and Mabel would walk there from Far Cotton so she could play the little harmonium at the chapel there. Mam used to hold her hand all the way there and back.

Mabel and me had to walk to Hardingstone every morning before we went to school to sell milk. We carried the milk-cans on a yoke across *weer* shoulders and in the winter we used to

---

Caption: Mrs Harriet Blason of Little Houghton with her children, Alfred and Doris, in the early years of the century. Doris learned from her grandmother the folksong 'False Young Men'. Mrs Loretta Smith, Little Houghton.

have to break the ice before we could put the measure in. There was an old lady lived at one of the thatched cottages as you go into the village. (They are still there.) We called her Moushy Sharman because she was little, like a mouse, and never had no teeth. She used to say 'Come in, moy dearsh and have shome tea and toasht.' *Mrs Rose Pearce*, Northampton (1875-1960).

'I went to a private school, Miss Risby's. We used to parade to St Michael's Church. I can remember horse races on the Race-course. One of the girls was driven to school in a brougham by a coachman from her home in Castilian Street, where the YWCA is now.' *Mrs E Carpenter*, Northampton (1890s).

'We lived at Maidwell. One day we were taken out of school to see a motor-car go by.'
Mrs Glanister, Northampton (1900s).

'Once a week we older girls went to the vicarage, where the vicar's two daughters taught us to knit and sew. We had some happy times there.

The one o'clock dinner bell was rung each weekday on one of the church bells, by Miss Parker. Everybody called her Lizzie. We children were allowed to go into the belfry with her, so long as we wore a hat. I can see her now. She was elderly and wore a black straw hat summer and winter, and her long black skirt swept the ground. She always wore a crocheted shawl which was meant to be black, but with age it had a greenish tinge. Horses were shod in the blacksmith's shed on Mondays and Fridays. The floor is wood cobbles, softer and warmer to the horses' feet when shoeless. You could get lots of jobs done there, such as mending saucepans and kettles and getting milk-pans soldered. We had to fetch milk from the farm every morning so almost everyone had a milkcan. The doctor was driven into the village every day from Wollaston by pony and trap. You could always see where he was in the village and ask him to come to your house. Then you had to walk to Wellingborough to the evening surgery to collect what he had prescribed. There was no National Health Service. You paid for everything as you collected it.

On Wednesdays and Saturdays a carrier came. You could give him your order and money and he would be there again in the afternoon with the goods.

In those days there was no water laid on, no gas or electricity and no playing round the village at night. We were quite happy to be at home with both our parents, sitting by a real fire. There was always plenty of toast. I doubt if nowadays children know what a toasting-fork looks like.'

Mrs L Papworth, Grendon, early 1900s.
Her father was a mole-catcher.

'I can remember being in the pram between Ashton and Roade, and my father coming out of the railway where he worked, to see the baby. My next memory is of him carrying me round the lane at the back of our house and picking me a dog-rose.

When I was six my mother was ill and I was fetched to stay with my grandmother in Roade and I remember how grandma walked up the three hills between the villages from side to side, zig-zag fashion, carrying her umbrella.

My brother and I used to go down the fields mushrooming quite early in the morning. They were gorgeous in flavour and texture. Today's are like eating leather. Mother used to take us gleaning in the holidays to get food for our hens, and how we enjoyed it, in spite of sore ankles. We spent the whole day gleaning, taking food and a bottle of cold tea with us. We used to go blackberrying, usually in lovely autumn sunshine. Sticking was nice too, gathering loose wood blown down in gales.

We always kept a pig and some hens and as my father was a good gardener, growing all vegetables and having fruit trees and bushes, we were almost entirely self-supporting. Mother made jam and pickles, bottled plums, damsons etc. and my father roped his onions and made pits for carrots, swedes, turnips and potatoes. The hens' eggs were preserved in waterglass in a large *pancheon.*

At Ashton we always had day-school and Sunday School treats, with games and races. We had country dances in the school at Christmas. To this day I know we had egg sandwiches at the summer treats and potted meat in winter.'

Miss Jessie Curtis, Northampton (1900s).

'On a warm sunny day with no wind, my mother used to unpick the mattress cover, which was made of ticking, and wash the feathers, spreading them out to dry on the henhouse roof.' *Mrs. Alice Rainbow,* Northampton (1898–1980).

'They took us in at school when we were four years old and we left on the day we were thirteen. We went to the headmaster and said "If you please, Sir, have I made me times?" and he looked at the register and said "Yes. I wish you all the best and hope you get on well," and he'd shake hands. But if you hadn't made your times they could compel you by law to stop another twelve months.

We had an Inspector come, a man called Harrison, and he used to come in 'ansom cab—we could hear the bell ringing as he come down the lane. The Attendance Officer was a man called Brown—he'd got a face as red as a turkey-cock and he was a retired sergeant in the police force. Once I'd bin away and he said to me "Where were you?" and I said "Please Sir, I had to mind the baby" and he said "The baby must mind itself. If you stop away from school your father and mother'll have to go to Northampton and it'll cost them five shillings."

There used t' be a man come with 'and-truck and he used to shout all the way up the village

> Kippers, kippers, tuppence a pair,
> They are to eat and not to wear

and every Good Friday an old woman called Eliza Bond, she was a woman of sixty years, she used to come with a great big clothes-basket full of hot cross buns, and under her white apron she'd got a money-bag tied round her.

She charged 'a'p'ny [a halfpenny] for a bun, and she used to come in and set the basket on the floor and say the same thing every year.

> One a penny poker, two a penny *tungs* [tongs]
> Three a penny fire-shovels, hot cross buns.

At that time we weren't s' many in family as we were eventually, but she always said "How many d'y'want, Mag?" So mother said "Well, Liza, I can't afford *above* six." That were thruppence. So Liza said "Well, there's the six—thruppence, and one in extra" so she give my mother seven.

(Many cottages had only open fires, with no means of baking, so Mrs Burt could not bake buns herself.)

When I was a boy, big people like Earl Spencer used to have a

---

Caption above right: Hardingstone Women's Institute line up before an outing in one of F and E Beedens' local buses. NL.

Below right: A group of children in Meadow Lane, Little Houghton, in the 1900s. The house, built of local limestone with ironstone at the corners, contained three dwellings, two downstairs and one above. Photographer, Mr Knight of Olney. Mrs Loretta Smith, Little Houghton.

sale in the woods, and people as were clever wi' the *billuck* [bill-hook] and wire, they made faggots and sold 'em thruppence each. A man come from Pattishall with two great big horses and a great load o' these faggots.

The big boys, they used to say to anybody as had got these faggots "Please will you give us one?" and if they said "No", they used to mutter as they turned away

> If yer dunt give us one, we shall take two,
> The better f'r us and the wuss f'r you.'
> *Mr William Burt,* Harpole (1899–1985).

'I was born at Brafield in 1918, the youngest child of five. As soon as I could carry a bucket of water, my job was to help fetch it from a tap about seventy yards away. All the water had to be carried into the house and out again. On Sunday evenings we had to carry about thirty gallons in, ready for washday, in buckets, baths and earthenware *pancheons.* The copper fire was kept going with sticks.

Mother then washed, scrubbed, boiled, rinsed twice, mangled, dried and then ironed for the family of seven, also four old people. I used to collect the washing from an old woman who lived in one room. I held my breath as I went in, said thank you, dived out of the door and let out my breath. The smell was dreadful, the bundle was full of fleas and had to be dropped into a bucket of water the moment I got it home.

Monday mornings were always busy. I had to go to one end of the village to collect skim milk for four old people at a penny a pint and to the other end to buy new milk for three people at threepence a pint. On Saturday I would collect butter from the farm for someone for one and threepence a pound. My reward was just a saying– *You'll have a wife when you're married.*

In winter the bed was warmed with a copper warming-pan. Many a time I have melted ice on the roof of the attic with my candle. The roof was about one foot above my head as I lay in bed. (The bedroom was open to the sloping roof, with no ceiling.)

There were ten houses in the End, nearly all old people, so I earned money doing errands, cleaning hen-places out, sticking, to save coal. From ten years old I would get a job on the farm in the summer holidays, for twopence an hour. All the money I earned went towards clothes and boots, with one day's treat up to London to see the sights and go to the Zoo. The first bike I had had no saddle, brakes, tyres or tubes. You just pushed on down the hill and hoped for the best. About ten of us boys had a lot of fun with that old bike.'   *Mr Ted Hollowell,* Cogenhoe.

This account shows how hard rural life was. Mr Hollowell married in 1944 and his wife's account shows that life was still hard. This is not a child's eye view, but makes a very interesting comparison.

'In 1944, when newly-wed, we thought we were very lucky to get a small cottage to live in. The kitchen had a broken-down Victorian range, the oven hardly got warm, and the room got no heat as it all seemed to go up the chimney. Being wartime, we could have no alterations done.

We had no sanitation, only an earth-closet about fifty yards away down the path, no drains inside, no gas or electricity. Someone gave us a Tilley lamp and we managed to buy a good oil-lamp. We also had a primus stove which was the greatest boon as all cooking had to be done with this and the sulky fire.

I had my first baby late in 1945, and had to boil the nappies in a bucket on the primus, where more often than not the water would boil over and put the blessed thing out. Like many more we had to heat buckets of water for a bath, which we had in an old galvanised bath in front of the fire, then cart all the water out, same with the washing. We managed at this little house for eleven years, which seemed like a dream, and in spite of my grumbles we were very happy.

A farmer from Brafield delivered milk to us. He used to hang his large milkcan over the handlebars of his old bike, with the measure hanging over the side. At about ten every morning, into the kitchen he would walk, pour the milk into the waiting jug, and tell us all the news. If you had a grumble or felt a bit down or the news was bad about the war, he would sing his favourite song—"Count your blessings". He had a very poor life as a boy. His mother had a large family to bring up. She would cook up bones for a bit of broth or have a pig's head and it would have to feed them for several days. His son was at the Grammar School.

He was a real character with a rosy plump face, blue eyes, a droopy moustache and always a kerchief tied round his neck under a collarless shirt, with old brown corduroy trousers tied up in the old-fashioned way under the knee.'

Mrs Janet Hollowell, Cogenhoe.

'Our stepmother used to put the newspaper upside down on the table so that we could not read it while we were eating. We had to wash outside in the yard – the water was icy in winter. Once she took a bread-and-butter pudding out of the oven and threw it at me. It stuck on my arm and burned it.'

Kettering lady.

'I can always remember at Christmas, how our Dad used to read to us. We only had one book in the house and that was Charles Dickens. If you'd got a good fire you had to turn the gaslight out because you couldn't afford to burn both.

So we would all sit round the fire—seven kids, mother and father, and he would read *A Christmas Carol* to us. Mum'd be got her arm round me, he would be got the youngest one on his lap, and we all knew what he was going to do.

When Marley rattled his chains, our Dad'd pick up the poker and rattle it along the guard and we used to think that Marley was coming into the living room.

And of course, parents never called each other by their Christian names, you know—it was always "man" or "woman", so Mum'd say "You fool, man"—laughing, you know—there'd be laughter in her voice. They were wonderful people, that they taught us to have a love of reading.

Mum was left a widow in 1926 and she had four boys and three girls. In that day and age, if you lost your husband and you were hard up, there was no Social Security, nobody coming to see if you needed food, blankets, clothing—in fact you felt a bit of an outcast. We had wonderful neighbours, though, considering they weren't much better off than we were. Mrs West who lived next door to us, she would put a *sprig-bag* [shoe-maker's nail bag] over the wall at night, either with coal or wood, cauliflower, cabbage, a few brussels. But no other neighbours knew. It was always done at night.

The food we had was stodge, bread mostly. Where women could cook on the fire they had to, and nearly everyone had an oval iron pan, and in this pan would go the *clangers,* suet rolls. One was made with pieces of meat or bacon, and onions—mostly onions—and the next one had black treacle in it. The third one was left plain and that was sliced up in the morning and fried in its own fat for breakfast. We were told that *"What don't fatten'll fill"* or *"That'll stick to your ribs."* I wouldn't mind a bit o' that now. We all lived to tell the tale.

As the older ones started work, although sometimes they

only worked two days a week, there was just a bit more money coming in, and then, Friday nights were always great. We used to have sixpennorth of faggots, sixpennorth of *chitlins* and *Tom Hodge* [the thick part of chitterlings] and a jug of gravy, all for a shilling. And we did get, through the year, a bit of fruit, or, Saturday tea-times, a fourpenny tin of pineapple, whereas before, that was just a Christmas treat.

We were always clean. There was no bathroom, but a big bath was brought into the living room on Saturday nights in front of the fire and we were all bathed in that. As we got older our Mum would stand by the kitchen sink and we all went in in turn and had a good wash standing in the sink. She rinsed our hair in vinegar to keep the nits and lice at bay.

My sister had some Russian boots, and she'd got very thin legs, so to keep these boots on she had to wind newspapers round her legs like puttees, and she had to wear the boots, winter and summer, till they fell off her feet. Whatever footwear there was, we wore, if we could possibly get our feet in, and sometimes the boys had the boots and went to school and sometimes the girls. There were no questions asked, because our Mum would not keep us at home if she could help it. If we could get to school we went and that was it. She believed in education and good manners.

We all passed for the Intermediate School, which was quite an achievement, but most of us couldn't go, because there was no money for uniforms and all that.

There was old Granny Smith at the top of Milton Street, deliverer of babies and layer-out of corpses. I don't suppose she ever went to school in her life. We used to watch her making lace at her parlour window. She had a lovely blue pillow on a bamboo stand. We weren't sharp enough to follow the sequence of the bobbins, but we used to like to watch the little bit of lace grow. She was quite a clever woman, but she couldn't read or write.

We used to play marbles in the street. You screwed a *dobby-hole* in the road with your heel and tried to get the marbles into it. And if you were lucky you had a *glarney*– a glass ball from a *spruce* bottle. You didn't let anyone win that off you. Kids couldn't do it today–play in the road–but then you could. The only vehicle that was in Milton Street was old Poll Tarry– George Tarry's horse. It used to bolt sometimes and we all used to rush out to sit on old Poll's head, while he got it to its feet.

And over the road here, where it says *Garage*, it was a

slaughterhouse. There was a butcher on every street corner and they used to slaughter their own. The drovers stood at the end of the street, in case a bullock or something got away because their big fear was that one would get on to the Racecourse. But occasionally, poor things, one would get away and we'd shout "Mad bull, mad bull" and chuck ourselves in our gateways at [the sight of] this terrified cow galloping through the streets.

When you came home from school and opened the door, you knew then that your mother would be there. She wasn't at work or Bingo or gossiping. She was there and there was the smell of the scrubbed table and hot toast with homemade lard on it. It was welcoming. You were home, and poor you may be, but you were wanted. It was a great thing. Fun-wise and morally, they were good days. It was marvellous really.'

Mrs Anne Toms, Northampton.

It is moving to hear of people like Liza Bond the hot-cross-bun-seller at Harpole and Mrs West, who helped others from the little they had themselves.

'The Reverend R W H Simmons was the vicar of St Andrews, in a poor area of Northampton, from 1948 to 1955. He cared deeply for his parishioners and one of his most frequent observations was "The poor help the poor".'

Mr V A Hatley, Northampton.

Some people were desperately poor. Children were kept indoors or in bed all week-end, their clothes pawned for a few coppers. School photographs of the turn of the century nearly always show one or two children who look undernourished and ill.

Food and Drink

'Tay-kettle-brorth [broth]–I've had it for breakfast many a time. It's hot water with pepper and salt. I used to run round the streets to get warm before I went to school.'

Mr Harry Rainbow, Northampton (1898-1979).

'On summer evenings we girls used to stand talking in the village street, till first one, then another would say "I shall have to go in and give Gran her *kettlins*." It was hot water from the kettle poured on bread.'   *Mrs Ward*, Kislingbury.

'I've known the time when we've gone home and had bread with tea poured on it, with a bit of sugar, and I've seen tears in my mother's eyes when she's had to give us such terrible food.'
Mrs Anne Toms, Northampton.

'Flour and water mixed together and fried in a pan—I don't know what they called it.'
Mrs Doris Robinson, Little Houghton.

'If any fish or meat had been boiled, they thickened the water with flour, cooked it and ate it. It was called *flurrups*.'
Mrs E Emmott, Little Houghton and
Mrs M Minney, Yardley Hastings.

'Our Gran saw a neighbour throw half a *bake-pudden* [Yorkshire pudding] in the ash-box and she come in and cried. It would have made us a dinner.
Miss Lily Littlemore, Northampton.

We were often hungry. Once I stole a parsnip from outside a shop and took it to a quiet spot and ate it raw. If we had a halfpenny to spend we took it to the shop and bought a rusk, never sweets. My grandparents in Cold Higham used to send us a hamper each year when they killed their pig, and at other times a sack of vegetables. It was a shame, as they were very poor, and it was not easy in those days to send anything right across the county to Irthlingborough by carriers and the railway.
   My grandmother was an independent and God-fearing old lady. My grandfather injured his hand at work and had one finger amputated. He was not able to work for a time and was given one shilling a week parish relief. Some years later, a sister died and left my grandmother ten shillings. She walked from Cold Higham to Towcester and paid back every penny.'
Mr Jack Davis, Northampton.

'Sometimes men couldn't work properly because they were hungry. They'd have to work all day on a piece of bread and an onion.'   *Mr Arthur Seckington*, Greatworth.

Many gardens had an apple tree and *'keeping apples'* were a valuable winter food. 'Them apples'll keep till apples come *agen,'* people used to say, and the local version of 'coals to Newcastle' was *'apples where there's orchards'*.

'In the early nineteenth century, adverts regularly appeared for "Finedon Dried Apples" at 20 shillings per box, which were available from "J Abel, Book and Musicseller, Northampton, on the same terms as from the Person who prepares them at Finedon".

The apples were set on trays and placed in a baker's oven some hours after the bread was removed. When the oven was required again for bread they were removed and gently pressed between thumb and finger, great care being taken that the skin was not punctured. This process was repeated for nine or ten days until the apple was only about half an inch thick. The processed apples would keep for months and were regarded as a great delicacy for dessert. . . . They were very hard, crab-like fruit, completely inedible raw.'

From *Finedon, Otherwise Thingdon,* pp. 142, 155,
by *Councillor John L H Bailey.*

At Great Doddington a preserve called *citronelle* was made from apples and lemon. The Northamptonshire writer H E Bates, in a typically lyrical passage, describes an old *'stun*-pit' [stone-pit], in the calcareous soil of which a man 'had everywhere planted fruit with great prodigality. . . . The scene was utterly idyllic. Time had covered the lacerated cliffs of stone with grass and thyme and wild rose and elderberry and odd bushes of hawthorn; above it rose the many fruit trees in their full bearing and prime . . . pears of many varieties . . . an apple that my grandfather called a *summerin'* apple . . . to be followed a little later by that queen of plums . . . the squarish apricot-like plum of incomparable flavour always known as the *Stanwick plum.* (Has it died too with the vanished world, I often wonder. . . .?')

The Vanished World, an Autobiography, vol 1, p 91.

'Our Gran had a damson tree and if there were a lot of damsons she used to put them down in layers with sugar in between and it all used to go to a *surrup*. It was lovely to eat in the winter.'
Miss Lily Littlemore, Northampton.

'Blackbirds eat fruit, so the men'd go out with a gun and shoot them. The women would cut out the bird's breast and grill it on toast.' *Mrs Loretta Smith,* Little Houghton.

For savoury dishes, vinegar was the poor man's sauce. In many homes it was on the table every dinner-time, perhaps for the same reason that meat was washed in vinegar 'to take the smell off' in hot weather.

Northamptonshire has few traditional dishes. The suet *clanger* varied from place to place. At Pury End it was a bacon, onion and *pay* [pea] dumpling with jam at one end, like the Bedfordshire clanger.

At (Earls) Barton Feast they still eat Leek Pie, made with pieces of pork, beef and leeks.

'Leeks grow well on the alluvial land of the river valley. A Mr Keach was the baker about fifty years ago. He used to make fifteen oval dishes of the pie, twelve of them for Eli Cooper at the Boot Inn.'   *Mrs Joyce Palmer*, Earls Barton.

Wellingborough is so famous for *hock and dough* that the town is locally known by that name, and people from villages in the area talk of 'gooin' ovver 'Ock'. It is a splendid dish, savoury, filling and economical, and for many years it was the regular Sunday dinner, cooked at home or taken to the bakehouse, in places all over the county. In Northampton it was called *'baked taters'* and was made with whatever meat you could afford, fresh or leftover, as follows. Cover the bottom and sides of a meat-tin with thickish pastry made with some suet and lard, and place the meat, part-cooked if necessary, in the middle, with potatoes, peeled and cut in half lengthways, standing up round the edge. Fill the spaces with sliced onions and a little gravy. Before foil was available, the tin was covered by another tin or left open, in which case the pastry would get a bit *crumpy* round the edges, but this added to the glorious smell and taste. Bake in a medium oven, or take it to the bakehouse.

'The fire was made of faggots, and the oven was cleared out with a *scuffel* [mop], then with a wet sack—a skilled operation. Church and chapel came out at different times, so one side of the oven was for "church 'uns" and the other side for "chapel 'uns". Outside the bakehouse was called *Yawnups* Corner.'
Mr Roy Payler, Kislingbury.

'It has been known for the Squire (of Little Houghton) to lean down from his horse and with his riding-stock lift the cover from a dish being carried to the bakehouse to see if there was one of his rabbits underneath.'
Mrs Loretta Smith, Little Houghton.

Rabbit, poached or otherwise, was often on the menu, but what you ate really depended on what sort of job the wage-earner had, as this rhyme points out.

> Ham and eggs for plasterers,
> Brickies, bread and cheese.
> What will the poor old painters do
> When the leaves fall off the trees?
>
> From *Mr William Jones*, Litchborough.

In most houses the table was set four times a day. Breakfast might or might not be a cooked meal. Dinner was the main meal of the day when children came home from morning school and most fathers returned from work. Tea was often just bread and butter, with jam, or salad in summer and cake if you were lucky. Supper was usually bread and cheese.

'Harry Dot the roadman had his dinner pinched. The bobby booked it down and he said "Was it beef or mutton, Harry?" Harry couldn't remember so he sent him home to find out.

The food was lovely then. The ingine-men [steam-threshers] took a cottage loaf–top for lunch, bottom for dinner, with a big bit o' fat bacon in. The ingine gev it a flavour. If you get a bit o' boiled bacon now, it hasn't got the flavour it had in them days. The lovely flavour's gone and the lovely smell's gone. Now what I should like for breakfast is a nice slice of home-cured bacon and a hen's egg laid in a manger or under a cow-crib, with a nice yellow yolk. Not from one o' them *cubs* [battery cages]. I don't hold with having hens in a battery – It's not natural.

I were brought up wi' the old Gran and the old Grandfather–he were born in 1849. When we started work in the morning, he used to fry the breakfast and he said "Get plenty o' fat down yer, boy. It'll grease yer ribs and you'll stand the cold." They lived on fat years ago and it didn't kill 'em and yet now, it'll bring on a coronary. There's a lot o' coronaries and a lot o' growths (cancers) and it's the food–I'm certain o' that.

Now how did they go on years ago with no fridges? I

Caption above right: Roadmen at Duston having a rest. NL NRO
Below right: Mrs Charlotte Beeby at the doorway of her grocery and sweetshop in Semilong, Northampton in the 1920s. A widow, she ran the shop with the help of her two widowed daughters, Em and Kit. They also looked after Aunt Suey, who was bedridden. 'I remember her singing hymns as she lay in bed. Her favourite was "Fight the good fight".' Mr Ray Grimes, Northampton. AC

remember Miss Luck when we went for the butter—she'd open
the well-lid and pull it up—it hung on a nail just inside the well,
and that were Nature's way. I think if you go against Nature you
go against God.'   *Mr Jack Meyer,* Little Houghton.

The Northampton Cookery Book was compiled in 1908 to raise
money for Doddridge Castle Hill Congregational Chapel. Recipes
and household hints were sent in by local ladies, many of them
the wives of local businessmen. Brice, Kingham, Adnitt, Lewis
and Trenery are among the names.

There are terms which are now seldom used—*eschalot* for
shallot;
a *quartern* of flour for three and a half pounds [a quarter of a stone],
. . . 'if a pinch of salt be added'.

There is a recipe for *collared head* [brawn], using a pig's head,
feet and hocks. This was always made at home in my husband's
family. Here are some more extracts.

'When bottling plums, you must tie each bottle down very hot
with a scalded bladder.'

'Oxgall rubbed into a carpet will restore the colours and make it
almost as new.'

'For frying fish. Fill the wire basket with the fish cutlets and
plunge it in [to very hot fat]. Never mind the commotion; hold
the pan high above the fire till it is quiet, lest it boil over. In one
minute the fish will be cooked. Tried and proved.'

And here is a recipe for 'Scripture cake'.

Four and a half cupsful 1 *Kings* IV 22	[fine flour]
One and a half cupsful *Judges* V 25, last clause	[butter]
Two cupsful *Jeremiah* VI 20	[sugar]
Two cupsful 1 *Samuel* XXX 12	[raisins]
Two cupsful *Nahum* III 12	[figs]
One cupful *Numbers* XVII 8	[almonds]
Two tablespoonsful 1 *Samuel* XIV 25	[honey]
Tablespoon *Jeremiah* XVII 11	[eggs]
Half a cup *Judges* IV 19, last clause	[milk]
A pinch of *Leviticus* II 13	[salt]
Season to taste of 2 *Chronicles* IX 9	[spice]
One teaspoon *Amos* IV 5	[leaven or yeast]

Follow Solomon's prescription for making a good boy,
Proverbs XXIII 14 ['beat with a rod'] and you will have a good
cake.

Book lent by *Mrs Joyce Embrey,* on behalf of Doddridge and Commercial Street United Reformed Church, Castle Hill, Northampton.

The recipe must have brought interest and amusement to a number of Edwardian ladies and their cooks.

At about the same time as this little cookery book was published, Granny Mayes was living in Little Houghton and telling her grandchildren these two verses, the mistress' genteel precept and the servant's vigorous retort behind her back.

> Where there is a little, take a little,
> And make a little do.
> Where there is a little, take a little,
> And leave a little too.

> May the Lord above send down his love
> And ten thousand rusty sickles,
> And cut the *thruts* of all the sluts   [throats]
> As *think much* o' the servants' vittles. [begrudge]

Home-made wine

The wine my grandmother made used to stand under the pantry shelves on the cold brick floor, and was offered to visitors as often as a cup of tea. She used whatever was plentiful, dandelions, elder-berries, parsnips, and for me she made 'stinging-nettle pop', a tangy drink of palest green, lovely on a hot summer's day. Herb-beer is a variety of it, and so is *dea* or *dia-drink,* made from the *dea-nettle* and agrimony. It was good for the blood and skin.

'The wastelands are a pretty sight, with their thick spangle of yellow dandelions. These flowers make an excellent wine, much favoured by country folk. Here is an old recipe.

To a gallon of water allow six quarts of dandelion petals, picked on a fine day, never in the evening when they are damp. Put the flowers in a large earthenware pan, pour over the boiling water and leave to stand for five days, stirring once. Strain the liquor into a pan, add the rinds of two lemons and two oranges and one ounce of ground ginger, then boil gently for an hour. Add four pounds loaf sugar, and stir till it has dissolved. Spread a piece of toast with yeast, float it on the liquor and leave for four days. Then strain the wine into a stone jar and keep for three months before bottling.'

Mrs Hilda Berry, Wroxton, near Banbury.

Mrs Berry, in her late eighties, sent her collection of wine recipes to her daughter in Australia, and a copy came to me from her daughter's friend, Mrs. Sonia Glenister, formerly of Banbury. As well as the more usual recipes there is cowslip tea for children, rice wine or saki, and 'an old Dutch liqueur called Van der Hum, a speciality of old farm houses in South Africa'.

There was also 'whisky wine', made with potatoes, wheat and hops, without yeast.

This is the one to watch.

'My Gran used to live in Oxford Street, near the *jitty*. Well one winter there were some men working on the road outside. It was bitter cold and Gran called them in to have a drop of her potato wine. Then they went out again and after a bit one of them said "Where's Charlie?" They couldn't find him, so they went to ask Gran and when she went to the door she found him in the passage, out stone cold. They had to carry him home.'   *Mrs Joyce Hancock,* Northampton.

Illness and Remedies

'Anaemic girls were taken out to the fields early in the morning to get the smell of the sheep' (at Ashton, near Roade)
Miss Jessie Curtis, Northampton

We look more carefully now at the remedies with which people once tried to heal themselves. My great-grandfather gathered mould from plants and rotting wood to put on cuts and wounds, many years before the great discovery of penicillin, developed from a mould. To be honest, he used cow-dung as well. A tarred rope hung over the bed helped me, they said, with breathing problems and doctors in my childhood treated patients with pneumonia by ordering hot poultices for their chests and backs, and, if they recovered, a 'pneumonia jacket' made of cotton-wool, from which a square inch would be removed every day till it was all gone.

There were bread poultices for tooth-ache and currant plasters for drawing out the *matter* from *gathered* wounds. Soap and sugar heated together was used for this as well.

'The only time I ever fainted in my life was when I had one of them put too hot on me.'

Mrs Anne Toms, Northampton.

'My mother cut her head open when she was a child in 1902, and the doctor stitched it up with an ordinary needle and black thread, because Grandma had no white at the time.

Mrs Loretta Smith, Little Houghton.

'A cure for chilblains on the feet was to dip them in the chamber-pot.'   *Mrs Dorothy Warren,* Yardley Gobion.

'One of my brothers had a very bad chest every winter, and mother used to make a jacket out of brown paper, the hairy sort, soaked in goosegrease and linseed oil. It smelt terrible, but he had to wear it all winter, sewn on him.'

Mrs Anne Toms, Northampton.

'The common thick brown paper is an excellent thing to be worn next the skin.'

Mrs Marsh, wife of the Bishop of Peterborough, writing to John Clare. Wilson J, *Green Shadows, The Life of John Clare,* p. 184.

'A layer of brown paper on the chest was used for travel-sickness, and a trip on the canal or a visit to [Stony] Stratford gas-works was recommended for whooping-cough.'

Mrs Dorothy Warren, Yardley Gobion.

'If one of the children had whooping-cough, our mother used to give it fried mice' (at Broughton).   *Mr Rowlett,* Kettering.

'A young boy who had consumption used to have to eat raw liver every day.'

Mrs Alice Rainbow, Northampton.

'Chickweed ointment is good for piles and the first nettles were brewed to make a drink which is good for spots.'

Miss Margaret Lattimer, Moulton.

'They used to squeeze the juice of *eyebright* [germander speedwell] into babies' eyes.'   *Mrs Sonia Glenister,* Australia.

'We bind sprigs of comfrey round horses' legs if they have a sprain.'   *Mrs Rosemary Eady,* Pytchley, 1983.

'Once some gypsies asked if they could pick some of the *penny-pies* that grow on the church wall, to make ointment. The real name is *pennywort.'*

Mr William Jones, Litchborough, 1983.

'If a pig is ill, turn it out near a hedgerow. It will usually find the right plant to cure itself. If a sheep has had a bad lambing, turn it into the ground elder.'

Mr A Broom, Tugby, near Leicester.

'My grandfather used to keep a lettuce leaf under his hat in hot weather. From time to time he would take it out and shake it. He was quite sure that this kept his head cool. He always had a potato in his pocket to keep rheumatism at bay.'

Mr Ray Grimes, Northampton.

'One of my ancestors had a lot of knowledge about herbs and was thought to be a witch.'   *Mr Jack Davis,* Northampton.

'In Flore Fields there used to be a house called *Nocolation.* It was where smallpox victims were given injections and nursed in isolation.'   *Mr A Clements,* Harpole.

'The *pesthouse* was where people with smallpox were taken, carried there by men who had had the disease already'.

Mr A Jones, Banbury.

There was belief in the healing power of gold, a wedding ring being rubbed on a baby's sore gums or on a *stine-eye* [a stye on the eyelid].

It was believed that washing the hands in water that had been used for boiling eggs or potatoes would cause warts to appear. The curing or charming of warts had to do with magic and the full of the moon.

Folklore

*'. . . a little girl with wart-encrusted hands
outstretched in the moonlight'*

'My grandfather said that before he died he would tell me how
to cure warts, but he died before he could do so. He'd go to the
cow-'us or shed, lay a penny on the wart and then a bent straw.
He said you must have faith.'   *Mr Ray Wykes,* Spratton.

The element of secrecy—going to the 'cow-'us or shed'—
continued even after the cure. Several people told me 'If you tell
anybody the warts come back'.

Thomas Sternberg in *The Dialect and Folklore of
Northamptonshire* (1851) *(DFN)* records the following:

'To cure a wart, rub it with a piece of meat, which must be
afterwards buried; and as fast as the flesh rots, the wart will
decay. Another for the same: take one of the large black snails
. . . rub it over the wart, and then hang it on a thorn. This must
be done nine nights successively, at the end of which time the
wart will completely disappear.' *DFN* p 166.

These two cures were being carried out well into this century.

'Warts were charmed away by rubbing them with snail's slime
or old meat [at Ashton, near Roade].'
            Miss Jessie Curtis, Northampton.

'From the age of four I started to get unsightly warts on my
hands. No-one wanted to hold hands with me and would only
hold on to my wrists. My mother bought wart-remover from
the chemist—all to no avail.

My Gran snorted and told me to come to her on the night of
the full moon. This I did and she took me into the garden and
shone a torch around. Soon she said "Ah, 'ere 'e be" and picked
up a huge black slug, which she bade me let crawl over the
backs of both my hands.

What an odd sight it must have been—a small, stout, middle-
aged lady and a little girl with wart-encrusted hands
outstretched in the moonlight, with this large slug sliding
slowly over the warts. I wasn't afraid, because my Gran to me
was peace and comfort.

After a while, Gran said "That be it then" and from her pocket she took a long thorn from the blackthorn hedge and stabbed it right through the slug. "Now, gal, when that slug dies, so will your warts" she said. Poor slug—it died somewhere in the garden and my warts dried up and vanished.'

Mrs Sonia Glenister, Australia.

This took place at Hornton, near Banbury, in the early 1930s.

Sternberg also records that witchcraft 'still holds a conspicuous place in our popular superstitions' (*DFN* p 145) and that 'the belief in fairies . . . still lingers among the rural population of Northamptonshire and South Warwickshire', (*DFN* p 132) also that 'the hell-hounds and their ghostly huntsman are still heard careering along the gloomy avenues of Whittlebury' (*DFN* p 131). Certainly John Clare, writing a few years earlier, was steeped in such lore.

I have heard nothing to suggest that these beliefs still remain, except the legend of the 'white lady' who is said to haunt the brook at Ladybridge, on Towcester Road, Northampton.

The *Bogeyman* is a different matter. Sternberg says '*The Bogie* was the household spirit' (*DFN* p 138). As children we half-believed that he lurked in the shadowy garden when we went to the outside lavatory in the evening, and we obeyed our grandmother's injunction to 'Hurry back in else the Bogeyman'll get you.'

Some beliefs recorded by Sternberg were still going strong for much of this century. Here are some of them, and some more besides, set down as spoken locally:

Animals, birds, insects

It's lucky if a black cat crosses your path, but if you kill one you'll have seven years bad luck.

> One crow sorrow, two crows joy,
> Three crows a letter, four crows a boy,
> Five crows silver, six crows gold,
> And seven crows a secret never to be told.

You must not kill a robin, because he tried to pluck the thorns from Christ's crown—that's how he got his red breast.

What you are doing when you first hear the cuckoo each year you will do for the rest of the year.

You must tell the bees the family news. A bee coming in to the house is a sign of a visitor. If a *money-spider* [a very small spider] settles on you, twirl it three times round your head and it will bring you money (*DFN* p 160).

Trees and Plants

'We used to hit a tree to drive out demons.'

Hardingstone lady.

If you pick off daisy petals and say 'He loves me, he loves me not' you'll find out one way or the other. If you put your cherry stones round the edge of the dish and say

> Tinker, tailor, soldier, sailor,
> Rich man, poor man, beggarman, thief.

you'll find out what your job will be or who you'll marry (*DFN* p 162).

(These are forms of plant-divination)

It's unlucky to bring may/lilac/keck/snowdrops/ivy into the house.

(All the flowers except some lilacs are white)

White flowers are best for a funeral.

'Pick up flowers, pick up sickness'
'Parsley goes nine times to the devil before it comes up'
'Plant parsley on a rising moon as near Good Friday as you can'

It's good luck to catch a falling leaf.

The moon

It is unlucky to look at the new moon through glass (*DFN* p 170). You must go outside and bow or curtsey to it, three times, some say. Turn your money over then it will grow as the moon gets bigger. If the moonlight falls on your face when you're asleep, you'll *'get too much o' the old moon'*, lose your wits.

Wells and springs

'I come off my bike and cut both my hands badly, and they never healed at all till I got some water from Becket's Well.'

Mr Ferdinand Pearce, Northampton (1868–1945).

'In Adkins Piece at Weston-by-Lois Weedon there was a little stone arch built into a mound. Inside the arch was a roughly-hewn stone basin which was filled with water from a mineral spring. It was called an *eye-well*, as people believed the water was good to bathe bad eyes with. From its colour I would say the water was rich in iron. A few old people still used it around 1920.'   *Mr Arthur Seckington,* Greatworth.

Iron and stones
You hang the horse-shoe open-end up so the luck will not run out.

'Horse-brasses were originally iron charms against witches.'
Mr Jack Davis, Northampton.

If you stand the poker upright in the fire-opening it will draw the fire up. [This was once a defence against witches coming down the chimney.]

'If I find a stone with a hole in it, I feel that it is somehow special, but I don't know why.'   *Mr Ray Wykes,* Spratton.

Sternberg gives this quotation from John Morton's *The Natural History of Northamptonshire,* 1712. 'Those [pebbles] that are perforated . . . the vulgar here are wont to use as amulets, hanging them up in stables, and at their bedheads, imagining they have a strange and wonderful efficacy against the powers of witchcraft.'

The house
If you visit a house, always go in and out by the same door, otherwise the friendship will be broken. If you leave your own house and then have to go back for something, sit down for a minute before you go out again. Never pass anyone on the stairs. It is unlucky to open an umbrella indoors or to put shoes on a table. Do not dry your hands on a towel being used by someone else or the two of you will quarrel. Do not accept gloves as a gift—it means a parting; always pay for them. Pay a small coin if anyone gives you a knife as a gift or it will *'cut the friendship'.* I can testify to the truth of the belief that if you break one cup, glass etc. you will break two more. Some people try to forestall this by breaking two matchsticks instead. Signs of death are a picture falling from the wall, a hole in the fire and a diamond-shaped crease in the tablecloth.

Fire
The sun shining on the fire will *dout* it. A fragment of ash fluttering on the grate is a sign of a visitor. If you burn elder wood

the devil will sit on your chimney. The fire will not burn brightly if someone in the house is dying.

The table
Crossed knives foretell a quarrel (*DFN* p 172). Two spoons in one saucer mean a sweetheart. If two women pour tea from the pot one of them will have a baby. It is bad luck to spill salt but you may avoid it by making the sign of the cross in the spilled salt and throwing it over your left shoulder. Never put salt on someone's else's food—'*Help to salt, help to sorrow.*'

Mirrors
A mirror is an ancient symbol of magic, being an image of oneself. Breaking one brings seven years bad luck (*DFN* p 172). Cover mirrors during a thunderstorm and open the doors to let the thunderbolts out.

Washing
'Wash on New Year's Day, wash your luck away.' 'Wash blankets in May, wash one of the family away.' 'If you wash on Good Friday, the water turns to blood.'

Friday
An unlucky day, perhaps because of the Crucifixion. On this day you should not turn the mattress nor cut your nails.

Death

'The dead-bell don't ring for somebody else every time'
Mr George Crowson, Helpston

In the days following a death, family, friends and neighbours were taken to see the dead person, lying on his own bed until the funeral, often with fresh flowers in his hands. The flowers, and those in the church and afterwards on the grave were often white. The body was prepared for burial by a local woman—*'the old death-monger'* I have heard her called.

'Salt was placed on the chest and on the feet of the dead person.' [Thorpe Langton, 1948.]

Mr A Broom, Tugby, near Leicester.

Children were brought in to touch the dead body, 'so they don't fear death' or *'so that the dead person should not come back to haunt them'.*

At a funeral in Kingsthorpe, Northampton in 1962, doors were left open. This was thought to be for the spirit to pass through.

'Down the fens, they won't put a dead body in a coffin till it's paid for.' *Mr George Crowson,* Helpston.

Sayings

'She looks as if she's bin pulled through 'edge backuds'

They speak for themselves, to mock, to console, and to comment on the things and people around us. Our speech is the richer for their vigour and plain speaking.

From the animal world
In and out like a dog at a fair.
Sue a dog and catch a flea.
> A warning against going to law or making a fuss over a small matter.

Neither *'ug, dug,* n' mutton.
> Neither one thing nor another (hog, dog, nor mutton) *Wellingborough.*

That's what killed my pig.
> That was the last straw.

She called him everything, from a pig to a dog.

He couldn't stop a pig in an entry/a passage.
> He is bow-legged.

You could run a pig between his legs and he'd never know it'd bin there.
> as above.

Our cat run up your entry.
> We are slightly related.

Cats in season and bean-setting time.
> Springtime. *Boddington.*

She's got as many whims as a wounded bear.
> A memory of bear-baiting.

You never see a young bird feeding an old one.

You are an ill-sitting hen.

Michaelmas chickens and parsons' daughters are not worth rearing.
> Chickens hatched at Michaelmas 29 September were too late to thrive.

If you want to live and thrive,
Let the spider run alive.
> Spiders were thought to bring prosperity.

Bodies and minds

You could put it in your eye and see none the less.
> It is very small.

It's better out than a poor man's eye.
> Said of something unpleasant brought to light.

It's beyond my thumbs.
> It's something I cannot cope with. *Harpole.*

I don't know whether I'm on foot or horseback.

What's bred in the bone comes out in the flesh.

'Ere's me 'ead and me bum's a-comin'.
> Said of someone walking with a forward stoop.

Arse over elbow.
> Head over heels. *Denton.*

The nearer the bone, the sweeter the meat.
> Said in defence of a thin person.

Once a man, twice a child.

Come day, goo day, God send Sunday.
> Lackadaisical.

He looks as if he could do with two pennorth o' God help him.

She can't see the length of a gooseberry.
He don't know A from a bull's foot.
> He is ignorant.

They're not sharp enough to give handbills out.
You might as well talk to the stones in the wall.
He wants gooin' over afresh.
One's *frit*, the other *daredn't*.
I'd as soon believe you can plait fog.
I'll tear fustian first.
You may as well throw muck at the moon.
When the sun shines both sides the 'edges.
> Never.

It's handle-me-carefully day.
Twenty-four carpenters round a bag o' chips.
> Too many cooks . . .

Such wood, such chips.
> Like father, like son.

He'd bite a nail atwo.
> He's in a bad temper.

She'd skin a flint for a *farden* and *spwile* a knife worth a *groat*.
> Farthing, spoil, fourpence.
> *Moulton.*

She'd skin a flea for a farden.
She talks as 'er belly guides 'er.
Men are all right so long as they've got a wife at home with her
head up the chimney.
> Like 'slaving over a hot stove'.

All sauce and no bottle.
> Without substance.

More nice than wise.
> 'Nice' is used in one of its old meanings, fastidious.

The creaking gate hangs longest.
> Said of an ailing person who outlives others.

That be damned for a tale.
> I don't believe it.

All there/All there with his acid-drops.
> Shrewd.

All to pieces.
> Distressed.

Warnings

Measure twice and cut once.
> Take care *eg* in carpentry, dressmaking.

Better goo twice laughin' than once bawlin' (weeping).

Do a bit and sit a bit.
> Good advice for the sick or elderly. *Helpston.*

You never miss the water till *the well runs dry.*
> *Little Houghton.*

It would be *present* death to go out in this weather.
> Instant.

A watched pot never boils.

Save your breath to cool your porridge.
> *Motteux P., Rabelais' Works* 'Spare your Breath to cool your Porridge.'

Don't do that else the fat'll be in the fire.

Sing *afore* breakfast, cry afore the day's out.

Neighbours and others

Lace curtains at the winders and bread and drippin' on the table.

She thinks she's everybody.

They were all there, noddin' and beckin'.

She thinks the sun shines out of 'is arse.

She makes the bullets for 'im to fire.

They try to weigh your corn with their bushel.

They're all tarred with the same brush.

There's bin a splash o' the tar-brush there.
> One of their ancestors was coloured.

He'd argue with an echo.

I wouldn't give him the time o' day.

Them as brings'll carry.
> Said of gossips.

They're only dung'll [dung-hill] bred.

Ho—'is mother's starched 'is shirt-tails.
> Defined simply as 'walkin' funny'.

I see you were dressed at Dame Tucker's.
> In ill-fitting clothes. *Kettering.*

I see you come from Desborough.
> Wearing many different colours. *Kettering.*

It's big enough for Mother Alderman.
> She was a very fat lady.

It looks as if it's bin sewed up with a 'ot needle and burnt thread.

She looks as if she's bin pulled through 'edge backuds.

He's got no more idea than the man in the moon.

Much wants more.

Comparisons

All dressed up like 'ambone with a frill round its neck.

All done up like an October lettuce.
> Needing a good deal of trimming.

She looks like 'aystack with a string round the middle.

She looks like 'aystack tied up ugly.

It (usu. a hat) looks like a pimple on a round o' beef/'aystack/a tomtit on a muckle [manure-heap].

Like a little old woman cut short.
> Said of a child wearing unsuitable clothes, or of a precocious child.

She's got teeth like coffin-nails.

He's puffin' like a broken-winded old *pismire*.
> Ant.

Om *cast* like an old *tup*.
> I'm as helpless as an old ram that has fallen on its back. The speaker had arthritis.

Like a pig in a fit.

Like a pig with one ear.
> Lopsided.

Squealing like a stuck pig.
> Pigs were killed by a knife-thrust in the neck.

Staring like a throttled cat.

She's like a bear with a sore head.

Like a dying duck in a thunderstorm.

Like an old *yoe* [ewe] dressed lamb-fashion.

It fits like a ready-made shirt on a wheelbarrow.

She looks like a bull in a pinafore.

You're like a man made o' worsted/smoke.

It stinks like a polecat.

He come rushin' in like a thousand o' bricks. in 'igh wind/gooin' to 'Ell to be burnt.

She rushes about like a pea in a pan/like a parched pea in a colander.

She's all *chopse* (talk) like a cod's 'ead.

> A play on the word chops [face].

She's as thin as a deal board wi' the knot knocked out.

It sounds like Rainbow's woodyard.

> It is very noisy. *Wellingborough.*

You sound like a *ship* on turnups.

> Like a sheep eating turnips.

It's like *yettin'* [eating] a pudden with 'airpin.

> Complaint of a Banbury man, given a small shovel to unload a cartful of coal.

The fire smokes like all Hell and two sticks.

He looks like death warmed up.

She's going like butter/dew before the sun.

> She is ailing.

He sleeps with one eye open like a Bristol carpenter.

> Meaning unknown. *Banbury.*

as white as the driven snow/as a sheet.

as black as your hat/old Bill's mother's/the ace of spades/the devil's nutting-bag.

as yellow as a guinea.

> Nearly always referring to the colour of a sick person.

as red as a turkeycock.

as blue as a whetstun.

> *Whetstone.*

as brown as a berry.

as fair as a lily.

as sweet as a nut.

as nice as pie.

as clear as a bell.

as right as rain/ninepence.

as cheerful as a cricket.

as happy as a sandboy.

as pleased as Punch.

as clean as a whistle.

as fit as a fiddle.

as tough as old boots/*whitleather* [see glossary].

as fat as butter/a *tunkey* pig [ibid].

as sour as vinegar/*varges* [ibid].

as thick as thieves/*duckpuddle* [ibid].

as bald as a *bolshin* [ibid].

as drunk as *cloey*/a fiddler [ibid].

as wet as tripe.

as hot as kitty.
> Meaning unknown.

as hard as the devil's toe-nails.

as soft as 'ap'ny carrot/pap.
> Poor quality carrots, sold for a halfpenny a pound.

as dull as ditchwater.

as wooden as a cowcrib.
> Bedfordshire.

as thin as a lath.

as fat as butter.

as weak as a rat/kitten.

as meek as a maggot.

as wet as tripe.

as dry as a bone.

as cross as two sticks.

as hungry as a hunter/*thacker* [thatcher].

as straight as a die/yard o' pumpwater.

as plain as a pikestaff/the nose on your face.

as happy as a pig in muck/as a biddy.

as miserable as sin.

as cunning as a wagon-load o' monkeys.

as quick as greased lightning.

as stiff as a crutch.

General

Cough, Julia, and make the baby laugh.
> Origin unknown. Said when someone coughs.

Ah well, this won't buy the baby a new dress or pay the old
woman her ninepence.
> I shall have to get on now.

Every so often.
> From time to time.

For the longest of whiles.
> For a long time.

When all comes to all/for good and all.
> Finally.

There's *allus summat.*
> There's always something—something will turn up.

Pick up every bit that has two ends.
> Don't waste anything.

You could go farther and fare worse.

Hopping the twig.
> Moving fast.

It's an *overlayer* for meddlers.
> Said when one does not wish to answer a question. See
> glossary for *overlayer.* The meaning seems to be keeping
> something hidden.

It smells to high heaven.

She's had a hard row to hoe.

You've got to eat a peck o' dirt before you die.
> An excuse for not-quite-clean food. A peck = two gallons,
> dry measure, or one-quarter part of a bushel.

Friday flit, not long sit.

as broad as its long.

as bad burnt as scalded.

It cuts both ways.

With the best will in the world.
> Willingly, if I could, but I cannot.

It's Martin's masterpiece.
> It's a mystery.

That's the chap as married 'Annah.
> That's the very thing.

Turn the sheets and thank God for clean linen.
> Said when bedsheets are not taken off to be washed, but
> turned round.

Never show a fool or a woman a half-finished job.
> *Litchborough.*

That's a job up Abington Street.
> That job must be done to a high standard. *Litchborough.*

The three coldest things in the world–
a *dug's* nose, a woman's knees and a man's be'ind.

Of devils and witches

It's the devil's own job.
> Said of any difficult job.

All hell let loose.
> Said of an uproar.

They kicked up hell's delight.
> They made a great fuss.

Seven stone six is witches' weight.
> Meaning unknown. *Spratton.*

A night fit for the lost souls.
> A night of howling wind and rain. *Rushden.*

She looked like a 'aunted witch.

She loves him like the devil loves holy water.

Illness and death

Bad *abed* and *wuss* up [worse].

Full of cold.
> Having a heavy cold.

My looks don't pity me.
> I feel worse than I look.

Love him out of life.
> Take care of him till he dies.

Put to bed with a shovel.
> Buried. *Piddington.*

Black follows green.
> Green, the fairies' colour, brings ill-luck or even death.

Open for a he, open for a she.
Open for a she, open for three.
> This chilling rhyme from North Leicestershire refers to the grave.

No pockets in shrouds.
> You can't take it with you.

Down to earth

See a man about a dog.
> Go to the lavatory, said mainly by men.

See my aunt.
See if the same old moon's a-shining.
> Go to the lavatory, often an outside one, said usually by girls and women.

I shall pee over nine hedges and sprinkle the tenth.
> Said when offered another cup of tea.

Red hat, no drawers.
All arse and pockets.
> Said of a fat old lady bending down.

Like a brick-built shit-'us [house].
> Large, heavily built, like a brick-built outside lavatory compared with a wooden hut.

There may be snow on the roof but there's fire in the hall.
> Answer to a comment about white hair.

There's many a good tune played on an old fiddle.

Change the name and not the letter
> e.g. when Brown marries Bates.

Change for worse and not for better.
Clay on sand is good for the land.
Sand on clay is money thrown away.
Short splice for iron,
Long splice for wood,
That's what makes both the joints good.
Cold-iron blacksmiths and shut-knife carpenters never go to Heaven.
Wise men nor fools
Can't work without tools.
> Mr William Jones, *Litchborough*.

In the following group, emphasis is gained in various ways, e.g. by repetition, by reversing the usual order of words, or, as in the first example, by leaving out a word (the).

Up hill and down dale.
> Soundly, thoroughly. She went for him [scolded] up hill and down dale.

Many and many's the time.
> Often.

For many a long day/year.
> For a long time.

Since married I've been.
> I've never missed paying the rent since married I've been.

It went to the heart of me.
> It went to the heart of me to see the kids crying.

Ever knew how to be.
> Often after the comment
> 'They're worse than animals'—They're worse than animals ever knew how to be.

I'll give you . . .
> An angry repeating of what has been said, or done, used as a threat of punishment.
> I'll give you tell me what you want.
> I'll give you stop out till this time o' night.

No, nor nobody else neither.
> This multiple negative is very emphatic.
> esp. with so much alliteration—all those 'n's.

Ever likely to be.
> You're ever likely to be cold.
> You don't wear enough clothes.

. . . and willing.
> There's plenty of room in the car. You can come and willing.

I never did.
> Expression of surprise. Well, I never did (see such a thing).

Every so often.
> From time to time. I give her room a good clean-out every so often.

Never so much as
> Not even. They're got a *gret* big garden, but they never so much as give us a cabbage.

None the more for that.
> Even so. She don't want me t' goo, but I shall goo, none the more for that.

for the life of me.
> In any way, at all. I can't see for the life of me why she don't give up that big 'ouse of *'ern* [hers].

The truth's not in her.

The Leather Industry and the Shoe Trade

'. . . and there is always the smell of tanneries, leather and shoe-factories'

The time is the early 1900s, the writer, Reginald Payne, a London surgeon and son of one of the owners of the old Northampton furnishing firm, in his autobiography *The Water-shed*. His words would still have been true fifty years later, but now we smell leather more rarely, and the unpleasant fumes of the old tanneries have gone. So with the old words—some may still be heard, others are remembered and recorded here, some are lost. The story begins in the tanyard.

OAK-BARK TANNAGE

'An old fellow from *Farrexton* told me that he used to take a horse and cart laden with oak-bark to a tannery in Northampton, and he tied his horse up at the old Red House in St James, where he could get a pint of *splits,* some bread-and-cheese, half an ounce of shag with a clay pipe thrown in, all for sixpence-halfpenny.'   *Mr A W Clements,* Harpole.

'The old fellow' came from Farthingstone. *Splits* is a mixture of ale and small beer.

The raw hides and skins were trimmed of hooves and horns and taken to the *limeyard,* where they were soaked in lime-pits to loosen the hair. Then, in the *beamhouse,* they were spread one at a time over the tanner's beam and scraped, with an *unhairing-*knife on the hair or grain side, and with a *fleshing-knife* on the flesh side. After further liming they were scraped again, this time with the blunt metal or stone-bladed *scudding-knife* to remove *scud,* remains of hair roots, fat cells etc.

One of two processes could be used to cleanse and open up the skin structure. In the alkaline process, called *bating, puering* or *mastering,* the hides were soaked in an infusion of bird-droppings or dog-dung.

'Dog-dung bates were still used in Northamptonshire in the early 1950s, and in Leeds ten years later.'

In the acidic process, called *raising* or *drenching,* an infusion of barley, rye or ash-bark was used, fermented by stale beer, urine or rotting pieces of hide. The hides were washed and worked over the beam, using the stone-bladed *scudding-slate.* This was the end of the pre-tanning process, which took anything up to six months to complete.

Tanning proper was carried out first in the *handlers,* tubs or pits containing spent tanning liquors in which the hides were moved up and down by the use of long tongs or hooks, for about a month. They were piled up to drain or *sess,* while the *ooze* or liquor was *mended* or strengthened.

Next, in pits called *layers* or lay-aways, the smoothed hides were placed between layers of ground oak-bark for nine to eighteen months or longer. The tanned hides were rinsed, smoothed with a *setting-pin* and placed in an airy shed for drying or *crusting.* Crust leather was the tanner's finished product.

The above quotation and information about work in the tanyard are from a monograph, *Post-Medieval Archaeology 15 (1981)* pp 161-175, *Leather Manufacture in the Post-Medieval Period with special reference to Northamptonshire,* by *Mr Roy Thomson,* Wellington Tannery, Raunds.

TANNING TODAY

'Sheepskins and lambskins are collected from the abbatoir or butcher while still warm, washed off and salted down to

Tanner's beam

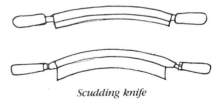

Unhairing knife

Scudding knife

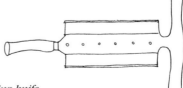

Currier's shaving knife

preserve them. When we are ready to put them into work, they are sorted into grades, *double-face,* with the wool on, for clothing; furrier grades, suitable for rugs, and fellmongering grades, which have the wool removed.

Skins for fellmongering are *broken-over,* using a blunt fleshing-machine, soaked and painted with a thick suspension of lime and sulphide. Then the wool can be *pulled,* that is, rubbed and pulled off the skin, then washed, spun, dried, baled and sent to wool merchants in Yorkshire.

The limed pelts are put into pits containing holding-lime or whitelime to keep them from the air. They are then de-limed, puered or bated and pickled-down to preserve them, and in this condition are quite stable and can be bought, sold and transported across the world.

The pickled pelts are sorted and the rejects and *spetches* or *glues* are sent to the fellmonger for glue-making. The thickest skins or *splitters* go to the chamois tanner, who splits them into chamois leathers, and the *skivers* are used for book-binding and fancy goods. The better skins are pickle-fleshed, hydroed and drummed in degreasing liquors and brine solutions. Then they are tanned, using chrome (basic chromic sulphate). After *horsing up,* on a frame called a *horse,* and ageing for a time, they are chrome-fleshed and either wet-wheeled [suedes] or shaved [grains].

The skins are re-tanned, with vegetable and synthetic tanning materials and *fatliquors.* After being *held on the horse* to drain, they are *sammed* [half-dried], *put-out, set-out* or *struck-out* to increase the area and flatten the skin. They are crusted-out, either by hanging on tenterhooks or by toggling. Toggles are also hooks. When quite dry they are usually held in the crust-store for a time to *come back* or rehydrate.

Suedes are conditioned or damped, staked or softened and dry-wheeled and *padded,* using a revolving plush-wheel. Grains are staked, *padded* (the word is the same, but the meaning entirely different) by brushing a pigment or paint finish on to the surface, glazed or plated to give a gloss, dry-drummed, trimmed and passed into the warehouse.'

Mr Roy Thomson, Wellington Tannery, Raunds.

'In 1948 there were about fifty tanners, dressers and merchants in the county. Today there are less than twenty leather works and their product is mostly leather for the uppers of shoes. Heavy leather for soles is bought in.

Bovine leathers are, with some exceptions, unhaired. Some leathers used for belting in textile mills—*hairy picker butts,* are dressed *in the hair.*

Tanning procedures are basically the same as they always were, though carried out by machinery. The term *beamhouse* is still used, as is *bating* and *fleshing.* Depending on the *weight* (thickness) the hides can be split to provide upper leather from the grain, and shoe-suede, clothing etc. from the flesh. When the skin is tanned it is ready for the leather-dresser.'

Mr T Cooper, Hardingstone (1984).

'As a twelve-year-old butcher's boy, I had to take buckets of blood to the leather-dresser, and for one process, dog-droppings were used. They used to advertise "Top price paid for best white". We lived in Currier's Yard (Irthlingborough).'

Mr Jack Davis, Northampton.

LEATHER DRESSING

'The term "currier" is used for a producer of heavy leather for saddlery etc. A leather dresser produces a range of lighter leathers. There are still a good number in the town and county and once were many more.'

Mr John Fookes, formerly of Edward Woodley and Sons,
Higham Ferrers (1984).

In Northampton their works were often tucked in around the shoe-factories, in streets where many of the shoe-workers lived. Nearly all the buildings were of the same red brick, but there was variety, with the two and three-storied factories, yards, loading-bays and streets of terraced houses. These, with the smell of leather and the thump, whine and rattle of shoe machinery were part of the Northampton scene for many years of this century.

Some businesses were started in a small way. In 1908, W Pearce and Company, the well-known leather-dressers of Great Billing, started business in a single room over a gateway in Burns Street, Northampton. Their assets were £40 and a bicycle. They bought in crust *sumac*-tanned skivers and prepared them according to the requirements of their customers. (Sumac is a Mediterranean plant producing a tanning liquor.)

'The feel or handle of a piece of leather depends on its subsequent use. Sole leather should have a mellow handle and a *cheesy* cut [readily cut with a sharp blade to give a smooth edge]. Any sign of tenderness should be avoided. Shoe upper

leathers should have a full round feel–they should fill the hand. Calf leather has spring–a certain resistance to bending. Glove leathers need *run*, the ability to stretch in one direction, so that they grip the hand without exerting pressure. In all cases a fine *break* is required, so that when the leather is folded grain inwards, the folds are narrow and uniform.

It is hard to be precise about the names of tools and processes. Both now and in the past, words may vary from town to town and from one works to another, or one tool may have several uses. The essential processes have remained the same for centuries and the sequence is as follows:

The leather, in crust form, hard and rough-grained, or *wet-blue*, tanned with chromium salts and having a bluish tinge, is washed to strip or clear the grain surface. It is pulled, piled and drained [pulled into shape, and left in piles to drain] before the important process of splitting and shaving to the required thickness. The skins or hides are placed in wooden drums and *wet-back* [neutralised], retanned, dyed and *fatliquored* [impregnated with animal and marine oils]. In the past the mixture was of neats'-foot oil, cod oil and soap.

After *pulling* and *horsing-up* to drain overnight, the skins are *sammed* or *sammied*, fastened to metal frames with toggling-clips or hung up by tenterhooks to dry.

If it is to be curried, the leather is *stuffed*, impregnated with warm dubbin, a mixture of beef or mutton tallow, cod-oil or *train-oil*, from the blubber of whales or seals. After *tabling*, scraping off the dried dubbin which has not penetrated, rolling and oiling-off, the *rounded* [trimmed] bends or butts are measured for sale.

If the leather is not to be curried, it is buffed and corrected, rubbed down to smooth out defects and scars. This is followed by padding on to the grain a mixture of pigments and resins to provide a base for a decorative finish. To *kiss* is to apply a very light grain. In days gone by, a *chalk-boy* rubbed in French chalk with a pad made from a *sprig-bag*, shoemaker's nail-bag, filled with oddments of leather. Tipping, angle-spraying and lacquering are the prosaic terms for finishing operations and the leather is then *pinwheel-measured*. The pinwheel machine is still in use in a number of places to measure leather in square

Caption left: Ten-year-old Jack Davis at the turn of the century in Irthlingborough. He had just left school for good and was working as a butcher's boy. Miss Betty Davis, Northampton.

feet. Bought in the crust for old pence per pound weight, it is sold in new pence per square foot, over a range of thicknesses measured in millimetres.

The *top-shop* is the store or warehouse where it is laid out for sale, often in a display of striking beauty.'

Mr John Fookes, Canada, formerly of Northampton.

Leather technology is (1989) taught at the National Leathersellers Centre, Nene College, Northampton.

The Hand-Sewn Shoe Makers

'They used to get five bob a pair for making them right through, and found their own grindery'

'We let our barn at one time to a man who worked at home. I was very young, so did not know what his job was, but he used to have his mouth full of small nails and pick them out one by one like lightning.'   *Mr Jack Davis,* Northampton.

'Some forty or more shoemakers worked at home in Harpole in the 1900s for agents of Manfield, Collier and Pinkards, who, I believe, did a London trade. Several of the old houses had no *shop* (workroom), and only one living-room, so the *snob* had his seat at the window, taking most of the light, and in winter, lit by a paraffin lamp.

The makers, welt-sewers, stitchers, finishers, all of them had to supply their own grindery—nails, hemp, wax, heel-ball, everything. As well as ordinary shoes they used to make *straights,* which had neither left nor right feet.

Often both parents worked, mother perhaps sitting on a stool, stitching shoes by hand, and rocking the cradle with her foot, or watching to see that the *shackles* [broth] did not boil over on the fire. No gas or electric light, no bathroom, no water on tap, a bucket lav., no future, but some of us made it.

It was not unusual to hear the *tappers* singing as they

Caption right: Welt-sewing by hand at R E Trickers' Northampton factory. Footwear is still made wholly or partly by hand here, as well as by machinery. Dr R Whittaker, SATRA, Kettering.

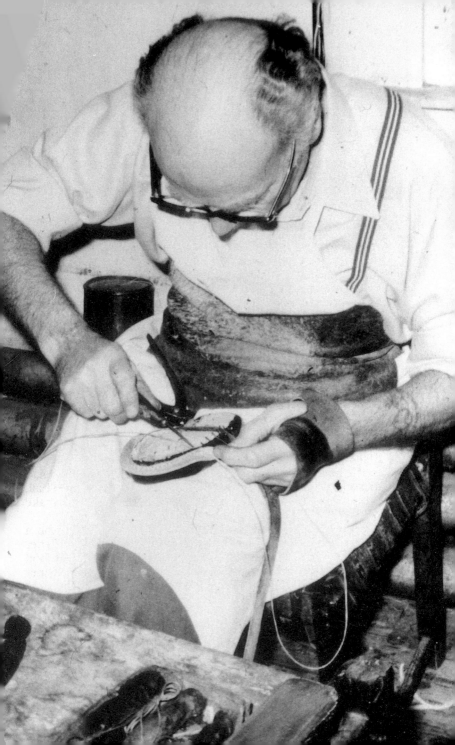

worked. In one *shop*, two men worked side by side and they'c
often sing a duet.'   *Mr A W Clements,* Harpole.

Mr Charles Marlow, a well-known local hand-sewn shoe maker,
gave me the following account:

'My grandfather "Boss" Loakes was born in 1854 and he was
the first trainer for the Cobblers when they played in the
Northamptonshire League. When they went on the beer, he
used to give 'em salts and get 'em round like that. And my old
Granny Loakes, she used to do the cobbling for the Cobblers—
she put the studs in the football boots. Charles Marlow was my
other grandfather and he walked in from Desborough
(Desborough's full of Marlows) when he was a very young
man, because they gave it out that there was work in
N'thampton. It would be about 1870. So he did the hand-sewn
and my uncles did it and I did it. They were all doing the hand-
sewn down Market Street, Northampton, where I was born.
My uncle Ted was one of the first to teach hand-sewn at the old
'Tec, which was the old Grammar School on Abington Square.
He used to make all the *cripple shoes* for Manfields.

Some people had places at the back of the houses where they
worked or a *shop* down the garden, but some just worked
upstairs in the bedrooms where they slept. The gaslight then
was just a flame, when they first had gas. Before that they had
candles.

They used to go in for canaries—they kept them company
while they worked. Some would keep a jackdaw in a cage, and
slit its tongue with a silver *tanner* [sixpence] so it would learn to
talk.

All the raw parts—soles, insoles, uppers, welts—come in
skips, and my cousin and me, we used to fetch it. Some o' the
men couldn't read or write, and my cousin used to read the
work-tickets to them. The women closed the uppers on a
closing machine downstairs and then took them upstairs to the
shoemaker. He put the insole on to the last first, because the
insole is like the keel of a ship—everything else is fixed on to it.
Then he started pulling over the uppers. The first big pull was
on the toe, with the *toe-puff* inside. That was called the *long
pull.* It was hard work, especially for Army or riding-boots. He
pulled over all the parts of the shoe, nailing them to the last as he
went.

When he'd got all the nails round he made the thread. The

ball of hemp was usually kept in an old tin with a hole in the lid. He pulled it out and measured it by the *fathom*–the distance between his two arms outstretched, from fingertips to fingertips. A fathom and a half'll do for a shoe, but for a seat and all there'd be two fathoms. The thread was several lengths twisted together and waxed. The wax was pitch and *Russian fat* or candle-fat, and he boiled it all together and mixed it up. Then he tipped it into a bucket o' water so it cooled down and went into a ball. He waxed the thread and put it across his legs and rubbed it so the friction melted the wax. Then he rubbed it round with a piece of leather, put it round a nail and pulled it longways till the wax worked into the fibres of the thread.

Then he put a bristle on–a hog's bristle years ago, but nylon later on. He twisted the bristle into the fine ends of the thread, made a hole with the awl and turned the threads back to lock them.

He made the stitch-holes in the leather with the awl, *riddled* it through and made the holes, then put both ends of the thread into each hole, facing opposite ways, so every stitch was locked. They never *got a machine out* [invented a machine] to do that. That's why you get so many complaints about the stitching coming apart in the machine-welted shoe. When they're done be hand, you never get anything back. You *sew* the uppers and *stitch* the bottoms.

He got a welt and started from the inside of the shoe, where the heel part was, and put the awl through the insole, upper and welt. He held the last on his lap with a leather strap, over the last and under his feet. He had a *hand-leather* to protect his hand as he pulled the thread through, and he went right round till he got to the other end.

When that was done he took out the nails that held the insole to the last, and put the bottom-filler in. Years ago it was felt–the felt you find on top of a hut, and they trimmed that up and put it in the middle of the sole.

Then he trimmed the uppers so they come level with the welt all round and stuck the sole on. They used to make their own paste from water and flour, or *dexter*–a yellow powder that they got from flax. Put the paste on, then stick the sole on and put a nail in each section to hold it, you see.

Then he stitched that round the welt, outside, with an in-and-out stitch, not the locking stitch. Next came a *piece-sole* and he trimmed it round, as near as he could to the upper, all according to how wide he wanted the welt. Then he tacked the piece-sole on to the insole, and put layers of heel-pieces–lifts–on and trim that round, buff it round with a buffing-knife to get it all level, then put the *top-piece* on, trim and buff.

Then he got a bit of emery and rub right round it to get it smooth. Then came *inking*–he got some beeswax or coloured wax and put some brown or black ink in. He had an *iron* which he warmed over a candle and just wheeled it round.

He buffed the soles and inked and waxed on top of that, and rubbed it down on his apron or whatever he'd got.'

Mrs Marlow said 'Sometimes they used a bone. I've seen my Dad do it with a ham-bone or a rib-bone. He used to do that at home when I was a little toddler. He used to do finishing at home. They used to have a candle there and heat the iron, and then he'd go round the edges to give a pattern.'

Mr Marlow went on 'They rubbed the sole with flour to *bring it up* white. There used to be white fronts and black waists and heels. The bottoms of shoes used to look lovely in the shops years ago.

They made *turnshoes* as well. They used to have the uppers inside-out and turn them inside when they were stitched. Then there were *straights*. The lasts for them were straight up the inside. The Romans wore straights–there were no left or right feet. . . . To make a last longer you just put a piece of leather on the front.

So when it was all finished, he put the shoes, perhaps two or three pairs, in a skip, and me and my cousin, we used to carry these skips between us to *Muster* Smith in Henry Street–he was the gaffer, They used to get five bob for a pair of shoes, for making them right through, and find their own *grindery*. In a week they'd perhaps do about seven pairs, some on 'em, but they worked all hours. This would be up to 1914. It livened up after that because the war come about and they wanted the Army boots.

There were grindery shops all up to the 'Course [Racecourse] and they sold nails, all different sizes. *Tingles* were the ones they put round the top-piece. Then there were brads and seat-tacks and balls of hemp, waxes and inks, eyelets and laces.

They called it *shopping it*–taking the work in o' Fridays. Then Mondays (Saint Monday they called it sometimes) they used to go on the booze and the women used to take the suits or whatever they could pawn up to Uncle Axby at the top of Market Street. They used to do the washing on

Mondays as well. And the men went on the booze till Tuesday.

Some on 'em went rabbiting or poaching if they couldn't get no work, and lived on what they could get *holt on* [hold of]. A shilling'd last 'em a good while—beer was about tuppence or thruppence a pint. But most of 'em had got work, because they were beginning to come in the town, the manufacturers were, and there was one at the bottom of Market Street—Sears', that was, before they had a fire and moved to Stimpson Avenue.

Wilson the builder, the one that started the firm, and all the big people used to come down Market Street to see me work. And Royalty used to come down St Michael's Road, the Queen Mother and King George VI, to see a fellow down there as used to make the hand-sewn. You didn't know they was in town— you'd never see them. They just used to stop outside his house and go in. He had their lasts there.

'My Uncle Ted was the first one to teach hand-sewn at the old 'Tec which was the old Grammar School on Abington Square. He used to make all the cripple shoes for Manfields.'

Mr Charles Marlow, Northampton.

'Mr Dobbs, the shoemaker'd get a little disc of leather and cut a little slot, then stick a clicking knife in the bench, hold the disc against the blade and pull — and there he had a shoe-lace.'

Mr E Drage, Bozeat.

'I can remember the shoemakers, on their days off, linking arms and marching across the Racecourse singing this song.

> We're on the booze, we can't make shoes,
> We'll all be 'appy today.
> I've pawned me ticker for 'alf a nicker
> At Jones's over the way.

> I've managed to borrer 'alf a dollar
> Orf my old woman today,
> And I know where to borrer some more tomorrer,
> So shout 'ip 'ip 'ooray.'

The lady who told me this rang off before telling me her phone number, so I could not ring back to see if she had remembered the other verses she mentioned. I was luckier with "The Ballad of Boughton Fair". All the verses are in a copy of the first volume of *Manfield Magazine,* 1929–1930, lent to me by *Mr Don Flower* of Wellingborough. Shoemakers traditionally attended Boughton Fair (held from the 25th to the 29th of June) along with cattle and horse-traders, gypsies among them.

THE BALLAD OF BOUGHTON FAIR

With his beard in his bib the stitchman wrought,
With his lapstone, leather and awl.
But he sometimes brushed from his clouded face
A tear, for the tears would fall.

And his hair on his drooping shoulders curled,
And his band round his brow was tied,
And he said 'Tis the eve of Boughton Fair'
And he stitched and stitched and sighed.

Then he said 'Come in' to a tap. She came.
And her eyes they were borage-blue.
And her hair like gold in the sunshine shone.
'I have scoured, Sir, the whole town through.

So you'll measure me, please, for shoes—and shoes
That will wear for years and years,
And you'll make me a pair that shall fit me well,
Of leather and thread and tears.'

'It is cruel to scoff' the stitchman said,
'At sorrow that none can allay,
But inform me, who, for the wonderful shoes,
Will, when I have made them, pay.'

'If it's pay you want, no pay you'll have,
Yet you'll make, all the same, for me
The finest pair that you ever have made,
For I read folks' thoughts' said she.

'T was at Boughton Fair, ten years ago,
That you lost what you prized the most.'
And the stitchman's face turned white as death,
Or the face of a sheeted ghost.

'And what did I lose?' he trembling said,
'Why, you lost me, father, there,
For I am the girl whom the gypsies stole
From the stall at Boughton Fair.'

And she flew to his arms and stopped his words
With kisses . . . at last he said
'I shall make them of tears, but they're bound to be tears
Of joy, and leather and thread.'

And at dusk they *wetted the candle-block*,
And his men their revels made,
And a loving hand on the stitchman's arm,
While they sang and joked, was laid.

And they raised a cup to Crispin old,
    And a cup to Crispin's heir,
    And a cup to the girl whom the gypsies stole
    From the stall at Boughton Fair.

And at dawn the happy stitchman wrought,
    As he'd wrought all the ten black years,
    And the shoes were made of leather and thread
    Of leather and thread and tears.

The shoemaker wore a leather bib to protect his clothes, and had a smooth stone on his lap on which he beat parts of the leather. To *wet the candleblock*, a lace-making term, is to take drink. Crispin and Crispinian are the patron saints of shoemakers.

Shoes were made entirely by hand until the introduction of the closing machines in the 1850s. These were similar to the domestic sewing machine and were used to 'sew and stitch' the prepared shoe components, giving employment to women in the many closing shops set up in living-rooms, bedrooms or barns, and later in 'sewing factories'. The following memoirs from the same magazine as the 'Ballad of Boughton Fair' give a good first-hand account of shoe-making based at Manfield's factory Northampton in 1875. Only pattern-cutting, sole-cutting and clicking [the cutting of upper leather] was carried out on the premises. The rest was done by workers in their own homes, or perhaps in small groups in backyard or upper room *shops*.

REMINISCENCES OF 1875

Mr A Nichols writes in the *Manfield Magazine*, 1930.

'It was a beautiful June day when I first saw the interior of the old factory on Campbell Square, surrounded by St Sepulchre's Church, the School and the Gaol now being demolished.

As a booking-boy, I remember a department called the *Work Out*, where Mr Warren, "the gentleman", gave out work to the women closers, Mr Smith, "the captain", gave out the class called "agents" work', the cheaper class, made mostly in the villages. Mr Williams, "the preacher" gave out the better class of *making*, and Mr Tom Caven, the manager . . . unpacked and examined hampers of agents' work from Abthorpe or some other village.

In the sole-cutting, the gentle Mr Philips was the manager, and in the clicking department, Mr Kidney, officer in the local

Volunteers. The pattern cutter was the late Mr G T Hawkins.

The "guvnor", Mr Philip Manfield (later Sir Philip), was a man with fine physique and carriage, and when in frock-coat and top hat looked every inch a gentleman. . . . Although about fifty-five years at this time, he would still take off his coat and run up the spiral stone stairs two at a time. Often his office light might be seen at 10 pm . . .

I recall these old offices of fifty-five years ago—three small rooms, that was all. In the first, a man, two youths and a boy. In the second, the principal and in the third, Mr Harry, Mr James (Mr Philip's sons) and the Lady Cashier. Once there was a sovereign short on a certain Saturday. One would never guess where it was discovered. The Cashier found it in the upturned tuck of her dress after returning home. Substitutes for phones in those days were zinc tubes connecting the office with the departments. On blowing down, a whistle sounded in the room at the other end.

About the year 1881, the writer was compelled for health reasons to rest at a seaside resort . . . Mr Philip sent personal letters in his own handwriting, with advice concerning health . . . and a gift, with more to follow if required. "You must rouse yourself and make up your mind that you will make the good out of it. If you cannot bear Sea Bathing . . . sponge yourself well and take short walks, don't tire yourself, and if your appetite is weak, get an egg beat up in a glass of sherry to take about 11 o'clock . . . and take some Epps' cocoa for breakfast. Try to get a little sleep after dinner, but above all, keep up your spirits. We are getting along fairly well. Lately but little has come in, but don't trouble about office work. Mr. Ellard is very good and will keep it under. Write again soon. With kind regards,

P Manfield."

My position was kept open till I was able to return.'

Now many years have passed since Mr Nichols wrote his account of Victorian shoe-making in Northampton at the Campbell Square factory, demolished in 1984 in the face of strong protest. Manfield became a household name, and so did that of G T Hawkins the pattern-cutter, whose old factory still makes specialist riding and climbing boots for a world-wide market. Out-working continued to the end of the century and beyond, as Mr Marlow's account shows. In 1931 the Rushden writer H E Bates gave a child's eye view of a sewing factory in *Charlotte's Row,* pp 16,25,26. Quintus the hand-sewn-shoe maker calls to the boy Adam.

'Will you go with the shoes to Daniel's?. . . . Sewn and stitched. You can remember that, four pairs sewn and stitched, can't you? They'll know. Can you *match* it if I sling them on your shoulder? . . .

Daniel's the sewing factory lay beyond a dark archway at the foot of twenty or thirty steps, where some dark buildings were gathered confusedly in a yard . . . filled with a drumming murmur of machines. As he pushed open the door of Daniel's, a low, one-roomed building next to an empty house, the murmur suddenly leapt out at the boy like an infernal thing, shrieking and moaning and hammering as if his presence were hateful. He saw a confusion of fantastic machines, whirling and quivering and gleaming in the gaslight, worked by white-aproned men with faces shining with dirt and sweat; there were little smoking pots of wax hanging over fierce blue flames and hundreds of boots piled up about the machines. . . . There was a rank odour of burning wax, and a machine which at intervals let out long shrieks more agonising than all the rest shrieking together. . . . Then a black individual with eyes gleaming white and a dirty rag round his neck, seemed to bear down on him from nowhere . . . and snatched the boots from his shoulders.'

Like Adam, the passer-by in Northampton could often hear the thump of the *bottom-stock* presses or *jumpers, the rough-rounders* and the whining *bottom-pounder*. Some factories were in St James, but most were in the densely-populated area just off the town centre–good buildings, many of them, with fine lettering and detail above their doors. In their hey-day in the first sixty years of this century, they made, for the most part, leather boots and shoes by the Goodyear welted process.

The Boot and Shoe Factory

THE DESIGNER AND PATTERN-CUTTER

The beginning of the work is Design and Pattern-cutting. After consultation with production and sales department, a number of last models are *set down,* approved as suitable. The lasts are made of maple, beech or plastic, in a shape which is longer than the foot and narrower in the *comb,* just above the instep. Elevations at each end are *toe-spring,* which allows for the rocking of the foot when walking, and *heel-pitch,* which accommodates the addition of the heel. *Sprung* and *dead* are terms for greater or less curvature at the front of the last. Both the designer and his steel marking tool may be called a *scriber.*

He draws a line down the centre of the last and makes a paper forme in the shapes of each side of the line. From the forme a working standard is made, from which the parts of the shoe are cut.

The design, made up in the required materials, is a *pullover.* A pilot or *pathfinder* line consists of several pairs of the new design, through a range of sizes. After fitting tests, a full set of brass-bound patterns are made in all fittings. Clicking-press knives can be cut from the patterns.

A shoe designer, Northampton (1970s).

'My grandfather worked at Miller Lasts in Arthur Street in Northampton when I was a boy in the Thirties. Grandmother used to get up at four in the morning and go down to the basement kitchen to make bread and get the water hot, ready for breakfast and grandfather's shave. He came down to the lovely smell of frying bacon and homemade bread. Then he went off to work in his old bowler hat and apron.

At twelve o'clock, Grandma took his dinner to work. The men ate outside in the loading bays and the women used to stand talking, waiting for the empty plates.'

Mr Geoff Roff, Easton Neston.

THE SKIN ROOM FOREMAN

'We make riding-boots, jodhpurs, walking, climbing and ski boots. We mainly use full-chrome leathers, oiled and greased. French calf is used for very expensive boots and it is about the best leather you can buy. In France the calves are not allowed to graze in the fields. They're tethered up in barns and store-fed, so you get no bramble or wire scratches—really, they're prime. *Veals* are skins from older calves.

First thing, when I start work, I collect the clickers' returns, the remains of the leather when the clicker has finished his job, and I credit him with his bonus, if he's got any bonus. I receive stock-sheets from the foreman, from which I fit up various clicking jobs with the right leathers.

When the leathers arrive at the factory, my job is to check them and put them on the skin-room shelves and in the *cubs–* open cupboards underneath. I go through the day, fitting different jobs up, searching different leathers out. Most processes are similar to those in other factories, but there is a treeing department for riding-boots. In the boxing department, the very best French calf riding-boots are packed in wadding. It wouldn't do to get them scratched.'

Mr Roger Wilson, Skin-room foreman,
G T Hawkins (1978).

THE CLICKER

'You read a skin like you read a book, and cut it up for what it's worth, as much as you can, as close as you can'

'I was just a little lad in the war, cutting linings for Army boots. I worked at George Webbs for forty-two years.

First thing in the morning, the foreman gives you a certain amount of leather, with information on the shoes he wants you to cut. You sort out the leather according to colour and shade. The next thing to look for is the quality and how much feetage there is. A twelve-foot skin would cut up into six pairs of shoes.

It was mainly cattle-skin, but linings were cut out of goat– even uppers were, sometimes. There was sheep, and I have cut horse even, and pig of course–you get suedes from pig. There was crocodile as well, though that's mainly ladies' work [for ladies' shoes] and we made primarily men's.

Leather comes in various forms–some was *stout,* some was thin. A tender skin split if you bent it over. *Plump* skins were softer and looser. A *pipy* skin has a loose surface. An ideal skin for upper leather was a nice, firm, medium-weight skin, about two millimetres. *Weight* means thickness. You read a skin like you read a book and cut it up for what it's worth, as much as you can as close as you can.

You cut the leather on the board with a knife which is just a handle with a blade in. The blade is made out of an old hacksaw blade as a rule. When you *fetch* the blade *out,* make the shape, that is, you use a grindstone, but after that you use a flat block of wood with a *buffing-strap* on one side and emery paper on the other. We call it a *rifle.* I know they call it something else out Wellingborough and Kettering way, but they're only country boys. You put the final edge on it with an oilstone and that makes a very good knife for cutting leather. Knocked on the

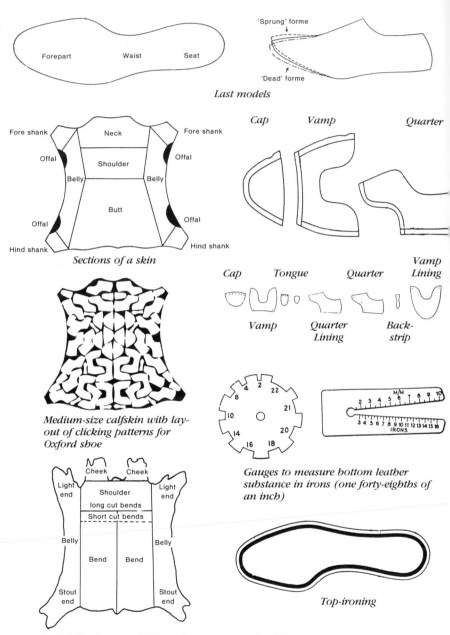

Forepart   Waist   Seat

'Sprung' forme

'Dead' forme

Last models

Fore shank   Neck   Fore shank

Offal   Offal

Belly   Shoulder   Belly

Butt

Offal   Offal

Hind shank   Hind shank

Sections of a skin

Cap   Vamp   Quarter

Cap   Tongue   Quarter   Vamp Lining

Vamp   Quarter Lining   Back-strip

Medium-size calfskin with lay-out of clicking patterns for Oxford shoe

Gauges to measure bottom leather substance in irons (one forty-eighths of an inch)

Cheek   Cheek

Light end   Shoulder   Light end

long cut bends

Short cut bends

Belly   Belly

Bend   Bend

Stout end   Stout end

Top-ironing

Cattle hide showing divisions for bottom-stock cutting

bench, it gives a certain ring, indicating a tempered steel. If it sounds flat, this would show a poor blade that would never hold an edge. As you stand by the board, you rock backwards and forwards on your feet, leaning over or slightly back as you cut round the patterns.

You start cutting the vamps first, six pairs of vamps, gradually working from the centre of the skin out towards the edges. That is the prime part of the skin—any waste should be in the flanks and *offal*.

So you cut up your skin, always matching pairs as you go. The upper is made of various pieces. For men's wear, there's the vamp across the middle of the shoe, the cap across the toe, quarters at the back, tongue down the front and backstrip at the back. It could be a backstay instead or a *moorcut*, cut all in one with the quarters.

The odd bits of leather are collected in an old sack and returned to the skinroom to be sold as fertiliser. The shoe components are examined, sorted and sent to the closing room.

An average figure of *pairage* cut per day might be a gross— 144 pairs. Some people could do a lot more. It depends what type of shoe it was and how fast you work. Tuesday is always a good day. Monday, you were getting over the week-end—by Friday, you're slowing down. If you have a good start on a Tuesday, you have a good week. Have a bad Tuesday and you're finished—it's too late after that to catch up.

Mr George Stinson, Northampton.

The 'country boys' in the Wellingborough and Kettering area call the knife-sharpening board a *rifle* or *rapstick*. The meaning of *rap* here is rasp. There is a Kettering saying, *'raping and scraping'*— scraping a living.

CLOSING

'It was always a joke that the first operation in the Closing Room is opening—counting and checking all the components sent from the Clicking Room. These are then stitch-marked and sent to Skiving, where the edges of the cut pieces of the upper are pared down to make a suitable edge for stitching. This was once the job of a hand-skiver, using a long knife, with the leather on a marble

---

Caption left: Sketches from Textbook of Footwear Manufacture, *J H Thornton, Northampton 1970.*

slab. The present-day machine is sometimes said to be *Going like the devil and not doing very much'*.

Closing is the preparation, fitting and stitching together of the prepared pieces. The closing machine can be of the flat or post variety, the latter, standing on an upright pillar, enabling parts of the upper to be stitched and kept in shape more easily.

Heavy footwear is *hand-stabbed* at the back and tabs.

ROUGH STUFF

In welted bottoming, the *bottom-stock*–soles, heels, insoles, welts and other parts are cut out from tough, durable leather in the Rough Stuff Room.

Terms used here are *slip-middles,* section between sole and welt in the *forepart* of the shoe, *top-pieces* and *seat-lifts,* all heel components.

Care is taken that all components are *fellowed, rounded* [cut] in pairs.

Before rounding, soles are wetted, partly dried, and put in a *mulling-cabinet* in warm, moist air. If rubber top-pieces [lowest heel-lifts, next to the ground] are used, these are attached by *cutlan* nails and cements.

MAKING

In the Making Room, two processes, lasting and attaching, take place.

In *hand-lasting,* the insole is tacked to the last by hand or machine, the upper being *pulled over* after the insertion of *toe-puff* and heel stiffener. This is done with a series of pulls with pincers in different directions, according to the shape of the last, in such a way that uniform tension is set up and the moulding of the last balanced. This is very important in bespoke and surgical work.

The upper is then pulled over the last in the waists with the *waist-drag.*

If the uppers are *set on the wood* [left on the last for a time] they retain their shape much better. Instead they may be *mulled* before lasting to make them more *mellow,* and set by heat afterwards. In machine-lasting, a pulling-over machine takes the place of the hand-laster, followed by other machine processes, and the uppers are *set* [shrunk to the last] afterwards.

Attaching. The first process is sewing in the welt, a strong, pliable strip of leather which strengthens the shoe and makes it

Closing Room, Allen and Caswell Ltd, Kettering, 1915-25. Standing, far right is Mrs Mobbs, the supervisor. NL, with acknowledgments to Mr W M Caswell, of the above firm.

watertight. In hand-welting, the sections to be used are tempered by being wetted and wrapped in cloth or sacking to dry and mellow. In the Goodyear welted method, the welt is sewn in while wet, and then beaten to bring it back to its original substance and close the fibres. It is dried and reduced by skiving. *Welt-butting* is the process of skiving the ends of the welt to meet the *seat.*

Bottom-filling. The completion of welt-sewing leaves a hollow space over most of the insole and this is filled in with a mixture of granulated cork and resin, and formerly with other substances such as leather waste. The *shank,* which acts as a bridge between heel and forepart, is inserted, the sole attached by stitching, and the seat is nailed on. The lifts (layers of the heel) are attached and the top-piece, the bottom layer, *slugged* (nailed round with slugging nails). *Breasting* is levelling off the front of the heel at right angles to the sole.

FINISHING

Finishing is a series of processes which includes trimming the edges of soles and heels, scouring the shoe-bottom, inking and burnishing, to present the shoe as completely finished as possible. *'Only an ink-boy'* was said of someone with little experience, both in and outside the shoe trade. *'He wants top-ironing'* was an ill-wish for an unpopular worker.

SHOE ROOM

In the Shoe Room, scuffs and wrinkles are hot-blasted, uppers cleaned and polished, sometimes to remove *spue,* a bloom appearing on finished shoes, due to the *migration* of chemicals to the surface of the leather.

'You could always tell a shoe-room girl because her shoes were never clean. They didn't bother about their own–they got fed-up with cleaning shoes all day in the factory.'

Mrs Lucy Marlow, Northampton.

Finally, when all defects have been dealt with, the shoes are examined, laced and boxed.

'As well as welted footwear, shoes are made by the *cemented process,* in which the bottom and sole are roughed and cemented and the two sections are compressed together.

In the *direct-moulded process,* unvulcanised rubber is put in a mould, which is then heated and subjected to pressure.

The sole is made and stuck on to the upper in one operation.

In *injection-moulding,* the lasted upper is positioned over a mould, and molten plastic injected into the mould. It sets in the required pattern, at the same time sticking to the upper.

Northampton, in common with other centres of footwear production, has suffered greatly from foreign competition and imports, and consequently overall pairage is much reduced. However, possibly the best bulk-produced welted footwear in the world is still made in Northampton.'

A factory manager, Northampton (1985).

Quarrying Stone and Smelting Iron

'I'll give a golden guinea to the first man who fills a cart'

Brown at Brixworth, grey at Geddington, laid in alternate courses at Blisworth, stone is a joy to the eye throughout Northamptonshire. Jurassic limestone, grey and cream with brown Northampton Sand ironstone, runs in a great sweep from Eastonon-the-hill in the north-east to Helmdon and beyond in the southwest, and has been extensively quarried for building stone and for iron ore.

In Helpston, the poet John Clare's native village, the Crowsons have been stonemasons for generations.

'Clare's tombstone in the churchyard – our people put that down, and in 1964, the centenary of his death, we re-lettered it. The cottage where he lived was one of a group of four or five. We made them all into one, modernised but looking old–his cottage is the kitchen now. We maintained Milton House and did a lot at Burghley. Stone has been worked here for centuries.'
Mr George Crowson, Helpston.

It has been won and iron has been smelted in the county for almost 2,600 years. A small bowl furnace with slag, found at

Oakley near Corby close to an Iron Age settlement of known date, about 600 BC, may be the earliest iron-working furnace in Britain. By the second century BC the hill-fort at Hunsbury, Northampton, was a major source of iron for the tribes of southern Britain. The site was abandoned in 20 BC. When it was quarried for ironstone from 1882 to 1887, workmen found domestic articles, iron weapons, blacksmiths' tools and slag from the furnaces and forges of more than 2,000 years before.

'We played as children in the track of the deserted nineteenth century tramway at Hunsbury, which carried ore to the furnace near the railway and canal. White violets grew on its banks, and we picked the yellow flowers of wild *bunny-rabbits* (antirrhinum) along the field-side path to the furnace cottages, where school-friends of ours lived. Mr James from Oxford Street, who had worked at the quarry with my grandfather, used to say that he had 'seen the roots of *twitch* (couch-grass), growing twenty foot down'. *Mrs Dorothy Grimes.*

In previous centuries, in Rockingham Forest, iron was smelted in charcoal furnaces until, by the reign of Elizabeth I, so much timber had been felled that laws were passed forbidding its use for charcoal-burning and the local iron industry died out. Stone was used solely as building material or for the making of monuments until, in the mid nineteenth century, the construction of cuttings and tunnels for railways showed the extent and value of the ore. A sample of Northamptonshire ore shown at the Great Exhibition of 1851 aroused wide interest. Locally, a quarry was opened at Wootton and the ore sent from Bridge Street Station to be smelted at Dudley.

This first venture was followed by the opening of quarries at Hardingstone and Blisworth and nine quarries around Northampton were opened in the 1850s. In time the quarries and some mines extended from Easton-on-the-hill in the north to Showsley in the south, and from Lamport in the west to Islip in the east. A group around Byfield and Charwelton was part of the Oxfordshire ironstone field.

At first the ore was taken to the nearest canal or railway and sent

to furnaces in the west midlands. Soon ironmasters built furnaces locally. The first was at Wellingborough, where Thomas Butlin built the East End furnace in 1852. There followed others at Heyford in 1857, Stowe and Finedon, 1866, Irthlingborough 1867, Islip 1871, Hunsbury Hill, 1873, Towcester 1875, Cransley 1877, Kettering 1878, Wellingborough 1886 and Corby 1910.

Some quarries and furnaces were in use only for a short time. The early quarries were worked by men using picks and shovels to remove the overburden of soil and expose the ore. This was broken up by explosives and loaded into carts to be taken to the nearest canal or railway. Later a considerable network of narrow-gauge tramways was constructed, on which small industrial locomotives hauled rakes of tipper-trucks to the furnaces. In the Nene valley at Cogenhoe, quarrying was in operation from 1858 to 1888.

'They used *pecks* (picks) and shovels, iron bars, chisels and sledge-hammers. The master on one of his visits said 'I'll give a golden guinea to the first man who fills a cart'. To do this, you filled a barrow with soil, pushed it along the planks, which were held on trestles fifteen to twenty-five feet above the ground, and springing as you walked, even more dangerous in a high wind, and tipped the barrowful of soil into the cart below. A Mr Mann from Cogenhoe won the guinea by filling six large barrows full, and as he was tipping the last barrow, both handles broke off. The same guinea has been handed down to my son, along with this tale.

I can just remember the nearby Whiston pit, which was worked from 1914 to 1921, and knew men who worked there. I was carried there *cock-hen-roost* (on a man's back or shoulders). The ore was blasted each day at lunch-time (mid-morning), dinner-time and evening, so that the dust had settled by the time the men got back to work. Then it was carried in trucks on the tramway, right down the fields, to the Cogenhoe to Grendon road, with a flag-boy to wave it across, and over the meadows to the Northampton to Peterborough railway line.'   *Mr Ted Hollowell*, Cogenhoe.

Mr Eric Higgs worked at the pit as a boy.

'I used to get there in the morning and light the fire and sometimes I was sent to Wellingborough to get the explosives. I came home with coils of fuse on the handlebars of my bike, sticks of dynamite in boxes on the carrier at the back and boxes of detonators in my pocket. Once the dynamite fell off. A man came along and started to help me pick up the sticks, but he soon ran away when I told him what they were.'

At about the turn of the century, steam shovels were introduced into the quarries and they in turn were superseded for certain jobs, such as removing the overburden, by the 'walking' dragline. This vast machine weighed nearly 2,000 tons and moved about on huge metal feet. The largest one, built in 1963 to work at Great Oakley quarry—near the site of the small furnace of about 600 BC—was a Ransome Rapier W1800, with a boom length of 282 feet and a bucket capacity of 30 cubic yards.

In the pick and shovel days a good man could remove one cubic yard an hour.

In 1962 the furnace at Wellingborough closed. It was the last of the Victorian works to go, leaving only Corby still in blast. By 1966 the four furnaces there were producing 2,500 tons of steel per day and this output increased when a still larger No 3 furnace was built. Corby, though, could not compete with the new coastal works having ready access to huge bulk carriers with their cargoes of iron-rich imported ore. In the spring of 1980 ironstone extraction ceased and the quarries and ironworks closed.

With acknowledgments to *Mr Ray Grimes,* Northampton.

The Railway

Down the Shed, round the Loop and over the Castle

The first railway station in Northampton was opened at Bridge Street in 1845, and five streets of small houses, mainly for railway workers, were built ten years or so later in the tiny hamlet called Far Cotton [the name means 'distant cottages']. In 1859 a small halt was built near the site of Northampton Castle and this was rebuilt and enlarged in 1881. Nearby St. James became the other railway district.

'I came to Northampton in 1912, when I was twenty years old, started on the railway and worked there for the rest of my life,

Caption: Navvies at Catesby. They worked on the construction of the Great Central Railway. NL, with acknowledgments to Leicester Museums, Art Galleries and Records Service, Leicestershire Record Office.

for the London and North-Western Railway, the London Midland and Scottish and then for British Rail. I wonder what folk would say now, if some trains had no toilets or even corridors. Lighting was by oil-lamps or naked gas-burners, the only way to keep warm was to hire a foot-warmer, and some coaches had wooden seats and floors of bare boards. A line of horse-drawn cabs stood in Castle Station yard and the Grand Hotel had its own coach to meet trains.'

Mr Jack Davis, Northampton.

Of the Far Cotton railwaymen, some worked 'over the Castle', but most were based at the Motive Power Department, where engines were *stabled* and maintained. This was quite an important place—not every town had such a department, and it stood, with its turntable, engine-sheds and office, near the canal, with swans gliding by the office window. It was known locally as 'The Shed'. Men going to 'book on' and children on their way to school converged in the old streets leading down to the railway, where the little alley-way to the Shed was just across the narrow road from the school gate, so close that engine-drivers could look into the classroom windows. The Shed stood at one corner of a *reversing triangle,* by means of which engines could be reversed in direction. The other corners were at Bridge Street Station and 'The Castle'. Lines between these points were collectively called 'The Loop'.

The fare round the Loop between the two stations was one penny, and this was the quickest and cheapest way to travel from St. James to Far Cotton. Both districts were on low-lying land and were often flooded. Porters at Euston used to call out *'Any more for Frog Island?'* as the Northampton train was ready to leave. Two other terms in common use were *a rough shunt* for bad luck or hardship, and *in the same link.* Literally this meant a group of men doing the same turn of duty, and figuratively, people with the same interests or characteristics.

Working shifts gave men time off during the day, and most kept allotments. Some of the ground was 'up *Thrup* road' [Rothersthorpe Road], within sight and sound of the Bank, the length of track coming out from the Castle, and as a train slowly pulled up towards the tunnel, they would straighten their backs and pull out their watches to see if 'she' was on time. Many kept pigeons, and a flock of these, wheeling across the smoky skies, was a familiar sight.

The *footplate man,* driver or fireman, could take a pigeon with him as he worked a train to its destination, releasing it there to fly home to 'Cotton'.

With acknowledgments to *Mr Peter Stoneman* for help with this section and for railway terms in the Glossary.

The Brewing Industry

Brewing

'The master's barrel was set aside'

It was once carried out in homes and farmhouses, and so crucial was the timing of the various processes that it was usually accepted that the housewife did no other work while brewing was in progress. Many farms had a brewhouse and sometimes a malthouse or maltkiln as well. The remains of an early seventeenth century maltkiln, with its floor of perforated bricks, can be seen at Church Farm, Newnham.

'This was once the Home Farm, the house of the estate steward. It supplied farm produce and malt for the manor houses of Newnham and Brockhall, the Thorntons being lords of the manor of both houses. The barley was warmed from underneath by steam from a boiler.'

Mr Robert Key, Church Farm, Newnham.

After malting, the barley was milled and was then ready for brewing.

'The brewer came once a year and stayed for a week. We had to have a licence to brew our own beer. In the brewhouse [a cellar] were two coppers with fires below them. The hogsheads which held the beer were made in the cellar and were too big ever to be removed. There were two openings in the breakfast room floor with wooden covers. The *snake* [metal pipe] and funnel passed down through the holes into the coppers. We children were not allowed down there, but we used to creep down to play with the froth. Enough beer was made to last for twelve months, and the master's barrel was set aside for his use only.

My mother said that the only good thing about the war (1914–18) was that there was not enough sugar and malt to make beer, and it was never made at home after the war.'

Mrs Fountaine, Pattishall.

A *bough-house* was a private house allowed to sell liquor at fair-time. The word, said to be obsolete *(EDD)* is still known at Brigstock, where there was such a house. A green bough, ancient sign of an alehouse, hung outside.

Beer was fairly cheap and was said to be almost a food in itself.

'Thatchers half-lived on beer—it had so much goodness in it.'
Mr Jack Meyer, Little Houghton.

'Harpole once had two bands—a beer band and a teetotal band. No love was lost between them and when they met in action, neither would stop playing.' *Mr A W Clements,* Harpole.

From about the mid-nineteenth century beer was brewed commercially in numerous breweries in town and county, their numbers reduced over the years by mergers, take-overs and closures.

For many years Phipps' Brewery and the Northampton Brewery Company, standing side by side, dominated the lower part of Bridge Street and employed many local people.

'The brewery girls used to stand outside at dinner-time wearing clogs and coarse aprons, with their hair tied up in scarves. They used to smoke, which was unusual for women in those days. The gateways where they stood had iron protections, shaped like sugar loaves, at the edges of the wall, to stop them being knocked by the wheel-hubs of the drays as they went in and out.' *Mr Ray Grimes,* Northampton.

The brewery product was locally approved.

> Phipps's beer is very good,
> Dulley's ent amiss,
> Bedford beer is damnable
> And Praed's is worse than—
> *Mr William Jones,* Litchborough.

Dulley and Praed were Wellingborough brewers.

Malting

'The only way to tell if it is cooked is to chew it'

'The bags of barley weighed sixteen stone each. Two bags weighed a *quarter*, and we kept fourteen hundred quarters in stock. The barley was dressed and cleaned, dried and stored in bins. Then it was steeped for forty-eight hours and the *steep* [steeped grain] thrown on to the floor in heaps.

Next day it was thinned out along the floor with the temperature at 60°F. It remained there for ten to twelve days, being turned with the wooden malting-shovel and *ploughed*– an action similar to hoeing.

The barley was loaded onto the kiln next. Two men with shovels filled the *bobies,* half-moon-shaped vessels with large wheels. The barley from the lower floor was loaded on to the kiln by means of skips on wheels, pulled up by hoist. The fire was lit at three o'clock.

The temperature next morning was 160°F and three men went into the kiln to turn the corn at six, twelve and three o'clock, by which time it was getting dry. On the third day, with the temperature at 210°F, the corn was turned again, and by three o'clock it was roasted.

For pale beers the malt has to be pale in colour. The only way to tell if it is cooked is to chew it. Now it weighs twelve instead of sixteen stone. Fires are shut in and left till next day, when the malt is run through a screen to remove the *cooms* [roots]. It is stored in a bin till required at the brewery and then weighed off to twelve stone and sent to the mill. Special shoes were provided, with canvas tops and string bottoms, to avoid crushing the malt. *Mr R French,* Northampton.

Coom is another word said to be obsolete *(OED).* Mr French makes no complaint about the extremely high temperatures in which men had to work. *The Malt Shovel* public house stood opposite the brewery. Like the nearby *Navigation Inn,* it has lost its name.

The Brewing Process

'The milled malt was moved by conveyor to a hopper above the mash-tun. Brewing commenced at 4.30am. In attendance was a brewer and his assistant. Mashing-in begins with milled malt, called grist, being fed into the mashing machine and mixed with water, always called liquor. Sugar is added at the same time, and quantities and temperatures are important. After standing awhile for conversion, the extract is run off, *sparging* slowly [being sprayed with warm water] to rinse out all the extract. The resultant liquor—wort—passes through the false bottom in the mash tun into the *underback*, via the Valentin arm [named after an inventor or manufacturer]. The mash tun now contains hot spent grains, which are removed by two men with shovels and sold to farmers.

The wort is pumped to the *kettle-house*. In the kettle, hops and more sugar are boiled, to extract bitterness from the hops, and Irish moss is added to clarify the brew.

The brew is turned out into the *hop-back*, and the liquid drawn off, leaving behind spent hops, to be sold for farm and garden use. The liquid is cooled and drawn off into fermenting vessels, Yeast is added, and during fermenting, some yeast is skimmed off to be saved for future use, but some, the *dirty head*, is left to act as a cover for the brew. This is later collected and sold. The *bright beer* is conveyed to a storage tank for barrelling and bottling.'   *Mr C Smith*, Northampton.

Coopering

'It always makes a cooper smile to hear anyone talk about a big barrel or a little barrel. A barrel holds thirty-six gallons.'

In Cattlemarket Road, Northampton, there once stood the cooperage and cask store for the nearby breweries.

'The beer-casks were made of oak, ideally Memel oak from Russia, which has a straight grain and is basically free of knots. The staves are cut to shape, hollowed on the inside with a *hollow-knife* and rounded on the outside or back with a backing-knife. With a *chive* [another knife] the cooper cuts a hollow in each stave to take a groove for the *head* [end of cask] to fit in. The staves are set round in a circle and a fire is lit in a *cresset* inside, to warm the wood so that it can be bent to shape. Then hoops of ash-wood are *driven* on to the staves with a trussing-hammer, and later metal hoops are put on with a hammer and *driver*.

It was hard work, and the cooper's shoulder-muscles some-times became permanently stretched as a result.

Jigger and *croze* are the names of two other tools used for making grooves for the heads. To *chinse* is to work rushes (bulrushes) into the grooves to make the head watertight. When needed, split rushes are also put between staves with a *flagging-iron*. The outside of the cask is shaved with a *downright*.

The smallest cask, a *pin*, holds four and a half gallons; a keg holds six gallons; a firkin, nine gallons; a kilderkin, eighteen; a barrel, thirty-six; a hogshead, fifty-four.

Sherry and port casks from the Continent were much bigger and of different shape. A *port pipe* was long and thin, a *puncheon* stubby. Bungs from the casks were removed with a *flogger*.'   *Mr Horace Tarrant*, Northampton.

'It was the custom on a Monday morning, maybe with a touch of boozers' gloom, for the *snobs* [shoemakers] to repair to a hill known as *Callowell* and there play cards and drink. On one occasion they ran out of beer and after some thought decided to draw lots as to who should go back to the village, borrow a horse and cart, go to Mannings' Brewery in Northampton and there ask to see a high-ranking man (who lived at Harpole) and ask for a barrel of beer on strap [to be paid for later]. This genial gentleman agreed and asked if a four-and-a-half gallon barrel would do? "No" said the snob, "make it a niner" and a niner it was. I was given to understand that the debt was settled to the satisfaction of all.'   *Mr A W Clements*, Harpole.

Now the two breweries and the cooperage have gone. The huge Carlsberg Brewery, which began production in 1973, occupies the site of the breweries, and the river Nene was re-channelled to make more room.

The product is lager—the word means 'store'—matured for many weeks after being made by fully-automated processes. In fact these processes are much the same as they were. The raw materials are still malt [and maize], water, hops and yeast. The terms *mash kettle, mash tun, wort kettle* and *bright beer* are still used. Spent grains are removed from the *laughter* tun (pronounced lawter) after settling. Sediments are removed after the wort has passed through the *whirlpool*.

The changes since 1973 have already given rise to a saying—'over the wall' or 'over the other side', meaning 'in the old brewery'.

With acknowledgments to *Mr Roy Scott*, Northampton, for his help in gathering and explaining the material.

The Grand Union Canal

'. . . plenty of blisters and hard hands'

The waterways of England and Wales carried commercial traffic for about two hundred years, from the 1760s to the 1970s. Northamptonshire, on the busy route between Birmingham and London, was crossed by the Grand Junction, later Grand Union Canal, from Braunston to Cosgrove, with an *arm* to Northampton from a junction at Blisworth. The canal runs through a tunnel, recently rebuilt, between Blisworth and Stoke Bruerne.

Working barges can still be seen among the pleasure-boats at Braunston, and there is a canal-side warehouse with a wide overhang from its roof, covering the towpath and part of any boat moored alongside. Here and there along the towpath can be seen incisions in the handrail of a footbridge or in one of the iron bands protecting the brickwork of bridges. These were made by ropes, in the days of horse-drawn boats—narrowboats—though the people who worked in them seldom used that name.

'My father and mother worked on the barges on the Grand Union Canal in their early married life, and one of their children was born on a barge, but I was the youngest, and when I was born they lived *on the land* at Milton.

In the 1920s and 30s I spent some of the school holidays on the barges, mainly looking after the horses. There would be one or two of them, perhaps mules instead of horses, because they were more sure-footed. When the boat came to a tunnel, the horse was led over the top, while a tug with a Diesel engine pulled the barge through. It was all wet and dripping as you went in, but you could see the light at the end. In the days before powered boats, they used a pole to push the boat through, or they were *legged* through. I've seen the horse lean sideways as it went under a bridge.

It was hard for the horse, pulling the barge, quite often two barges (the second one was called the *butty*), for twenty miles a day. Some people took care of their horses and liked to *dinks* [decorate] them up, but some worked them very hard.

They used to swing the nose-bags in the canal to dampen the oats and corn, otherwise when the horse blew down its nose, it blew half the grain away. Once, one of the nosebags came up with an eel hooked in it. They used to fish for eels at night—four feet long, some of them were, and as thick as my arm.

Some of the barge people kept a dog—for catching rabbits, mainly, and they'd go in the fields themselves and take a few potatoes and swedes. They pulled ducks in off the canal with a piece of bread tied to a string, and there were never many ducks' eggs in the reeds either, I can tell you. But on the other hand, the barge people were always blamed for anything that went missing—it was always their fault.

The barges carried coal very often, from Coventry or Nuneaton to London, mainly to power stations. Then there was timber, and grain to Whitworths at Wellingborough, and lighter cargoes as well—Ovaltine from King's Langley and tinned milk from Aylesbury to London—right into the docks sometimes.

If it was coal they had to wheelbarrow it—the man and the woman, both used to *muck in* and load the barrows and push them up a plank on to the bank. The woman worked as hard as the man, and when the barge was moving, she'd be peeling potatoes, preparing the meal or knitting or sewing while she steered the boat.

Everybody had to take a hand at that—someone had to be there all the time. You steered on your time off. If it was straight there was nothing much to do, but there was no getting away from the smoke if it blew over you.

There were two little steps just below where the tiller was, with a trap door above and in the winter you could stand or even sit on the steps and put your arm up to the tiller. Even tiny tots had to stand on a stool and steer. Boys and girls—everybody had a job. The boys spliced the ropes, and when they wore out, they'd make fenders of them, to hang over the side of the barge to protect the paint, if it caught a bridge or a lock-gate. It was hard work turning the windlass at the locks. The boys used to jump across—I've done it many a time, but it was a long way down. They didn't wear life-jackets, you know—they just used to fall in and out of the water like dogs—I never heard anyone say "Be careful".

My mother was brought up on a barge, She never learned to read and write, but later on, they used to leave the children at a school so many days a week and pick them up on the way back. Some of the teachers were very good to the barge children, and it wasn't easy because the barge people used a

Caption right: Welton. A horse towing a barge and butty and wearing a nosebag.
NL

language of their own, with different words. I can't remember them now.

It was very cramped on the barge. Walk down three steps and keep your head down. On your left was the coal-fired range with a brass rail round it. I don't know how they didn't get burned. It was very hot down there. Often one woman would cook for two barges, and they'd put a kettle of water on top of the boat in hot weather to get warm—anything to save having the range on too long. They cooked mainly stews and things like that, and they kept the food in a cubby-hole at the end, in tall brown containers with lids.

They used to put the buckets, painted in traditional colours and patterns, on top of the boat. A man at Banbury did the painting. And they were very fond of plates with a lace pattern round the edge. They hung them on the walls with a ribbon tied through the holes to hold them in place when the boat rocked. All the brass was polished and shiny—the women were very houseproud. They worked in black clothes and kept their best things in a box under the bed. It was a double bed and usually three or four people slept in it. There were quite a lot of children in some cases, often six or eight. My father was one of eight.

My mother made all the clothes—most of the women did. Shops were few and far between, so they made most of the things they needed, like pegs, themselves. My grandmother wore a bonnet, black in winter, white in summer.

I didn't find much really bad language. They used to swear a bit—you could hear them as you passed some of the boats. They never wanted to slow down too much at the *winding-holes* [bays in the bank for turning] or they were moaning about the weeds. They drank quite a lot—the men particularly. They'd stop at night at one of the pubs, like the Navigation Inn at the Arm end, and down a few pints. They always knew where everybody else was, where he'd be, where he was going, where he'd come from and when they saw a barge coming, they knew instantly who it was.

Families stuck together and brought the children up strictly. As the sons grew up they took another boat—it was nearly always a family business. There were very few arguments or rows. They were very knowledgeable, very adaptable. There was usually no doctor, no nurse, no vet. within call, so they had to know what to do themselves. And there was no time for hobbies—the lads played football a bit. It was a hard life in many ways—plenty of blisters and hard hands, but you rarely heard them complain—they'd always got another job to do.'

Mr Bill Cherry, Northampton.

In earlier times, life and language could be very rough. A barge-girl's comment on something which could have been worse was *'There'll be no rippin' o' guts (even), if there's kickin' of arses'*, and it was said that a single pregnant girl might end up in the Cut, perhaps with a butty towed over her.

But there were gentler memories.

'We lived by the canal at Stoke Bruerne, just by the bottom lock. You could look across to the big house at Stoke Park through the trees. A family called Burns lived there, and in the very bad winter of 1895, when I was six, the canal was frozen over for sixteen weeks and none of the barges could move. The Burns family used to make coppers full of soup two or three times a day and anybody who was out of work could go and have some.

Just below the bridge they fixed the horses to the ice-breaker. There must have been more than twenty of them—they stretched, sometimes one horse, sometimes two abreast, right down past the next lock to the wooden-topped bridge below that. It was a sight—all those horses with their drivers, then the steam-boats following behind, as close as they could get, then the horse-boats. They kept going, up and down, day and night, to keep it open till it thawed.

All the boats had to come through Blisworth tunnel. The fare for the tug to pull the boat through was sixpence for an empty boat and a shilling for a full one. Sometimes when there was no wind, the smoke and fumes were shocking.

The boat people didn't get much money, you know. A boat with a ton of cargo got a farthing a mile. The boat would carry thirty tons, but it doesn't work out much, does it? They carried coal, long ash poles which they took to London to be made into cotton-reels, loads of corn, beer, which Phipps sent from Northampton to Coventry, limestone, ironstone from Blisworth to Hunsbury Hill furnaces, then the pig iron from Hunsbury Hill to Birmingham, groceries, and sometimes gunpowder. When that was carried, there would be a red flag on the mast. The horses worked hard. Some were well-fed and the women used to crochet frilly hats for them, to keep the sun off, but some were poor things.

My Dad, John Timson, worked on the canal for forty-six

years. He was a *lengthman*, responsible for keeping the hedges and towpath clear on his stretch of the canal. My grand-dad, John Janes, lived with us and he used to sit outside the cottages as he got older. All sorts of people came by in those days—hawkers, tinkers, tramps, Spanish onion-sellers and an Italian with a barrel-organ and a monkey that sat on his shoulder. When someone he recognised came along, my grand-dad would say "Come on, mother" (to his daughter) "time for a cup of tea". He had been a farm labourer all his life but he could read and write. He came from Tring, and the Rothschilds provided a school there. I used to fetch him his shag and his beer. It cost threehalfpence a pint.

The lavatory was on the other side of the canal from our cottage. The quickest way was over the lock-arm—there was a little handrail. One night my sister and I were going to cross, when one of the neighbours' boys, a bit simple-minded, said he'd carry my sister across. He picked her up and they both fell in the lock-pound. I screamed and shouted till people came running and pulled them out.

Every place had someone people went to when they were sick, and by the canal it was my mum. She had all sorts of remedies—one was the puffball mushroom. They used to collect and dry it and keep it in a jar, to use for stopping bleeding. One man came in with a massive gash down his arm from an accident on the canal. He swore the puffball saved his arm. An old tramp came to the door with a poisoned toe. My mother bathed it and put on this country ointment. Years later he came back to see my mother and was told she was very ill. He said that he just wanted to thank her for saving his toe. A few days later she died.

The boat people were a mixed bunch. Some were clean, some were dirty. Some were honest and some were thieves. Most of them never learned to read or write. They always said *oinons* instead of "onions" and they didn't like oinons if they could get any lecks. They always had tea in a basin, and would ask for "a cup of *tay* in a basin, *plase*". One of the boat people lodged with a widow in Stoke Bruerne once. Come Christmas he said "What about Christmas dinner, then?"

Well, she wasn't very bothered, and said "Get a fowl out of

Caption left: John Janes, retired farm labourer, outside his son-in-law's cottage by the bottom lock at Stoke Bruerne, before 1914. Miss Margaret Lattimer, Moulton.

the run and you cook it". He managed to kill it, but he'd never cooked a fowl before, and he just stuffed it in the oven, feathers and all. Poor woman, the fumes nearly suffocated her.'

Mrs Lucy Emery, Milton Malsor.

Mrs Lucy Emery was the wife of George Emery, Lord Hesketh's thatcher. They married in 1916. Most of the above account was published in the *Chronicle and Echo,* Northampton, on the 14th November, 1979, written by Matthew Engel with the assistance of *Mrs V Proctor* and *Mrs Emery's* niece, *Miss Margaret Lattimer,* who also lent me the photographs.

I feel certain that the 'country ointment' was comfrey ointment. See p. 27.

Lace-making

'She had some lovely bobbins, bone and wood, with the names all on them.'

The art of lace-making was probably brought to England in the sixteenth century, by lace-workers from France and the Netherlands seeking refuge from religious persecution. There is a pleasant and persistent legend that Queen Katharine of Aragon, divorced by King Henry VIII and banished to Bedfordshire, taught the local women. In fact, nothing certain is known of this.

We are on firmer ground in 1698. A Parliamentary Petition of that year (quoted in the *Victoria County History,* vol. 2, p. 337, Abington Park Museum Library) shows that there were then five hundred and ninety-one lace-makers at Towcester. Nearly one hundred years later, the *Universal British Directory* of 1789 says of Northampton 'Its principal manufacture is shoes, and next to that, stockings and lace'. The main centres locally were Olney, Newport Pagnell, Hanslope, Towcester, Wellingborough and Yardley Hastings. Towcester remained an important centre, with Paulerspury and Spratton, and lace-making was carried out in most villages and in Northampton.

Caption right: Mrs Scott of Pury End with her daughters, Florence, Mabel, Ida and Rose, later Mrs Foster. All their dresses and lace collars were made by Mrs Scott, and she taught these skills to her daughters. Mrs Brenda Slack, Pury End.

'We used to do the *Lady's Fancy,* the *Fan* and the *Spider,* and there was the *Seven* and the *Fourteen* and the *Eighteen-plaited.* Mother made them all, and several sorts of lace-collars. She had some lovely bobbins, bone and wood, with the names all on them.

There used to be a lace-buyer come to Towcester every month, and he had a room at the Talbot Hotel, and people took the lace there. So I used to go down, and the older people in the village used to give me their lace to take. I remember Mother saying, the first time I went "The lace-buyer always gives a ticket for a woman to have half-a-pint o' beer if they want, but you won't have that, so you take it in thread instead."

He used to have a box, blue-lined, and all the lace you took had to be wrapped in blue paper, so it wouldn't go yellow. He wouldn't accept it if it *wadn't.* And he sold the thread and the pins. I've heard my mother say that the first pins had no knobs and you'd get sore fingers. And this *Lady's Fancy,* he used to give us fourpence a yard for that, and the *Seven-plaited* was tenpence, and the collars half-a-crown. It was badly-paid work, it was, for the work as was put in.

I should say you'd find a piller [pillow] in everybody's house that were poor people. All the women in the town [village] had to do it, and all the girls had to learn. I detested it. My mother used to say, when I come from school, "Now sit down and do your piller-work. The sooner you do it, the sooner you'll get out to play." She used to set me four *heads* [patterns] a night.

I was sorry afterwards that I done away with the piller. I'd 'ad s' much of it when I was little, so I got rid of it. But I kept some of the parchments [patterns] for a long, long time. They were all skin parchments–they were lovely. I burnt 'em–it was a shame. My brother made mother a *horse* [wooden frame] to protect her piller in. It was a beauty and I burnt that. And mother had got a nice bobbin-wheel, for winding the bobbins on. My brother stripped it all down and painted it oak colour. But I destroyed that as well.

My children, all three of them, they used to stand and watch the Gran doing the piller, and they used to say to her "Gran, can we do a stitch now?" and she told 'em how to put the thread over and under and all the rest. They'll talk about it now,

Caption left: George Emery was the husband of Lucy Emery, John Janes' grand-daughter. He was Lord Hesketh's thatcher and is seen here thatching at Milton Malsor. Miss Margaret Lattimer, Moulton.

standing by the Gran, doing the stitch. Yes, Ted an' all, though he was a boy, he had to come in and do a stitch for his Gran.

I always remember, when I worked at Towcester, a person sat next to me and she was gooin' t' be married. She had every bit of her underlinen trimmed with lace, and my mother done it all, every bit. And her petticoat had the *Eighteen–plaited* at the bottom. I see [saw] her years afterwards, and she told me as when she had her first baby, she took the lace off her petticoat and put it on the christening robe. So she said "Your mother's lace is still goin' strong".'

This is the transcript of a tape-recording made by *Mrs I Smart* of Greens Norton in 1979. The lace-maker, *Mrs M Swain*, lived in Greens Norton all her life.

'There was a lace-making school at Ashton (near Roade) and my grandmother was sent there at the age of five. I still have a tablecloth she made for my mother about 1900. She made insertions about three inches wide and leaves for decorating dresses. Her fingers used to fly, and on dull days she used a lamp-like glass to reflect light from the window. Many women in Ashton used to make lace in those days, to eke out a living, and the lace was collected by an agent from Olney.'

Miss Jessie Curtis, Northampton.

The following is an account of the lace-school at Spratton in about 1840. (The date is not made clear.)

Girls there left day-school at eight and joined the lace-school. Their hours were from 6 am to 6 pm in summer and from 8 am to 8 pm in winter. They were allowed half-an-hour each for breakfast and tea and an hour for dinner. Each girl had to stick ten pins a minute or six hundred an hour, and if, at the end of the day, she was five pins behind, she had to stay an extra hour. . . .

Eighteen girls sat round the table, three to each bottle [light-reflecting glass] their stools being upon different levels, the highest nearest the bottle. In the daytime, as many as thirty girls, and sometimes boys, would work in a room about twelve foot square, with two windows, and in the winter they would have no fire for lack of room. If a girl's pins fell short she would go round the room singing

Polly or Betsy, a pin for the poor.
Give me a pin and I'll ask no more.

NNQ 1886, p 641

That must have come as a welcome relief from the cramped

position in which the girls had to work. Some were so stiff at the end of the day that they had to be carried upstairs to bed. Some wore special corsets which held their bodies more upright, as they sat in winter round the *candle-block,* a tall stool, its top or *holeboard* pierced to take the nozzle, a wooden candle-socket, adjustable in height, in the centre, and sockets round the edge for the *flasks* or *flashes.*

These were long-necked glass globes, filled with water. There were usually four of them and each acted as a lens, reflecting the light of the single candle. Three to five girls could work fairly comfortably round one candle but there were often more, the older and more experienced having the better seats, the *lesser lights* sitting behind.

Each girl worked at a stuffed pillow, held on her knees or on a wooden *horse* or *maid.* The pattern was laid on the pillow and pins stuck in to follow the design. The threads, each wound on a bobbin, are worked round and between the pins, the bobbins hanging down in front, with glass beads or other ornaments to add to their weight and keep the threads lying straight. In cold weather the workers sometimes had *firepots* of earthenware, brass or iron, filled with hot ashes or charcoal, placed near their feet. Summertime, when they worked outside, must have come as a blessed relief.

The old French or Flemish lace-names were sometimes used, but often local names took their place, so Torchon, a coarse but attractive lace, became *beggar's lace* and *Bucks Point,* said to be the most beautiful of all English lace, was based on the laces of Lille and Mechlin. *Blonde* was made from natural silk, and *yak,* usually black, was made with thread produced from yak's hair.

A *bud* is a small component part of a pattern. These pattern-names are still known locally: *cat's face; crown; Fertility; Kat-stitch,* used for wire-ground, a background pattern; *Little Dick; lover's knot; Old Trot; old wheel; pheasant's eye; Prince of Wales' feathers; running river.*

The inner edge of the lace, to be sewn to other material, is the *foot* or *footside,* the outer edge the *turnside* or *headside.*

The pillow may be round, square or roll-shaped, and was covered by a *butcher-blue* cloth, to help keep the lace white. A *worker* or *drawcloth* may hang down the front of the pillow to take the friction of the moving bobbins. A *drawter* keeps the finished lace clean.

The pins were made in factories at Hardingstone, Milton Malsor, Stony Stratford and Long Buckby, in factories owned by a

Caption: *A beautiful Victorian photograph of unknown date. A lacemaker works at her pillow in front of her cottage in Spratton. NL*

family called Lever. The earliest pins had no heads and workers made their own from sealing-wax, or from *sweethearts*, the burrs of the plant goosegrass. A Greens Norton lady still uses *burrhead* pins.

Bobbin-making is an art in itself. They were made mainly of fruit-tree wood, and for extra weight had *spangles* [glass beads], pewter or wooden rings, nuts shells or lucky charms. Here are some bobbin-names, descriptive of the various designs used: *bird-cage, cow-in-calf, church window, mother-in-babe*. In all these four designs, the shank was hollowed out into tiny compartments, or made in sections, with a smaller bobbin inside. *Jack-in-the-box* was also made in sections, usually of light and dark wood; *the fairing* was of bone inlaid with metal; *dumps* or *bob-tailed* bobbins were of wood only; *old maid* was plain and thin, and the *yak* was a large heavy bobbin, used for making worsted lace. There are many more names to be found in books, but all the above names are still known.

Lace Tells

'Nineteen long lines hang over my door'

Most lace makers could not read or write, and to help them keep count of their pins and patterns, a collection of rhymes and songs grew up, some based on local folk-tales. Like all work-songs, they helped to prevent boredom and kept the rhythm going. I heard the following *tell* sung by Mrs Doris Robinson of Little Houghton and her daughter, Mrs Loretta Smith. Mrs Robinson was eighty years old and had heard the village lace-makers sing it when she was a child. It is a simple round for two workers, to the tune of 'For he's a jolly good fellow'.

> The bobbins are twisting and twirling
> With a murmuring, buzzing sound.
> The bobbins are twisting and twirling
> Around, around and around.
>
> Then all up, all up, all up,
> A-coming, a-coming, a-going,
> The bobbins are twisting and twirling,
> All up, all up, all up.

From Yardley Hastings

> Twenty pins have I to do,
> Let ways be ever so dirty,
> Never a penny in my purse,
> But farthings five and thirty.
> Betsy Bays and Polly Mays,
> They are two bonnie lasses.
> They built a bower upon the tower,
> And covered it with rushes.   *(Wright)*

The compiler thinks this may refer to the rush-bearing ceremony.

> I had a little nutting-tree
> And nothing would it bear
> But little silver nutmegs
> For Galligolden fair.   *(Wright)*

He adds 'But who Galligolden is, is not clear.' It is clear that it is a most beautiful name.

> Nineteen long lines hang over my door,
> The harder I work, the shorter my score.
> The more I do play, it sticks at a stay,
> So come, little fingers, let's twink away.
> There's twinkum and twankum and five to your four,
> Them as are done first, they may give o'er.
> My shoes are to borrow, my true love's to seek,
> I cannot get married till after next week.
>   *(Freeman, Wilson, Wright)*

An old gentleman of eighty cycled the three miles from his home at Kempston to see Mr Fred Hamer and his wife in Bedford. He recited to them a complete version of *The Wedding Day,* which is to be found in Mr Hamer's collection of folk-songs, *Green Groves.* Here are three of the twenty or so verses of this lively and lovely song.

> Nineteen long lines hanging over my door,
> The faster I work, it'll shorten my score.
> But if I do play, it'll stick to a stay,
> So ho, little fingers and twink it away,
> For after tomorrow comes my wedding-day.
> My shoes are to borrow, my husband to seek,
> So I cannot get married till after next week,
> And after next week it will be all my care
> To prink and to curl and to do up my hair.
> Six pretty maidens so neat and so clean
> Shall dance at my wedding next Monday morning.

Down in the kitchen, the cook she will run,
And tell Mr Bellman to ring the ting-tang.
(Hamer, Wilson, Wright)
Ting-tang is still used for the smallest bell of a peal.

One moonlight night as I sat high,
Waiting for one to come by,
The boughs did bend, my heart did break
To see what a hole the fox did make.
(Freeman, Wilson, Wright)
Freeman also says that this tell was collected in Oxford by J O
Halliwell-Phillipps. It is a rhymed version of a folk-tale, usually
known as *The Oxford Student* (K Briggs and R Tongue).

The student and a local girl were lovers. She was pregnant and
beseeched him to marry her. He told her to meet him in the apple-
orchard near Divinity Lane. Arriving first at the meeting-place, she
climbed a tree and sat down to rest on a branch. Soon she saw the
light of a lantern in the darkness and heard her lover's voice. But
another man was with him, and they began to dig a hole. As she
watched and listened she realised they were digging her grave.

MR FOX

Nineteen miles as I sat high,
Looking for one and two passed by.
I saw them that never saw me,
I saw a lantern tied to a tree.

The boughs did shake and I did quake
To see what a hole the fox did make.
The fox did roar and I did see
The fox made a hole to bury me.

(Hamer, collected from Mrs White, Bedfordshire.) These chilling
words are short and plain, coming straight to the point as old
ballads do.

Wright records an unpleasant *tell* chanted to mark a *glum*, a
period of silence, when even looking up was forbidden. This
lasted until a certain number of pins were worked—in this case,
thirty-one, the number doubled if the rule was broken.

Dingle, dangle, farthing candle,
Put you in the stinking dog's hole
For thirty-one. Speak or look off for sixty-two.
See book-list for authors and books on pages 342-346.

Wetting the Candle-block

This was the term for drinking and eating together on the lace-makers' holiday. In the north of the county this was at *Catterns*, the feast of St Catherine on November 25th, and elsewhere at *Tanders*, St Andrew's Day, November 30th.

On that day, Olney people congregated 'in one another's *housen*' to eat *thrummety* (see glossary) and drink metheglin, a drink made from honeycomb.

At Spratton there was a *barring-out*, the girls from the lace-school chanting

> Pardon, mistress, pardon, master,
> Pardon for a pin.
> If you won't give us a holiday,
> We will not let you in.

There were similar customs at Stoke Goldington, where they made sweets called 'black buttons' and at Ecton on St Thomas' Day, December 21st, when the mistress 'was turned out in a frolicsome manner'.

As all these holidays were in winter, they played indoor games, one of them, bob-apple, being similar to the Hallowe'en game played in the north, except that pieces of apple and candle were stuck on the four points of the bobbin-winder, the blindfolded player risking which she got in her mouth.

Mr Charles Higgins, squire of Turvey, whose birthday was on *Tanders day*, always gave figs to the revellers, and they played games till midnight at Yardley Hastings and then partook of *Tanders* cake and tea. There was *Tanders* cake at Milton Malsor too, and they rang the church bells in celebration.

Kettering *Cattern* cakes contained caraway seeds, and the revellers sang

> Rise, maids, rise,
> Bake your *Cattern* pies.
> Bake enough and bake no waste,
> And let the bellman have a taste.

The evening there was spent in singing and dancing, and eating 'stuffed boiled rabbit, smothered with onion sauce'. At Hanslope, though some lacemakers worked all night, so as not to lose money, the goings-on next day 'often exceeded the bounds of prudence'. This may have been because the young men joined the games, one of which was jumping the candle-block. Is this the origin of the nursery rhyme

Jack be nimble, Jack be quick,
Jack jump over the candlestick?

The men who made the bobbins for their women-folk often took great pride in decorating and inscribing them. They become love-tokens, prized possessions for children who usually had few if any toys, memorials to the dead, records of great events. Blessings, warnings, prayers and curses find a place on their tiny surfaces. Spelling is erratic. Very few work-tools can be so appealing.

Here is a lively collection from *The Romance of the Lace-pillow*, pp 144-174 *(Wright)*, with places or explanations on the right.

Sarah Berrell Bozet haged 8	Bozeat
Faby (Phoebe) Tarry Yardley Hastings 1859	
I love thee as the glad bird loves the freedom of its wings	Deanshanger
I wants a husband	Olney
Don't list love	enlist. Many a girl lost her *chap* when the recruiting party came. Lavendon.
Don't tell my mother	Newport Pagnell
I love the boys	Hanslope
If I love a lad in Eavenstone, that's nothing to nobody	Ravenstone. The maker of the bobbin made a mistake in the first letter.
Vote for Althorpe	Paulerspury
Wait for the waggon	Hanslope. This was a popular song.
Love Jesus whilst you are young	Deanshanger
I do love dear Jesus	Hanslope

and my favourite

Jesus weept John XI 35	Olney
Sarah Dazeley hung 1843	(at Bedford Jail) Lavendon

Northamptonshire lace was sold even to Queen Victoria.

'Her most gracious Majesty the Queen has been pleased to honour Mr Rose, lacemaker and gold blonde worker of Paulerspury, Northamptonshire, with an order for a white lace scarf, veil and setter [perhaps *settee*, head-covering] to be made of Paulerspury lace'.

The Northampton Mercury and Northampton Herald,
16.6.1847 (NL).

Caption: Miss Betsy Gibbons of Pudding-bag Lane, Paulerspury, making the Paisley Pear pattern and, on the left, Miss Julia Reed. Abington Park Museum, with acknowledgments to the Curator.

But as the years passed, the cottage craft of pillow-lace making fell into decline. Machine-made lace from Nottingham was much cheaper, and the 1870 Education Act required all children to attend school. In 1878 Mrs E M Harrison, wife of the newly-appointed vicar of Paulerspury, was disturbed by the poverty she found in the village and surrounding area. She used to make 'a copper pail of ox-head soup' and serve it to the schoolchildren at her back door as they came out of school. Encouraged by her husband, she set about reviving the local art of lace-making, which had almost died out. She went to see Mrs Rose, widow of the 'gold blonde worker', who had no love for lace-making because it had kept her husband away from home so much. Other lace factors made similar journeys.

'Our great-great-uncle, Mr Brown from Paulerspury, used to go to France periodically to collect lace-patterns. The kitchen floor was scrubbed and the patterns laid on it to be copied.'
Misses F and G Brown, Paulerspury.

Mrs Rose still had all her husband's parchments, and grudgingly sold them to the vicar's wife for five shillings, instead of 'boilin' 'em all down for glue' as she had intended. Mrs Harrison said 'I put them all in my apron and carried them home rejoicing to my husband'. She found two lace-makers who had not forgotten the art—Miss Betsy Gibbons of Pudding-bag Lane, and Miss Julia Reed. Before long, Paulerspury lace was once more being made.

In 1891, Alan Cole, in his *Report on Northamptonshire, Buckinghamshire and Bedfordshire Lace,* commented –

'Almost every cottage in Paulerspury has a pillow-worker, and probably there are at least a hundred and thirty workers more or less engaged in making lace.'

The Revd and Mrs Harrison continued to encourage the work until the vicar died in 1910, and his widow left the village. It was about this time that Mrs Swain's mother in nearby Greens Norton was making the *Lady's Fancy,* the *Fan* and the *Spider* and the *Seven, Fourteen* and *Eighteen-plaited.*

The material for this account was taken from *Mrs Harrison and the revival of lace-making in Paulerspury,* by Ann Lovell, in the library of Abington Park Museum. I acknowledge with thanks the help given by Miss J Hodgkinson, Keeper of Social History of this Museum. My thanks also to Mrs I Smart and other lace-makers of Greens Norton.

COUNTRY PEOPLE

The Village Bakery

'About 1900 my grandfather Robert Green was carpenter, wheelwright and journeyman, following in his father's footsteps, at Holcot. He lived with his family in a stone-built, thatched cottage with a brewhouse attached. There were sides of bacon hanging from the living room ceiling, the attic was stacked with apples stored for the winter and in the cellar were hams being cured in brine, barrels of ale from the brewhouse, stone jars of honey, brown *pancheons* of eggs pickled in isinglass, and bottles of parsnip, cowslip and damson wine. Across the road from the yard was an orchard, the sawpit, timber shed and pigsties, a paddock for the horses and six beehives.'

Many of us have a memory or folk-memory of such a cottage, and perhaps a deep-seated reaching back to that ordered, hard-working, home-based way of life, in a place where for centuries, our forebears had lived before us.

We know that there was another side. While Mrs Green worked in her well-stocked cottage, Jack Davis 'stole a parsnip, took it to a quiet place and ate it raw'. Those were the days when

Caption left: Shepherd and dog watch the sheep at Moulton Grange, Pitsford. NRO

men drove cattle for long distances over empty roads. Others sowed the seed, sometimes by hand, mowed the grass and *thacked* the ricks, gathered in the harvest and feasted afterwards, judged what the weather would be and made *hurks* in the field to shelter *mothers* and lambs from the winter cold. They bedecked their daughters for May-day, revelled at their feasts and fairs, and at Christmas flocked to church or chapel and opened their doors to the mummers. But most of the time they worked, as Robert Green did in his carpenter's shop with 'the half-moon window at one end'.

'In the forge he made wheels, gates and iron fittings for carts and carriages, and shoed his own horses. His work took him to other villages, mending farm fences and gates, restoring pumps and making benches for the little schools. When there was a death in the village he worked through the night making the coffin, to avoid having to put his other work behind.

He was also the carrier, and with his horse and trap would fetch goods from Northampton or take people to Brixworth railway station. Here are some items from his accounts.

Scratch (*cratch.* See glossary)	6*s* 6*d*	(six shillings and sixpence)
Sharping saw	3*d*	
Manger rail	3*d*	
Turning bung for churn	6*d*	
Repaired wagon-hovel roof	2*s* 6*d*	
Turning Handel for Scope [scoop]	6*d*	
Diging Dirt and carting for thatchers	2*s* 3*d*	
Stopping Gaps down Little Field, 5 posts, 10 rails, nails and time	10*s* 6*d*	
Poney to Northampton	4*s*	
Miss Coen had Bounce to go to Hannington	1*s* 6*d*	Bounce was a pony. Miss Coen's father was Rector of Hannington.

His younger daughter, Polly, looked after the pigs, hens and Uncle Ted's cows. Here is an extract from her accounts of their progress.

Miss Middleton had calf
Old Sow had 12
Little Black had 8
Prick ear had 10
Black Eiffer sold, £3.2.6*d*
Set 13 eggs under red hen Good Friday 12 hatched . . .

'She also did dressmaking, and made me my first Sunday-best dress. It was of brown velvet with collar and cuffs of hand-made lace. I had never had such a beautiful dress. Our everyday frocks were dark serge with white pinafores over them. We had black boots with little round buttons that were so difficult to do up, even with a buttonhook.

On Sunday afternoons, Grandad and Auntie Polly took us for a walk, usually round the Mere, a narrow road between Walgrave Road and Brixworth Road. There was a spinney along there called the Fox Covert and Grandad would point out the different trees and flowers and name the fields– *Millborough, The Leys, Mill Close*. Hannington *Mere* was a muddy bridle road, now under the water of Pitsford Reservoir.

Aunt Polly's sister married Harry Ellis, who took over his uncle's bakery in Holcot. I am their daughter.

A door, with an iron bell hooked on the inside, opened into the bakehouse. There were long wooden dough troughs with hinged lids along three walls, the lids being used as work-tops. The brick oven, about nine feet square, with walls two feet thick, was built out from the back wall. The base was four feet above ground level with one cavity under the fire-door for the ashes, and another under the oven door for the kindling sticks. The fire was on the floor of the oven in one corner and the thickness of the walls, base and roof kept the oven always hot. In the evening, Father put bricks in to heat the beds, and at night a big black kettle of water which would be boiling for the morning cups of tea.

The "over the oven room" had lines across for airing clothes, and a bath. The water had to be carried up in buckets and kettles, and father had knocked a small hole through the wall, through which the water could run out.

Father started work at 5 am, unbolting the door so that the men going off to work on the farms could buy "Woodbines" [cigarettes] or ½ an ounce of shag. Then he lit the oven fire and prepared and baked the loaves, which he later carried round the village in a wooden two-wheeled truck. In the afternoons he made cakes, weighed flour into quartern [28 lbs] bags for sale in the shop and mopped out the oven with a *slopper*, a long-handled mop made by cutting up strips of sacking and tying them to the handle.

Friday was pork pie day. The local butcher delivered half a pig which my mother boned, cut up and put through a chopping machine. The bones were put in a big iron pot in the oven to boil for three hours for the jelly, and the head was cooked for *collared head* [brawn] which was sold in the shop.

Our shop was open from 5 am to 10 pm (11 pm on Saturdays) with no mid-day closing. If the bell rang while we were eating our dinner, mother put her plate on the range and went to serve. There was no electricity or gas in the village, so most women relied on the bakery to get the Sunday dinner cooked. The men brought the dinners in as the church bells began to ring, then gathered at the *Old Payne Tree* for a chinwag. "My old woman's bad again with a hacking cough." "Poor old Jeremiah's gone then." "Sar'ann's got another young 'un." "The best thing for scaly leg [in fowls] is paraffin oil. It works a treat, old Obby said." At twelve o' clock they went to fetch back the dinners.

On Mondays the women brought the remains of the joint surrounded by potatoes and onions in the baking-tin lined with suet pastry. One old woman always picked out a hot potato from her tin for me, much to my mother's disgust, as her hands were filthy, but my granny said *"It takes a peck before it kills"* and I was too young to bother.

It was an all-night job making hot-cross buns for Good Friday. There were far too many to keep in the bakehouse, so all the furniture was moved from the living room and the floor covered with newspapers to lay them on.

Our shop sold almost everything—pins, Fairy dyes, lampwicks, *pollard* [spoilt grain ground for pigs]. Nothing was prepacked—the customers brought jugs for vinegar, a cup for castor oil, buckets for corn. Sugar was weighed from a barrel, butter and lard cut from large slabs and bacon sliced with a carving knife. The tall glass jars in the window held pear drops, bulls' eyes, brown and white stripes, extra strongs and slabs of toffee.

On Mondays the washer-woman came and worked in the wash-house where there was a copper with a fire beneath it. Ironing was done on the kitchen table by flat irons heated on the fire and rubbed with emery cloth and rags.

Every Saturday night we were given a tablespoonful of

Caption above right: The bakery and shop at Holcot in 1917, with 'H Ellis, A M Ellis, Nancy and me. The shop was open from 5 am to 10 pm with no mid-day closing'. Mrs E Rouse, Desborough.
Below right: The Limes Farm at Farthinghoe, with the pump in front. 'There was no piped water.' Miss Barbara Adkins, Banbury.

Parishes' Food and the dreaded brimstone and treacle. For sore throats we had a sock soaked in horrible-smelling goose-grease round our necks and eucalyptus on our hankies.

My mother and father must have been very tired by night-time, but they never went to bed without having one game of bezique.

The village bobby lived two miles away at Walgrave. He served Hannington, Old and Holcot as well, riding on his bicycle between the villages. I don't think he had much crime to cope with, but he spent a lot of time hauling us back to our parents for *scrumping* apples, for which we got a good hiding.

We looked forward for weeks to May-day, and on Easter Sunday morning, all the children at church were taken after the service to Miss Coen's garden to search for Easter Eggs she had hidden among the shrubs and flowers.

My old Grandma lived in a cottage next to a farm, and she lay on a sofa all day, pegging rugs. Every few minutes she would bang a tin tray to frighten away the mice.'

Mrs Elsie Rouse, Desborough.

One of the memories, from the turn of the century onwards, are of those pieces of ground, measured in poles, known locally as *the lotments.*

'I can remember an old man wearing a smock and kerchief, red for work and white on Sundays. He lived in Shenington, and there was a place there called Grimes' barn, used by those who had allotments and grew corn. It was stored there, and in turn, folk would thresh it with a flail, and winnow it in the machine there for all. I can remember this Henry Hiorns working at the barn in his smock.'

Mrs Hilda Berry, Wroxton, near Banbury, born 1895.

'My dad had a thirty-pole allotment in two strips, and he grew potatoes and a few onions and greens on one side, and the other side was for wheat or barley, sometimes beans, to change the ground, you see.

When I was in my teens and started keeping a pig or two, I used to help him with the allotment. We cut the barley or beans with a *fagging-hook* and tied 'em up in sheaves. Quite a few chaps used to do the same, and take 'em to one of the small-holders. There were all these little cocks—wheat, barley and beans, all labelled. Then they had the steam-*thrashing* [threshing] tackle come along, and they used to have pretty well a day, thrashing all the allotment-holders' corn.

Then they had the wheat ground, so they'd got some flour for home-made bread. At Cuttle Mill they used to grind barley for animals. So we had our barley-meal for the pig, and of course, the straw was its bedding. And the beans, well, sometimes they were sold to the farmers for horse-feed. They're good protein you see, for working horses.'

Mr Percy Foster, Pury End.

'They all had an allotment. My husband once saw a donkey and a bullock pulling a plough on one of them.'

Mrs E Wood, Weedon Lois.

'I can remember several of the old chaps having two allotments as well as a big garden at home. One was still digging at ninety-two, and going four miles to Bedford on his bike to fetch his bread.' *Mr Maurice Boston,* Wilstead, Beds.

Farming

The Farm at Farthinghoe

'The farmers wore breeches and gaiters to market. The ladies wore long dresses, just off the ground.'

Dorothy Deeley was born at The Limes Farm, Farthinghoe in 1893 and compiled this account with the help of her daughter, *Miss Barbara Adkins* of Banbury.

'In the kitchen was a large range on which water was heated, and all the cooking was done on this until oil stoves came to be used. It was black-leaded once a week and all the steel parts and the fender scoured with emery-cloth till they looked like silver. The kitchen, back kitchen, dairy and all back places had stone floors and in some farmhouses all the downstairs rooms had flagstones.

The wash-house was across the court. It had a hearth with a large open chimney—you could see the sky above. Wood only was burnt on the fire, and there was a hook on a chain for holding the big iron boiler which heated water for washing the milk utensils and for boiling a ham in summer. Or a brass kettle was hung on it for jam-making. At the back of the hearth was a baker's oven. It was lined with bricks, and a faggot of wood was lit inside to heat it. When it was hot the wood was scraped out and the loaves or cakes put in to cook.

There were two coppers (this was once the brewhouse). On wash day, fires were lit beneath them, inside a heavy iron door, and the washing was boiled in them, covered by wooden lids, and stirred with a copperstick. The big wash was done only once a month—I suppose that is why brides used to have dozens of everything. The washing took two days and the ironing most of the week. We had lots of white pinafores and blouses with frills, which were crimped with goffering irons.

Furniture was big and heavy, often made from mahogany. There was a brass bedstead in the main bedroom and iron ones in the smaller rooms. In the spare room was a half-tester bed with a deep red canopy, curtains and a matching valance with yellow bands.

There was no piped water or sewage disposal. Water for the village came from the village pump or wells in gardens. Our drinking water came from a well in the place where the milk was cooled. It was a good spring which rarely ran dry. There were two privies in the garden. One had three wooden seats, including a small one for the children. We had to have a lantern to light the way in the dark except when the moon was shining.

Milking was done by hand. The cowmen wore milking-smocks and caps worn back to front, and sat on three-legged stools and milked the cows into wooden buckets. A man with two buckets on a yoke over his shoulders carried the milk to the cooler-house. Here the milk was put through the cooler, a square container with tubes filled with water pumped up from the well. It ran over these tubes into churns underneath, and these were taken to the station in the milk-cart and sent daily by train to London.

The milk retained for butter-making was taken to the cool dairy and poured into shallow leads. The wooden buckets with metal bands on the outside were scoured every day with wood-ash and well-scrubbed inside. The milk was left in the leads till next day and the cream skimmed off with a brass skimming-dish. The skimmed milk was drawn out from the leads and fed to the pigs and calves. The cream was salted for a day or two and then churned in a small wooden churn by hand. This churn was kept in the well in hot weather. There was also a very large churn that was a fixture in the dairy and was turned outside in the courtyard by a shaft through the wall, driven round by a horse, Old Blossom. When the butter was formed and was ready to be taken out by hand, the buttermilk that remained was run off and used for making scones or given to the calves and pigs.

The butter was washed in brine and kneaded in a butter *kiver*, a wooden oval container, and knocked about by wooden *scotch hands*, to squeeze out all the remaining brine. Then it was made up into 1lb and ½lb blocks to be taken to Banbury and sold to shops. Some, for our own use, was made into fancy shapes–arum lilies, leaves etc.–and some was salted down for use in the winter when there was not so much milk. This was done by putting the butter and layers of salt in large red earthenware vessels and tying them down with greasproof paper. They were stored then in the cool dairy, which was below the level of the other rooms down several stone steps. It had a stone floor and was shaded outside by trees. There was a pump of good spring water and a drain, as the floor had to be swilled down every day. The ladies wore pattens over their shoes when working in the dairy or when going out in the wet. There were no wellingtons in those days.

Above the dairy was the granary, reached by stone steps, and there was also a *mealhouse* in the courtyard.

About the end of May it was sheep-shearing time. The sheep had to be *dagged*–have all the dirty wool cut off, and were washed in the *washbrook*. Part of a stream was lined with brick, and the sheep were driven through it, controlled by a man with a crook. Then they were sheared by hand–it took a long time to shear a flock. During the summer they were dipped in a sheep-dip containing insect-killer to kill the maggots. A policeman came to see that it was done properly and to issue a certificate.

Rooks were a great nuisance in the spring as they ate the growing corn. Boys were employed in the fields to scare them off and farmers had rook-shoots in their own and each others' fields. Some people made rook-pies.

Haymaking and harvest were very busy times, and it was all hands to the pump then. More men were taken on, and women too. The grass was cut by a horse-drawn mowing machine and left to dry in rows or made into haycocks. Then a horse-drawn waggon with four wooden wheels was loaded with hay picked up with a two-pronged pitchfork and pitched up on to the waggon. This was made into a hayrick in the field or rickyard and later thatched.

At harvest-time the only machinery was the binder, pulled by a horse. This cut the corn and bound it into sheaves, and men following behind stood the sheaves up into stooks or shocks. After drying for some days they were pitched on to the waggons and made into ricks on staddle-stones to keep away the rats, or taken to the barn for threshing. The women from the village would then go gleaning, and when all was finished there would be a Harvest Supper in the farm kitchen for the farm workers and their wives. After the fields were ploughed, the women would work at stone-picking and hoeing.

Threshing was done in the barn by a steam-threshing machine belonging to a family who went round the district working for the farmers. Quite a number of workers were needed for this dusty job and farmers would lend each other their men. They were paid six shillings a day, a much higher rate than their usual pay. In one of the buildings was a winnowing machine, for separating the chaff from the corn. This was tipped down from above the manger into a trough below for the horses to eat with their oats.

In the winter pig-killing was another busy time. A man from the village or the local butcher would come to do this. After the pig was killed its hair was burnt off with straw and it was cut up in the wash-house. The two flitches and the two hams were cleaned and salted and put in the leads. After a few days, a special mixture of salt, dark brown sugar and black treacle was put over them and they were turned every day in this mixture for several weeks, then drained, and hung up on hooks from the beams in the kitchen to dry. Lastly they were covered with a cloth to keep clean, and when any ham or bacon was needed, they were taken down and slices cut from them. These tasted very different from the ham and bacon bought today.

Animals to sell were taken to Banbury Market on Thursdays, by two men from the farm, one walking behind and one in front. Calves with net muzzles would be put in a cart and the

---

Caption right: Mrs Amelia Deeley, the farmer's wife, holding two chicks. She is wearing pull-on sleeves and a home-made hat to keep her dress and hair clean and to shade her face. Miss Barbara Adkins, Banbury.

cow walked behind. Flocks of sheep and herds of cattle were driven through the town and penned in the streets. The farmers wore breeches and gaiters, as they did on the farm, with caps or bowler hats. The ladies wore long dresses, just off the ground, and black woollen stockings with laced-up or buttoned-up boots. In cold weather they wore cloth gaiters. The roads were very muddy in winter, so they had to hold up their long skirts.

We had a trap and a big black horse called Motor, because he went very fast and was a high-stepper. In the winter we all had to be well wrapped up and had thick rugs, as it was all open. We had what was called a gig-umbrella, which was large enough to cover six people. The one who sat next to the driver had to hold it up when it rained—no light work when it was windy as well. Later we had a tub or governess cart and a smaller pony called Penelope. These traps were made to order by Mr Sirman the coach-builder in Banbury. When in the town we could not leave the horse and trap in the street, so we had to put up at a hostelry which had a waiting-room and toilet. If we went into Banbury by train and did not have the trap, we hired a hansom cab to take us home. There was a brougham for hire in the village to take people to weddings and funerals. There were also waggonettes which held six to eight people and brakes holding twenty people. These could be hired in Banbury and had two horses each to pull them.

It was a tremendous thrill when motor cars first came. We used to run out to the road when we heard one coming. They did not run quietly. These early cars were open-topped, but had a hood at the back which could be put up if it rained. The driver had to stop and get out to do this. The ladies wore large motoring-veils, which covered their large hats and tied under the chin. In dry weather the roads were very dusty and when a car came along there was a terrific cloud of dust, so people had to turn their backs to the car.

Most villages had carriers visiting them on market days, and sometimes twice a week. They had horse-drawn covered carts, and would take anything into Banbury to be repaired—harness, shears, buckets etc. and crates of eggs to sell in the market or at one of the shops. The carrier would take our grocery order to the shop and the errand-boy would take the box of groceries to where the carrier had left his cart, usually by the Town Hall, and put it in the back of the cart. Nothing was stolen from it. The horses were stabled and fed at one of the pubs. The carrier took people to town from the villages and then home at night.

Each May Day the schoolmistress brought round the May Queen, dressed like a bride with a veil and bouquet, and carried in a chair by the older children, who all had bunches of flowers, and they collected money for their 'treat'.

At Whitsun there was a Club Feast in the Clubroom, when the money that had been paid in all the year was given out.

A set of swing-boats came in the summer and set up outside the pub.

At Christmas the mummers came round to the houses and performed their play of St. George and the Dragon. Usually a local family did this and they went to other villages as well.

Occasionally a German band came in the summer—this was one man playing a brass instrument. Sometimes a man with a barrel-organ came, with a monkey or dancing bear. Tramps used to come quite often, on their way from one workhouse to another. Sometimes we gave them food, or hot water with tea and sugar in their tin can. Occasionally they spent the night in the stable or cow-shed, but not often. This was not encouraged.'   *Mrs Dorothy Adkins*, Banbury.

Motor, Penelope, Old Blossom and their counterparts were still all-important on turn-of-the-century farms and elsewhere.

Horses

'They are very clean animals. They won't eat out of a dirty bucket, and they hate pigs.' Mr J Morley, Clipston.

'When we lived at Irthlingborough in the early years of the century, the miller delivered flour to the baker in a huge van drawn by six white horses, and Phipps' drayman had a splendid pair of black ones. It was a thrilling sight to see the horses which drew the fire-engine galloping along. The firemen were in brass helmets with axes in their belts.

Once some big trees were felled and carted away on timber-carriages drawn by a string of horses harnessed one behind the other. On winter afternoons the ploughman and his team could be seen plodding their weary way homeward after a hard day's work, and we would watch the blacksmith shoeing, if we had time.

Before I started work at the age of ten, I sometimes used to help my father, who was in charge of the railway horses at Irthlingborough Station. I was not much higher than their legs. They had to pull very heavy loads, and a chain-horse was needed to help them up the steep cobbled road outside the goods yard. As well as dray-horses, there were parcel-van horses and one that was used for shunting.

My uncle at Brington was the carrier to Northampton on Wednesdays and Saturdays, calling at Nobottle and Old Duston. He took any kind of stuff for a copper or two, and people for threepence. He used to put up at the Woolpack in Bridge Street, and always came down Gold Street, Marefair and Black Lion Hill at a smart pace. Once he was charged with "furious driving".

I used to go and work with him as a boy, fetching loads of grain for pig-feeding from Walker and Soames' brewery at Long Buckby. And we used to go on horseback to the harvest fields. I was very proud to be allowed to lead the horse from shock to shock, calling "*hol gee*" ["come toward"—turn to the left] and "*gee back*" [turn right] to warn the man on top of the load, and then take the full load to the stackyard.'

Mr Jack Davis, Northampton.

Not all were working horses—Northamptonshire is a hunting county. The Pytchley and the Woodland Pytchley hunt in the north of the county, the latter in the wooded areas which were once part of the great forest of Rockingham. There are two other royal forests, Salcey and Whittlewood, as well as other tracts of woodland.

'I can remember seeing a string of horses coming back from exercise at six in the morning, with a groom leading each horse and a stud groom wearing yellow gloves. When I first came to Greens Norton I noticed how well-spoken the children were. This was because their fathers were employed by the Grafton Hunt and they learned to speak quietly in front of the gentry as their parents did. Their mothers often did the laundry for the

Caption above left: The blacksmith's yard at Potterspury in 1900. Mr Sydney Smith is the blacksmith, his brother-in-law holds the horse's head and his father looks on. The blacksmith and his father are appropriately named Smith. NL, with acknowledgments to Miss Miriam Smith, Potterspury. Negatives held by Mr J D Clamp, Greens Norton.
Below right: The Pytchley hounds meet on a cold day in Pytchley village. NL

Hunt people. In winter they laid a white cloth on the table and put the folded clothes on it to dry.'

Mrs Ivy Smart, Greens Norton.

One of the Grafton Hunt's most ardent followers was William Seckington, born at Weston-by-Lois Weedon in 1869. This graphic account, in beautiful handwriting, was written when he was fourteen. Lightly punctuated, it sounds rather like a present-day race commentary.

'The Grafton Hounds met at Astwell Mill on the 19th of January 1883. Amongst those present was Lord Peneryn the Master, and Sir Robert Loder, MP.

They first tried Astwell Spinney after searching it about for a few minutes it was thought there was not a fox in it. The huntsman, Frank Beers . . . began blowing the hounds out the fox lying close to the hedge around the spinney in long grass the hounds come trampling over him if he would have layed still they would have went away saying they could not find but as the last few come over him he jumped up in sight of all and through the spinney with hounds at his tail but they soon lost sight of him.

Went into the Wappenham Road turned into the fields on the left and crossing the line just as a train was coming they had a narrow escape . . . but the driver seeing the danger slackened the train the passengers having a good view running the same direction for a little way but passing over the hill as if for Weedon which they went to at a rattling pace and through the churchyard and straight on to *Cathanger* and Oakley bank to Plumpton Wood and by then it appeared to tell on many of the horses as they had come at such a rate they kept on a little farther the scent being anyway besides good Reynard had got so far in advance that they could follow no longer leaving him for another days sport a good many turned for home their horses being *knocked up*. The fox must have been a good one to get so far before the hounds.' William followed the hunt on Old Jack, his father's 'market-trap horse'.

'Gorse or furze is called "*furzen*" by the hunting fraternity. The rest of us call it "*fuzz*".'

Mr Arthur Seckington, Greatworth.

Pigs

'Ah, Thomas, get thee to thy pigs'

The pig was a valued possession for anyone who had space for a sty and some household scraps and vegetable peelings as a basis for its food. When killed it would provide the only meat that the poor ever tasted, and good food for all.

'What we tried to do, if we could, was to have two pigs. We sold one to the local butcher just round the corner—no middleman or anything o' that—and we used to reckon for that one to pay for the feed for the next, so you had one in the house.

The pig was killed on a *cratch* or *scratch*, a wooden frame, and the meat was salted in a salting-lead. It was like a trough, lead-lined. You put in two flitches, one on top of the other, with the meat side up, and rubbed salt in—quite a lot o salt. And then, in the shoulder pieces, you'd have saltpetre, and round the bones, and the same with the hams—you'd put in saltpetre. You kept it in the salt for about three weeks, and half-way through you had 'em out and put the top one in the bottom and the bottom in the top.

Then, after about three weeks, it was hung up in the house. There are the hooks, there, where they used to hang the hams—on those beams. Some people had a strong wooden frame on the ceiling and pushed the flitches on to it, and the hams hung in the chimney corner.' *Mr Percy Foster,* Pury End.

'*Hug's-pudden,* that's what you make when you have a pig killed. You skim the *chitlins* [small intestines], with groats—grits, some people call it—and blood and bits of fat meat. You shape 'em like a horse-shoe then and boil 'em in a pot. They call 'em black puddings today, but we called 'em hugs-pudden.'
Mrs Rose Foster, Pury End.

The more perishable parts of the pig, the 'chitlins', liver, kidneys etc.—*pig's fry*—were eaten first, then some meat was eaten fresh, and scraps and trimmings used to make *collared head* [brawn] and pork pies. Neighbours shared out their bounty as each pig was killed, thus making the food go further, and the practice is neatly set down in this little verse from Rushden.

> Health to the man who kills a pig,
> And sends his neighbours fry,
> And after that a leg of pork,
> And then a big pork-pie. *Mr R Cowper.*

Hocks were used for that tasty and filling Wellingborough dish, *hock-and-dough* (see p 21) and the bristles were put to good use by the local shoemaker, twisted into the ends of his thread for stitching.

'A brother of Gran's, Thomas Harrison, worked for the Squire of Hornton, near Banbury, as a pig-boy. He was ten years old and loved horses. Every morning the men lined up in the farmyard, waiting for the Maister to give them their jobs for the day. The Squire would go down the line of men and boys, and Tom, being the youngest, was always the last. "Please" he would think every morning, as he stood there cap in hand, "Please let him send me to the stables to help with the horses". But no, it was always "Ah, Thomas, get thee to thy pigs".

He had to wait eight years before he became a groom. Then he was a coachman, and in his late twenties he was a coachman to a titled family in Derbyshire, and there met Sarah, the lady's maid who became his wife.'   *Mrs Sonia Glenister,* Australia.

Commoner even than the pig-sty, in both country and town gardens, was the henhouse. Like pigs, hens could be fed in part on scraps from the kitchen and garden, and provided good food in return. Woe betide them if they did not. If putting a *pot-egg* under them did not work, there were more drastic remedies.

'My father's family have lived in these parts for some three hundred years. I can remember my grandmother, a hard-working woman and quite a case. Her favourite words were "them old *galluses*" (see glossary), which she applied to just about everything from her children and grandchildren to the animals and birds on the farm. She once had some hens which wanted to sit rather than lay, so she put them in a sack, chucked them in a stream and *pruggled* them [stirred them about] with a broom. That would make them old *galluses* lay, she said.'
Mr Maurice Boston, Wilstead, Bedford.

Sheep

'What's the trouble then, shepherd?'

Away from the farmyard now, and out to the open fields and the peaceful sheep.

'I started work on the farm in 1912, looking after the poultry, looking after the cows and horses. Then the Great War started, and when I came back, I took on the duties of a shepherd. You understand that on a farm there was the waggoner, the cowman and the shepherd. They were the three carrying the biggest responsibility.

The busiest time was when they were lambing. We used to keep them in a little enclosure and feed them there, and then in three or four days we took them on to new pastures, because them little lambs, they were weakly, and you couldn't *travel* 'em till they'd got stable.

I was only knocked over once by a mother sheep. It was towards eventide. She'd given birth to two lovely lambs, and I said "You're not stopping here tonight. I'll put you under cover". So I picked the lambs up and cuddled 'em under me arm, and I walked along thinking she'd foller me, which they usually did, and all of a sudden she knocked me as far as from here to the corner of this room. I dropped the two lambs, and she come and stood over me–all them years ago and I can see it now–and her eyes were GREEN. But I put her in. I was me own master on that job.

When lambs are born, or are about to be born, you never take the sheepdog. But when they got on their feet I used to take him and he walked beside my knee. Well, as I was walking off, I knew this mother was gunner do as she had done when the lambs were born. When she come for me, the dog's great jaws closed right across her face. It was something as I never wanted to happen. I've been knocked over be [by] the rams times [many times], 'cause they could be very nasty, but I was only knocked over once be a female sheep.

There were times, when they were lambing, when the veterinary surgeon had to be called in, and he used to say "What's the trouble then, shepherd?" and I said "Well it's *beyond my thumbs* this morning".

We used to take the sheep down to the mill-race at Harpole Mill, and each *mother* was strapped round the neck, and two men threw them into the mill-race, and two others used to pole 'em under with poles anything from twelve to fifteen feet long. That was so the wool was clean. Now that sheep-washing has been gone near sixty years. They accept the wool as it is now.

The first time as I was there at shearing time to catch the sheep for the shepherd and bring it out for him to shear, I brought what we knew as a *two-shear* ram. And when I'd

done up the fleece, he said "Boy", he said, "bring that over 'ere and we'll weigh it". And the shepherd had cut off that sheep nineteen pounds of wool. Lincoln Longhorns, they were. I've never seen that breed of sheep for twenty year.'

Mr William Burt, Harpole.

'John's aunt has a woollen shake-up bed made by her mother and the children. Her father was a shepherd and was allowed to take home odd bits of sheeps' wool. Her mother used to wash it, and they would all sit round and fluff it out, and make cushions, pillows and beds with it.'

Mrs Loretta Smith, Little Houghton.

'My grandmother came from Medbourne, near Market Harborough, and she taught us these sheep-counting numbers.

een	one	eendick	eleven
teen	two	teendick	twelve
tethery	three	tetherdick	thirteen
fethery	four	fetherdick	fourteen
fip	five	bumpkin	fifteen
shater	six	eenbumpkin	sixteen
rater	seven	teenbumpkin	seventeen
coter	eight	tetherbumpkin	eighteen
commoner	nine	fetherbumpkin	nineteen
dick	ten	jinkit	twenty.'

Mrs Margaret Fookes, Great Billing.

The first five numerals are similar to standard numbers. *Dick* and *jinkit* are like French *dix* and *vingt*. Welsh drovers pastured their sheep in Northamptonshire on their way to London and the east coast. Welsh numerals to ten are as follows: *un, dau/dwy, tri/tair, pedwar/pedair, pump, chwech, saith, wyth, naw, deg.*

'Shepherds and drovers put a pebble in their pocket for the highest number to which they could count, and then started again.'

Mr Jack Davis, Northampton.

'When I was at school I learned that the camel was called "the ship of the desert". I imagined them being kept in flocks by the Arabs. There were *ship* all round us in Boddington.'

Mrs Ruth Hill, Boddington.

Caption above left: The three Westaway brothers shearing at Prince Rupert's Farm, Sibbertoft, 'One brother was killed in the first war'. NL. With acknowledgments to Mr Eric Westaway, Naseby.
Below left: Brackley Wool Fair, 1912. NL

The Seckingtons of Stonehouse Farm

'After tea, the basins were breaded . . .'

'My grandfather, George Seckington, was born in Middleton Cheney probably about the year 1820. He was a farm labourer and very poor, but eventually became the tenant of Stonehouse Farm at Lois Weedon. An old man who had worked for him told me that it was his practice to go to Brackley to fetch waggon-loads of *grains*, barley-waste from brewing, for the pigs. They reckoned to leave Weston soon after 4 am, even in winter, once when the snow in places came up to the horses' bellies.

The reason for the early start was to get home in time to work on the farm while it was still light. I have heard it said that each day after dinner his wife would wash up and then lay the tea. At three o'clock she put the kettle on—the great old copper kettles then in use took some time to boil—at half past three tea was made, and she would stand at the window watching for her husband to cross the yard. Then she poured out the tea, so that he could sit down and drink it, with no time wasted. After tea the basins were breaded—bread was broken into basins which were then filled with milk and set on the hob of the fire-grate to warm. At eight pm. they took their bread-and-milk and went to bed.

My father, Alfred Seckington, was born in 1843 and married three times. His first wife died at the age of twenty-six, leaving two sons, William and Mark. William was very good at reading and writing and loved to keep records of village happenings, about a hundred years ago now. This is his account of Queen Victoria's Golden Jubilee in 1887.

'The fiftieth year of Her Majesty's reign was commemorated here with every manifestation of loyalty and respect. The village was all astir from early morn till late at night. At five in the morning a long and glorious peal was given, and at 7.30 the church choir ascended the tower and there sang the National Anthem. At 10.30 a procession was formed at the schools and marched to church. At 12 o'clock *about 200 males* sat down to dinner in Mr Hatton's barn, which had been most beautifully decorated. Simultaneously *some 100 males* partook of dinner in the Baptist schoolroom. Mr Chamberlain and Mr. Tomkins gave "The Queen", which was received as heartily and loyally as possible.

At 1 o'clock all adjourned to a field where a variety of amusements were indulged in, the chief being a cricket match between the Upper and Lower village, when the latter gained an easy victory, Mold batting exceptionally well. Punctually at 5 o'clock a programme of sports commenced and lasted for three hours, ending in a tug-of-war between the two villages, Lower Middleton winning easily.'

Arthur Mold became a renowned county cricketer. The italics are mine.

'William and Mark were my half-brothers, many years older than me, but we always got on well together. When his second wife died, my father later married for the third time and I was born at Thenford Hill in 1901. One of my earliest memories is of seeing the old bull pick up a gate on his horns and throw it in the air.

I started school at Middleton after my seventh birthday. It was a rough place in those days. The kids seemed to have one idea in life–to fight and throw stones, and the grown-ups weren't much better. A boy of fourteen from a rough family stole a watch from the pocket of a roadman's coat. It was his first offence, but he was sentenced to five years in a reformatory.

After my father died we went to live in a thatched house at Helmdon. The children were more friendly there. Then I went to Towcester Grammar School, fees two guineas a term and buy your own books. I went by train, leaving home at 7.30 am and getting back at half past five. The discipline was grim, the headmaster believing in the cane and plenty of it. I left school at fourteen and got a job in the gardens of Moreton [Pinkney] Manor. I started to take sandwiches for my dinner, but my Aunt Poll soon put a stop to that. She was cook at the Manor at the time, and she had me in the kitchen and fed me like a fighting cock.

After my illness in 1919 my uncle Mark offered me a job at Stonehouse Farm. The first day's work was threshing wheat out of the barn. I was sent up on the *mow* [heap], pitching sheaves across to the *box* [threshing-drum]. At first you are pitching from the roof of the barn, but as the stack gets lower, you are pitching uphill. Towards four in the afternoon, with about half-an-hour's work to do, I was almost exhausted, when a voice said "Give me that fork, boy. You've had about enough" and he told me to sit down. I was too tired to speak. I have never forgotten that act of kindness. It is fresh in my memory after seventy years.

One day I went stone-picking on the clover in Sulgrave Ground. It was very early spring, and a lovely sunny day. Away in the far distance I could see a tractor at work—too far to hear the sound of the engine and dwarfed in size by the distance, it looked like a huge beetle crawling up and down the field. But there was something else—a sense of wonderment that I should be there at all, alive, out in the sunshine, in the midst of these peaceful fields, when I might so easily have shared the fate of thousands of my generation who lay in Flanders fields.

A winter job I liked was boiling beans for the cows. The beans were kept in the granary. In the floor was a large funnel and from it a pipe went down into the brewhouse below. I had to measure out the beans, pour them down the funnel and then fill the copper with water. Each bucketful had to be pumped, carried across the yard and lifted up into the copper. Then I laid the fire in the fire-hole and lit it at tea-time. Next morning the beans had cooled off to a sort of jelly. I harnessed old Sally to the pig-cart, collected various old washing-*trays* (tubs) churns and buckets, dug the beans out of the copper into these vessels, loaded everything into the cart and took it to the cowyard.

It was a common custom years ago to graze the cows on the roadside, and that was another of my jobs. I used to keep them out about two hours in the morning, and then turn them into a field. It wasn't too bad with the older, quiet cows, but if you had a few restless young heifers among them, you could run your legs off. About half a mile out of Weston was a field called *Poor's Lot,* with several small iron gates. One morning one of the cows stuck her horns in the bars of a gate and lifted it on her head. She panicked off down the road, and all the herd pelted behind her. After about half a mile she managed to shake the gate off her head, and I chased about, rounded the herd up and put them in the field. Then I had to carry the gate back and replace it.

The bull was not grazed up the road with the cows. He was turned loose up the cow lane to find his own way up the field, the gates being left open for him. One morning he hung about

Caption right: Mr Mark Seckington (c1865-1933), farmer, of Stonehouse Farm, Lois Weedon. Mr Arthur Seckington, Greatworth.

near the cowhouse, so I was told to drive him up field. I took the old dog with me, though he wasn't much use with cattle. Towards the centre of *Adkins Piece,* the bull suddenly turned round and began to bellow at me and then gored his head in an antbank. Obviously he was in a very bad temper, and I didn't feel at all happy. Then the old dog flew at the bull, jumped on his neck and hung on for all he was worth. I bolted for *Wheatlands* gate, got over it mighty quick and felt very grateful to that old dog.

Once when I was setting up stooks in *Osborne's Wild,* I saw a fox leave the wheat and start towards me across the field. I picked up a stone and crouched behind a stook. When I straightened up, there was the fox only about fifteen feet away from me. He was a real big one, grey-furred, probably an old dog-fox, and a savage one. I expected him to run for it, but he turned and faced me and bared his teeth. We both stood still for some seconds, and thinking it most advisable to put a bit of space between us, I very slowly walked backwards. He watched me go and then went quietly on his way.

There used to be a thatched *hovel* in Moreton Fields. The walls were thick slabs of timber and there was a deep thatched roof, old and crude, but a warm haven for cattle in winter. One day, Sankey and I sat in there eating our vittles and he pointed to the beam over our heads and said "That's where Billy Robinson hung himself. Them marks is where they cut the ropes to get him down". A grim story, but it never put me off my dinner—I was too hungry.

Once we *farmed* [cleaned] out this old *hovel.* It came some hot and thundery weather, and the heap of manure we had thrown outside became covered in literally hundreds of mushrooms.

The great farm waggons always held a fascination for me. My father had two—a Northamptonshire waggon with straight *reaves* (see photograph) and a Cotswold waggon with curved ones. They were made by local craftsmen working with handtools and some had been in use for nearly a hundred years.

The Depression was the cause of me having to come off the land. The guaranteed prices of corn dropped and the bottom

Caption above left: Mixed farming at Jackson's Farm, Helmdon in 1930.
Below left: Haymaking at Jackson's Farm, Helmdon, 1930. The girls are in 'the Northamptonshire waggon with straight reaves', side-pieces increasing capacity and serving as seats. Both from Mr Arthur Seckington, Greatworth.

literally fell out of farming. I spent the rest of my working life as a self-employed shoe-repairer, but when I retired, we came back here, not far from where I was born.'

Mr Arthur Seckington, Greatworth.

The following is a miscellany of Northamptonshire rural life, starting with a memory of the Culworth gang, who carried out highway and other robberies for a number of years in the south-west of the county, perhaps near Mr Seckington's 'peaceful fields'. Four members of the gang were hanged on the 3rd of August 1787.

'My father's grandfather went to Northampton to see the Culworth gang hung. They had threatened the lone places. When I went to Greatworth Hall to farm, fifty years ago this year, every door had a chain on and every window was shuttered. It's a lone place down the fields.'

Mr S Adkins, Greatworth.

'Tramps and railway labourers used to sleep in mangers. When the first binder appeared, the farm labourers smashed it so that they should not lose their jobs.'

Mrs E Wood, Weedon Lois.

'Harry Griffin from Badby used to go to Northampton Market and bring back a herd of about forty cattle. When he got to Newnham, he'd stop and go in the pub for a drink, and the cattle just grazed outside with the dog to watch them. They didn't stray far–they'd walked twelve miles already.'

Mr Cox, Newnham.

'The people used to gather together to hear my grandfather Hines read the newspaper. Not many of them could read.'

Mr Jack Davis, Northampton.
Information from *Mrs Boyle*, Harpole.

'I was a schoolgirl in the first World War. There were no buses in those days, and I walked from Ashton to Roade Station, caught a train to Northampton and walked to the General Hospital to have my tonsils out. Afterwards I walked back to Castle Station, went by train back to Roade, and then had to go to bed at my grandmother's for an hour. Then I walked home to Ashton, and my mother and father came to meet me, with the cat walking behind.' *Miss Jessie Curtis*, Northampton.

'When I was a child in Winslow (Buckinghamshire), a gypsy woman came to the door to see my father, who was a churchwarden. She had had her baby in a *hovel* [barn] but it was baptised in church as she wished. We came to Alderton and farmed there for many years. There were a lot of gypsies there. It was near a drift road and the gypsies used to prefer these green lanes, and they'd sleep in a *hovel* nearby. Some had bears and used to make them dance.'

Mrs Fountaine, Pattishall.

'There was a man at Brafield and he was a poacher. He done nothing only poach—that was his living. I never knew him work at anything else. Well then, the Squire made this man a gamekeeper. They used to give him the corn to take up to the Firs to feed the pheasants and he used to go into Brafield pub and sell the corn to folks as had got fowls and drink the money.'

Mr Jack Meyer, Little Houghton.

'The way to catch pheasant is to put down wheat soaked in whisky. They get as drunk as fiddlers and you can shoot 'em easy then.'

Anonymous, Spratton.

Walter Silsby of Bozeat

'He knowed all the woods round 'ere f' miles.'

'Well, according to what I can make out, he (his father) ran away from home when he were about fourteen. They couldn't do a lot with him when he were a little boy. There used to be him and another boy lived next door, in a yard up the other end o' the village, they poked a hole through the bedroom wall, so when they used to go *scrumping* carrots and that out the *garden-field* [allotment], they could swap 'em backwards and forwards.

When he got a bit older he started catching rabbits. Well, that time o' day, it were a big estate all round Bozeat, and they catched him when he were quite young, and he had to go orf t' prison f' that. When he come back, they got on to him so he went away from home and lived wi' one of his old uncles. And he were another sich character, so that started his days o' poaching. So it went on from there. They used to do a bit o' pheasant-shootin' when it were moonlight. When it was dark they'd goo *lung-netting* (long-netting). Course they all had to go to jail for it, that time o' day. But they wadn't always able to catch 'em—they wen' away, you see. Sometimes they used t' go *up the hay-country*—up London way.

My father come back from London one day, and a bloke lay fast asleep with his back up agen a *stun—'eap* [stone-heap] at the side o' the road, and he'd got a new pair o' boots. He'd took 'em orf, I presume, because they hurt his feet. And father said "They're a better pair o' boots than mine" so he sat down and took his own off and set 'em aside and put the old man's pair on. But afore he got home he'd got blisters on his feet and wished he'd never a pinched 'em.

He knowed all the woods round 'ere f' miles. Sundys, we alwus used t' goo for a walk round the fields and these were the times he used t' tell us all these little ditties. He'd say "I had a month f' shootin' 'are on 'ere".

There's a field between Bozeat and Wollaston and father said "I stood there one Bozeat Feast Sunday night with an old muzzle-loader. I'd got twelve hares round me and it took me a good while to pick the biggest one out. Then when I shot it the police were in the field behind me so I got a month for that."

Then one day he were out w' the old muzzle-loader and they lost the 'ammer. So they put the cap on and found an 'are in the forme and he held the gun while his mate tapped the cap with a *pibble* [pebble] to knock it orf. And still they got the hare.

They were comin' for him to do a month one day, and the policeman as come t' fetch him didn't know him. Father stood outside in the yard, 'evvin' a bit o' bacca and the policeman said "Could you tell me where Mr Silsby lives?" He says "Yis—he lives in that house there". The policeman goes over and father went down to Castle Ashby station and on the train and up t' N'thampton and that night he were in Harlestone Firs wi' the lung-nets (long-nets), catching rabbits.

We lived in an old thatched house in what they called Spangle Row. Spangles were the glass beads they used to fasten to the lace-bobbins. There were two houses but we had one for a kind of spare barn, and they'd bin out one Satdy night when I were a little boy—I can just remember that—and when I looked in the barn that Sunday morning there were three hundred rabbits, all lay in rows. They'd all been gutted and packed up to go away. They used t' put them in hampers and get the old feller as used t'tek the milk down, t'tek them to Castle Ashby Station and put them on a train to N'hampton t' be sold.'

Mr Harry Silsby, Bozeat.

Remembering

'Shift the cairvin's, coz.'

'When you go to ingine rallies now you see a lot of old agricultural machinery, like the threshing tackle and the steam plough. It was all being used on the farm in my time.

A man was on the ingine when I were a boy–a little bloke– they called him Peggy. He hadn't got a real artificial leg–it were an old bit o' wood. And Om [I'm–I have] sat on the plough with him, and when there's bin a lot o' *twitch* [couch-grass], Om seen him poke it off with his wooden leg, and we're bin singing "We plough the fields and scatter". Om bin about wi' that ingine bloke when I should 'a bin at school.

Then there was the cultivator–some on 'em called it the drag–we called it the *scuffle* [hoe, harrow]. And there was the *straw-jack* [straw-elevator]–the stuff that used to come out was the *cavin's* [refuse of threshed corn, chaff]. And the old bloke used to say "Shift the cairvin's, *coz*". He called everybody coz.'

(Shakespeare uses this word as a form of 'cousin'. *King John* 111, 3, 21.

Elinor. 'Farewell, gentle cousin'.
King John. 'Coz, farewell'.)

'Right up by that farm they got the ballast out of that hole to make the railway up on an embankment, and at Horton, the *Spoilbanks,* along the *bullock road,* that's what they threw out of the cutting. The men who come here to build the railway, they lodged in the old Reading Room. Some relative of mine, as come from Northampton in the 1840s, she lived there.

There's a pond in the field they call *Stunpit* [Stonepit] and it were very deep. George Bason said that were a limepit. They were getting the lime out, and it were on a spring, and the water come in and they had to get out. They didn't have time to get all the kit out.

There's a barn up the Lodge with four posts in, and the name of a firm who put a windmill up–a grinding mill, but there's no date on. It says *R J Peel, Southwark*. There's still some gears–a big dog-clutch and a pulley, and four pillars, right from the top of the barn to the bottom.

There was a *washbrook* and they done away with that after somebody got drowned in it. You know *Braff* [Brafield] windmill. That had horse-gears–a horse went round and did the pumping. I always like Brafield better than Houghton, because most of the chaps as worked on the farm when we were kids, they were Brafield [men] and we were always in with them. Bill Parsons used to say "Brafield chaps are the best farm workers I've ever had in my life". Of course, they were a little more precise at Houghton. They thought Brafield folk were a bit on the rough side.' *Mr Jack Meyer*, Little Houghton.

'Time we thacked it, boy.'

'While the ground was lying *foller* [fallow], our old gent [father] 'd go round sowing mustard with a *seblit* [seed-lip]. It's a seed-basket shaped to your body, with a harness round your neck. He fixed his eye on a mark on the hedge and walked forward, using his left hand with his right foot and vice versa. The seed was in sacks round the edge of the field, and I used to go behind him with a bucketful. I could see his arms going left and right, and the seed like feathers cutting an arc and falling to earth. He sowed it with two fingers and a thumb. When the mustard was six to ten inches high, he ploughed it in to enrich the ground, and let it lay dead *foller* till the following season.

You sow grass seed with one finger and a thumb, on a dead-still day with no wind, else it'll blow into '*eps* [heaps]. If it's heavy grain, you whop it on fairly thick.

A *fiddler's* a seed-box with a handle, and as it turns, the bow throws the seed out. A seed-barrow has one wheel and a drill-box. A flat iron wheel turns a cog on to the drill and a row of brushes throws out the seed.

When the grass was fully grown we did the mowing with a horse and mowing machine, starting at the hedgerows and working towards the middle of the field. At the end of the

---

Caption left above: William Berry steam-threshing with a Marshall engine at Hall's Farm, Ravensthorpe in 1921. NL, with acknowledgments to Mr P Clifton, Long Buckby.
Below left: The Red Lion at Little Houghton. NRO

mowing, we got a wooden rake and raked the *hedgebacks* [the cut swathes of grass nearest the hedge] and went round the other way with the mower to finish off the field. Well, after turning it a couple of days, we swep' it into heaps with a horse-sweep, till we'd got enough for a staddle. The staddles were built by hand, and after the hay had matured, we drew them into the rick with a long horse-drawn chain.

After the rick had stood there three *wiks* or *above,* the old gent used to say "Time we *thacked* it, boy", so we used to come down with a load of wheat-straw generally, tip it in a heap and wet it thoroughly. We had a board for beating the straw on, and then my job was to draw it into handfuls and *mek* what we called *yelms* with it. Father stacked nine or ten yelms up at an angle to each other, to mek it easier for the thatcher, and tied a cord round them. This bundle of yelms was known as a *bottle.* Up on your shoulder, up the ladder on to the rick. The edge of the ladder was a straight-edge from the top of the rick to the bottom. Father started at the right-hand side of the rick and called it a *stelch* [as much thatching as could be done without moving the ladder] from top to bottom. He thacked it then, yelm after yelm, one on top of th'other, then he took the wooden *prickers,* made of ash or elm usually, about three feet long, stick 'em in and bind the yelms down.

We always called the cattle-shed out in the field the *starvel.'*

[Perhaps from *Starve-all,* a field-name, denoting poor soil.]

'My grandmother kept the dairy and got up at half past four in the morning to sterilise the bottles. When I was a little boy it was my job to cut the straws for the school milk. If the butter wouldn't *come* [form] my granny threw half-a-crown in. The dairy floor was lower than the ground outside. Granny called the outside level the *deadman,* and said it kept the dairy cool.'

Mr Ray Wykes, Spratton.

The sowing of seed broadcast was being carried out in the 1940s.

'The Moggerhanger man is living on the stack.'

'Harvest time, you had to leave the oats in the shock to hear the church bells ring three times, for three Sundays in fact. Three sheaves a side for oats, four for wheat. My grandfather was a stickler for this and he'd make you pull down the shock if there were more. The rows had to be dead straight too. He would sight along with his stick to see if they were straight. If you had a big tall stack, they used to ask if you could see the roundabouts going round at Bedford, some five miles away. If the stack started leaning so it had to be propped, the saying was that *the Moggerhanger man was living on the stack.* I never did find the reason for this.'

Mr Maurice Boston, Wilstead, Bedfordshire.

Moggerhanger is a village in Bedfordshire.

'A very serious type of dog . . .'

'We lived at Moulton where my father was the village policeman. We had a pedigree Airedale bitch, a very serious type of dog called Spider because of her long legs, very much my father's dog. He always took her with him on night duty— once she chased a poacher across three fields and brought him back. It wouldn't be allowed nowadays.

Once father came home in the late evening and left Spider in the yard, going back on duty on his own for some reason. After a while the old man next door came out, to go to the closet [lavatory] at the bottom of the garden. He hated the dog and would have kicked her if he'd dared. She followed him down the yard and just sat outside the closet. All night she sat there and he daren't come out. He had to stay there till morning.'

Miss Margaret Lattimer, Moulton.

A good working dog was needed by many country-dwellers, and the *dog-man* plied his trade accordingly. Miss Lattimer said it was reckoned that '*you could get a good dog for eighteenpence and stand a quart*' [have change for a quart of ale].

'She comes steady out of the hole when she has young . . .'

It is well-known that dogs, cats, horses and some farm animals will, for reasons of their own, make friends with some people and have nothing to do with others. 'The waggoner, the cowman and the shepherd' knew how to persuade animals to respond to them, in part by calls and other sounds.

'We called the cows by saying "Cup, cup". The boys used to go down on all fours and the cows would come wandering towards them. Sheep will come for a whistling or hissing sound. You rattle tins to settle a swarm of bees.'

Mr Ray Wykes, Spratton.

Some people, not all of them poachers, can call wild creatures. A man from Oundle can call pheasants and moorhens, a Newnham man can call hares, and someone from Finedon can entice hares to him and pick them up. *Mr Fred Golby* of Duston said

'One night a burglar alarm went off at Upton Hall. It brought out about twenty hares and a deer.'

'Gran, working in her kitchen with all the doors shut, could hear "the old dog-fox up on Blacklocks. If you're still", she would say, "not just quiet, but still, the crayturs'll come to you".' *Mrs Sonia Glenister,* Australia.

'October is a good time. You keep out of the wind. I saw the plovers rise and then the *bitch-fox,* swerving over the field and wriggling on her belly. She comes steady out of the hole when she has young and bolts out when they're older. I called her and she came to within about thirty yards. The pups'll come nearly to my feet. I just like to look at them, that's all, but poachers come in fast cars from London. They get between twenty and thirty pounds for a fox-skin.'

Mr Ted Hollowell, Cogenhoe (1985).

The Weather

'George Longland and a little bent man called Hallelujah, they knew all the weather signs.' Mrs Sanders, Piddington.

Still an important factor in our lives, in the past it was much more so. Weather lore is part of our inherited knowledge.

It is natural to look up into the sky if one is wondering what the weather is going to be. High, broken cloud in a pattern like that on a mackerel's back foretells unsettled weather.

Mackerel sky, mackerel sky,
Not long wet, not long dry.

When the cloud begins to break up after rain, it will clear *if there's enough blue sky to make a Dutchman a pair of trousers.* The colour of the cloud is important. *White sunset, windy night,* but

> Evening red and morning grey
> Are two good signs of a very fine day.

A better-known version is

> Red sky in the morning, shepherd's warning,
> Red sky at night, shepherd's delight.

These pleasant words are usually very reliable.

Wind makes *mares' tails* in the sky, and occasionally the formation known as *Noah's Ark,* a great boat-shape across the sky, a sign of rain.

There seem to be few local sayings about the sun. *The morning sun never shone all day* is another form of *Fine afore seb'n, rain afore leb'n,* and its opposite.

That *parish lantern,* the moon, foretells rain if its arc is tilted back—a *piddling moon,* they call it at Spratton.

> When the moon is on its back
> Then the weather will surely crack.

At Helmdon they said that *a Tuesday moon brings rain,* and also

> Tuesday new moon and Friday full
> Allus did rain and allus 'ull [will].

A Sunday moon brings a flood before the month is out, they said at Milton Malsor. Elsewhere it was *Wet Friday, wet Sunday,* and also *Wet Sunday, wet wik* [week].

Throughout the year, the weather on certain days was believed to indicate the weather to come during the next weeks or months, as on St. Swithin's.

> If Candlemas Day be fair and bright,
> No more winter is in sight.

or   Winter will have another fight.

> Where the wind is on Candlemas Day,
> There it will stay till the end of May.

> If at Candlemas it be rain,
> Winter is gone and won't come again.

Candlemas is the second of February, and two lovely names for snowdrops, which bloom at about this time, are *Candlemas bells* and *Mary's tapers,* from the Purification of the Blessed Virgin Mary, on the same date.

February is a rainy month, hence the rhymes

> February-Filldike, be it black or be it white [rain or snow]
> and   February weather all mire and muck,
> Three white frosts and then pack up.

The next month is changeable–*March Manyweathers*–and, *as many fogs in March, as many frosts in May,* the saying went. In the days before weather forecasts, and when most people could not read or write, these sayings were useful warnings and reminders.

> By Saint David and Saint Chad,
> Plant your beans, weather good or bad.

The church calendar was better-known than it is now, and everyone would understand from the rhyme that broad beans should be planted by the first or second of March.

> When April blows its horn, [is windy]
> Keep your hay and sell your corn.

The forecast here is for a scanty grass crop followed by a good corn harvest. A *lambing-storm* is a sudden squall in early spring, soon followed by sunshine. One spell of weather which needs no prediction is the *blackthorn winter,* a cold spell every April when the blackthorn is in blossom. Once it falls, the weather warms up, though they're not too sure about it in Little Houghton, where they say

> Let may be early, let may be late,
> It's sure to make the old cows quake.

I think it refers to the may-blossom and not the month. At Abthorpe they say that

> A cold May and a wet June
> Makes all things come in tune.

The blackthorn winter is nearly always balanced by warm weather in Autumn, *St. Luke's* or *St. Martin's little summer.* These dates are 18 October, though the warm weather is often nearer the beginning of the month, and 11 November, by the present calendar, in use since 1752.

'One old inhabitant told me that he always went to the crossroads at 11.30 pm on Old St. Martinmas Eve, 23rd November, and the weather that prevailed during the half-hour till midnight would indicate the weather for the next three months' *Rev B L Evans, The Story of Milton Malsor,* p 233.

In the same village they celebrated *Garland* (May) *Day* on Old May Day, the twelfth of the month, until 1906.

And so to Christmas. It is widely believed and probably true that a mild winter is unhealthy. *Green Christmas, full/fat churchyard.* Though some said that *if the sun shone on the apple trees on Christmas Day,* it foretold a good crop, this was not the general opinion.

> Sun on Christmas Day.
> Few good apples and little hay.

At Milton Malsor they were even more specific.

> Christmas Day bright and gay,
> Gather your horses and go and get hay.
> Christmas Day ragged and rough.
> Sit by the fire, you'll have quite enough.

THE BEHAVIOUR OF ANIMALS AND BIRDS [and rain-beetle]

It is a sign of good weather if rooks build high in the trees.

> Rooks high, it will be dry,
> Rooks low, winter will show.

If rooks make for home early, bad weather is on the way, and *if they sit at the tops of trees, facing the north wind, snow is to come. A host of rooks breaknecking* [flying wildly about] *is a sign of rain.*

> If the cock goes crowing to bed,
> It will rise with watery head.

> If the cuckoo comes to a leafless bough,
> Keep your hay and sell your cow.

This saying, with its indication of a cold April, perhaps the blackthorn winter, seems to confirm the one about April blowing her horn. Both predict poor summer grazing.

Sheep bleating in the evening is a sign that a storm is on the way (Piddington). *If sheep graze in the middle of the field, bad weather will follow,* meaning they are stocking up with food before having to shelter under the hedges (Tugby, near Leicester). *Cows lying down is a sign of rain,* meaning they are keeping a patch of grass dry (Piddington and Banbury).

> Cattle on the hill, water for the mill,
> Cattle in the hollow, water to follow. (Cogenhoe)

Another sign of rain was the appearance of the rain-beetle [the

long-bodied shard-beetle]. It was sometimes kept in a jar full of
soil, and would wriggle out when rain was due. It was also said in
Bedfordshire that *if one was killed, it would rain for forty days.*

'That wunt rain fer an hour. I've just had a look at me rain
beetle'   (Bedfordshire).

VILLAGE FEASTS AND THE WEATHER

Arter Desborough Feast, you can shut your doors (13th
September).
On Milton Feast, shut your door at six (14th September).

'*When Milton Feast comes, you can shut your door.*' I can
remember people saying this as we walked home from the fair
in *Half Croft.*'

Mrs Kathleen Fuller, born and bred in Milton Malsor,
then living in Ontario Canada.

Fine Rowell [Rothwell] Fair (starts on the Monday after Trinity
Sunday), *wet Kett'rin' Feast* (29th June).
Hardingstone snow-feast, Wootton crow-feast (20th November,
23rd April). And to make the point clear, they used to shoot a
crow and hang it up at the feast, one less to eat the newly-sown
seed.

Mr Jack Davis of Northampton, born in 1893, remembered
lines from this poem being recited by the father of one of his
friends when he was a boy in Irthlingborough. He managed to
collect them together as follows, and thought that the poem dates
from 1826.

SIGNS OF FOUL WEATHER

The hollow winds begin to blow,
The clouds look black, the glass is low.

The soot falls down, the spaniels sleep,
And spiders from their cobwebs peep.

Last night the sun went pale to bed,
The moon in haloes hid her head.

The boding shepherd heaves a sigh,
He sees a rainbow in the sky.

The walls are damp, the ditches smell,
Closed is the pink-eyed pimpernel.

[poor man's weather glass]

— Country People —

Hark how the chairs and table crack,
Old Betty's joints are on the rack.

Her corns with shooting-pains torment her,
And to her bed untimely sent her.

Loud quack the ducks, the sea-fowl cry,
The distant hills are looking nigh.

How restless are the snorting swine.
The busy flies disturb the kine.

Low o'er the grass the swallow wings.
The cricket, too, how sharp he sings.

Puss on the hearth with velvet paws
Sits wiping o'er her whiskered jaws.

The smoke from chimneys straight ascends,
Then spreading back, to earth it bends,

The wind unsteady veers around,
Or settling in the south is found.

Through the clear stream the fishes rise,
And nimbly catch the incautious flies.

The glow-worms, numerous and bright,
Illumed the dewy dell last night.

At dusk the squalid toad was seen,
Like quadruped, stalk o'er the green.

The whirling wind the dust obeys,
And in a rapid eddy plays.

The frog has changed his yellow vest,
And in a russet coat is dressed.

The sky is green, the air is still,
The mellow blackbird's voice is still.

The dog so altered in his taste
Quits mutton bones on grass to feast.

Behold yon rooks, how odd their flight,
They imitate the gliding kite,

And heading downward seem to fall
As if they felt the piercing ball.

The tender colts on back do lie,
Nor heed the traveller passing by.

In fiery red the sun doth rise,
And wades through clouds to mount the skies.

'Twill surely rain, I see with sorrow.
No working in the field tomorrow.

These verses bring together some of the bad-weather signs already mentioned, including the *breaknecking* of the rooks. The first line is striking. Clare, who knew all about weather in all its moods, writes of '*hollow winds and tumbling floods*' in the September poem of *The Shepherd's Calendar*, p 110.

Fairs, Feasts and Charities

'My father was a shoemaker, one of the fastest in the village, but he couldn't get work, and there was no dole, you know.'

'Statties,' hiring fairs held by statute, were important events in the village year. Farm workers hoping to be hired carried scythes and sickles, and had plaited cornstalks in their jackets or smocks, dairy maids had buckets and stools, housemaids carried mops. There was all the fun of the fair besides and ale flowed freely for those with a little money to spend.

The village feast, the patronal festival of the church, was a much more decorous affair, but none-the-less was an eagerly awaited holiday. Greens Norton Feast was held on a Monday between the 6th and 12th of September.

'Towcester band used to play on the Sunday night for Norton Feast, and they always finished up with "Christians Awake". Billings Roundabouts used to come as well, and Norton people who lived away always used to come back for the feast if they could.' *Mrs Ivy Smart*, Greens Norton.

'Village life was a lot different years ago. The best things that happened were the village feasts and the Club feasts. The

Caption above right: Springtime at Helmdon. Mr Arthur Seckington, Greatworth.
Below right: A march of the Towcester Oddfellows and court Live and Let Live, Ancient Order of Foresters. The occasion was the proclamation of King George V in 1910. NL with acknowledgments to Sponne School, Towcester.

Bluebell was the headquarters of the Foresters, and the Exeter Arms the headquarters of the old Friendly Society. They used to have their dinners every club day, and their feast was the first Sunday after the 29th of June. The band used to play down the village with scarfs and staves to celebrate it. The whole village took part, but only the club members attended the dinner. It was baked at the bakehouse.'

Mr George Crowson, Helpston.

'There was a clothing club at Alderton. People paid so much a week and the Duke of Grafton contributed money and gave four or five hundredweights of coal to his tenants at Christmas. He gave land for a chapel on condition the services did not clash with the ones at church, and he had a rule that men must be off the allotments by ten on Sunday morning so that they would not be late for church.

The Sparrow Club paid threepence a dozen for dead birds and a penny a dozen for eggs. This was because the sparrows nested in the thatch and spoiled it.'

Mrs Fountaine, Pattishall.

'Our patronal festival follows the first of November, and we always had the roundabouts come. At that time there was no such thing as the government helping the hospitals or the deaf, or the blind, so we had committees to organise charities. There was a service on the Sunday, and our church could not hold all the people who wanted to go. There was a collection for the hospital, and the chap who owned the roundabouts, on a certain evening he gave all the profits to the hospital. From time to time, someone would give five shillings so all the children could have a free ride.

The Sunday following the Quarter Day, you'd see all the people at the Co-op, and on the stroke of nine from the church clock, they used to open the bake-'us door, and the charity's trustees were there with a great long book with the names in. The baker stood there with a great heap o' loaves behind him, and as the trustees called out the names (if it had been me, he'd have called out "Widower William Burt") the baker threw a loaf across the street and if you didn't catch it it went on the ground.

Then there was the coal charity. When my father was on the senior list—you had to be married and over thirty, the coal *higgler* came. He was a trustee of the Methodist Chapel, a grand man–I respect his name. And I can remember him coming to my mother and saying "Maggie, my gal, I've brought you some coal" and she said "What coal, Joe?" and he said "I've got seven hundredweight, my gal" and my mother said "I've never had s' much coal since married I've bin" and she said to me "Get that thrup'ny bit and give it to Mr Frost". And this man, who was the Methodist, he said to my mother "You have this for your children. I'm all right. They want this thruppence, not me".

In them very hard times, the gentleman at the Hall started a soup-kitchen, on Tuesdays and Fridays. If you'd been at our school, in the boys' cloakroom, you'd have seen a three-pint can with a cap hanging over it. We used to go straight from school in the afternoon down to the Hall, and the governess used to dish this soup out, and believe me, it was *thick as duckpuddle* with meat and vegetables. When I got home with ours, my mother had always got a pint of boiling water to make it go farther. I'm going back now *hard on* eighty years.

My grandfather and grandmother had a white ticket for Tuesdays, and I used to go and fetch their soup, and help them eat it, and my mother and father had a blue ticket for Fridays. You didn't know where the next meal was coming from. People used to be kind, and my word, you were glad of it, because work was very bad. My father was a shoemaker, one of the fastest in the village, but he couldn't get work, and there was no dole, you know. The only thing was the Poor Law, Wellingborough Road [the workhouse]. I hope this country will never see again what we saw when we were children.'

Mr William Burt, Harpole.

Here is a selection from the thirteen verses of the 'Newnham Benefit Club song'. For sheer exuberance and Victorian wordiness (each verse has a different chorus) it takes some beating.

THE NEWNHAM BENEFIT CLUB SONG

The Newnham Benefit Club has been
    From childhood's earliest day
To me a happy joyful scene
    Which ne'er can pass away.
        Chorus–Upon this anniversary
            We will be glad and free.

Benefit—a meaning in that word
   There is we dearly love.
'Tis wafted far around, 'tis heard
   And by the hosts above.
            Let us then praise the King of heaven
            For benefits that He has given.

Respect for age should be the rule
   Impressed upon us all;
   Of every other learned at school
   By lads both big and small.
            Ye old and young today rejoice
            In our society with one voice.

Thus this society began
   Like a little seed at first,
To benefit the labouring man,
   Though earth, alas, was cursed.
            But thankful hearts indeed are ours,
            For sending us such prosperous hours.

Our banner let it proudly wave
   Sobriety and peace,
March on with hearts of virtue brave,
   Let not our gladness cease.
            Then we in chorus all will cheer.
            And not get overcome with beer.

We will lay up for winter's store,
   When sickness lays us by,
Prepare for death to ope the door
   to a bright Eternity
            Brother clubmen here we meet,
            And must too at the Judgment seat.
                  J Castell, printer, Daventry.

A copy of the whole song was sent to me by *Mr Robert Key,*
Newnham.

Characters

'All them characters are gone now.'

A miscellany now of warmly remembered people of a kind which most people say is not to be found now.

'Old Crook was old in 1892. He had an old-fashioned wooden leg with an iron stump. When he was drunk he used to fall down in the street and frighten people, because he couldn't get up again, and appeared to be dead. Once he went to the outside closet and sat down, his wooden leg sticking out in front of him. They were communal places and when someone else came in, in the dark, and stumbled against the leg, this man shouted out "Who left this bloody wheelbarrer in 'ere?"'

Mr Roy Payler, Kislingbury.

'His name was Pep Horne. A farmer near Irthlingborough let him live in one of his barns down a lonely lane, and he must have lived on fish caught in the Nene, and perhaps a rabbit or hare he managed to snare. He made a little [money] by selling mushrooms, blackberries and watercress. We children often saw him, but he interfered with no one.'

Mr Jack Davis, Northampton.

'There were two brothers known as Smack and Bagus in our village years ago. I have never known how they got these names, but from childhood that is what they were called. They were thatchers—a team—Bagus up the ladder, Smack making the *burdens* and carrying them up to him. As they got older, Bagus was always upright with a tendency to lean back a bit. Smack bent forward. They always walked along with Bagus, upright, in front, Smack behind, leaning forward, clutching the lapels of his coat with both hands. Whether they were going *'um* from work, or to church, or to their allotment, they always walked the same. They used to tread every footpath once a year to ensure that none should be closed.

When they were in their late sixties we had a flu epidemic. Both got it and Bagus died. Smack was too ill to go to the funeral, which upset him, and when the mourners got home they found that he was dead too. Everybody seemed to make the same comment, "Well, he always followed Bagus".'

Mrs Ruth Hill, Boddington.

'There was an old chap from Grimscote, he'd been married three times and had eleven children in each family. In the pub he bet a gallon of beer that he'd got some celery in his garden "as a tall man couldn't reach standing on tiptoe". He had. It was only just out of the ground.' *Mr William Jones,* Litchborough.

'Back in the last century, the Post Office in one little village in South Northamptonshire was kept by an old lady. Outside the Post Office was a bank alongside the road, and that's where she hung out her washing. One winter's day, with snow on the ground, she hung her washing out to dry, and among other things was a pair of real good old flannel bloomers. The local lads came along and tied up the bottoms of the legs with string and then filled them up with water. It froze later on in the afternoon, and the old lady found that her bloomers were not only frozen stiff, but frozen to the line as well, and she couldn't get them off. So she enlisted the help of a farm labourer, and this man told me he managed to get them off the line, but daren't try to carry them in case they snapped in two, so he wheeled them indoors for her on a wheelbarrow.'

Mr Arthur Seckington, Greatworth.

Village Sayings

Most villages had a local rhyme or saying. Here are some of them (see also 'Sayings' commencing on p 34)

Brafield

Denton folk don't know when they're told,
Houghton folk know before they're told,
Brayf'll folk know when they're told.

Deanshanger

The place where the moon changes.
The place where old moons go to be cut up into stars.

Eastcote

The village carrier, nearing Eastcote and Astcote, would call out 'Eastcut, Arscut and any badly bruised'.

Grafton Regis

A local legend is that Grafton stands on a hill made by nine churches buried below.

Great Houghton

Great Houghton folk, wicked people,
Sold their bells to buy a steeple.

Harpole

Ask/tell Billy Leek
Harpole leeks, Duston sneaks,
Kislingbury long-necked onions.
Billy Leek who lay down to hear the grass grow.

Holdenby

It shines like *Olmby* on a dark night.
Holdenby House is an Elizabethan mansion with large windows.

Hornton, near Banbury

Hornton in the valley, Horley on the hill, Snotty little Drayton and bloody *'Anull* 'Ill.
Hanwell Hill was the scene of a battle in the Civil War. Of nearby Cropredy it was said 'Blood ran down the gutters like water'.

Irthlingborough

Good ringers and singers,
But poor *'um*-bringers.
Said of a family of choir-members and bell-ringers, who never brought much money home.

Little Bowden

Little Bowden, poor people,
Leather bells and a wooden steeple.

Little Houghton

Houghton for pride and poverty,
Brayf'll [Brafield] for money and muck.

Moulton

Moulton images
Is this a pun on 'molten images'? But 'In 1799 the rector sold . . . the two ancient glebe closes and Ymagis Wood'. Baker G. *Hist. of the County of Northamptonshire 1822-30* p 41.

Naseby

Naseby children
Old people in their second childhood. Long-living was common here.

Northampton

Far Cotton, nicknamed New Zealand, later Frog Island. It was separated from the town by the river.

Northampton *(continued)*

Kingsley, called Sloper's Alley

Debtors were said to go there because it was separated from the town by the Racecourse. If they could not pay, they would say 'You'll have to run me round the Racecourse'.

St. James people had a saying, 'It's enough to drive you up the 'ill'

To Berrywood Mental Hospital, later St. Crispins.

Olney

If you can hear Olney buzzer,
It will rain within three days.
Said at Cogenhoe.

Piddington

Hackleton *bolshers* locked up in a den Daren't come out for Piddington men.
And vice-versa at Hackleton, of course. *Bolsh* = sit down heavily, throw oneself down.

Rothwell

You sound like a Hospital man.
Said to someone with a cough. Jesus Hospital is an Elizabethan alms-house, where old people once had to attend church at 8 am and often coughed throughout the service.

Slapton

Slapton [also Spratton] where fools happen,
Thrupp, where they bring 'em up.
Rothersthorpe, among other places, was called Thrupp.

Souldrop

Souldrop air and Sharnbrook water Makes a man live, here and hereafter.
Both Bedfordshire villages, Sharnbrook just over the county boundary.

Weekley

She guz all round Weekley to get to Warkton.
Said of a long-winded person.

Wellingborough

It looks black over *Cookna.*
Weather saying. Cogenhoe is a few miles to the west.

Wolverton

Piano and herring
Proud but poor, living on herring, once a cheap food, and having a piano in the parlour.

Can you discarn 'er?
Men leaving the carriage works after a day's work could
see Hanslope church, several miles to the north, if it was
light enough. It was a sign of Spring when they could first
'discern her' in the evening.

Yardley Gobion
Yardley skegs
Come to Pury to suck eggs.
Taunt shouted by boys at Potterspury school when boys
from Yardley Gobion went there. *skeg* = bullace, wild
plum, but is here used as a shortened form of 'suck eggs',
hence 'fools'.

Yardley Hastings
Half-sharp and hardly,
Say the bells of Yardley.
Said at Little Houghton.

The following interesting rhyme was sent to the *Northampton
County Magazine* in 1929 by *A Milton* of Wadenhoe, who said 'I
well remember my father repeating this to us as children. He died
in 1924 at the age of eighty years'.

Thorpe and Achurch stand in a row,
Lilford and Pilton and peevish Wadenhoe.
Onicle [Aldwinkle] the Chronicle stands by the waterside,
Islip is nothing but malice and pride.
Thrapston, white horse,
Titchmarsh the cross,
Clapton the clay,
Barnwell, Kings highway.
Armston on the hill,
Polebrook in the hole,
Ashton blows the bellows,
Oundle burns the coal.

PEOPLE AT WAR

'We lost forty-six men out of a village of nine hundred.'

These accounts of war speak best for themselves with no comment from me.

The Boer War

'I can remember them coming back from the Boer War in 1903. My mind's so vivid—I can see them getting out on the Green—there used to be the big old elm there—and they had hats like the Australians wear now, with a broad rim, turned up one side. There were seven went and seven came back, and my mother taught me that old song, *'See the conquering hero comes'*, and I stood on the green and sang that song and I had many a penny singing it after that.

Mr William Burt, Harpole.

Caption left: Private Albert Eyles, his wife Emm and their son, Gordon. Emm lost her husband in the war and Gordon died of pneumonia when he was four. Albert was the baby in the frontispiece.

The Great War, 1914-1918

'In my boyhood days a troop of yeomanry was formed in the village. As far as I can remember there were fourteen of them under Mr Wartnaby–he was the lieutenant. They used to practise on the horses in Cave's Close. He trained these men for the Northamptonshire Yeomanry and at the outbreak of war they went to France and into the trenches. There's only one– Tommy Dexter–left in the village now. Mr Wartnaby promised them that if he and they got back to Clipston he would roast an ox on the Green. He didn't come back. He was shot.

Mr J Morley, Clipston.

'In my boyhood days there was the Althorp Troup of Volunteers, under the supervision of Earl Spencer. There'd be about thirty from '*Arpull* (Harpole) in it. My father was one of them and he used to take me when they went to Althorp House. They used to give us great batch loaves and a lump of cheese. It was a meal enough to last us the next day, but we had to walk home.

One day this man came from the Reg'lar Army with a red sash over his shoulder–rank o' sergeant–and he said to the instructor "There's going to be a war. You'll no longer be called the Volunteers but the Territorials, and when the war starts, you'll be the first line of defence". It all came true. The men all went. My father did and he was a man of forty.

Then the letter came saying that Private John Leeson had been killed. That altered everything. In them four years, every so many weeks, just before six o'clock, unless the family went to the Methodists or the Baptists, or never went anywhere, they all came into church, from the youngest to the old, all in deep black, for a memorial service, because another man had been killed. We lost forty-six men out of a village of nine hundred, and seven in the second war.

The numbers of wounded was terrible, and a lady in the village used to collect eggs for them. We youths all had an area we used to go round every Friday night and say "If you please, would you give an egg for the wounded soldiers?" A gentle-man used to come to *Arpull* with a great hamper on a bike. We started this before they came to Berrywood (St Crispin Hospital, where war-wounded were nursed). People used to

invite those who could walk, into their homes for a cup of tea.'
Mr William Burt, Harpole.

Other servicemen were nursed at Barry Road School in
Northampton, and a group of young boys from the East Street area
nearby, carrying wooden guns, used to go from door to door
collecting food, especially eggs, for the wounded. They sang this
song, recorded elsewhere as *The Gloucester Boys* and *The
Bermondsey Boys.*

> We are the East End boys,
> We are the lads that drink no beer, no beer,
> We earn our *tanners* (sixpences), we know our *manners*,
> We are respected wherever we go,
> We are the East End boys.
> When we go walking down the Broadway line
> Doors and windows open wide, wide.
> We can hop, we can skip,
> We can dance the Irish Trip
> We are the East End boys.
Song sung by *Mr V Cook,* Northampton.

The following words were sung to the quick march of the
Northamptonshire Regiment.

> We are the old Northampton boys,
> Swinging a leg, swinging a leg
> (or *swinging the lead,* feigning illness)

> We are the old Northampton boys,
> Swinging a leg today.

> Hard up, hard up, some poor beggars are hard up,
> Hard up, hard up, other poor beggars are broke.

> Back the Bays, steady the Greys and let the Northamptons
> pass

Mr Frank Lay, a blacksmith's boy from Greens Norton, volunteered three days after the outbreak of war, giving his age as
eighteen. He was sixteen, and served in Egypt, the Dardanelles
and on the Somme, winning the Military Medal and coming
through 'without a *scrat*'. He told his story in the richest South
Northamptonshire accent I have ever heard, and it was recorded
in 1974 by Mr R Bicknell, who gave a copy to Mrs I Smart. Both
allowed me to take a further copy, which I gratefully acknowledge.

'I brought 'em all back'

'I volunteered the seventh of August 1914. I went to Egypt until they went on the Dardanelles. I went in the landing there. We were in the backing-up-force—we were out at sea, and as soon as they forced a landing, we *swoped* (swept) in on the boats and my God, that were a bloody do. I hadn't got nothing, neither hat, nor rifle nor equipment—nothing. They snuff all the bloody lot off us.

As we got the boat in, it'd be damn near as long as Greens Norton from the shore, and I don't know how long I was in the water. We was all swimmin'—men, horses, some dead and some yelpin' and a few gettin' away with it. Somebody collared hold on yer and you were bloody near drowned.

And, my God, when us got out, the ruddy clothes, they rubbed me that there sore, with the sea-water in the khaki, I was red-raw from head t'fut, as it dried y' see. Being so hot, and we sweat—it were just like being rubbed with emery-cloth. My God, I thought—I shall never get out o' this.

However, I went right through, and went back to Egypt and finished up in France. I went straight up on the Somme on the sixteenth of August, 1916, in the big push. That were me first time in action in France, and I tell you, we got wiped out. There were only this one lieutenant and the adjutant and a bloody colonel left in our mob. They cleared the whole issue out. This medal (the Military Medal) "for bravery in the field", I had that on the Somme. I very near had to take command in B Company, and we were cut off for three days and I brought 'em all back. There were only twenty-seven left out of eight hundred. The lieutenant, he'd never bin in the line before, and when he was posted to our platoon, we used t' sing "And a little child shall lead them". He wanted to know how long we'd bin there, and I were the oldest, and I said "Up and down this bugger f' two years".

Well, I come home on leave on New Year's Day 1919, and I went to N'thampton to be presented with that medal. There were seventeen of us went up f' different medals, DCMs and one thing or another. There were crowds up there, 'cause it was a big day, y' know. There was a crowd of women and men just behind where we stood. The Rig'mental Sar' Major the Rifle Brigade, he reads all this here lot out, when you joined the army, what theatre of war you were in.

These 'ere women bawled out "Poor buggers" they said

"went all through the bloody war for a bloody medal. You ought t' give 'im two". And do you know, when I got this 'ere medal, them women bloody near lynched me.

It's a nice medal—silver, it is. That other's the Victory Medal.

I come through wonderful well—never had a *scrat*. I was one of the luckiest ever went in.'

Mr Frank Lay, Greens Norton.

I did an extra guard duty to hear the nightingales sing

'I enlisted in the Royal Fusiliers, a regiment in which discipline was harsh. I expect it had to be, to turn civilians into fighting soldiers in a few weeks. I got into trouble twice for being unshaven, once in England at 4 am with no lights in the hut and later in a front-line trench when we hadn't even a drop of water to drink, let alone shave.

We could see No Man's Land and the enemy lines by periscope. Sometimes there was only a little shelling and machine-gun fire, sometimes intense bombardment for days and nights on end, and in the big attacks it was hand-to-hand combat.

In the mining area around Lens, we came upon whole villages empty and abandoned, the gardens still full of hawthorn and lilac. The empty ground became covered with poppies—each Armistice Day it all comes back. When we were advancing through a wood devastated by shellfire, I came across a bed of narcissus that had survived. I have always loved them since then. Once I did an extra guard duty to hear the nightingales sing.

This was one of our marching songs.

> We are Fred Karno's army, [a music hall character]
> Whatever good are we?
> We cannot fight, we cannot shoot,
> We cannot do PT.
>
> And when we get to Berlin,
> The Kaiser he will say
> "Mein Gott, mein Gott, what a bloody rotten lot,
> What a bloody rotten lot are they".

Once I had a Blighty(home) leave which ended a few days before Christmas. How hard it seemed to go back to war.

I was married while on a few days' leave after the Armistice. Mabel and I had been sweethearts since before the war. She lived just across the street, in the house where we have lived ever since. She kept house for her father, and before we knew her name, my grandmother used to say "That little Sixteen will make a good wife for someone". Times were very Spartan—one of our wedding presents was a loaf of white bread.'

Mr Jack Davis, Northampton.

The standard loaf at the end of the war was dark in colour, made from rye flour.

Letters were all important in both world wars. Very few people had a telephone. Here are some written to Ferdinand and Rose Pearce of Far Cotton, Northampton, their daughter Alice and her fiancé Harry, himself serving in France, during the Great War.

Dear Firday and all,
Just a few more lines hoping they will find you and all at home in the pink as it leaves me in the best of health and strength. Well we are off across the water tomorrow—France, I think it is. Well I don't suppose it matters where it is so long as we can get a few rounds into them pretty quick and finish them off so that we can get back home and be our old selves again. Now whenever you see Emm (his wife) I want you to buck her up and tell her the war is going along all right and will soon be finish, then I am sure it will bring a smile on her dear face.
We had our full medical and full service kit inspection yesterday. Well Firday I will be sure and let you know where I am as soon as I know. Good luck to you, Rose and Alice. Your ever-loving brother, *Albert.*

On Active Service with the British Expeditionary Force 9.9.17.

Dear Rose and all,
At last I have time to write you a few lines hoping they will find you all in the pink of condition as it leaves me quite alright.
Tell Firday I came across old Micky Newman the town reserve goalkeeper the other day and by the look of him he

Caption left above: Crimean war veterans awaiting a visit from King George V and Queen Mary at Northampton in 1913. NL
Below left: Bread supplies being delivered to an Army billet in Rushden in the 1914-18 war. Food hygiene was not a priority. NL with acknowledgments to Mr Kenneth Mobbs, Bristol.

hasn't stopped any shots here. I suppose Emm and the boy look you up occasionally. What do you think of him now–gets quite a topper they tell me. How is Alice's Harry going on–I hope he's quite alright still.

Well Rose, things are a bit hot here at times but hope to soon quieten things with our Big Bill, the name we have christen our gun. The work isn't bad now that we have got settled, going on 9 in the morning till 9 the next, then we are relieved for 24 hours. One good thing, we get our food pretty regularly, but there isn't any pudding–just the stuff you want. Well we must be thankful for what we get, considering the hard times. I don't think I dare say any more, so must close. From your ever-loving brother *Albert*.

Dear Mother, Dad and sister (an affectionate greeting from a soldier billeted with the family)

Sorry I could not write before as I did not settle down until last night. We got to a little place called Tiptree about 4.30 and were walking about trying to find a Billit. We did at the finish–a Blooming empty house, one what had just been left by a german countess and here we had to spend the night. It was nine o'clock when we got in and we had had no tea, so we set to work to get some supper. Then we retired to bed which was three Blanketts on a hard wooden floor. There was no fire. I was as cold as ice all night and had not a wink of sleep.

The worst part of it was we had no grub, only a chunk of bread and jam, but Oh Ma, for a bit of your Apple pudding.

But still think all is well now as they moved us to a nice little thatched roof cottage and there are two nice daughters. I am thumbs up with one, so Alice my little pigeon, it is all up with you for a time.

Your affectionate *Harry Gidley* (not Alice's fiancé).

40081 Sgt J W Riddington, 1st Northants, BEF, France.

Dear Harry,

Thanks for the parcel containing my watch, which I received at the Base some six weeks ago. It seems like six months. I'm still in the pink. Sgt Dunkley also is quite well. We had the good fortune to be drafted together, to this Battalion, and mighty proud we were.

Well we got here after a rail journey of about forty miles in twenty-six hours and detrained in earshot of our own artillery.

We moved the same night up to the Regiment who were resting three miles behind the line, in some old disused trenches. Thus I spent about three days, then up we went 'over the top and the best of luck'. Our people sent up a mine and Fritz gave us a few trench mortars, bombs, bullets and what not. We were changing our position in the trench and I was leading man when suddenly something shoved a hole in the parapet and I got a neck full of dirt, but the man third behind me got something else and behind him three or four were killed. I found nothing to upset me very much until our men crept back over the parapet, wounded, with holes in their faces, eyes out, and saturated with blood and to see men laying in bits in the trench.

But you get used to most things. We've been up again since then, and I'm still OK. But some of the old 2nd/4th Battalions (The Northamptonshire Regiment) touched out—Daniel, Youle, White and some others but I don't think any were killed.

In between times we move back to villages or woods behind the lines where we live in barns or bivouacs and spend the days sloping arms by numbers etc. This drill, though a trifle monotonous, is wonderfully smartening. When our time is more fully occupied, discipline necessarily slackens a little, and if not watched, troops tend to regard privileges as absolute rights. During a rest, a regular series of parades restores the standard.

For some time past, I believe, this Battalion has been promised a month's rest, and after several false starts, this has now happened. One day we packed off, marched a few kilometres and were picked up by an army of motor-buses. We are now miles and miles back, right out of all the sights and sounds of war, in a pleasant little village. So here I am, living a life of peace and ease until the motors shall return and shove us up again. Here the fields are in cultivation, the places are clean, the people are clean, and life runs smoothly as can be.

You can get Madame to do your washing, you can procure eggs and milk in any quantities. Orchards predominate and no.5 platoon (mine) have permission from the billet owner to help ourselves. Très bon.

Alf Dunkley is in Duston War Hospital. Well, so long. 2/6d enclosed to defray what you expended on my watch.

Yours to a cinder, *Jack*.

Jack Riddington died as he had seen other men die, and Albert never saw Emm and the little 'topper' again. He was killed by a shell four months after the letter to his sister Rose.

Harry Gidley came home, lying helpless and immobile with rheumatism in the bottom of an Army truck—a legacy of the water-logged trenches and battlefields. Mistakenly believed to be on a charge, he was taken home when his escort realised their mistake and dumped in the hallway of his parents' home. His mother restored him to reasonable health by rubbing his body every day with hot whisky and dosing him with the same.

Alice's fiancé Harry was taken to hospital in Scotland suffering from 'trench feet', recovered and married Alice in 1919.

The Second World War
1939-45

'Four of us milked a cow once'

'The war came and we had to plough up the grassland to produce more food—thirty-seven acres under the plough. I had nearly a hundred acres all told. I had to join the Observer Corps and work sixteen hours at that, Saturday and Sunday nights, and it was hard to get labour.

I applied for a land-girl to help with the milking and when I met her at the station and said "I presume you can milk?", she said "Four of us milked a cow once". She came from Wellingborough, out of the Ideal Clothing Factory. She had had four months training, sowing potatoes. I had to teach her and I must say she took to milking very well. Instead of paying her overtime I used to let her have the weekends off in the *highest* of hay and harvest.

We had two evacuees—one was a rascal from the East End of London and he was a terrible case. Fell in the horse-trough next door to the dairy.

The first Saturday night he was here I said to him "It's time you went to bed" and he said "I haven't seen nothing yet" so I said "What do you want to see?" and he said "Well, I thought there'd be a fight. My mum and dad always have a fight on a Saturday night". Ten years old he was and riddled with TB.

After the land-girl left I had two Italian prisoners from the camp on Farndon road. First boy was a doctor's son, taken prisoner after two months. Poor boy. One day I said to him "What have you got for your dinner?" All he'd got was a strip of pudding—looked like Yorkshire, no bigger than three fingers, and a little bag of currants. The wife said "We've got a few potatoes and a drop of gravy". When I gave it to him, tears ran down his cheeks. He'd never come in the house to have anything, but we always found him a bit of something.

Mr J Morley, Clipston.

We would not have missed it for anything

Working on the cornstack could be dicey. As you picked up the sheaves, mice and rats would run in all directions. One girl ended up with a mouse going up her leg and running round her waist. After that we copied the men and tied string round our trousers, just below the knee.

The meals at the hostel were very filling, but the pack-up left much to be desired. Cheese and spam OK, but peas on bread-and-butter with beetroot, put up the night before—ugh.

Discipline was very strict. We had to be in by 10.30 in the summer and 10 pm in the winter. Our social life usually meant a trip down to the local with a sing-song round the piano. Sometimes we had social evenings in the hostel when the local lads, soldiers from the camp and the Yanks from Grafton Underwood and Benefield were invited. Then we had the old wind-up gramophone with all the old favourites by Glen Miller and Joe Loss. We hardly lived in the lap of luxury—the dormitory had a concrete floor and there were two coke stoves for heating. We slept on two-tier wooden bunks (no springs) with mattresses. There were no mats on the floor.

Our memories of those days are of satisfying work, lots of laughter, even when the news was bad, and some wonderful friends. We would not have missed it for anything.

Former Land-girls (Women's Land Army) *J Shiells* and *J Blades*, writing in the magazine of the Brigstock Historical Society, by courtesy of *Mrs Simons*, Secretary, and *Mr JE Bailey*, Brigstock.

− *People at War* −

'We picked the photographs up and handed them in for his next-of-kin'

'I volunteered for the Regular Army in 1938, after Munich, when Chamberlain came back and said that there was "peace in our time".

When war came in 1939 I went out with the British Expeditionary Force in the 7th Guards Brigade of the Third Division, under Major-General B L Montgomery, as he then was.

When Belgium was invaded in 1940 the Division was sent to Louvain, and from there played a major part in fighting the rearguard action which enabled most of the BEF to be evacuated from Dunkirk. At Louvain I was wounded in the face, and nursed at a convent by the nuns. I was a platoon sergeant, and when I came back all my platoon except the truck-drivers had been killed on a minefield.

We went back into Europe a few days after D-Day. I was then in the 1st Battalion the Grenadier Guards Armoured Division. We had to anchor off-shore for two days because the sea was too rough for a landing. The ship was attacked from the shore and from the air. We were glad to get off.

We went ashore in tank landing-craft. There were dead bodies and smashed-up buildings. I remember the dead cattle with bloated bodies, and the smell. The fighting was close—the Germans were only a hundred yards away.

Our first big advance was from south of Caen to a place called Cagny. It was a terrible battle. We lost a third of our tanks. It took twenty-four hours to get six miles through the cornfields, being mortared and shelled.

The biggest advance was from Normandy to Brussels. We liberated Brussels on the evening of 3rd September 1944. The people went wild, climbing on our tanks with flags and champagne that they had hidden away. We could only stay a few hours.

There was a pause then. We had to capture the bridges at

Caption above left: Winter in the Ardennes, 1944-45, and a well-earned mug of tea for a group of Grenadiers of the Guards Armoured Division. Sgt L J Vickers holds his mug under the kettle. Mrs Iris Vickers.
Below left: A rest on the road in Bukit Tima for Sgt R E Grimes seated, with sweat-rag, and his two mates. They were from the 40th Armoured Brigade Workshops, REME, providing maintenance services for the troops on Singapore Island in 1946, after the Japanese capitulation in 1945.

Eindhoven, Grave and Nijmegen. The Guards captured the bridge at Nijmegen and it was called Grenadier Bridge from then on. Just before we got to the last bridge, at Arnhem, the Germans flooded the plain. But we crossed the Rhine and the Siegfried Line, and then there was a long campaign through Germany to a place called Stade and on to Hamburg and the Kiel Canal. There was a concentration camp at Stanisbostel. It stood on top of a hill, guarded by the SS. We were in the river valley below, and we had a lot of casualties there, just before the war ended. It was hard that men should die like that, just at the end. We saw the inmates of the camp, like skeletons and full of disease.

We let the Russians take Berlin alone, because of all they had been through in the defence of their country. There were British, French, Americans and Russians there. We were in Berlin for the Victory parade, with Monty and Marshal Zhukov.

After that I was posted to Bonn and in March 1946 I was demobbed at the Talavera Barracks in Northampton.

I had seen a number of my friends killed. One was blown up by a booby-trap left under a dead cow on the road. His body landed in a field, and photographs of his family were thrown out of his wallet and spread on the ground around him. We picked them up and handed them in for his next-of-kin.

Mr Leslie Vickers, Northampton.

'After Dunkirk some troops were billeted in Kettering Road, in the Exeter Hall, I think. I remember them standing about, sitting on the kerb and walking down Abington Street. There were all nationalities and they wore all sorts of uniforms, whatever they could find. Some had no shoes. They were still showing the shock and stress in their faces.'

Mrs Iris Vickers, Northampton.

CHURCH AND CHAPEL

'Stoop low to hear us; listen to our cry'
From a poem by *Mrs Rose Clarke*, Barton Seagrave

The Christian faith has enriched the oral tradition, bringing great words and music into the daily lives of rich and poor alike. The lord of the manor together with his humblest labourer and their families listened Sunday after Sunday to the majestic seventeenth century English of the Bible and the Book of Common Prayer, perhaps in a church built of fine Northamptonshire stone, standing in quiet beauty as it had stood since Norman or even Saxon times.

Or a nineteenth century shopkeeper or artisan sat among his apprentices as they listened to a local preacher, who had perhaps walked miles to take the services in a chapel, small and plain in the village street, large and confident in the town. They would sing one of Charles Wesley's hymns, or, later in the century, 'one out o' Sankey', that collection which struck such a chord in the hearts of so many ordinary devout men and women. Such people used sentences from the Bible or from prayers or hymns as part of their everyday speech, and could probably sing in harmony even if they could not read or write.

'When I was a girl and used to play the piano in the front room on Sunday nights, and all the family stood round and sang, people used to gather outside and we used to open the window so they could join in.

Then in the first war, we had a shop in Lutterworth Road, open till eleven o'clock at night. I've often been so tired when we shut the shop that Ted has had to take my shoes off for me. But the Cheshire Regiment was billetted in the streets round about, and the Welsh boys used to gather round the lighted shop window and sing.'

Mrs Mabel Lineham, Northampton.

'In the year 1868 there occurred one night a spectacular display of shooting stars. The handsewn-shoemakers at Kislingbury had their own Glee Club, a name which did no justice to some of the music they sang, though not many of them could read, write or read music. On this night they were hastily summoned into the village street and they stood there with faces uplifted to the starry sky and sang "The heavens are telling . . ." from Haydn's "Creation".'

Mr Roy Payler, Kislingbury.

The Salvation Army, too, brought faith and music out into the streets, their bands valiantly playing and their singers singing in all weathers. They took copies of *The War Cry* into the pubs, and help and comfort to the poor and downtrodden. Churches and chapels themselves, as well as being places of worship, provided, as they still do, a meeting-place, a school, sometimes teaching adults as well as children, and a centre for varied activities. Then there were the outings. Casual clothes were not worn, as the photograph on p 174 clearly shows. Those of us who were children in the Depression remember the excitements of concerts and plays, and the winter bazaars with their decorated stalls and [magic word], Refreshments. The Sunday School Treat was the highlight of the summer, especially for children who never had a holiday. A half-day was allowed from day-school and we went, with our mothers and friends, by train, or in Mr Waddilow's soft-drinks lorry, to Blisworth or Hartwell, where a field had been wonderfully prepared for us, with stalls of small toys, sweets and bottles of *spruce* [lemonade] with glass marbles in their necks. There were races and a scramble for sweets and the joy of communal eating in the open air ('In the barn or schoolroom if wet') and the ride home through the quiet countryside, singing and clutching our trophies, or, if very small, leaning sleepily against our mothers. Nothing else was ever quite like it.

Caption left: Mabel Eyles aged seventeen in 1895, when she used to play the piano and sing hymns by the open window for all to join in. Mabel was the girl on the left in the frontispiece.

Here are some more memories.

'The children used to meet at a pub and marched up to the chapel, and, as they were really poor in those days, most of them, people provided clothes to make them respectable for the service. Little girls had white caps and tippets [capes] in summer and grey ones in winter. They had to keep their feet together so they shouldn't shuffle them about. They were given awards if they were good, but if they misbehaved they had placards put on them—LIAR, TRUANT, TALKING and so on. Another punishment was to make them stand on a form and put their first two fingers in their mouths. After school, members of the congregation used to take them home for a good dinner.'   *Miss Kathleen Coales,* Market Harborough.

'There is a house at Clifton known as Sore-finger Chapel. It was built as a chapel by a man who bought up plaited straw for the Luton hat-trade.'

Mr Angus Dudley, Clifton Shefford, Beds.

'There was one vicar who used to say "If you don't attend church I'll take the thatch off your roof".'

Miss Barbara Adkins, Banbury.

'Three generations back, my family came here from Gayton, and my great-grandfather was a ringer when he came, and until I had to give up through ill-health, there was always one of the family ringing the bells. My grandfather said to me "You know, boy, there was a place for each of them five bells. The first was the *sacrament bell,* the second was the *gleaning bell,* The third was the *club bell.* If the people in the village saved coppers, and—you believe me—that was all they could save, it was backed by somebody in the church. The fourth was the *pancake bell,* always rung on Shrove Tuesday at eleven o'clock, and the fifth was the *death-and-sermon* bell. That bell was *pulled-up* when there was going to be a sermon, and rung as a *passing-bell* for all parishioners. Pulled up? Well, the bell is in a great wheel. It goes backward and forward till it stands up like a great wine-glass."

When I came out the army, the man who was the *village man,* he was killed in action in 1916, and they asked me if I would take on his duties—helping christen babies, marrying young people and burying the dead. In those years I laid nearly five hundred people to rest in the churchyard. There was never a wedding or a funeral but I was asked to go and have a cup of tea. When I look back on my life I think "Well, you can claim that for all those years you were the *village man*".

Before we had TV and radio, on great national occasions, there used to be a service in the church. The first I attended as a choirboy was the death of King Edward VII, and the door of the church had to be left open and they stood up *agen* the door outside. And [even] the humblest people were in black. When the Coronation come it was just the reverse–all the people dressed up as best they could.

They didn't seem to get on together, the Church of England, the Baptists and the Methodists, until 1922. All three churches had good choirs, and the choirmaster of the Baptist chapel– they had a wonderful choir down theer–he said "Can we have a meeting at my house?", and I was chosen from our choir–I've been in 'Arpull choir since 1909. We had that meeting and after that the choirs all sang together. In 1925 we sang the Messiah. The relationship between the churches was really wonderful. I always say it was one of the most wonderful things in my life-time'. *Mr William Burt*, Harpole.

'I have seen hard-drinking, hard-swearing men remove their hats and caps when they sang Christmas hymns in the *Live and Let Live* public house.' *Mr A Clements*, Harpole.

'My Gran (who lived at Hornton near Banbury) used to tell of the Methodist preachers who held open-air services on the village greens in the last century. One day she and her brother were listening, and the preacher asked if anyone would follow him and go overseas and help spread the Word to the heathen. Gran said her brother's eyes were like stars and he said "I'll come with 'ee, Maister". The preacher said "Go and make your farewells, and bring only as much as you can carry in your hand".

So Gran and her brother went home and found their mother just taking the bread out of the oven. When told of her son's intentions, all she could manage to say was "It's a good thing you've got some fresh bread to take". He went away and never came back. He died of fever in Spain'.
Mrs Sonia Glenister, Australia.

'When we had our first wireless set, I can remember my mother's rapt face as she heard the hymns she loved coming apparently from thin air.' *Mr Jack Davis*, Northampton.

Caption above: An outing by brake for Kingsley Park Methodist Church Women's Meeting, 1900. Casual clothes were not worn. Mrs W Mundin and Mrs G White. Below: Potterspury Band of Hope about 1910. On the right is the Revd Plant and on the left, his curate, the Revd Goldberg. NL with acknowledgments to St Nicholas Church, Potterspury and the Revd E H Lurkings, Vicar.

'The rector of a local village in the last century was also a JP, and he was noted for the stinging sentences he handed out. He also rode to hounds and one day, jumping a wide brook, he came off his horse and landed up to his waist in mud and water. There was a local boy standing on the bank, and the rector yelled to him to come and pull him out. The chap looked at him thoughtfully for a minute and then he said "Waal, you wunt be warnted till Sunday. You may as well stop where y' be", and he went off and left him'.   *Mr Arthur Seckington*, Greatworth.

'He was a good roadman. He came round on Sundays before morning service and cleaned up all the streets. It wasn't part of his job'.   *Mrs Crowson*, Helpston.

About sixty years ago the Sunday School superintendent used to keep a blazing fire going on a cold winter's day and all the poor children from the cottages nearby could go in and get warm. Perhaps they had to say a prayer as well.

After church people used to go for walks round the village. Everybody knew the hedges where violets grew and where to find cowslips in the wood. The seasons dictated the Sunday walk—it had been the same for generations. It's not the same now. Somehow we have lost our caring nature. When we all went to Sunday School we knew what was right and wrong.
     Mr William Jones, Litchborough.

You know the missionary William Carey who went out to India? Well, in the old Baptist manse at Clipston a group of men sat up all night and cooked a joint of beef over the fire to eat— while they planned how they would send him there.

My wife and I first went to the chapel when we were four years old. My wife was a Sunday school teacher all her life and I am a lifedeacon at eighty-six. We were within a fortnight of our Diamond Wedding when she had a severe stroke on the Sunday afternoon. Her last words were 'I shan't go to chapel tonight'.   *Mr John Morley*, Clipston.

I remember a gypsy wedding held in the porch only of St. Mary's church in Banbury. The bride's hair was a cascade of black curls hanging down to her waist.

My mother was brought up by a childless uncle and aunt in 'Culluth—Culworth. Uncle George and Aunt Sarah-Ann Watts had to pay a year's tithe to the vicar on Christmas Day. Everyone in the village had to respect the vicar—women and girls curtsied and men and boys touched their caps. Mum's friend was called Ruby Gulliver and each time Ruby met the vicar and curtsied, he would pat her on the head and say 'Ah, the price of a virtuous woman is far above rubies'. It was years before Mum and Ruby knew what 'virtuous' meant. I remember so well my mother's Wesleyan severity against those who did not work and save.

I remember at the age of three or four, going to the Railway Mission Hall on the corner of Merton Street, Banbury. I can only remember going there on cold snowy days when, inside, a coke stove glowed red and sometimes white-hot. We watched magic-lantern shows—soldiers marching off to war, and one which remains clearly in my mind, of a girl waving her soldier boy goodbye, and then receiving a telegram to say he had been killed and of her falling sobbing over a rock. Of course it was a silent film and each slide was followed by a caption which was read out loud by the older children. We sang the old hymns from the Sankey book—'Tell me the old, old story' was one— and at the end we lined up and were given mugs of boiling hot cocoa and so were sent home.

From the Railway Mission I graduated, once I could sew properly, to 'sewing for the heathen in Africa'. On Saturdays we went along to the Bluebird boarding-house in Bridge Street, where Mrs Gillett sat in one of the rooms, and we all gathered round her, sewing these dreadful shirts. In my memory she is like Queen Victoria, encrusted with jet beads. While we sewed she read the Bible to us and we had to remember a text. Each Easter we sewing girls were invited to Woodgreen where Mrs Gillett had hidden chocolate eggs in the garden. We could keep those we found.   *Mrs Sonia Glenister,* Australia.

In the 1920s my brother, sister and I attended from an early age at Eastcote Baptist Chapel. The whole of my childhood was conditioned by a Sunday devoted to three attendances there. The annual outing to Wicksteed, though, was an unqualified privilege and eagerly looked forward to. A busload of excited children and accompanying grown-ups was deposited inside the gates by Mr Kirton and then there were swings and slides, boating, model train rides and the garden to admire and then the tea.

In what seemed a vast area, this was laid out on long, white-covered tables and here various parties assembled at stipulated times to have their meal. What remains as a vivid impression was the spontaneous singing of the grace, throughout the building. It was no subdued 'For what we are about to receive' but a full-throated rendering, each table louder than the one before, and, what with standing up and sitting down, the whole must have resembled a musical sea. There was enough zeal in reserve to sing on the way home.

Sermons were long in those days. One rather fiery and theatrical character sprayed saliva to the detriment of those close to the pulpit, and I think that Eastcote probably holds the record for sermons based on Elijah and the prophets of Baal. But I do not denigrate the loyal service of lay preachers which continues in an unbroken line to the present day.

Mr Harry Saunders, Eastcote.

We lived in Broughton across the *pad* (path) from the chapel. If I slept late, I would be awakened by the strains of the 'Hallelujah Chorus', belted out by the organist, who nodded his head vigorously at each 'Hallelujah'. Then the ritual of the Sunday dinner. Everyone—yes, everyone in the village, except 'the quality' had a roast, mostly beef surrounded by delicious meat-gravy and saturated Yorkshire pudding. This was taken to the bakehouse by the menfolk, walking carefully, carrying the tins, sometimes holding them with felt pads.

Later on, mother said 'Time now', and went to put on the vegetables. As I walked down the twisty lane, I could smell the glorious aroma of all the sizzling beef and golden puddings. I must be sure to get the right one. The baker would open up the big, black oven and slide in the huge shovel. 'No, that ent yourn, my duck, yourn's pork this week'.

After dinner we would retire for an hour into the sitting-room to talk of the week's doings—so many problems got sorted out then. Then to Sunday School and Bible class down the elder-bedecked lane to the Rectory. In the drawing-room, two tall windows looked out on the sleeping lawns. The Rector's wife sat graceful and straight on an upright chair, the sunlight making a halo of her upswept hair. She would pick up her Bible and in her beautiful voice would begin the lesson. We never dared to fidget or giggle. If we did she would pause, raise her kind eyes and we would feel ashamed.

Mrs Rose Clark, Barton Seagrave.

Caption: Sellenger's Round, a country dance, at Broughton in 1926. Mrs Rose Clark, Barton Seagrave.

CHILDREN AT PLAY

Children's Games

Now you're married I wish you joy
First a girl and then a boy,
Seven years old, a son and daughter,
Now's the time to kiss one another.

PLAYING WITH THE BABY

Fingers and toes are natural playthings and most families know some very simple words and rhymes to amuse the baby, perhaps making up their own. 'Clap-a-*dannies*' is a good start, and for an older baby, the tickling game 'Round and round the garden like a teddy bear'. With two small pieces of paper stuck to your forefinger nails to bring about the vanishing trick you can play

> Two little dicky birds sitting on a wall,
> One named Peter, one named Paul,
> Fly away Peter, fly away Paul,
> Come back Peter, come back Paul.

Many rhymes, like this one and 'This little piggy went to market' have echoes of our rural past, and reflect a child's natural interest in animals and birds. These themes will run through his childhood, in game and nursery rhyme and fairytale, the last resting places of much ancient lore.

My eldest grand-daughter, when she was at nursery schoo
learned this modern finger-rhyme

> Tommy Thumb, Peter Pointer, Timothy Tall,
> Ruby-ring and baby small, fingers all.

My grandmother taught me a much older one.

> Thumper, Lickpot, Longman, Leanman, Littleman.

An endearing little rhyme from Little Houghton evokes a timeless
picture of mother and toddler by the fireside.

> Warm *dannies,* warm *dannies* [hands]
> Folks is gone to plough,
> If you want to warm your *dannies,*
> Come and warm them now.

> From *Mrs Emmott,* Little Houghton
> and *Mrs Minney,* Yardley Hastings.

A fireside favourite of my grandmother's was the first verse of the
following, and *Audrey Smith* of Grendon told me the second
verse.

> Jeremiah, blow the fire,
> Huff puff puff,
> Jeremiah, blow the fire,
> Huff puff puff.

> First you blow it gentle,
> Then you blow it rough,
> Jeremiah, blow the fire,
> Huff puff puff.

Another tickling game is 'Creepy mouse', known in 1689, when J
Carlile in *Fortune-hunters,* p 25, says '. . . not so old but I can play
at Creep-mouse yet. Creep mouse, creep, catch her'.

A lock of hair, the forehead, nose and mouth provide the door-
furniture for the following.

> Ring the bell, knock at the door,
> Lift up the latch and walk in.

The baby likes being bounced up and down on one's knee, the
bouncer perhaps saying *'Gee up Neddy to the fair'* or going
through the whole nursery rhyme. And when at last the *miller-
man* comes, throwing his *sleepy-dust* in the baby's eyes, then

rhaps, if he is a lucky baby, he may hear a lullaby, tenderest of all ongs for children, as he falls asleep.

HAND PLAY RHYMES

Here are some hand-play rhymes for children playing together, the first two involving intertwining the fingers of both hands, palms upward or downward to make a table with knives and forks, a looking glass and a cradle, or a church with people inside.

Here's the lady's knives and forks,
Here's the lady's table,
Here's the lady's looking glass
And here's the baby's cradle.

Here's the church, here's the steeple,
Open the gates and see all the people.
Here's the parson going upstairs,
Now he's in the pulpit, saying his prayers.

A clapping game, played with a partner, goes like this–

My mother said that I never should
Play with the gypsies in the wood
If I did, she would say
'Naughty little girl to disobey'.

–and another. I cannot remember whether we clapped or not, but we certainly declaimed it with gusto.

My mother told me that she would buy me
A rubber dolly if I was good,
But when I told her I kissed a soldier
She wouldn't buy me that rubber doll.

This is a rhyme from Stamford, accompanying finger-tapping on the table.

Go to bed, Tom. Go to bed, Tom.
Get up in the morning
And twiddle your drum.

Cat's cradle, a very old game is really *cratch-cradle.* The *cratch* is the box-like shape made by two players looping string between their fingers. The word is still used locally for various rectangular objects–mangers, chicken-runs and frames for pig-killing. Cf Fr *crèche,* a cradle.

Other hand-games are played with flowers, the best-known. 'He loves me, he loves me not' is a form of plant-divination, but 'Grandmother, grandmother, jump out of bed' is just, I hope, for fun.

'You pinch through the stem of a grass called wild barley, about an inch from the tip, and when you push up with your fingers, the head will spring off.'   *Mrs Ivy Smart,* Greens Norton.

A game using a sprig of privet is played by girls today.

'You get a sprig with all the leaves on—"the tree in summer". Press the leaves close to the stem—"the tree in winter". Push the leaves up and off. As they fall they are "April showers" and on the ground, "May flowers".'

Miss Clare Haynes, Northampton.

In March 1978, the *Chronicle and Echo,* Northampton, published letters from readers about their childhood games. Of eleven letters on one page, seven described imaginative games, requiring little or no equipment.

'The games we played years ago were mostly imagination. . . . I remember the long summer holidays we would be in the fields all day playing "houses" . . . we marked out rooms with stones, hung old lace curtains on the hedge, all the bright broken bits of china were put around. Dolls were old woollies tied up, meals were *egg-and-bacon,* clover, sweetbrier, sloes, crabapples. Some days as a treat we took up bottles of lemonade crystals . . . our mothers knew we were safe and happy in the fields.'

Mrs M Whitney, Yardley Hastings.

'We used to play *Fairy Gardens* in the fields, marking out little gardens with stones and putting wild flowers and leaves in them. Then there was *Old Firms.* We played this in the street, along the pavement, with boxes of all sorts of things we borrowed from home. It was like a street market.'

Mrs Joan Hassett, Northampton.

HUNTING GAMES

'In Ecton in the 1920s there were no street lamps and no traffic, and in the dark evenings boys and girls would meet near the Co-op yard, and half of us were the foxes and the others were the hounds. The hounds gave the foxes a few minutes start in the darkness, then they crept silently down the street and in and out of the yards. It was pitch dark. I often felt a shudder. Then we called '*Blow your horn or we won't follow*'. We crept into yards and corners and then, in the stillness of the night, we would hear a low howling and find a fox crouching in the dark. He had to join us hounds and search for the others. We would go into the blacksmith's yard where there were many hiding-places, through the churchyard, down the village to the spinneys and back . . . and into the cowshed. We could hear owls and farm animals and bats flying about the street. The creepy thrill of moving about in the dark and jumping with fright when we found a fox thrills me still. Oh for those days back again'.   *B C Smith,* Northampton *Chronicle and Echo.*

We used to play a version of this game, without the exciting call, through the *jitties* of Far Cotton after dark. The game was called '*Fox and hounds*' at Kislingbury and a horn was used by the 'foxes'.

'We played *hare and hounds,* chasing the "hare" across the fields'.   *Mrs F Goodman,* Braybrooke.

'There used to be two go off as the "fox" and we used to go up over five fields to *Arpull* Cover and shout

"Oller if you're far away,
Whistle if you're nigh"

We're bin up them fields till ten o'clock at night—dark nights, too'.   *Mr William Burt,* Harpole.

A good hunting game could be played in an ordinary open playground.

'It was called "*Stag*". The catcher tried to catch any one of us "stags", who then held his hand and helped catch. Soon the line of boys and girls with linked hands stretched across the playground, trying to catch the free stags. The danger arose as the line grew so long that the ones at the end were thrown across the playground or against a wall, as the line wheeled round.'
Mrs Dorothy Addicott, Hardingstone *(Chronicle and Echo).*

A chasing game known in Northampton and Kettering began with the words

> Stag-stag-a-rony, my black pony,
> Touch my finger, touch my thumb,
> Touch the ground and way I run.

Another was called *Release,* because captured players brought back to base could be released if touched by one of their own side. In some places this was called *Chelease.* Could this be from Fr. *je* [I] or *jeu* [game], perhaps *'je laisse'* [I let, allow].

Tiggy or *Ticky* was the usual name for touching games, Latin *tegit* [he or she touched].

> 'In *Ticky-where-you're-touched,* if the one who was *on* [the chaser] touched you, you had to hold the place where he touched with one hand and *tick* somebody else.'
>
> *Mrs F Orrin*, Kingsthorpe, Northampton *(Chronicle and Echo).*

Even more interesting are the games *Tiggy wood* and *Tiggy iron.* If you touched wood or iron you were safe from capture. Trees and the wood from them were once held sacred [cf. the saying '*Touch wood*' to avoid ill-chance] and iron was believed to be a protection against witchcraft.

Sanctuary could also be claimed by touching a base agreed before the game and shouting '*Stone*'. This sounds like the sanctuary offered by holy places. Ripon Cathedral had sanctuary stones surrounding it, each a mile distant.

A temporary halt or breathing-space in chasing and other games could be obtained by calling '*Kings*' in Northampton and holding up the right hand with fingers crossed. The words *Pax, Patsies, Exes* or *Crosses* were used in different parts of the county.

STICKS AND STONES

These were nearly always to hand and cost nothing. Bats and even balls and tops could be made of tree-wood.

> 'Most boys made their own [tops] out of wood or cotton-reels, with a boot-stud at the bottom and a picture on the top.'
>
> *Mrs Goodall*, Far Cotton *(Chronicle and Echo).*

Tippit, tip-cat, tit-tat, tip-tap, cattie, cat-and-stick and *cat-and-dicky* are all names for the game of hitting a short stick with a long one.

> 'My favourite game was *diabolo.* I think the craze began when I was about twelve years old, about seventy years ago. You held

one stick in each hand—they were joined by a piece of string about arms' length. You put the wood, which was like an old-fashioned cotton-reel, waisted in the middle, on the stick and moved your arms up and down to get it whirling. Then throw it high and catch it on the stick.'

Mrs Dorothy Addicott, Hardingstone *(Chronicle and Echo)*.

Cannon was a popular game, with some of the elements of both cricket and rounders. Sticks or the long, old-fashioned clothes pegs called dolly-pegs were set up against a wall as a wicket, and if a player knocked the wicket down, he ran round a pitch to try and reach home before his opponent set it up again.

The traditional pattern of *hopscotch* was chalked or scratched with a stone on the pavement. The player bounced a ball, or more often, kicked a stone into each numbered shape in turn and hopped after it. (See sketch on page 186.)

For *duckstones,* a large stone or *meg* was set on a larger one, or on top of three stones, to be knocked off by yet another stone. Some form of chasing followed.

Cock-a-roo-stick
A child stood with his foot on a tin while the others hid. When he went to find the others he had to get back before an opponent kicked the tin.

Rin-tin-tin
Named after the 'wonder-dog' of Thirties films, this game involved kicking a tin full of stones away from base without being struck by an opponent's ball.

Are these two games a memory of the barbarous Shrove-tide sport of cock-throwing, carried out at some public schools and elsewhere, in which sticks and stones were thrown at a cock tied by its leg to a stake? The one who killed the bird carried it off as a prize.

Hopping cockerels
Players hopped across a space with folded arms, while others pushed them to make them lose their balance.

Marbles
Games with marbles were very popular for many years and sometimes played by men as well as boys. The marbles were sold

Hopscotch

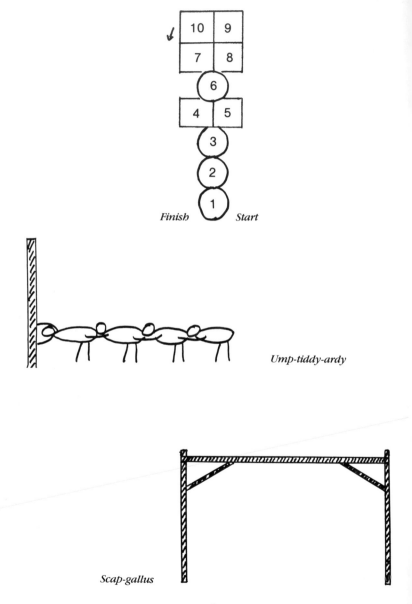

Ump-tiddy-ardy

Scap-gallus

in sixes, later thirties and could be of clay, marble *[marlies]* or glass *[glarnies]*. They could be rolled along the gutter on the way to school, the object being to *peck* your opponent's marble with your own or to get within a *hand's span* of it, the winner taking both, or perhaps a stake of buttons. Marbles were rolled into a hole in the game of *dobs, dobby-hole* or *chockhole*.

> See here where the shepherd boys played,
> Here's a ring for the marble, a hole for the chock,
> And a *cat-gallows* not a yard high.
>
> *John Clare*, MS Poems

A *cat-gallows* is a simple jumping frame made of two vertical posts with another laid across. An elderly man at Everdon a few years ago called it *scap-gallus* [escape the gallows], an allusion to its shape.

'. . . things we found lying about'

'We had to get all the amusement we could from things we found lying about. A cocoa-tin made a hand-warmer. You knocked holes in the top and bottom, popped some old rag inside, put a light to it, put the lid on and ran as fast as you could, holding the tin so that the air was driven through it. The fun was to get it burning slowly so that it warmed your hands and left a stream of smoke behind you. If it got too hot you dropped it in the gutter.'

> *T J Clarke*, Hackleton *(Chronicle and Echo)*.

Two tins with a hole in each and threaded on to a length of string made a 'telephone'. You spoke into one tin and the sound seemed to travel along the string to your friend listening with her ear to the other tin. If three played, the one in the middle could make a variety of interesting sounds by running the tin's lid along the string.

'A pig's bladder blown up with a straw served as a football.'

> *Mr Ted Hollowell*, Cogenhoe.

'We made our best whistles from *keck*-straws (cow parsley) and hip-shooters from a stem of *keck* cut between joints. With a mouthful of ammunition, this couldn't fail. The ammunition was haws when they are small and green. We made various kinds of implements to propel them. One was a short length of ash with one end split. You pushed in the hip, opening the split, and finger and thumb pressure forced it out. Another kind was made of elder and a piece of bone from Mum's old stays.'   *Mrs Ruth Hill,* Boddington.

'You make shooters from *keck*-stems and may-buds and another sort from elder wood and a steel bone from ladies' stays. To make a *David's sling* you need a piece of soft leather from the tongue of a boot. To this are fixed two thongs of a leather bootlace, one four inches longer than the other. This was twisted round the middle finger and the other just held. A pebble is placed in the pouch and whirled round the head. At the right time the loose thong is released, and the outstretched arm must point to the target which the missile will follow.

To play *Pin-a-dip* you place cut-out pictures, which were scarce seventy years ago, into a thick book. A pin is inserted into the tightly-held book. (Boys kept pins in their lapels then.) If a picture is disclosed, it's yours. If not, hand over the pin.

For a *peep-show,* you obtain a shoe-box, stick pictures round the inside, and cut-out figures on the base. Now make a hole in the narrow end and paste tissue paper over it. You charged a fag-card or a marble to look at the show.'

Mr A Jones, Banbury.

'We made *coulter-pins* [catapults] with a *forket* [a forked stick] and *bagging.* That's what we called the leather strips.'

Mr Ray Wykes, Spratton.

'We had a doll once, between the six of us, a wooden doll as our Dad made, and that was the on'y plaything we ever had.'

Mrs Rose Pearce, Northampton, 1875-1960.

CHOOSING SIDES

In school playgrounds, amid unremitting noise and Breugel-like activity, the children performed their rituals, determining who should be *on,* if it were a chasing game, or who should start first. Choosing sides, especially, was an important preamble and often took as long as the game itself. Sometimes counting-out rhymes were used.

> One potato, two potato, three potato, four,
> Five potato, six potato, seven potato, more.

— *Children at Play* —

Eena meena macker acka
Rary dominacka
Chicka oacha acha packa
Rom rom push.   (Kettering)
Ink, pink, pen and ink,
You go out because you stink.

The following counting-out rhymes were used in Northampton schools in 1984.

Ip dip do
The cat's got flu,
Mother's got the chicken-pox
So out goes you.

Ippa dippa dation, my operation,
How many people at the station?

One potato, two potato, three potato, four,
How many people knocking at the door?

Black horse, white horse,
Which horse is your horse?

Three fine horses in a stable
One of their names is Marmaduke Jinks.

I went to California, far, far away,
I met a senorita and this is what she say,
'O shaky, shaky, shaky, shaky all you can,
And if you cannot shaky, then do the best you can'.
Miss Ruth Nichols, Northampton.

Two older rhymes now, the second one from Dorset, where Mrs. Chamberlain's grandfather was born in 1819.

Corum, borum, bingle, lock, three wires in a clock,
Sit and spin and turn the wheel, diffy, daffy, man afield.
Mr Scott, Pury End.

Intery, mintery, cutery, corn, apple-seed and apple-thorn,
Wine, brier, limber, lock, three geese in one flock,
One flew east and one flew west
And one flew over the goose's nest.
Mrs I Chamberlain, Northampton.

Another way of choosing sides was *clipping up* [OE *clypian*, call or name]. The two leaders walked towards each other, heel to toe, the one filling the last space, with his toe covering his opponent's, was the winner.

Nowadays there is another ritual carried out quickly, expertly and in silence. The leaders face each other and at the same instant make a hand-sign as follows:

A clenched fist represents stone,
a flat hand, palm upward, paper,
two fingers pointing forward, scissors.

Scissors can cut paper, stone will blunt scissors, paper can wrap stone, so one of each combination is the winner. Placing the hand in an umbrella shape represents a bomb, and under certain circumstances is the ultimate winner.

Miss Carol Brown and *Miss Ruth Scott*,
Delapre, Northampton.

SKIPPING GAMES

After *clipping-up*, there were shouts of 'No end' and 'First end' referring to the rope-ends, everyone wanting to skip, not twirl the rope. There were several variations of a simple jump over the rope, each having its own rhyme. The simplest, with the rope swung under the feet only, was

Eeper weeper, chimney sweeper,
Had a wife and couldn't keep her,
Had another, didn't love her,
O-U-T spells out.

'*High low water*' was a simple raising and lowering of the rope as the players skipped. In a modern version, a girl swings the rope in a circle and is either a witch or a fairy. Accordingly, anyone whose foot catches the rope is 'out'–or allowed to play on. In '*Snakes and ladders*' the rope is shaken vertically to make it snake along the ground, or held with one end high and one low.

'*Over the moon and under the stars*' involves twirling the rope several times over the head and under the feet.

Information from *Mrs Grace Riches,* Northampton.

Except for the questions, all the following rhymes have a strong stress when the skipper jumps the rope and a weak stress for the balancing jump in between.

Who shall I marry? Tinker, tailor, soldier, sailor,
Rich man, poor man, beggar-man, thief.

What shall I wear? Silk, satin, muslin, rags.

Question not known. Salt, pepper, vinegar, mustard.

How shall we go to church? Hansom cab, wheelbarrow, muckcart.

> Blackcurrant, redcurrant, raspberry tart,
> Tell me the name of your sweetheart.

> Andy Pandy, sugardy candy,
> French almond rock,
> Bread-and-butter for your supper,
> That is all your mother's got.

> The wind blows east, the wind blows west,
> The wind blows over the cuckoo's nest.

> Nebuchadnezzar the king of the Jews
> Bought his wife a pair of shoes.
> When the shoes began to wear,
> Nebuchadnezzar bought a chair.
> When the chair began to break,
> Nebuchadnezzar bought a snake.
> When the snake began to sting,
> Nebuchadnezzar bought a ring.
> When the ring began to rust,
> Nebuchadnezzar fell in the D-U-S-T.

This rhyme and the following one could be chanted at a fairly fast rate to accompany *scutters*. The rope was shortened so that it could be twirled as fast as possible and the skipper jumped with both feet, with no balancing jump.

> Old Daddy Dixon's a nice young man,
> He tries to *learn* you all he can.
> (ME *lernen,* teach)
> A-reading, a-writing, arithmetic,
> And he don't forget to give you the stick.

> When he does he makes you dance
> Out of England into France,
> Out of France into Spain,
> Over the hills and home again.

Bumps were slow jumps, the rope passing slowly, to the rhyme

> What ho she bumps,
> She's got the mumps.

Then there were the rhymes for skipping all together in one rope, either running in and out, to the words *'In the river, on the bank'* or from a standing start, to any of the following rhymes and to encouraging cries of *'Keep the pot a-boiling'*

> All in, a bottle of gin,
> All out, a bottle of stout.

> All in together, girls,
> Never mind the weather, girls,
> When I count twenty,
> The rope must be empty.

And from Little Houghton.

> Charlie, Charlie stole some barley
> Out of the baker's shop,
> The baker came out and gave him a clout,
> And made poor Charlie hop.
> > *Mrs Loretta Smith,* Little Houghton.

Children in the 1950s and 60s skipped to these rhymes.

> Teddy bear, Teddy bear, go upstairs,
> Teddy bear, Teddy bear, say your prayers,
> Teddy bear, Teddy bear, put out the light,
> Teddy bear, Teddy bear, say goodnight.

> I am a Girl Guide dressed in blue,
> These are the actions I must do,
> Salute to the king, bow to the queen,
> And pray for the soldiers on the green.
> > *Mrs Alison Grimes,* Rothwell and
> > *Mrs Joan Bradley,* Northampton.

Below is a modern rhyme.

> I'm a little bumper car, number forty-eight,
> Pop round the corner before its too late.
> Shut the gate.
> > *Miss Ruth Scott* and
> > *Miss Carol Brown,* Northampton.

BALL GAMES

Some were played against a wall, preferably one without windows. Nearly all the corner houses in the older streets had stable-yards at the back, the walls blank except for the hayloft door high up. Here we played *Donkey, Sixes* and *Twelves,* games in which the ball was thrown up to the wall and caught with six or twelve contortions of the body. *Sixes* and *Twelves* could be played between two players without a wall, and, at Little Houghton, *Sevens* had an accompanying rhyme.

> Plainsy, clapsy, round the world to backsy,
> Touch your heel, touch your toe,
> Touch the ground and under you go.
>
> *Mrs Loretta Smith*, Little Houghton.

Playground games included *London* and various other throwing and catching games the names of which are now forgotten. Many people remembered *Queenie,* and it is still being played, in an even more elaborate form.

'One girl stands with her back to the rest and throws a ball over her shoulder. Whoever catches the ball keeps it hidden and all chant

> Queenie, Queenie, who's got the ball?
> Is she fat or is she tall/small?
> Or is she like a tennis ball?

Queenie turns and tries to guess who has the ball. If she calls "Dustbin" to a girl, she thinks that girl has not got the ball. If she is wrong, she is out, and the "dustbinned" girl becomes Queenie.

Players may move the ball around among themselves. If they get too close together Queenie may call "Split the cake". She can also say "Queenie's going to market" and "Queenie's coming back" and then rush through the group to try to see the ball. Saying "Queenie's lost the ball/her budgie" she picks out one player and *ferrets* her by running round her, trying to see the ball.' *Miss Ruth Nichols*, Northampton.

A girl could play this game on her own, bouncing a ball under her leg.

> One two three a-lairy,
> My ball's in the dairy,
> Don't forget to give it to Mary,
> One two three a-lairy.

In some versions the last line was 'and not to Charlie Chaplin'.

PLAYGROUND GAMES

The boys played *Jump* or *Ump-tiddy-ardy* or *Jumpety-whack* or [at Wellingborough] *Bung the bucket*, as in the sketch on page 186. The other side leap-frogged on to the bent backs, the best athlete going first. Each shock-wave was very hard on the boy next to the wall, in fact, I am told that sometimes another boy stood back to the wall as a buffer.

Girls played a gentler game. One child stood sideways to the wall, her arm forming an arch under which the others, holding hands in a line, passed, singing

>The big ship sails through the Alley-alley-oo
>On the first day of September.

When all arms were crossed and linked, they sang

>Dash, dash, dash, my blue sash, (or
>Dip, dip, dip, my little ship).
>Sailing on the water
>Like a cup and saucer
>Dash, dash, dash,
>(Dip, dip, dip).

As they sang, they lifted and dropped their linked arms, and on the last word, let go.

The following is an action game.

>Poor Roger is dead and is low in his grave,
>Low in his grave, low in his grave,
>Poor Roger is dead and is low in his grave,
>Ee ay low in his grave.

>They planted an apple-tree over his head
>Over his head etc.

>The apples got ripe and they all fell off.

>There came an old woman a-picking them up.

>Poor Roger got up and he gave her a knock.

>It made the old woman go hippety-hop.
>*Mrs Grace Nicholls, Miss Grace Carr,* Northampton.

Then there were guessing games–

Here come three broken-down merchants
>What is your trade?

The merchants mimed their occupations and those who guessed correctly became the next merchants. The same game was sometimes called

>I'm the old woman from Botany Bay.
>What have you got to sell us today?

Her wares had to be guessed and were always exotic, as befitted someone from the other side of the world. A later

version had the words 'Have you some work for me today?'
In the Kettering area, *Three old men from the work-'us* may
have been similar. All, clearly recall the past.

A line-game played at Little Houghton was

> All in a row, bendy-bow,
> Shoot the pigeon and kill the crow.
>> *Mrs Loretta Smith*, Little Houghton.

What's the time, Mr. Wolf? was well-known and popular. The
wolf behaves gently at first, answering 'One o'clock, two o'clock'
etc., and then suddenly shouts 'Dinner time', turning and chasing
the children who have been creeping cautiously after him. This is
akin to the behaviour of the wolf in sheep's clothing and in the
story of Red Riding Hood.

Even more alarming is the man-turned-wolf in *Sheep, sheep,
come home*. Thus the shepherd calls the sheep and they
answer 'We're afraid'. 'What of?' asks the shepherd
ungrammatically, and the children say 'The wolf'.

> The wolf's gone to Devonshire
> And won't be back for seven year.
> Sheep, sheep, come home.

Again the children slowly follow, until suddenly the
shepherd turns into the wolf and chases them.
Mrs M Gibson, Denton; and *Miss Grace Carr*, Northampton.

RING GAMES

> I sent a letter to my love,
> And on the way I dropped it.
> One of you has picked it up
> And put it in your pocket.
> Tisn't you, tisn't you. . . .

She touches the backs of those in the ring and gives a good push to
the one she decides has stolen the letter, and both players run
round the outside of the circle to gain the empty space. This is the
form of most chasing games played in a ring, such as '*This is my
friend's seat*', played indoors, '*Stroke a bunny*' and '*Fire on the
mountain, run, run, run*'.

Choosing a partner
Attractive to watch and pleasant to listen to, these games brought
to a child's world a hint of future joys and perhaps of past customs

as well. Not surprisingly, some involve chasing. The first is very
well-known.

Poor Mary sits a-weeping, a-weeping, a-weeping,
Poor Mary sits a weeping on a bright summer's day.

O pray, what are you weeping for, are you weeping for,
    are you weeping for,
O pray what are you weeping for, on a bright summer's day?

I'm weeping for a sweetheart, a sweetheart, a sweetheart,
I'm weeping for a sweetheart, on a bright summer's day.

O pray, get up and choose one, and choose one, and choose one,
O pray, get up and choose one on a bright summer's day.

> The farmer's in his den, the farmer's in his den,
> Ee-I, Ee-I/Ee-I-endy-O, the farmer's in his den.
>
> The farmer wants a wife, the farmer wants a wife, Ee-I . . .
>
> The wife wants a child, the wife wants a child, Ee-I . . .
>
> The child wants a nurse, the child wants a nurse, Ee-I . . .
>
> The nurse wants a dog, the nurse wants a dog, Ee-I . . .
>
> We all pat the dog, we all pat the dog, Ee-I.

> > Oats and beans and barley grow,
> > Oats and beans and barley grow,
> > Do you or I or anyone know
> > How oats and beans and barley grow?
> >
> > First the farmer sows his seed,
> > Then he stands and takes his ease,
> > Stamps his foot and claps his hand,
> > And turns around to view the land.

The last two songs were still being sung, in 1989.

> In and out the windows, in and out the windows,
> In and out the windows, as we have done before.
>
> Stand and face your partner/lover,
>   stand and face your partner/lover,
> Stand and face your partner/lover as we have done before.
>
> Follow her to London, follow her to London,
> Follow her to London as we have done before.
>
> O why can't you catch her, O why can't you catch her?
> O why can't you catch her as we have done before?

Here come the bluebirds through the window,
Here come the bluebirds through the door.
Here come the bluebirds through the window,
I-tiddly-I-dum-day.

Take a little bird and dance together,
Take a little bird and dance all day.
Take a little bird and dance together,
I-tiddly-I-dum-day.

> Rosy apple, lemon and pear,
> A bunch of roses she shall wear,
> Gold and silver by her side,
> Here comes . . . to be her bride. (sic)

A Hardingstone lady told me this lovely little rhyme, but we were in a crowded room and I did not learn her name.

The next game, which we played in the 1920s and 30s, is recorded in *NNQ* (1886) p 270 and is taken from *MS Notes of Midland Folklore* by John T Page. It was known, with variations, in many parts of the British Isles.

> O this pretty little girl of mine,
> She cost me many a bottle of wine,
> A bottle of wine and a guinea or two,
> To see what my little girl can do.
>
> Down on the carpet she shall kneel,
> While the grass grows in the field,
> Stand upright upon her feet,
> And choose the one she loves so sweet.

At the end of a choosing game called '*Sally Waters*' John T Page records this verse.

> Now you're married I wish you joy,
> First a girl and then a boy.
> Love one another like sister and brother
> And never lose time by kissing one another.

We used to sing a similar version, after almost any choosing game.

> Now you're married I wish you joy,
> First a girl and then a boy,
> Seven years old, a son and daughter,
> Now's the time to kiss one another.

and also
> Now you're married you must obey,
> You must be true to all you say,
> You must be wise, you must be good,
> And help your wife to chop the wood.

The next rhyme strikes a different note.

> The wind, the wind, the wind blows high,
> The rain comes pattering down from the sky,
> She is handsome, she is pretty,
> She is a girl from the London city,
> She goes courting, one, two, three,
> Tell me what his name might be.
>
> — — says he loves her,
> All the boys are waiting for her,
> Let the boys do what they will,
> — — loves her still.

The words of the next game are disturbing.

> Wallflowers, wallflowers, growing up so high,
> We're all the ladies, we shall have to die,
> Except — —, she's the only one,
> She can hop, she can skip,
> She can turn the candlestick.
>
> So turn your back, you saucy cat,
> And say no more to me,
> For if you do, I'll chop you in two,
> And hang you on the tree.

This seems to have been a song sung by lacemakers at *Catterns,* their annual holiday on St. Catherine's Day, 25th November. T Wright in *The Romance of the Lace Pillow,* p 196, records a similar version, of which the last line was

> Turn, turn, turn your face to the wall again.

This line appears in a verse from Milton Malsor.

> Try, try, try again,
> Turn your face to the wall again,
> If at first you don't succeed,
> I'll hang you on a tree.
>
> *Mrs Dew,* Milton Malsor.

This verse, in fact, is an intriguing amalgam of a well-known precept for success and lines from the lacemakers' songs, that last line very chilling indeed.

MEMORIES

The next account brings us forward in time to the Thirties, and a childhood spent in Semilong, Northampton.

'My grandparents lived a little way away, in Knightley Road. I can see my grandmother now, in her boots, long dress and black beads and her husband's old cap, sitting in the rocking-chair, making a peg-rug from old coats, trousers and dresses, cut into lengths and pegged on to a piece of sacking. She made a new one every year, because these rugs got so full of dust and dirt that it was impossible to clean them. To me, as a child, their house smelled of bread pudding—not so cosy though, as my other grandparents' house at Newport Pagnell.

This grandfather had been groom to the Duke of Bedford, and had married grandma when she was a parlour maid at Woburn Abbey. The duke had set them up in a sweet-shop at Newport Pagnell.

I loved my grandfather, and when I sat on his knee, I could see that his walrus moustache was stained half-way up with tea. He used to take a beaker of tea to bed and drink it at intervals through the night. They were upset when I went to live in Semilong, but it was better for me in one way. The kids in Newport were very rough—I could never go out to play—but in Naseby Street it wasn't long before I joined in. They used to call me Cockney.

I remember boys and girls taking the *May-basket* round from door to door, and we went to Midsummer Meadow to see the Maypole dancing. In the summer we used to have the *Old Firm*. We brought out old toys and other things that were finished with and set them out along the kerb like a street-market. The idea was to sell them if you could, but no one had much money, so it was mostly swapping.

Then in the autumn we played *Sparking Hoops*. We had these old iron hoops and hit them with a stick, backwards and forwards along the ground till they sparked, and then let them go. The winner was the one whose hoop ran farthest with sparks flying before it started to roll back.

There were rows of straight streets with *jitties* in between, and it was a custom to put our hands into the stand-pipes in the *jitties*. Sometimes there was something inside—buttons, cotton-reels, perhaps a farthing. Often they were just full of earth, but we always put our hands in, just in case.

There were street-gangs, always at war with each other. We played in Paddy's Meadow but we kept well away from Bell Barn and Scarletwell Street. To go down there—that was real blood.'   *Mr Geoff Roff,* Easton Neston.

THE LANGUAGE OF PLAYGROUND AND STREET

'Ad yer eye full, Polly-long-frock?'

Fatty, Skinny-Lizzie, Sparrer-legs, Four-eyes, Lamp-post, Bloodnut, Lighthouse—these are just some of the names we uninhibitedly called each other. The two last refer to redheads.

Behaviour which deviated from the acceptable was briskly dealt with by cries of 'Swankpot, Copycat, Scarebaby, Cowardy-custard, Kick-a-donkey, Mardy or Mardy-arse'. If you were not quite fresh you were a stinkpot; a short jacket was a bum-freezer. The best defence was to shout back—'Ad yer eye full?' or

> Stare, stare, y' rotten pear,
> Tell y' mother t' cut y'r 'air.

If you were smaller than your tormentor, or naturally timid, or outnumbered, it was best to call up reinforcements. Big brothers and sisters were a godsend, even if they would not come. You could always boast about their warlike nature and issue an ominous 'You wait'.

> Mind y'r own business,
> Eat y'r own fat,
> And don't stick y'r dirty nose
> in my best 'at

dealt with interference and there was nothing much that could be said in answer to

> Sticks and stones'll break my bones
> But names'll never hurt me.

There were tricks to catch the unwary. On the first day of the month, having said 'rabbits' on first waking up, you had to watch out for someone rushing up and saying

> Pinch, punch, the first day of the month

and suiting the action to the words. You had to take evasive action and come back at them with

> Punch, kick, for being so quick

unless they had remembered to say 'No returns'.

Turn a deaf ear to the verse

> Adam and Eve and Pinch-me
> Went down to the river to bathe,
> Adam and Eve got *drowned*,
> Who do you think God saved?

There were other Biblical references.

> And the Lord said unto Moses,
> 'All Jews shall have long noses,
> Excepting Aaron, he shall have a square 'un,
> Excepting Rebecca, she shall have a pecker.'

Ignore at all costs the tempting question 'Would you like to come to my party?' If you said 'Yes', the response was

> Custard and jelly and a punch in the belly,
> That's what you'll get at my party.

Custard and jelly, rather than fruit and cream, was the regular birthday treat.

To be sure you weren't being tricked about something, you could demand the assurance

> Me finger's wet, me finger's dry,
> Cut me throat if I tell a lie.

and, if all else failed, there remained the dire threat 'You wait–I'll *scrag* you'.

When a horse and cart came along, boys would rush to hang on the back for a ride, till the driver was alerted by the shout from other children *'Whip be-ind, mister'*. If the horse was white, the ancient belief that it would bring good luck was perpetuated by the simple rhyme

> Good luck to you, good luck to me,
> Good luck to everyone I see.

In *The Pattern under the Plough,* ch. 19, George Ewart Evans records this belief, and Iona and Peter Opie, in *The Lore and Language of Schoolchildren,* pp 206-208, give nineteen sources for it. The horse generally was venerated for its strength and swiftness. It was a fertility symbol and was sometimes worshipped.

We also had a repertoire of traditional rhymes which we recited, chanted or sang. Some were known in the last century and some may have been rhymes for games. Many include Christian names.

> O Jemima, look at your uncle Jim,
> He's in the duckpond, learning how to swim.
> First he does the backstroke,
> The he does the side,
> Now he's under the water, swimming against the tide.

> Sally go round the stars, Sally go round the moon,
> Sally go round the chimney-pots on a Sunday afternoon.

Grandmother, grandmother Grey,
May I go out to play?
Don't go near the water
To shoo the ducks away.

Knives and forks, plates and dishes,
Here comes Sally with her calico britches.

Good boy Bartle, who made your britches?
Daddy cut them out and Mammy put the stitches.
Mrs Florence Fookes, Northampton.

Go to church, get the birch,
Go to chapel, get a rosy apple.
Mrs Grace Nichols, Northampton.

Our Doll's a fine fat gal,
Our Doll's a bold 'un.
Our Doll's got a brand-new frock
Made out of the old gal's old 'un.   *Author.*

or

Ol' Jack Smith's a goodly lad,
Ol' Jack Smith's a bold 'un,
Ol' Jack Smith's had some trousers made
Out of his father's old 'uns.
Mr Ray Wykes, Spratton.

Paddy on the railway, picking up stones,
Along came an engine and broke Paddy's bones.
'Hey' said Paddy, 'that's not fair.'
'Well' said the driver, 'You shouldn't be there.'

Listen, listen, the cat's a-pissin',
Where, where? Under the chair.
Hasten, hasten, fetch a basin,
No, no, fetch a po,
Too late, too late, the cat can't wait,
And now the floor's in an awful state.
Mr Ray Wykes, Spratton.

Old Mother Martin's dead—how did she die?
One finger up, one finger down,
Tangled in her frilly nightgown,
One bloody nose, one shut eye,
One broken chin, one mouth awry.
Oo how awful.
Mrs Grace Nichols, Northampton.

It was the custom between the wars to give a half-holiday on Friday afternoon to any class which had made perfect attendance during the month. Woe betide anyone who had had to stay away, and so spoilt his classmates' chances. The lucky ones streamed triumphantly out of school at dinner-time (no school dinners then) and when safely out of earshot would yell

> Half-a-day today, the cat's gone away,
> The monkey's up the chimney pot and can't get away.

At Cottingham the children *barred-out* the headmaster, and said or sang

> Oh pardon, pardon, Master, we do not care a pin,
> If you won't give us a holiday we will not let you in.

Elections were very exciting, with rival gangs of children roaming the streets singing and shouting. This telling verse, from turn-of-the-century Market Harborough, was sung to the tune *Nuts-in-May*.

> Tariff reform means work for all,
> Work for all, work for all,
> Tariff reform means work for all,
> Chopping up sticks in the workhouse.

One Northampton electioneering song varied from district to district.

> Vote, vote, vote for old Maloney,
> He comes knocking at the door,
> For Maloney is the man and we'll have him if we can,
> And he won't come voting any more.

Lieutenant-Colonel Cecil L'Estrange Maloney was Labour MP for Northampton 1928-31.

> Vote, vote, vote for good old Pamely,
> Throw old Ashford in the Cut,
> If it wasn't for his liver we would throw him in the river,
> And he won't come voting any more.

Mr Pamely and Mr F Ashford were respectively the Labour and Liberal candidates for Far Cotton Ward. No words were wasted at Kettering, where they sang

> Our man for ever-O
> Yourn in the river-O.

MORE SWEET MEMORIES

Most of us had a halfpenny to spend on Saturday morning, and we gathered round the sweetshop window in earnest consultation. We had to choose with care. There would be no more money till next week, unless we could wheedle one more halfpenny on Wednesday, when the Misses Tilley sold *scrapings* [from the sweet jars] or *siftings* at their little shop for a farthing a bag.

Our Saturday halfpenny would buy one ounce of cheap *peps* [sweets]. *Jockey clubs,* named after a perfume, were scented and came in pretty colours. You got more *tiger nuts* or *locusts* [locust beans] but they were not very sweet. Mostly we settled for *dabs and suckers,* brown lollipops to dip in a triangular bag of *kali* [white or coloured sherbet, with which you could also make fizzy drinks] or *Spanish* [licorice] and kali. On non-sweet days, it was back to an apple, if we were lucky. Those who were unlucky would gather round and ask for the core. Often the answer was 'There aint gunner be no core'.

Games for Grown-ups

'The ring of steel on steel could be heard all over our village.'

Spinning the trencher was a firm favourite at chapel socials and the like. Players sat in a ring, each having a number, and one spun the trencher, usually a wooden collection plate, in the centre. When it had almost stopped spinning and was wobbling to a halt, he called out one of the players, who rushed out to pick it up before it fell. Simple as it sounds, it generated considerable tension and called for both skill and speed.

'At the Pig Club suppers in Kislingbury they used to play *Quakers' Meeting.* It started like Follow-my-leader round the room, each person placing finger on chin and not allowed to speak or smile. Then they were told to go down on one knee, still with fingers on chins. When all were in position, the leader gave the first one a hearty push and all fell down like a house of cards.'   *Mr Roy Payler,* Kislingbury.

Outdoors, marbles was for many years a pastime among men as well as children.

'*Pitch and Toss* was played at the Crown and Anchor at Cogenhoe. Small stakes were set in the ground, and players stood eight yards away and tossed a penny at the stakes.

For *Overs and Unders* men stood at the roadside placing bets on the number-plates of motor-bikes and cars, when they were few and far between. 1, 2, 3 and 4 were Unders, 6, 7, 8 and 9 Overs. The last figure of the number-plate was the one that mattered. The stakes were cigarette cards, fag-ends, sweets or marbles, sometimes pennies. If the number was 0 or 5, all lost. Sometimes we had to wait half-an-hour for something to come along the road. We used to post boys on the gates so they could see them coming and shout to us.'

Mr Ted Hollowell, Cogenhoe.

Played in inn-yards and on grass verges, *quaits* [quoits] was popular for many years.

'The ring of steel on steel could be heard all over our village.'
Mr A W Clements, Harpole.

SONG, DANCE AND SEASONAL CUSTOMS

Folksong and Dance

'Better to get married than die an old maid'

In some of the remoter Northamptonshire villages older people can still sometimes be heard singing old songs, in working men's clubs and in a few mercifully simple village pubs, with tables of plain wood, chairs that look like old dining-room chairs and beer drawn from the barrel.

The songs may be local ditties, old music-hall numbers, Victorian or Edwardian ballads or anything else they like. Favourites are or were *The Miner's Dream of Home, The Old Rustic Bridge by the Mill, If Those Lips Could Only Speak.* This was locally believed to refer to an early nineteenth century Countess Spencer who died young, leaving her husband with '*only a beautiful picture in a beautiful golden frame*'. The most-loved over the years has probably been *The Farmer's Boy.*

Caption left: 'A man called Botterill had the two colours.' He represents the darkness of winter and the light of spring, as did the two-headed Roman god Janus. He and the other Plough Monday singers performed for the last time in Harpole in 1913. Many such ancient customs died out in the Great War. This is an historic photograph. Mr William Burt, Harpole.

Now and again there may be heard a fragment, half-remembered, of a much older song. Perhaps there will be no singing at all. If you enquire, all you may be told is 'Ah, we do sometimes' or 'You'd have to be here when the boys from . . . come over'. Information from *Audrey Smith*, formerly of Grendon.

Here and there, though, there may be someone ready to talk and sing.

'When us went t' the pub at night, all reckoned t' pay a bob as didn't sing (everyone who didn't sing had to pay a shilling) and that found us beer f' the night. You'd get some o' the old blokes, singing the old songs, and some o' the young uns an' all, as picked em up orf the fathers an' that sort o' thing. We used to 'ave some really good nights, Fridy an' Satdy.'

> The other night we'ad a lecture on the green,
> Wi' one o' the finest fellers you ever seen,
>> 'E says 'All you fellers 'ere,
>> You're much too fond o' beer'
> An' 'e spouted like a penny magazine.
>
> Then we wen' orf t' the *Magpie on the Stump*
> Because e' fairly gave us all the bloomin' 'ump,
>> 'E says 'What d'y' think o' me?'
>> An' I said 'Not much, you b . . .'
> An we give 'im such a duckin' at the pump.
>
> Now our Squire, 'e's one as likes a bit o' fun,
> An' when 'is son and heir was twenty-one,
>> 'E gives us all a treat,
>> There were nuts and cakes to eat.
> An' the kids they 'ad an orange and a bun.
>
> *Mr Frank Lay,* Greens Norton with my thanks to
> *Mr R Bicknell* for recording this rhyme and
> *Mrs Ivy Smart* for lending me her tape.

These rough verses from *The Village Pump* give a down-to-earth picture of village life, with the lecture on the green, often political or religious in content, and of value to people in isolated villages, the paternalistic Squire whose simple treat would have been greatly relished, and the splendidly-named pub, which has an important place in our oral heritage. Since ancient times, communal singing, eating and drinking have helped to keep people together, in the home, at work, in church, on village green, in city hall and of course, in the pub.

Mr Lay was quite right about 'the old blokes, singing the old songs and some o' the young uns an' all, as picked em up orf the fathers and that sort o' thing'. This was the way that knowledge was handed down in the days when few people could read or write.

'Granny Coombs sang a song to me when I was a child, and she used to say, "I learnt that song from my Granny and now you're learning it from your Granny" (Hornton). The song was

> "Theer was an old 'ooman as I've heerd tell,
> She went to market, her eggs for to sell,
> She went to market all on a summer's day,
> She fell asleep on the King's highway.
>
> Along came a pedlar, his name was Stout,
> He cut her petticoats around and about,
> He cut her petticoats up to her knees,
> Which made the old 'ooman to shiver and sneeze. . . ."

That's all I can remember.' *Mrs. Sonia Glenister,* Australia.

The next verses, with their repetitions and fol lol diddle diddle dols go on to tell how the old 'ooman thought she must be someone else when she woke up in short skirts, and found that even her little dog did not recognise her. This song is in several collections, and we learned it at Far Cotton School but the two grannies learnt it by word of mouth.

In the quietness of her home in Little Houghton, Mrs Doris Robinson sang a number of songs she had learnt as a child, Mayday songs mostly, written rather than traditional, and one verse of *The Horseboys' Song*.

> Early in the morning at the break of the day,
> We pick up our *haunches* and we go on our way,
> We plough a straight furrow from then until now,
> We're four jolly ploughboys and we follow the plough.

A *haunch* was a thick piece of bread with a bit of fat bacon, or a small piece of cheese and an onion–the ploughman's lunch. A similar verse was sung at Cogenhoe on Plough Monday.

Then, without preamble, except to say that she had learnt it from her grandmother, Mrs Robinson sang this delightful song called *False Young Men*.

My — Grand - ma lived in yon - der vil - lage green. A

nic - er old la - dy — never was seen. She — al - ways caut - ioned

me — with — care of all false young men

to be - ware. Tim - my ay tim - my um tum

tim - my um - per tah of all false young men do be - ware.

Music for 'False Young Men'. With acknowledgments to Audrey Smith, folk-singer, formerly of Grendon.

My grandma lived on yonder village green,
A nicer old lady never was seen,
She always cautioned me with care
Of all false young men to beware.   (stress on 'young')

Timmy ay timmy umtum timmy umpa ta
Of all false young men do beware.   (after each verse)

The first came courting was little Jimmy Green,
A nicer young man never was seen.
But the words of my grandma ran into my head,
And I couldn't hear one word he said.

Said I to myself 'There must be some mistake.
What a fuss the old folk make.
If the boys and the girls had all been so afraid,
Grandmamma herself would have died an old maid'.

The next came courting was handsome Ellis Grove,
We met one day with a joyous love,
With a joyous love one needn't be afraid,
Better to get married than die an old maid.

False Young Men has been recorded only twice before, in Lancashire and in the Thames Valley. (F Hamer, *Green Groves*, English Folkdance and Song Society, 1970.) Most other references to it are in America.

Mrs Robinson's aunt Maud married an American Mormon missionary early this century. He had first fallen in love with her when she was a beautiful twelve-year-old girl, had 'spoken to her parents' and, returning to America, had waited several years until he could ask her to marry him. She emigrated to America with other members of her family, including her shoemaker father. The family prospered and grew, settling in various parts of the United States. I cannot help wondering if this is how the song came to be known there.

Dancing as well as singing was remembered by Mrs Robinson.

'The Booth was a big barn with an earth floor where we used to dance to the music of a fiddle.'

More often the memories are dim.

'We used to dance the *Swedish Drill* and the *Shutlanger Clap Dance*. I'm not sure what this was, but my mother used to know all about it. We danced it on *Oak-apple Day.*' (29th May.) *Miss Jessie Curtis*, Northampton.

'Once at Badby in the late 1950s or 60s we went into a pub for a drink after the men had finished [Morris] dancing, and we got talking to an old man who remembered the figures of a country dance in which he took part in his younger days. We think it was probably *Haste to the Wedding*'.
Mrs Margaret Hamer, Bedford, widow of Fred Hamer.

One old gentleman had memories of a lifetime of dancing.

'And this old gal told us how to do it'

'We used to do country dancing at school in Thrapston before the first World War, then in 1918 we come to live in Titchmarsh–there were ten of us–and the place was trying to get back to something like it had been before the war. They used to dance then, especially at Titchmarsh Feast, when they had several nights of dancing.

So we got the dancing going again and we had a good team and really enjoyed ourselves. We used to go all over the county. In 1925 we danced on Lady Lilford's lawn–she was a friend of

Cecil Sharp. Then Sylvia Thursfield from Cransfield EFDSS (English Folkdance and Song Society), she got to hear about an old lady of eighty in one of the almshouses who knew the steps of *Trip to the Cottage*. So this Mrs Dudley taught us the steps.

Miss Stella Skinner come to teach in Titchmarsh in 1930 and she was interested in dancing. We used to go round the WIs and we went to Islip and someone said "Why can't we do *Johnny Fetch Your Wife Back*?" And this old gal told us how to do it.

We went to dance at Delapre Abbey and it was what they called a Criticism Dance, but we could never take it seriously. George Jeffs was the fiddler and when it come to my turn I led on—cream flannels, white shirt, green and yellow colours— well, I slipped down on to my knees and then it started to rain. We laughed all the time we was dancing. When it come to the Criticism, the judge said "That was the team I liked. They didn't look down at the floor to see where the pattern were. They just enjoyed the'selves. Titchmarsh are the winners."

It was the same at Kettering Grammar School. We had a team of people from sixteen to sixty years old, and these 'ere young gals, they was laughing. We raised the roof. The judge there said we were the only team to bring the place to life.

Now the *Nottingham Swing*, they danced that at Benefield and so did we in Titchmarsh. We went to the Great Hall at Oundle and this lady from Benefield said "Oh, you don't dance it like that", and I said "We do. This is the Titchmarsh version". And Fred Hamer, as was blind, he come there to call *The Ploughboy*.

Now *Moll in the Wad* was danced on a village green at the side of a forest, and the story goes that, when it was over, the fiddler walked off into the forest and was never seen again. So when we used to do it, the fiddler would walk off first and disappear, into the kitchen or somewhere.

We kep on dancing till 1933, then they all moved away or got married, except Jack Colman and me. But Miss Skinner and me, we paired up and danced all through the war. The parson used to play the piano. We represented Northamptonshire five times and I've been to the Albert Hall fourteen times.

We danced *Hunsdon House, The Merry Milkmaid, Old Mole, Christchurch Bells, Tom Pate, Rufty Tufty, Gathering Peascods, If all the World were Paper, Bonny Breast-knot, Hole in the Wall, Wringing the Dishcloth, Marching through Georgia,*

Hunt the Hare, Parson's Farewell, Circassian Circle, Goddesses, Flowers of Edinburgh, Jenny Pluck Pears, The Rose Tree, Nancy's Fancy, Newcastle and *Mary and Dorothy.*

The last dance I called was at Benefield on the 26th March 1977 and I could only see a third of the way down the room. I'm blind now and live alone. I'm eighty-four, but they're not ready for me yet up there–haven't sent for me yet anyway. There was a man once who died and went to Heaven and when they asked him where he come from he said "Titchmarsh" and they said "Well, come in. You're the first we've seen from there".

Dancers from all over the county will have no difficulty in recognising the lively speaker as the late *Mr Don Spendlove*, who added:

'Sometimes somebody'll say "How d'you spend love, then?" and I say "Come here and I'll show you".'

In John Clare's *Collection of Songs, Airs and Dances for the Violin* (1818), the following titles are the same or similar to those Mr Spendlove knew. *Lady's Breast Nott, Flowers of Edinburgh, Christchurch Bells.*

The following dances are named by Mr Barry Lewis, formerly the Midlands Development Officer, EFDSS, as 'collected in Northamptonshire'.

From Titchmarsh	*Trip to the Cottage*
	The Rose Tree
	Nottingham Swing
	Hunt the Hare.
From Islip	*Johnny Fetch Your Wife Back*
From Warkton	*Tom Pate*
	Moll in the Wad, transcribed from *NNQ* 1905.

Singing and dancing were an important part of many of the rituals which in ancient times marked the stages of the agricultural year, slowly changing over the centuries to become yearly holidays or customs which brought welcome relief from the hard labour of field or farmyard.

Seasonal Customs

In 1952 children from the village school in Kislingbury recorded, in their scrapbook of village life, this custom for the first day of the year.

> '... the children would get down the Bible and dip their fingers, or sometimes a silver key, into it. Whatever verse their fingers touched would be their motto for the year.'
>
> Information from *Mr Roy Payler*, Kislingbury.

Plough Monday, the first Monday after Epiphany [6th January] was the beginning of the ploughing season. Here is a ploughboy's song from Wollaston.

> Think of a poor ploughboy, only once a year,
> Give us tuppence ha'penny to buy a pint of beer.
> If not that, tuppence will do.
> If not that, three ha'pence will do.
> If not that, a penny will do.
> If not that, a ha'penny will do.
> If not that, well, God bless you.
>
> *Miss I Walker*, Wollaston.

'Boys in Irthlingborough in the 1890s used to make a lantern from a swede with a lighted candle inside and slits for eyes, nose and mouth. They blacked their faces and chanted this song as they went from door to door.

> Tinker, tinker, ploughboy, only once a year.
> Please give us a ha'penny, there's a good old dear.
> If you haven't got a ha'penny, a farthing will do.
> If you haven't got a farthing, God bless you.

The last time we went, another boy and I were told "Go round to the back door and I'll give you a penny". We did this and he set his dog on us.'   *Mr Jack Davis,* Northampton.

'They went in the pub and sang "The Farmer's Boy", and years ago they used to pull the plough round the village.'
          Mr Jack Meyer, Little Houghton.

In Far Cotton at about the same time they dressed as old plough-men, in smocks and wide-brimmed hats.

'We used to black our faces, put on old clothes and go round
and sing this song.

> The ploughboys come round and what do they say?
> We're all jolly fellows that follow the plough.
> With a *haunch* in our pocket away we do run,
> We're all jolly fellows that follow the plough.'
>
> > *Mr Ted Hollowell*, Cogenhoe.

'The boys used to come round in their parents' old clothes,
with blackened faces. You had to guess who they were'

> *Mrs Sanders*, Piddington, 1930s.

'The men had black faces and some were dressed as women.
They could come in and eat any food that was about.'

> *Mrs Loretta Smith*, Little Houghton.

There were similar customs at Milton Malsor, Naseby, Kislingbury
and Braybrooke, where it was called *Plough Moggin Night.*

'They had their faces *reddled* and partly covered with lace.
They sang a song which began *Pity the poor ploughboy* and if
people would not give them money they daubed red sheep-
dye down their doors.'   *Mr John E Bailey*, Brigstock.

The Plough Monday celebrations, with their elements of disguise,
painted faces and a certain amount of licence are akin to the
mummers' plays and have a very long history. They are probably
connected with the midwinter rites performed by ancient people
to ward off darkness with the lighting of fires [the swede lantern]
and to celebrate the lengthening days. The contrast of light and
darkness, black and white is vividly brought out in this account
from *Mr William Burt* of Harpole.

'If it could all be put down, it'd give me a lot of pleasure. I've
lived here all my life and I wouldn't like to see it lost. After the
first war it never started again. That's a custom gone.

They were five quite ordinary men, simple men—they're
wasn't a ploughboy among them. They walked the villages on
Plough Monday—a real hard day, starting in the morning about
eight o'clock and getting home about ten o'clock at night. They
used to dress up. Three of them blackleaded their faces, and
there was one, his face one side was white with whitening and
the other side was blacklead. His high hat was black one side

and white the other. He had one trouser leg black and the other white. He had one white shoe and one black. They always went to Althorp House and when the butler answered the door he said "I don't like the look of you—you're a two-faced man".

And then another man was in hunting pink and another was dressed as a clown. My father and two uncles had their faces blacked, and a man named Botterill had the two colours. I was fourteen when they performed the last time (in 1913).

It was always on Plough Monday. This was the time when there were no tractors—it was all done by horses. Well from autumn onwards the horses had a slack period. They done bits o' carting, but not their regular work of ploughing. The soil had lain dormant after they planted the wheat in the autumn. Well, from this time on [Plough Monday] the waggoner brought these horses back and got 'em in trim for the heavy work of hauling the plough. It took three good horses, when it was put in the ground about eight inches, to turn the furrow.

With the coming of the self-lift plough it lost its meaning— you just hit it on the back and you're away.

They sang four songs. Yes, I'll sing them for you—it'll be a pleasure. I've got a powerful voice at seventy-four.'

Mr Burt's voice was powerful and tuneful and he sang the four songs with pleasure. There was *Hail Smiling Morn,* very popular in its time and always sung at Christmas in our family; one which included the line '*Victoria's a noble name—we'll have it yet again*'; another which also sounds Victorian, and the following much older song, *Dame Durdon.*

> 'Twas on the morn of Valentine,
> The birds began to prate.
> Dame Durdon's serving maids and men,
> They all began to mate.
>
> And Tom kissed Molly, Joe kissed Dolly
> And Dorothy Draggle-tail,
> And Kitty was the charming maid
> To carry the milking pail.

'. . . and they said to this two-faced man as they called him, "We don't want no *bibberin'* in this" and they sang them four songs time after time. There was a Methodist they went and sang to, and he was always very kind to them—a man named Ebenezer Bramley at Harlestone. He said to them once—he gave them some light refreshments—"I dare say if I asked you men you

could sing *The Hallelujah Chorus* or *The Heavens are Telling*"
and they all told a deliberate lie and said yes, they could, and
they didn't know a thing about it. As a matter of fact, they were
glad to go round to get those little bits of money, you know.'
                    Mr William Burt, Harpole. Transcript of a tape-recording
                    made by *Mr and Mrs D Ballard* in 1974.
           I am grateful that they allowed me to take a copy.

The expectation or request for payment–the quête–is a much
later addition to the performance of a rite, or yearly ritual, which
had changed in character through the centuries.

The making of pancakes on Shrove Tuesday, the beginning of
Lent, was heralded by the ringing of the *pancake bell*, as at
Harpole, or the general ringing of church bells, as at Kislingbury.

Anne Elizabeth Baker in her *Glossary of Northamptonshire
Words and Phrases, (GNWP)* 1854, vol 2, p 374, records three
'salutations, which vary in different districts'. Unlike '*Dame
Durdon*', they are not explicitly about love-making.

> Good morrow, Valentine.
> First its yours and then its mine,
> So please give me a Valentine.

> Morrow, morrow, Valentine.
> First 'tis yours and then 'tis mine,
> So please give me a Valentine.
> Holly and ivy tickle my toe,
> Give me red apple and let me go.

> Good morrow, Valentine.
> Parsley grows by savoury,   [the plant savory]
> Savoury grows by thyme,
> A new pair of gloves on Easter Day,
> Good morrow, Valentine.

'The custom of making presents of gloves at Easter . . . is noticed in
Bishop Hall's *Satires*, 1598. . . . They who could repeat "Good
morrow, Valentine" before they were spoken to, were entitled to
a small gift' *GNWP*.

> 'In times past the young people, especially the girls, would
> throw Valentines in people's doors and run away. It was also a
> day for playing pranks.'   ***Kislingbury Scrapbook*** 1952.

> On Mothering Sunday above all other,
> Every child should dine with its mother.

(This pleasant little couplet is found in *GNWP*, vol 1 p 33.)

Many do, bringing flowers and gifts in the traditional way.

Palm Sunday, commemorating Christ's entry into Jerusalem, when branches of palm were strewn in His way, was called *Fig Sunday* in my childhood and we had a dish of figs for Sunday tea. Pussy-willow is locally called palm, and still picked on this day.

Beating the bounds or *possessioning* often took place on Holy Thursday, the day before Good Friday. People walked round the parish boundary, so that everyone knew where this was, to ensure that no land could be taken without the people's knowledge. To preserve this knowledge as long as possible, young children had it knocked into them.

'The youngest child was pushed in the hedge.'

Mrs Fountaine, Pattishall.

On Good Friday, many shops and places of business closed for the day or employees were given time off to attend places of worship. In the streets children sang

> Hot cross buns, hot cross buns,
> One-a-penny, two-a-penny, hot cross buns,
> If you have no daughters give them to your sons,
> One-a-penny, two-a-penny, hot cross buns.

The tricks played on April Fool's Day are probably a survival of ancient celebrations of the spring equinox.

On Rogation Day (the date is variable)
'A procession makes its way from the church, led by the priest, and goes by spring and stackyard and in the fields, to ask God's blessing on the wells and springs, the fields and growing crops. Then they all go back to the church.'

Mrs Taylor, Weston-by-Welland, Market Harborough.

I was moved by the beauty and piety of these words.

'No sound was so entrancing as that of the *May-garlanding.* At the first sound of "We've brought you here . . ." we would be at the front door to see the children with their garlanded basket with its leaves and flowers and ribbons. It was no good telling us that it was only a clothes-basket, or that the canopy and back was made from a hoop and a tablecloth, or that the may was really blackthorn, or that the children had only come for money. The children had come with their garlanded basket because the countryside was singing, because the trees and the flowers were awakening, and to remind us of a joyful England that welcomed the seasons. Something was calling—something that I could not understand.' [This joyous evocation of May-day in the 1890s is from *The Watershed*, p 19, the autobiography of Reginald Payne, a London surgeon and a member of the former Northampton furnishing firm (see page 45).]

'In my childhood days in the 1920s we always looked forward to May-day. The night before, we went round the village asking for spring flowers, mostly flowering currant. Then my Dad would make me a garland, hoop-shaped with a doll in the middle. On the first of May we would rise early, put on our white dresses and wreathe garlands in our hair . . . then we went from house to house, singing the May-garland song. We used to go to Delapre Abbey and sing to Miss Bouverie. She made us very welcome and gave us refreshments. We always looked on May-day as a very happy day. My Dad said he felt the same when he was young, and it was from him that I learned the song.

> 1. A branch of may I brought you here,
>   Before your door it stands.
>   It's well set out and well spread out
>   By the work of our Lord's hands.
>
> 2. Now take the Bible in your hands,
>   And read a chapter through
>   And when the Day of Judgment comes,
>   God will remember you.
>
> 3. A man is a man, his life's but a span,
>   He flourishes like a flower.
>   He's here today and gone tomorrow,
>   Cut down in half an hour.
>
> 4. And now I have sung my pretty maid's song,
>   No longer can I stay.
>   God bless you all, both great and small,
>   I wish you a merry month of May.

Mrs Leah Clarke, Hardingstone, in a letter to the *Chronicle and Echo*, Northampton, March 1978. These verses are well-known in many parts of Northamptonshire and in some other counties as well.

The next song was sung by *Mrs Gray* of Brigstock at the age of eighty-five, in about 1968, and another local lady remembers her mother, born in 1880, singing it to her when she was a child. Two verses are very similar to verses 1 and 2 above, and are omitted.

The remaining four verses are numbered to follow those of the Hardingstone song, for easy reference.

> 5. We have been rambling all the night,
>   And the best part of the day,
>   But now we are just returning home,
>   We bring you this branch of may.

> 6. Arise, arise, my pretty fair maid,
>   From out your drowsy dream,
>   Steal down into your dairy room,
>   To fetch a bowl of cream.

> 7. If not a bowl of your sweet cream,
>   A tot of your brown beer,
>   And if we should stop to tarry in the town,
>   We'll come another year.

> 8. The clock strikes one and we must be gone,
>   Or else the day will be over,
>   So pretty fair maid, good morning to you,
>   And we wish you a joyful May.

Mr John Bailey, Brigstock.

Verse 5 refers to the custom of young men and girls spending the night of May Eve in the woods, returning with green branches which they set in front of houses.

The carrying of green branches continued at Wymington.

'Girls used to go from door to door carrying a branch of hedgerow decorated with bunches of flowers, ribbons, cards, pretty articles and bells that jingled as the wind blew.'

Mrs Millicent Wright, Wymington.

Songs known by Miss Ivy Walker of Wollaston and Mrs Elsie Rouse, born at Holcot, include versions of verses 5 and 6 above. Both songs have another attractive verse, Wollaston's a rather better version, again, numbered to follow on.

> 9. I have a bag on my right arm,
>   Draws up with a silken string,
>   Nothing does it want but a little silver
>   To line it well within.

Caption above right: May-garlanding at Braybrooke. Children hold the decorated hoop and the basket containing four dolls. Mrs F Goodman, Braybrooke. Below right: Jack-in-the-green, who took part in the May-day procession at Broughton in the 1920s. He is the Green Man of folklore and this little sketch, drawn from memory by Mrs Rose Clark of Barton Seagrave is the only 'sighting' I have. It is of great importance.

Jack-in-the-green

Wollaston has the following verse as well.

> 10. The hedges and the fields they are so green,
> As green as any leaf.
> Our Heavenly Father waters them
> With his heavenly dew so sweet.

Mrs Flower of Farthingstone sang this verse in the 1900s.

> Remember us poor Mayers all
> For thus we do begin
> To lead our lives in righteousness
> Or else we die in sin.
>
> *Mrs Ivy Smart,* Greens Norton.

The May-garlanding, as it was usually called within living memory locally, was recorded by Anne Elizabeth Baker in 1854.

At Polebrook the last few days of April are employed by the Queen of May and her juvenile attendants in gathering what flowers they can procure from the meadows, and in calling at the houses of the principal inhabitants to beg flowers, the gift or the loan of ribbons, handkerchiefs, dolls etc with which to form their garland. This being arranged on hoops, . . . the youthful maidens assemble on May morning and carry the decorated garland round the village preceded by a fidler, and the following quaint old song . . . is sung . . . at the different houses and a gratuity is collected' (*GNWP* p 424).

The 'quaint old song' had nine verses, of which five are similar to verses 1, 2, 5, 6 and 7 above. Two verses recorded by Miss Baker from Moreton Pinkney are similar to verses 9 and 8 above (*GNWP* p 426). Verses 10 and 9 above resemble the Hinwick May-day Carol collected by Lucy Broadwood.

> *English Traditional Songs and Carols,* 1908.

There were other songs—every village had its favourites—traditional or perhaps written in the last century.

'At Broughton we used to sing *Joan to the Maypole, Come Lasses and Lads* and *Now is the Month of Maying,* and dance *Jenny Pluck Pears* and *Parson's Farewell.* The May Queen was crowned on the village green and we danced round the Maypole. The boys and girls met for tea—salmon sandwiches, slabs of fruit cake, iced buns and an orange—and then went to the sports.'   *Mrs Rose Clarke,* Barton Seagrave.

At Cold Ashby there was a pleasant song with a lovely dancing tune.

Come along and dance with me,
'Tis the first of May.

People gather on the green,
All have left the town-O,
Hawthorn crowns our lovely queen,
She's the fairest ever seen,
Blossoms deck her gown-O.

Cold Ashby W.I.

An unusual song at Cogenhoe had this first verse.

O butterfly stop for a moment, I pray,
Have you seen a boy with a jacket of grey?
He's taken my three little birdies away.

Mrs Janet Hollowell, Cogenhoe.

Mrs Doris Robinson of Little Houghton knows a number of May-day songs, one of which admonishes those who will not join in the celebrations.

He who will not join our song
Does his nature grievous wrong.
Flowers bright no delight
Bring to his distempered sight.

The flowers bright were often whatever was available, but some people were specific.

'We used to start from the school at nine o'clock, and we'd got our brush handles all decorated with *gillies,* white arabis and bluebells. Our first stop was the Rectory.

Mrs Foster, Pury End.

'The smallest girls carried posies on sticks, the flowers being crab-blossom, *smell-smocks* and *gillivers.* The Kislingbury Scrapbook. *Mr Roy Payler.* Flower-bedecked sticks were carried at Brafield also.

Lots of flowers were needed at Grendon and Titchmarsh, where they were used to decorate a carriage and a cart.

'Mrs Spencer sent a groom with a horse-drawn carriage, beautifully decorated by the mothers, in which the Queen and her attendants rode round the village. The youngest children rode in a cart lent by a farmer, with a man to drive the horse. They all had a beautiful tea.'

From the memoirs of *Mrs L Papworth* of Grendon,
recorded by *Audrey Smith.*

At Ashton the girls carried their garlands round to the outlying farms.'   *Miss Jessie Curtis,* Northampton.

The striking flowers of Crown Imperial were used at Little Houghton and other places to crown the garland.

'They dressed the garland with the flowers of May, crowning the top with Crown Imperial. In my garden I still have descendants of those very flowers. (At Balscote, near Banbury.)
Mrs Hilda Berry.

In the blacksmith's garden at Broughton was a plant we always used to wait for. It was the Crown Imperial, a lily-like plant which was always, always ready for May-day. It would be placed on the top of the *green man's* frame and used to nod as he bowed in time to the singing. It was never picked till the *green man* needed it. I think the frame was made of willow, very heavy, covered densely with greenery, only the eyes visible. Two boys used to walk with *Jack o' the green,* one each side, ready to lift off the frame by the handles when Jack got tired. The greenery had a pungent smell, I remember, and when Jack bowed repeatedly in time to the music, it was almost hypnotic. I remember the sense of awe when the boys were dressing the Jack and the sweet, heavy smell of the greenery. The other name for him was the *old man of the woods.'*

Mrs Rose Clark, Barton Seagrave.

This compelling account is the only first-hand one that I have, although there was a *Jack in the green* at Boughton also. (*Boughton in the 1880s.* Charles E Kimbell.) Jack was a feature of the chimney-sweepers' celebration of May-day in earlier times and became confused with the King of the May and with Robin Hood. The shape of the frame is similar to the edifice built on the rush-cart in the rush-bearing ceremony of some northern counties.

He reminds me of summer days in Far Cotton Rec. when the grass was mown and we used to play 'houses' with it. We also, without knowing, played a much older game, covering one child with the sweet-smelling grass till he was completely hidden. Then we would cry '*Green man, green man, arise*' and he would spring up, shaking the grass away and chase the rest of us. This symbol of nature's springtime wakening after being hidden in the winter recurs in folklore and legend, and is a well-known inn-name to this day. Boys, in various costumes, or in ordinary clothes, often took part in the processions and dancing.

Two little girls called May Baxter and Florrie Webb, who lived in Far Cotton in the 1890s, set out before school one morning, in great excitement, to go round May-garlanding. They had their basket and doll and 'hoops decked with gillyflowers' but they were very small and could not remember the words of the song. But they were Methodist children and knew plenty of hymns, so they duly greeted the householders with a few verses of '*Blessed assurance, Jesus is mine*'. Blessed assurance indeed.   Information from *Mr Alan Fookes,* Great Billing.

The Morris

'They lack a font. And the curat is not in orders and is reported to be a morris dancer.'

Complaint to the Bishop of Peterborough by the parishioners of Canons Ashby in 1578. *NNQ*, 1884, vol 1, p 57.

'The Morris dance is performed in Northamptonshire by six or eight young men, gaily decked out with ribands, buttons etc. and with a great number of little bells attached to their legs: each carries in his hand a strong round stick of about a yard in length.

The dance, which is of the most picturesque character, consists of a series of rapid evolutions, changes of posture etc., accompanied with brandishing and clashing of the staves and flourishing of kerchiefs. The clown or Tom Fool has generally an old quilt thrown over him, plentifully hung with rabbits' skins. . . . In his hands he holds a stick with an inflated bladder attached. . . . This, together with the piper, completes the set'.

Thomas Sternberg, DFN.

Miss A E Baker was more interested in what they wore–

'blue or red ribbons, or blue and orange; five rosettes were placed on the scarf before, and five behind, with one on each hip. Their hats were also decorated with rosettes and streamers of the same coloured ribbons. On their legs they often had as many as six rows of bells. . . . It has been thought desirable to

record these vestiges of our popular pastimes the more minutely, as, from the change in the tastes and habits of the people, and the growing refinement of the age, they will soon disappear altogether. . . . *GNWP* 1854, vol 2, pp 30-32.

In fact, the last entry referring to Morris dancing in any of the county newspapers in this part of England was in the *Banbury Guardian* of 5th June, 1888. Prior to that, there is one reference to a Blakesley side [team of dancers] in 1747 and one at Towcester in 1766. All references from that date onwards are to Brackley sides. (From a monograph, *An Interim Checklist of References to Morris dancing in local county newspapers,* part 1, 1733-1914, Keith Chandler, 1983.)

I remember the Morris dancers about seventy years ago. I can't remember whether it was in Kettering or Broughton. They wore breeches and white shirts crossed with ribbons and they carried handkerchiefs, not staves. I think they danced to the music of a concertina.   *Mrs Rose Clark,* Barton Seagrave.

Morris dancing was done at school, before 1914. We all wore broderie anglaise dresses—dark girls had pink sashes and hair ribbons and fair girls wore blue. One dance was with sticks and one with handkerchiefs, with bells on our wrists and ankles.
Mrs Gladys Sharp, Kettering.

We were trained by the Rev Pitchford of Lamport Rectory in the 1920s. He was very interested in old music and songs and used to travel round the countryside collecting them. [He was the father of Denys Pitchford, writer on nature topics under the pseudonym BB.]

At first we used to practice in the attic at the Rectory with the pattern chalked out on the floor. We'd got one fellow as was rather flat-footed and the floor used to shake. We were doing a dance one evening and the servant came up and said 'Mr Pitchford, the wardrobe has fallen on Mrs Pitchford in the room below'. So the Rector sent some of us to go down and put this wardrobe right again and get Mrs Pitchford out of trouble. We didn't know where we were when we went on to grass. It took us twelve months to learn our first dance. We danced to the music of a harmonium and we wore the ribbons and bells and

---

Caption above left: Children dancing around the Maypole at Little Houghton.
The boy in the centre is Desmond Williams. Mrs Loretta Smith, Little Houghton.
Below left: The Brackley Morris, date unknown. NL

did the stick-dancing and the 'Baccy-pipes', long church-warden pipes. The Rector had a *fond* saying 'He never breaks them' but he didn't tell the crowd they were made of iron. The local blacksmith made them. We won first prize with that. I can remember we danced *The Flowers of Edinburgh* and *Shepherds' Hey* and once in a big display, *Sellenger's Round*. Once we danced at Belvoir Castle in an All-England competition, and once we toured the east coast.

The sword-dancing was nowhere near as polished. We used to have a 'victim', blind-folded and in a red jersey and we finished up with the points of the swords all together.

Mr Cecil Howlett, Market Harborough.

An Oxford graduate teaching at Magdalen School in Brackley in the 1960s talked to two old gentlemen who knew some of the dances. Knowledge is passed on by word of mouth and by teaching and learning, even if there are no recorded performances. There had been sides at Hinton-in-the-Hedges and at Badby. Local sides performing, among other dances, traditional Cotswold Morris are the Brackley, Northampton and Moulton Morris Men. From ancient times the Morris has been an exclusively male ritual. The leader of the side is the *Squire*, the treasurer the *Bagman*. The *capers* [leaps] of the dancers, their resounding landings and the knocking on the ground with staves are thought to have once been efforts to wake up Mother Earth to renewed life in Spring. Ribbons and other decorations are a form of disguise.

The revival of interest in Morris is of very great value in keeping alive one of our most ancient customs, especially when great care is taken to work sensitively with local dancers and musicians whose knowledge of the steps and bowstrokes has been handed down for generations.

One of the highlights of the summer, especially for children who never had a holiday, was the Sunday School treat, with its tea and games in the field. At Kislingbury it was even more exciting because of a remarkable processional dance which took place at the annual treat of the Baptist Sunday School.

'All the scholars, teachers and friends linked hands and danced all round the village. The first two in the line held up their arms to form an arch and the last person lead the whole line through. She would help to form the next arch and so on. This threading dance wound its way round workers in the field, through gates and all round the village, in and out of houses, gathering more dancers as it went. Stops were made at all the big houses and everywhere where someone was ill or aged. The dance was called *Threading the Tailor's Needle,* and had been performed for as long as anyone could remember. It was performed for the last time in 1923. As they danced they sang these words, to the tune of 'Here we go round the mulberry bush'.

> Hold up, hold up your gates so high,
> And let King George's men go by.
> It is so dark we cannot see
> To thread the Tailor's Needle'.
>> *Mr Roy Payler,* Kislingbury.

'There was a similar dance at Hook Norton in Oxfordshire and they sang

> Tailor's blind and he can't see
> To thread the tailor's needle.'
>> *Mrs Ivy Smart,* Greens Norton.

At Kislingbury, like the two little girls in Far Cotton, Northampton they sang Sankey hymns as well [from *Sacred Songs and Solos,* Ira D Sankey]. Many of the tunes are lively and joyful.

On 29th May, 1660, Charles Stuart re-entered London after the ending of the Commonwealth, and was later crowned King Charles the Second, amid great rejoicing. *Oak-apple Day* recalls this event and also the time when Charles was forced to hide in an oak-tree after his defeat at the battle of Worcester in 1651. When Northampton was rebuilt after the Great Fire of 1675, the king gave a thousand tons of timber, including oak, from his forests of Whittlebury and Salcey. His statue, standing above the portico of All Saints Church in the centre of the town, is crowned with a garland on Oak Apple Day.

'On Lammas Day, the first crop of ripe corn was made into bread and taken to church,'   *Mrs E Wood,* Weedon Lois.

Lammas is OE *hlaf-masse,* loaf-mass.

'The sheaves were left in the field for three bells—for three Sundays.'   *Mrs Barbara March,* Kettering.

> 'We've ploughed, we've sowed,
> We've reaped, we've mowed,
> We have got our harvest home.'
>> *Mrs Fountaine,* Pattishall.

This song was sung as the last load of corn, decorated with ribbons and boughs, was brought triumphantly home. This was the first verse.

> Harvest home, harvest home [often pronounced *'um*]
> Two plum puddings are better than one.
>
> *GNWP* vol 1, p 310.

Mr Robert Key of Newnham has a manuscript, undated, and headed '*Written for William Gossage's Harvest Home*', signed by Elizabeth Key, probably about 1860. The writer was an unidentified MM. Here are the first two and the last verses.

> A simple song I fain would sing
> Amongst our merry cheer,
> And honest thanks in it would bring
> For this most plenteous year.

> The farmers' fields with golden grain
> Right nobly have been drest,
> And now the harvest home again
> Our toil and care has blest.

> Good harvests be our Master's lot,
> 'Hurrah, boys' once again.
> Whilst plenty dwells within his cot,
> He'll not forget his man.

After the harvest came the ancient privilege of gleaning, as old as the Old Testament story of Ruth. It was a godsend to the poor and to country people generally, and was usually governed by local custom.

'At Ashton a field was not ready for gleaning until three sheaves of corn left in a stook in the middle of the field had been taken away on the farmer's orders. No-one could enter a field to glean until the church bell was rung at eight in the morning. I well remember the pleasure of working in the open air, with a bag for short ears tied round my waist.

> *Miss Jessie Curtis,* Northampton.

'A woman called Betsy Swann was the gleaning leader.

> *Mrs Fountaine,* Pattishall.

'They were all in charge of the ganger, who decided where they should all go, and when. She rang the church bell at 8 am for the far fields, until twelve noon, then at two till four o'clock for the near fields, and again in the evening. The women and girls filled sheets marked with a scrap of their frock material and carried them home on their heads. They took the grain to the mill to be ground into flour. Duston and Kislingbury always quarrelled about a field at Upton. One day both gangs arrived together. They swore and shouted and brandished their sheets at each other.'   *Kislingbury Scrapbook* 1952.

'On Thursday afternoons throughout October, the baker's oven was kept going for the use of women who were gleaning, so that they could take a meal there to be cooked'
                    Mr Roy Payler, Kislingbury.

'At Brafield a gleaning woman gave birth to a baby behind an iron fence. The child and mother both survived.'
                    Mrs Bedford, Cogenhoe.

Gleaning for some was a stark necessity, for others a pleasure, despite sore ankles from the scratchy stubble. It was a job that children could do and they had to do it.

'Children used to stay away from school after a strong wind to gather fallen wood, to visit [Stony] Stratford Fair on the second of August, to take dinners and drinks to their fathers in the harvest fields, to glean and to go to a meet of the Grafton Hunt if anywhere near.'   *Mrs Dorothy Warren,* Yardley Gobion.

> Poor girl hard at work in the heat of the sun,
> How tired and warm you must be,
> Why don't you leave off as the others have done,
> And sit with them under the tree?
>
> Oh, no, for my mother lies ill in her bed,
> Too feeble to spin or to knit,
> And my poor little brothers are crying for bread,
> And yet we can't give them a bit.
>
> How could I be merry and idle and gay
> When they are so hungry and ill?
> Oh no, I would rather work hard all the day
> My little blue apron to fill.

From *Miss I. Whitney,* Moulton,
part of a poem which her grandfather, born 1847,
in the Hungry Forties, used to recite.

There is no traditional celebration of Hallowe'en in Northampton-shire, except among the Scots at Corby, where the children don't beat about the bush, but sing

The sky is blue, the grass is green,
Give us some money for Hallowe'en.

Mrs Alison Grimes, Rothwell.

The ancient peoples who greeted spring and summer with floral fertility rites held autumn and winter festivals in which the lighting of great fires played an important part. Cattle were slaughtered and roasted, because the pasture would no longer feed them, and the fires ritually dispelled the darkness.

The bonfires lit in memory of Guy Fawkes and the Gunpowder Plot came much later but fitted into the tradition.

Mrs E Carpenter of Bostock Avenue, Northampton, in her nineties, and *Miss Grace Carr,* of Northampton, remembered this song being sung. The last two lines were sometimes sung on their own and are known at Kettering.

Guy Fawkes and his companions
Did the plot contrive
To blow the King and Parliament
All up alive.

By God's providence they were caught
(or he got caught, he got catched)
With a dark lantern, lighting a match.
Holler boys, holler boys, holler for the king.
(or God save the King)
Holler boys, holler boys, make the bells ring.

I am not sure of the meaning of this rhyme.

Half a loaf to feed the post,
A pennorth o' cheese to choke him,
Half-a-pint to swill it down
And a jolly good fire to roast him.

Mrs Dew, Milton Malsor.

I have not heard the version of the local rhyme at the end of the Guy Fawkes song from Northampton recorded in *The Lore and Language of Schoolchildren,* Iona and Peter Opie, p. 282, though Miss Carr knew it.

We sang this, as did *Mrs Carpenter* .

Guy, Guy, Guy, hit him in the eye,
Hang him on a lamp-post and there let him die.
Umbrella, down the cellar,
There I saw a naked fellow,
Burn his body, save his soul,
Please give me a lump of coal.

If a lump of coal won't do,
Please give me a ha'penny.
All round the Market Square
And up and down the Drapery.
When I get to Mercers' Row/Marefair/a firework shop
I'll stop and spend me ha'penny.

On St Thomas' Day, 21st December, widows could go from
door to door, asking for alms in a song or rhyme which began
'Pity the poor widows. . . .'   *Mr John E Bailey,* Brigstock.

Tom Bates, the old blind fiddler, used to play in the old streets of
Far Cotton at Christmas time. My grandmother could remember
only that he played and sang 'God rest ye merry, gentlemen' and
said he always sang 'A-ey New Year instead of Happy'. She
supposed that it was because he had no teeth. She and the other
children used to go to Delapre Abbey singing carols and remembered with appreciation that they were given hot drinks and
mince-pies there.

Quite a different note is sounded at Balscote, near Banbury.

'We girls used to go through the churchyard scattering hemp-
seed.'   *Mrs Hilda Berry.*

This was plant divination, supposed to reveal their future sweethearts. For some, a more practical hope was not for a sweetheart,
but for a Christmas dinner.

'At Christmas 1904 Michael Perkins, who kept a small general
shop in Irthlingborough, ran a raffle which was threepence to
enter. Each entrant had to shake three dice and cast them, the
highest scorer winning a turkey. I was twelve years old and I
had left school at ten and was working for a butcher. I gave all
my earnings to my mother as we had a large family. There was
no hope of raising threepence till my boss sent me on an errand
to Thrapston market, and gave me sixpence for the return train
fare.

I kept this and walked the sixteen miles, and was artful
enough to time my return to agree with that of a train. All went
well till another butcher I had seen in Thrapston passed me
with his horse and cart at the top of Crow Hill and told my boss
when he got back that he was mean to make me walk. I was for
it when I got back, but he did not ask for his sixpence back.

We gathered together on the appointed night and when I
had my throw I got two sixes and a five, which was not beaten

or equalled. I thought of how pleased my mother would be when I got home with the turkey.

Then it was found that one man who had entered had not turned up, and after we had waited some time, another man said "Let this boy throw for him—he is the youngest". I did so and beat my own score with three sixes. It was many years before I knew what turkey tasted like, the first time being in Belgium in 1918 when the officers of my unit treated us to a good Christmas dinner.'   *Mr Jack Davis,* Northampton.

'The lord of the manor provided a new coat and a pair of boots at Christmas for the poor children of Helmdon. There is a field called Poor's Lot at Weston-by-Weedon and the rent from it provided bread at Christmas. Nowadays it is given in groceries at the village shop.

Mrs E Wood, who has lived at both villages.

'I have all the respect in the world for the young men at the Methodist Chapel and the Baptist Chapel. Every Christmas, out of their own pockets, they found a dinner for their scholars. The Methodists used to send their dinners (to the bakehouse) in great big pans, with great lumps of meat on and batter puddings and baked potatoes. There were baked plum puddings in a big tin. And we Church scholars never got nothing.   *Mr William Burt,* Harpole.

'At Kislingbury in the last century, Christmas suppers were held by the choir and bell-ringers, the football club and the pig club. "Poor people over seventy" were given a tea by the Male Voice Choir, and the old people themselves provided the entertainment, as people did in those days.

Alf Jeffs always sang

> Poor old Jeff is gone to rest,
> We know that he is free.
> Disturb him not but let him rest,
> Away down Tennessee.

"Rocked in the cradle of the deep" was Jim Baseley's contribution, and Joe Starmer's was

> When we were boys together,
> It's a time I shall never forget,
> The schoolhouse by the heather
> In childhood where we met.

Most of these old people were born not long after the Napoleonic Wars. Dan'l Ward always sang

> 'Fore I was born, some years ago,
> When George the Third was king,

That was all he could remember, and he sang it over and over again. Apparently the concert was never complete without Tom Pebody's rendering of

> Will y' lend me mother a saucepan,
> Will y' lend me mother a spoon?
> For she's to have some visitors
> To tea this afternoon.

> Will y' lend me mother half-a-crown
> This morning, Mrs. Burke?
> And mother says she'll pay y' back
> When father gets some work.'

> *Mr Roy Payler*, Kislingbury.

Everybody enjoyed the singing and they sang some of the songs year after year.

The Mummers

Not many people could remember much about the mummers, who once went round from door to door at Christmas and performed their odd, pantomime-like play inside the houses.

'I've heard of them, but there's nobody to ask now. *You never miss the water till the well runs dry.*
> *Mr Jack Meyer*, Little Houghton.

'We're gooin' a-mummerin', people used to say.'
> *Mr Ray Wykes*, Spratton.

'Up to 1919' at Sulgrave; 'Until the 1920s' at Moulton; 'We called them the *merry-actors.*' *Mr John E Bailey*, Brigstock.

'I was very frightened of the mummers. I wouldn't look at them, so I don't really know what they looked like—only that they fought. One of the men fell down—he was killed—and that frightened me. They collected money and they used to dress up—one of them had his face blackened. I think it was to do with George and the Dragon. We heard them tramping along and my father would say "Here's the mummers coming" (at Farthinghoe).'   *Mrs Dorothy Adkins,* Banbury.

The great Christian festival of the Nativity retains elements of earlier pagan rites, which the early Christians wisely recognised as having much in common with their own belief. Primitive people feared the darkness and cold of winter when the cattle were slaughtered, no crops grew and Nature seemed dead. Their rites were prayers for the conquering of darkness and death and the return of light and life. To this end they brought evergreens into their huts to ensure their survival and ritually acted out a killing and restoring to life, the essence of the mummers' play.

There are two players who fight, one being killed, and a third, a magician or priest, later a doctor, who brings the dead man to life. The names of the two fighters are often those of heroes or kings. Later plays had words as well as actions and included a fair amount of horse-play, and also the *quête* or request for money.

I was very fortunate to be introduced to *Mr John E Bailey* of Brigstock, who told me the text of the Brigstock play. The fight between the two protagonists is not directly mentioned, nor is the raising of the dead. The fight with the dragon is perhaps allegorical – the overcoming of evil. Some verses may be missing.

THE BRIGSTOCK MUMMERS' PLAY

In comes I, never bin before,
Three *merry-actors* at your door.
By your leave I will come in,
Bolt, dance, fiddle and sing.   (Meaning of *bolt* unknown)

In comes I, Beelzebub,
On my shoulder/under my arm I carries a club,
In my hand a dripping-pan,
Don't you think I'm a jolly old man?

In comes I, Prince Charming/Champion bold,
Once I wore three crowns of gold.
I fought the dragon to the slaughter,
By this means I won the King of Egypt's daughter.

Hold your tongue, you foolish fellow.

In comes I, the Doctor.

What, you the Doctor?

Yes, I am the Doctor.

What can you cure?

Ixy, pixy, palsy and gout,
Pains within and pains without.

There was an old woman, three score years and ten,
She lost her head, I gave her a pill
And brought it back again.

My hat is lined with cats-skins,
It is but very thin.
I wish you'd give me something
To line it well within.

Your pockets full of money, your cellars full of beer,
We wish you a merry Christmas and a happy New Year.

This fragment from Pury End bears resemblance to a verse above.

> The cock sat up in the yew tree
> As we went clattering by,
> With a jug of beer and a pork pie,
> The Christmas singers are very dry.
>
> The roads are very dirty,
> My shoes are very thin,
> Tell the missis and master
> To slip a copper in.
>
> *Mr Percy Foster*, Pury End.

Cp also the last verse of the Wollaston May-day song, pp 220-221.

In the Harpole Mummers' Play, the hero is King Charles and another character makes an appearance. This is the popular Fool.

THE HARPOLE MUMMERS' PLAY

> In comes poor old Beelzebub,
> In his hand he carries his club,
> In his hand a frying-pan,
> Don't you think he's a handsome man?
>
> In comes King Charles, we'll all unite,
> Through all England he did fight,

Slew the dragon, conquered all,
And saved poor sinner from his fall.

In comes Doctor, ten-pound Doctor,
Ten pound is my fee,
But being as you're a friend of mine,
I'll only take five pound of thee.

Doctor.   Here's a pill, young man, and if this doesn't operate by
six o'clock tomorrow morning, you'll be a dead man.
Arise, young man, arise.

Big-head   In comes I who's never bin yit,
With a big 'ead and a little wit,
'Is 'ead's s' big and 'is wit's s' small,
Yet 'e'll do 'is best to please you all.

They sing.   Though we're not s' very dry,
We'd like to taste your Christmas pie,
Though we're not s' very dear,
We'd like to taste your Christmas beer.

Fol lol lol lol
Fol lol lol lol la.

This is the transcript of a tape-recording made for us by *Mr
William Burt* of Harpole in March 1983, two years before his
death. In his lifetime he had seen the last performance of the
Plough Monday men and of the mummers and had remembered
the songs and the play for us many years afterwards.

THE GREENS NORTON PLAY

The splendid Greens Norton play was recorded in 1972 by *Mr R
Bicknell,* a newcomer to the village, who spent a convivial
evening with his neighbour, *Mr Frank Lay,* then aged seventy-
four, village blacksmith and veteran of the Great War. The old
gentleman talked freely and another collection of memories was
in the bag. Mr Bicknell gave a copy to *Mrs Ivy Smart,* and they
generously allowed me to have a copy.

Mr Lay, in his splendid local accent, starts his account as if he
were one of the mummers standing outside a cottage door, on a
winter's night, many years ago.

'You knock on the door f'r a start and ask them if they want the
mummers.

'D'y' want the mummers t'night?' Then the old man and woman come t' the door.

'Yes, come in, *bwoy*' [boy].

'Ere we goo then, we'll start, then. Missis, shove that table *a* one side so we're got some room.' Then the *fust* [first] man, he comes in.

> I open the door and I enter in,
> To see your face when I get in,
> Whether I sit, stand or fall,
> I'll do my duty to please you all.
>
> A room, a room, a garret room,
> A room t' let me in.
> I'm neither one o' the ragged sort,
> Nor one o' the royal kings.
>
> And if you don't believe these words I say,
> Step in King George and clear the way.
>
> In comes I, King George,
> King George is my name.
> I have a sword and pistol by my side
> And sure to win the game.

his opponent
> Sure to win the game, sir?
> It's not within your power.
> I'll cut you up in inches
> In less nor [than] half a hour.
>
> Who, sir? You, sir? Draw your sword and try.

King George kills his opponent.

> Is there ever a little doctor in the how? [house?]
> Yes.
> Call him in.
> Follow me. Come in, Dr Brown.
>
> In comes I, Dr Brown,
> The best little doctor in the town.
>
> And how did you become a doctor?
> By my travels.
> Where are you bin in your travels?
> Over England, Ireland, Scotland and Spain,
> Up over the hills and back home again.

And what did you see in your travels?
A dead *dunkey*, stuck with straw,
Kicked a blind man through a nine-inch wall.

Well, how much will you cure this man for?
Ten pound if he's rich and five if he's poor.
He's very poor.
Five pound.

I'll give him an *ellican-pellican* pill.
It'll goo down like a wheelbarrow
And he'll rise up like a *peck*-axe. [pick-axe]
Arise, Sir John.

Come in, little Devilly Dout

In comes I, little Devilly Dout.
If y' don't give me some money
I'll sweep y'all out.
Money I want and money I'll have,
If y' don't give us money
We'll sweep y't'y' grave.

Come in, Big-head

In comes I, old Big-head,
Wi' my big head and my little wits,
My head s' big and my wits s' small,
But I'll sing you a song as'll please you all.

They all sing   O ring-ting-ting and a drop more drink
To make the ol' kettle sing sounder,
A drop for you and a drop for me,
An' a drop for Punch an' Judy.

The apparently ordinary request, as the players come in, to 'shove the table *a* one side, so we're got more room' is part of an ancient ritual. Sometimes a player would come in with a broom and literally sweep a clear space before the play began. It is thought to be a memory of ritually bringing order out of chaos, of creating a circle of safety into which the unknown powers outside in the darkness could not come. It is echoed by the repeated word 'room' later in the play, the words 'clear the way' and the threat to 'sweep y' t' y' grave'. The 'dead *dunkey*' is a horse image, the horse being a symbol of strength and fertility. The *'ellican pellican* pill' was elecampane, from the plant *horse-heal* [inula helemium], used as a tonic and stimulant.

Mr Lay, knowing nothing of these mysteries, but thoroughly enjoying himself, took every part in turn in a matter-of-fact way, making no distinction between the characters. This, again, may be a style of great antiquity, from the times when the play was not a drama but a rite, performed each year to ensure the rebirth of nature and the continuance of life. Mr Lay then described the costume and disguise.

'The first man, he's got a bowler hat on and a black face and a few red spots and a red nose, an old swaller-tail coat an' a walking stick. Looked like a tramp. An' the king, he'd got some fancy paper put across him an' this 'ere little ol' wooden sword, a pistol hanging on a belt. Dr Brown, he's got a silk hat and a long frock-coat and a bag.'

The Badby Mummers' Play has eight merry-actors, the Champion, John Fenn, Molly, the king's mother, the Turkish Snipe [Knight], the doctor, Fool and Father Christmas. It was recorded by *R J E Tiddy,* in *The Mummers' Play,* Oxford (1923), pp 222-3. Mr Tiddy, a Classics don at Oxford, was killed in the Great War.

A cassette recording of the Sulgrave Mummers' Play was made by David Parry, MA and Marion Jones, MA, BLitt. It is a long and interesting play, recounted by a man who took the part of Molly before the 1914–18 war. There is a 'sweeping-round' verse and three references to a horse.

'We moved to Sulgrave and I remember the mummers there quite well. They used to come one day about Christmas. My father was very interested in them. I remember him going outside and seeing the mummers. He came back and asked us if we would like to see them, and they came in. They were very weird and really frightening. They didn't say much–they acted. The characters had nasty, vicious ways, and they wore masks and peculiar dress. One had a broom and swept the room before they started the play. I was not a child, but fourteen or fifteen years old at the time, but I was frightened'.

Mr S Adkins, born in 1900, now of Greatworth.

PLACES AND PEOPLE

The Origins of
Place-names and Field-names

Up the rig *an' down the* thurrow,
That's the way t' Wellin'borough.

Our Northamptonshire speech, it seems to me, is rather like the county itself, not widely known nor instantly recognisable, but with its own unassuming appeal, gentle in the countryside, bustling in the towns.

Whether we speak Standard English or still use some dialect, our speech had its origins in Old and Middle English (OE and ME). The first of these was the language, really a series of related dialects, of the Angles, Saxons, Jutes and Friesians who invaded this country in the fifth and sixth centuries. Their homeland was the Danish peninsula and an area south and west of it, and their main objective in coming to Britain was to find good farming land. Some of the Angles sailed up the winding Nene to the fertile river-valleys and drove most of the Romano-British people already living there, away to the west. Few British [Celtic] words

Caption left: Chestnut avenue and grazing sheep at Flore. It was once a common custom to graze animals on roadside verges. C F Allen, 11 Market Square, Northampton.

survive. One is *brock* for badger and there is the place-name Crick and river-name Avon.

The newcomers' language was Mercian, a sub-division of Anglian, and some of our oldest place-names are those of their river-valley settlements, including Oundle, Thrapston and places with *ing* in their names, Orlingbury, Wellingborough, Billing, Kislingbury and others. *Ing* goes back to several sources, often meaning *dweller* or *follower*. Anglian settlement is also shown by place-names in *cote*, cottages; *dun* [don], hill, hill-pasture; *ham*, homestead; hill; ley [OE *leah*] pasture or land cleared from forest; *tun* [ton], farm; village; *well*, spring, among others.

Most of our surviving dialect words, many of them farming terms, date from this far-off time. *Thurrow*, in the little rhyme above, is a local form of furrow [OE *furh*]. When an old gardener says his lettuce is 'nice and *frem*', firm and crisp, he uses the local form of *frym*, vigorous in growth. Then there are the various forms of *hus*, house, *cow-'us*, *'en-'us*, *duffus* [dovehouse], among others. *Herriff*, goosegrass, is from OE *hegerife*, and *slon* for sloe is from *sla*, with its plural *slan*.

Next in importance in the making of our speech is the Scandinavian element. The 'Great Army' landed in East Anglia in 865, after some years of plundering forays. The invaders were mainly Danes from Jutland and the Friesian coast, and they were now looking for land. After years of warfare, Alfred the Great defeated the Danes in battle and by siege at Ethandun [Eddington] and was able to impose a division of land, in the *Treaty of Alfred and Guthrum* (886). The Danelaw, Guthrum's kingdom, was to be bounded on the south and west by the Watling Street (A5) in what is now Northamptonshire, with river-boundaries elsewhere.

South-west of the road was English Mercia. The frontier-road was a dialectal as well as a military and political boundary. The people who lived on either side of it spoke different, though related languages, and this difference can still be heard. Travel only a mile or two south of Towcester and you will hear, among older rural speakers, a rounded *r* (retroflex r-colouring is the exact term) in such words as *learn, corner, butcher*. You may hear a half-humorous '*ooman* for woman' and there is a local saying

'Ood, 'ard 'ood, stood in the barn all 'inter'.

As if to make up for this loss of *w*, it was added to words like *boy, boil, spoil*, which, with the local vowel sound, became *bwie, bwielt, swpielt.* These forms, though, are also known at Wellingborough and perhaps elsewhere.

A few years ago in Silverstone I heard a lady whose dog had died say '*Us* was heart-broken' and a few miles farther south, at Croughton, an old roadman once said 'It *be* 'ard work down there—it *be* all up 'ill'. At Banbury, *bist* is well-remembered for *be-est* '*Wheer bist gooin?*', Where are you going?

None of these forms is heard north-east of Watling Street. Dialect words from south-west of the road include *mawkin* for scarecrow, *lease* for glean and *flidger* (near Towcester) and *fledger* (near Banbury) for a fledgling bird.

Place and field-names are almost all of OE origin.

In the rest of the county, in what was the Danelaw, are found place-names in *by*, village; *toft*, homestead; and *thorp*[e], farm. More rarely, the same word, in form *trop*, from which comes *Thrupp*, is of OE origin, and Northamptonshire, being a border area, has both forms. Loatland Wood near Braybrooke is from a rare O Norse *laut*, probably meaning 'incline', and *lundr*, wood, hence 'the wood of the hollows'.

Dialect words of Scandinavian origin include *gline*, glance secretly or furtively; *kell* for caul, sometimes used also for a cataract on the eye; *laughter*, pron. lawter, a sitting of eggs; *pismire*, ant, and the very well-known shoe-trade term *skive*, to pare the edges of leather. *Tek* and *mek* for *take* and *make* can be heard at Spratton, Daventry, Kettering and Bozeat, probably the southern limit of this sound, heard throughout the north of England. *Rig*, in the little rhyme, is a form of 'ridge' common in the north, but known in this county. As time went on the two races intermingled. Some place-names became Scandinavianised.

> 'We know that in the tenth century Badby was called in-differently *Baddanburh* and *Baddanby*. . . . Other Northamptonshire examples of the same change are to be found in Naseby, Thornby and Kirby (Hall) in Gretton. . . . Much the most likely explanation of the Ashby names is that they represent earlier Ashton names. . . .'
>
> *PNN* pp. xxii, xxiii.

OE *burh, burg* means fort or fortified place, often referring to a Roman fort.

The two languages had merged into one by the time that the next great invasion took place in 1066.

The Norman Conquest brought another language to England. Norman French was derived from Latin and influenced by Scandinavian, as English had been. The conquerors spoke a different language from that of the conquered. Yet it was William's agents who provided a matchless record of life in eleventh-century English villages, from their names down to the last fishpond and pig, as they painstakingly gathered information for the Domesday Survey. Most present-day Northamptonshire villages are recorded in the Domesday Book, finished in 1086, nine hundred years ago.

Locally we have the O Fr. *salceie* 'abounding in willows' as the forest name Salcey, and Delapré, 'in the meadow'. Later street-names were prefaced by le—*le Collegelane, le Marehole* [Mayorhold now] and *le Berwardstrete*. This was one of the oldest recorded street-names and must have been where a keeper of performing bears lived. The loss of this name a few years ago is regrettable, especially as no steps were taken to preserve it in any way. Kettering, as well as Northampton had *le Newelond,* and Wellingborough, *le Chepyngstede,* 'the market place'. Cf the 'Chipping' villages of the Cotswolds and elsewhere.

In the country, villages acquired an addition to their names, as barons of Norman descent were given land and overlordship. So, in Barton Seagrave, Weston Favell, Thorpe Mandeville and else-where, a Norman-French family name, perhaps Anglicised as time went on, followed the English or Danish place-name.

Present day local pronunciations often go back to an older form of a name. Older people who still call Ashton, near Roade, *Ayshen,* are using the name recorded in 1311. Similarly, Chelveston was *Chelston* in 1689 and all the following local names, still used or known, were recorded at various dates from the fifteenth to the eighteenth centuries. *Deynton,* Denton; *Halston,* Harlestone; *Olmby,* Holdenby; *Raanstrup,* Ravens-thorpe; *Rance,* Raunds; *Rowell,* Rothwell; *Sylson,* Silverstone; *Sowgrave,* Sulgrave; *Sisheham,* Syresham.

Local Speech

By this time the slow intermingling of the speech of Norman French and English had brought into being a common language, Middle English, which was being written in many varieties as well as being spoken as early as the fourteenth century. London speech rose to prominence with the growing importance of the city itself, and was becoming accepted as standard. At this point, Northamptonshire had a part to play. London English was influenced by the speech of workers moving to the capital from our own county and from Bedfordshire and Huntingdonshire. Those who stayed at home carried on talking in their own way, so regional dialect and Standard English grew up side by side for many centuries, the one eroded and the other strengthened by such factors as the Industrial Revolution, the growth of transport, the spread of education and, in this century, the influence of the media.

How much remains? Something like the following conversation may—just—still be heard, somewhere in Northampton, by those who have ears to hear.

'Allo, stranger—aint see yer f'r a good while—are yer bin bad?

Ah, a bit *middlin'*, what wi' *the screws* and *the face-ache.* 'ow a you then, gal?

Well, bedder'n I were two *month* agoo with all that bronical trouble. I were *abed* a week wi' that, y' know. 'Ow's your chap these days?

Oo, 'e's up the lotment most o' the time now 'even when *it rains*—one thing, we do get some nice taters—not like some on 'em you buy—all gone *sapy.* It all 'elps—things don't get no cheaper.

No, they don't gal—makes yer *frit* t' look at some o' the prices.

Yis—I reckon kids' clothes'r about the wust. Our gal 'as a job t' manage with 'er *bab,* but we 'elp 'er out—*a bit of 'elp's worth a lot o' pity,* they say, don't they?

Ne' mind, we wouldn't be without 'em, would we?

I dunno s' much, some days. 'Ere, are yer got the time? Taint *five an' twenty* to, is it, yit, 'cus Om got me bus t' catch—I shall be late *else.* Om godder get our tea and give our Terry *'isn* when 'e comes in and see as everything's cleared up. . . .

'Ere, 'ang on—doin' a lot o' *scrattin'* about, aint yer?

Yis, well, I goo out with our Glad, y' know, a Satdys, and shiz a bit p'tic'lar. You should see 'er *glinin'* about. I don't want 'er t' think Om *slummocky,* even if we do *live in muck and comfort* sometimes. Anyway, shladder goo. T'da.

T'da, ma duck. 'Ere's y' bus *a-comin'.*

Dialect words are disappearing fast, but most of the ones in this exaggerated passage are well-known. Older forms of speech are seen in *the face-ache* [toothache]; *the screws* [rheumatism]; *five-and-twenty; it rains,* rather than 'it is raining'; *abed, a-comin'. Bab* is an older form than babe or baby; '*I were*' is from ON *ek var*

[I was]; *hisn, hern, ourn* and *theirn* were once the correct form, as *mine* still is. The double negative–'things don't get no cheaper'– was once accepted. Shakespeare used it from time to time, as in *The Merchant of Venice,* when Salarino says 'Not in love neither?' (1 i 47) and Lorenzo 'Nor is not moved with concord of sweet sounds' (V i 84). Notice also 'two *month*'. Singular rather than plural is often used for year, week, foot, yard, mile. The verb 'to be' is used for 'to have'–'*are* yer bin bad'. The present tense is often used for the past–'aint *see* yer f'r a good while'.

Here and there some older usages remain, perhaps only as a memory, very pleasing to the ear.

> 'I grew the cyclamen from seed *before* the window. . . . We used to walk from Collingtree to Rothersthorpe to visit our auntie, and she used to say "Come on in, my wenches" and she'd sit us down on stools and give us bread-and-butter and home-made blackcurrant jam.'   *Mrs York,* Northampton.

> 'People would go to their neighbours' doors and call "Are yer *within*?" '   *Mrs Loretta Smith,* Little Houghton.

> 'When the children made too much noise, my grandfather would say "*Done, done*". ["Have done."]'
> *Mr D Pattison,* Rushden.

These terms are clearly of the past. Some words which are slipping out of everyday use at the present time, to be replaced by others, are these. Readers may know others or may not agree with my findings.

Ashbox, barber, charabanc, closet [lavatory], clothes-horse, coal-hod, false, used of people, finger-post, flashlight, form [bench], frock, gramophone, hark, looking-glass, mangle, nightgown, night school, nosegay, pillar-box, pudding-bag street, rooster, scurf, slaughterhouse, springtime, summertime, wintertime, vexed, wadding, wash-house, wireless, yard [garden].

The Oxford English Dictionary, complete text (1979) lists the following words as rare, archaic, obsolescent or obsolete. It is difficult in some cases to be precise, but they are known, often used, in Northampton the county and its borders today. Some have a different meaning from their standard one. All are listed in the glossary.

Rare, *backen, fetch, starved.* Rare *or obsolete, hinder time.* Archaic, *whit, wunt.* Obsolete or dialect, *fur, keach.* Queried as obsolete, *bring up, quick.* Obsolescent, *baver/bever.*

Obsolete, *about, act, apern, aside, bate, bethink, budget, bullies, burgoo, chitty, dough* v., *else, ett, farden, flagbasket, give it in, gret, jalop, leer, madhead, pigeon, present, say, snitch, stomachful, street, thrail, tret, wallop, wed, wibble, wicket, word* v. Listed as obsolete in *EDD* are *bough-house, wicker.*

Though in general the daily use of dialect words and usages lessens all the time, the sound of local speech survives quite strongly. It is characterised by long vowels, sometimes of a rather toneless quality, the running together of words—'*Shladder goo*' and a falling intonation at the end of a sentence.

In Kettering, Wellingborough and the other smaller industrial towns of that area, there is a very distinct local accent, once joyously celebrated by Mr. Reginald Norman.

> *'. . . the rich mine you struck so long ago.'*
> *RWN* of Rushden.

In July 1956, Mr Raymond Parkin, editor of the *Northamptonshire Evening Telegraph*, wrote to Mr Reginald Norman.

> 'Can you supply about 20-30 words . . . in the local idiom to go under each of these drawings by Nev? (Mr Peter Nevitt of Wellingborough). What I should like is for the pointed comments of *Air Ada* to be quoted wherever readers foregather. I am assuming that you have not exhausted the rich mine you struck so long ago. . . .'

Born in Northampton in 1901, RWN lived in Rushden from the age of five. He contributed at least one thousand two hundred pieces of verse—'the rich mine'—to the *Rushden Echo and Argus*, and some thousands of Air Ada's 'Conversation Pieces' for the *Northamptonshire Evening Telegraph*.

He died in 1962, and in his obituary, approved by RWN himself two years earlier, Mr Parkin wrote

> 'No-one ever caught more exactly the manner of speech of the native-born Rushdenite or set it out phonetically with such skill.'

He had an enthusiastic following, and people still talk of him today with great affection. Here is one of his verses and four 'Conversation Pieces'. *Air Ada*, in Nev's drawings, is the one 'with 'er mouth alwus open', her friend Mawwud the silent listener.

With acknowledgments and thanks to *Mrs L Norman* of Rushden.

"Nye sez, 'No Missiz,' I sez, 'We ent noways posh,' I sez. 'Nitent much ovome wheer yaw frit t'walk on the carpit, alean on a cushion cairse ya wrinklit,' I sez."

" 'Vellike men is abit awkud nownagin,' e sez. 'But women what ent s'young as what they was is difficult mawsley awlus,' e sez. Thole faggut."

"Yis, Mawwud, artreed washtup the dinner things, I toldim e ant scoured the bottoms utha sawwuspans, ne sez, 'Oh,' e sez, 'nammye spozed t'polish the swearword andles anawwul?' e sez. Thole faggot."

"No, Mawwud, if traird gits bad, them what ent sairved note 'll git on bet nurrus whats bin a bit keerful gal."

Air Adas, with thanks to Mrs L Norman of Rushden, whose husband Reginald (RWN) was Air Ada's creator.

AYYA BINNON YOLDY?
HAVE YOU BEEN ON YOUR HOLIDAY?

Allo gal, ows things agooin?
>Hallo gal, how are things going?

Betchenerd my bitta noos—
>I bet you haven't heard my bit of news —

Lor, what's appened t'yer nawwuz?
>Lord, what's happened to your nose?

Yent bin gooin on the booze?
>You haven't been going on the booze?

Juss come back frm Yarmuth, ayya?
>Just come back from Yarmouth, have you?

'Ot it were, anall, I bet.
>Hot it was, as well, I bet.

Sunshine meksha roldy, dawnit?
>Sunshine makes your holiday, doesn't it?

Lungs there's awlus plenty tet.
>So long as there's always plenty to eat.

We booked up soon arter Chrismus,
>We booked up soon after Christmas.

Worthin—plairce called 'Oshun Voo'
>Worthing—place called 'Ocean View'.

Yuh, an now my chapsa sayin
>Yes, and now my husband's saying

Zow a dawwnt wanna goo.
>As how [that] he doesn't want to go.

Were, thas juss like men, gal, ennit?
>Well, that's just like men, gal, isn't it?

Maddim like it every year.
>I've had him like it every year.

Wussna kids—withem yuknawlus
>Worse than kids—with them you can always

Cloutum one asida thear.
>Hit them one at the side of the ear.

Were, we'll goo—we awlus are done.
>Well, we'll go—we always have done.

Summut, ennit, tevva rest?
>It's something, isn't it, to have a rest?

Sevvin grub got ready for yer,
>It's having food got ready for you,

Thas the bit what soots me best.
>That's the bit that suits me best.

Slovely, ennit, tave no cookin?
>It's lovely isn't it, to have no cooking?

No need turry, tatta coo,
>No need to hurry, to have to queue,

Yuh, an when we're ad *we* grub, gal,
>Yes, and when we've had our food, gal,

Thrent no washin up t'do.
>There isn't any washing up to do.

Were, sno good, I slatter goo, gal, kent stan *chopsin* ere all day,
>Well, it's no good, I shall have to go, gal, I can't stand talking here all day.

Fowern come an thrent no dinner,
>If *ourn* [ours, my family] come, and there isn't any dinner,

Dawwunt know what Dad'll say.
>I don't know what Dad'll say.

Were, s' lung, gal, glad I seed ya,
>Well, so long, gal, I'm glad I saw you,

Yuh, I'm gotta jine this coo—
>Yes, I've got to join this queue,

Nif I kent come round fore tholdy,
>And if I can't come round before the holiday,

V ellike think to senja voo.
>I'll very likely think to send you a view.

Ent, shent, kent are the well-known local forms of isn't, shan't, can't. The time is July, 1949. There are still queues, four years after the end of the war.

Field and Minor Names

'There's Ten Furlong, Middle Furlong, Lambcuts, and there's a field at Brafield called London Way—well, the bullock road went to London, didn't it?'

Children from some two hundred schools in the county assisted in the collection of field-names for *The Place-names of Northamptonshire (PNN)*, published in 1933. How good it would be if another survey could be made now, fifty years on. Hundreds of fields and stretches of woodland have been lost in the various towns' expansion schemes, but some of the names are still remembered, and may be preserved in the names of roads on the new estates.

The Wrongs, a farm at Sibbertoft, is named from the furrows of the old open fields which had existed for centuries. In the open field the unit of cultivation was a *land*, a strip of land, one third of an acre in area. Furlongs—the word is common in field-names— were not lengths, but areas, groups of *lands* with the furrows running parallel. At *The Wrongs* these furrows curved or twisted in some way, or were ploughed crookedly, which is what the name means. The same effect is sometimes why a field has *Rye* (wry) in its name.

Some names have to do with the level of the land. *Hanger* [OE *hangra*, a wood on a steep slope] and names like Hanging Houghton, Deanshanger and Shutlanger, 'wood where shuttles were got' denoted first, a slope and later, a wood. OE *hlinca*, another word for 'hilly slope' gives the field-names *Links*, *Lynches* or *Lunch*. The hill in question may not be a very big one—it just seemed so to the ploughman plodding up and down in the mud. *Rowler* is OE *ruh law*, 'rough hill', while *Smith* in a field-name may mean 'smooth'.

Hunger or *Hungry* refers to the type of soil and so does *Catsbrain*, rough stony clay. *Pike* is a piece of land running to a point and *pightle* can have the same meaning, or, like *pingle*, can mean a small enclosure. A *slade* is a valley [OE *slaed*] *Balks* were grass strips between furlongs. A small field, especially one near a farm or manor, is a *close*, locally *clus*, and a meadow next to it may be given the same name, so Ten Acre Meadow need not be of that size, but is next to Ten Acre Close. Animal names are quite common—fox, *neat* [cattle] and *'ug* [hog] and so are the names of crops, including flax [sometimes *flex* or *lin*], hemp and woad [*Wad*]. *Mere*, sometimes in the form *more*, is a boundary [OE *land-gemaere*] but *mor* is a swamp. *Spring* in a name may be a spring of water or new growth in woodland. *Stockings* are lands reclaimed from woodland.

A name such as *Poor's Lot* or *Charity* shows that the rent from the field was used for charity. A distant field was sometimes given the name of a battlefield or place overseas. A *washbrook* was used for washing sheep or clothes. Here then are some Northamptonshire field and minor names still known at the present time.

Alderton

> Rag Fair, Rags were fetched from Northampton and sold as fertiliser.

Ashton

> Bar Hill, Barley Hill *PNN*. Gunhole, from an Anglo-Scand. woman's name, Gunhild *(PNN)*

Barton Seagrave

> Goosepasture, later Gas Street and then Meadow Lane.

Boddington, Upper and Lower

> Blackdown; Buckle, Buck well *PNN*; Cleavers Ground; Leatherpits; Old Herden; Peasland, Peasground and Pedley, all places where peas were grown; Peewit; Pingle; The Crook; The Pleck.
>
> *Mrs Ruth Hill*, Boddington.

Bozeat

> Fish Alley; Pudding-bag Lane; Spangle Row.
> Gripes Hole; Fulwell; Roses Span; Banley (beanfield) Voting Field; Linchills; Dungee; Smith Hill (Smooth Hill *PNN*) Stoken Hill; Kape Mere; Pundle Close; Tow Mowing; Canada; Oxground.

Brackley

> Stockings.

Braybrooke

> Ainsborough; Banky; Charity, Flevells; Foxcroft; Foxholes; Game Fold; Granny's; Hovel Field, Lower and Top Hooks; Kestings; Madcraft; North and South Hermitage and Hermitage Meadow; Over Corner; Poor's Close; Prospect; Purgatory; Puddin' End; Realms; Spion Kop; Tofts and Little Tofts; The Caudells; The Seeds and Big Seeds.
> From a field-map filled in by local farmers in 1975, sent to me by *Mrs F Goodman*, Braybrooke.

Brigstock

> Break Hill; Cockerhead, cock clearing *PNN*; Hungry Hill; Larbrook, Old Head Hill; Samby Sykes, O*Esic*, a water-course; Silver Hill; Sudborough Great Greens; Van Diemen's Land; Catshead Wood; Cherry Lap Wood, *shenele lappe*, c 1300, which may mean 'bright clearing or wood' *PNN*; Harry's Park; Farming Woods, prob. a piece of woodland held at a

ferme (rent) *PNN*; Laundimere Woods, OE *landgemaere*, boundary; Maunterley Wood, may be a compound of *manteltre*, the big wooden beam forming the lintel of an open fire place + *leah*. *PNN*; Stephen Oak, a boundary tree; Stubby Stiles, Path or stile by the place which has been *stubbed* (various meanings of which one is 'cut down to the roots' *PNN*); Luscotes Lodge, OE *hlose*, pigsty + cote. Pigsty cottages; The Bocase Tree, a boundary tree. The church tower, below the spire, is Saxon, and was perhaps built as a refuge in the great forest of Rockingham which once covered the area.

Mr John E Bailey, Brigstock.

Brixworth

Bretch Close and Meadow Bretch = land broken up for tillage, *PNN*; Damsel and Damsel Meadow, Demmeswell, *PNN*; Brackenborough; First, Second and Third Kid; Salthills.

Mr Peter Alcock, Brixworth.

Clipston

Acre Dykes; Bellropes. Rent from the field provided an endowment for supplying bellropes for the church; Brierley Dam; Nineteen Boys, said locally to be so-called because it took a man and nineteen boys to *spud* thistles in the field, but cp. Fr. *bois*, wood; The Twitch. Couch-grass, OE *cwice*, is widely called *twitch*; Water Balks.

Mr J Morley, Clipston.

Cottesbrooke

Ashes; Shutterdown. This village is in Pytchley Hunt country. The following are names of spinneys left when woodland was cleared, or planted to give cover to foxes and gamebirds. Cotthill; Foalfoot; Harwich Home; Ketchlow; Mitley; Moss Hall; Pitmore Hill; Pole; Rickleborough. Also Smallthorns Wood and Drummer's Hole Copse.

Mrs Pamela Wykes, Spratton.

Easton-on-the-hill

Slate Drift. The village is near Collyweston, where slate was mined.

Farthinghoe

Cockley Break; Crabull, Crab well; Ham; Oven; Rough Piece; Stonepit Close. There was also an osier bed here in the early years of the century and a pond where the Rector bred trout.

Miss Barbara Adkins, Banbury.

Finedon

Shitten Alley. The Tainty, the tenter yard, where newly milled cloth was hung.

Mr J L Bailey, author of
Finedon, otherwise Thingdon.

Furtho

Crowgrove; Eyrr Stocking.

Great Doddington

Cut-throat Lane.

Great Houghton

The old green lane.

Greatworth

Dairy Ground; Langlands; Obble; Over Mead; Ovver Ground; Poor's Close; Riding Gale; Seed Close; The Aughms. Fields which have lost their boundaries are Bondage; Irons Corner; Redground. The last two fields were once quarried for ironstone. Two house names are Bacon House and The Wickets. *Mrs Pamela Carpenter*, Greatworth.

Greens Norton

Brickle Ground; Modley Gate. OE *mot-leah*, clearing where meetings are held. *PNN*.

Harpole

Banky; Big and Little Pikes; Blackleys; Callowell [bare hill]; Damons and Bottom Damons; Flitnill. Flithill in Braybrooke is 'dispute hill'. It lies on the parish boundary; Foxholes; Grimy; Halfway; Heygates Cleaf; Holts 1, 2, 3 and 4. Hillymere; Lakes 1, 2, 3 and 4, perhaps from OE *lacu*, small stream or pool; Martin's Goal or Gold; Mere, first and second; Metcraft; Neats Hill; Row Dykes. OE*ruh*, rough; Scarborough; Seeds Ground; Slade; Stockin Leys; Town Pool; Ungerull. Hunger Hill; Wookull. Wook Hill; Wung 1 and 2 and Scrivens Wung (small enclosure, often of marshy land); From a field-map lent by *Mr A Clements*, Harpole.

Gadshill; Little Tongues; Riding Hill; Summerhouse.
Mr William Burt, Harpole.

Kimbolton

The Stattis. The hiring fair was held by statute.

Kislingbury

Blakemore; Blithe Meadow; Bury Grass; Charity 1, 2, 3 and 4; Dukes Green; Knitter's Grave; Lakes; Marehead, from its shape; Pride's piece; Spout Furlong; Stockwell; Team Spout, a stream; The Camp, a bridle road to Hunsbury.

Mr Roy Payler, Kislingbury.

Litchborough

Christmas Hill; Corporation Close—it belonged to the Corporation of Sons of the Clergy; Cuckoo pen; Dark or Devil's Corner; Elderstumps; Lower Breeks; Lunch; Marthern, may thorn; Paradise; Pinfold, penfold, an enclosure for animals; Stunpit, stonepit; Warfren, Way Furlong; Winkles.

Mr William Jones, Litchborough.

Little Houghton

'There's *Ten Furlong, Middle Furlong, Lambcuts* and there's a field at Brafield called *London Way*— well, the *bullock road* went to London, didn't it? Then there's *Double Hedges* and '*Angulls* [Hang hills], weren't there, and there's a field against Billing Station called the Windmill Field, so I says t' Dick Hollowell, 'D'yer reckon there was a windmill in there?' and he says 'I'll show yer' so we went down, and old Dick—he's a droll old boy, y'know—'There y'are' he says 'you see that round bit—now that were the base o' the windmill'. I says 'Well, blow me' and that were the Windmill Field. Lord knows how many year ago that's bin.

Rodyshus Spinney—they're getting it down now— and back o' there, there's a field called *Catsbrain,* up *Cracknuts* way. *Deadlands* goes nearly up to *Spoilbank,* and between there, that's *Claxwells,* and the other side, that's *Stackyard.* Then there were *Sauceridge*—it were fourteen acres, then there were *Little Furlong* and '*Ell Edge.*

They've just found a well in the old rickyard. I pumped water out o' that well for years (at a hand-pump) and never knew where it was, but the old Grand-dad, he knew where it was. A man drowned

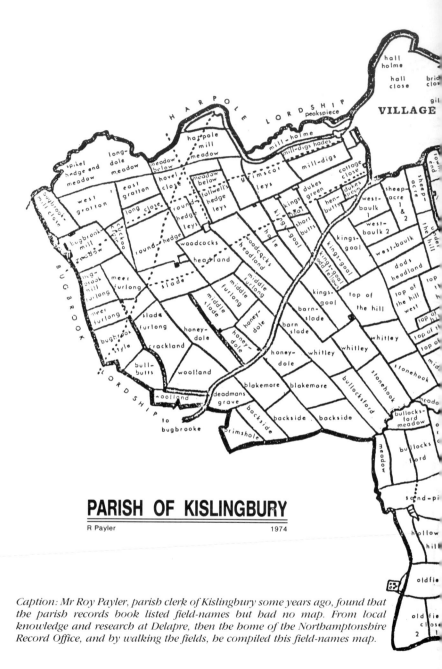

PARISH OF KISLINGBURY

R Payler   1974

Caption: Mr Roy Payler, parish clerk of Kislingbury some years ago, found that the parish records book listed field-names but had no map. From local knowledge and research at Delapre, then the home of the Northamptonshire Record Office, and by walking the fields, he compiled this field-names map.

himself in that well–lived in the *Mere*. When we walked through the rickyard years ago, if there was no water for the animals, we'd give it a pump.

Well, I were in a pub at Brafield one night, and old Jim White–he were a poacher you know–and he were telling us all the names of the fields, 'cause he worked on a farm. And when old Jim White died, Harry Kent, he says 'Ah we shan't a nobody t'tell us now what the weather's gunner be, nor the names o' the fields, now old Jim White's gone'. Old Jim had been an old poacher, y'see'.

Mr Jack Meyer, Little Houghton.

Also from or near Little Houghton

Campions Ground; Collier's Dip, a dip in the land between Denton and Yardley Hastings, where a Miss Collier lived. This modern name was formed in the same way as many ancient place-names were, by a combination of a personal name and a natural feature. Great Brington was *Bryni's farm, PNN*. Glass Bottle; Kingcraft or croft; Nine Springs; Ox Ground; Pert'nells, Big and Little; Snipe; Tay Bridge; Washbrook; Wolluth, Top and Bottom, Walworth.

Mrs J Evans, Mrs Loretta Smith, Little Houghton.

Milton Malsor

Anchor Terrace, where anchorites or hermits lived, Rev B L Evans, *The Story of Milton Malzor*; Clannell; Hempland; Hob End; Stockwell; Workhouse Yard.

Moulton

Big and Little Stocking; Botany Bay; Catbanks; Crow Close; Great and Little Grove; 'Ug'ole, Hoghole; Keresy Mere; Lowsy Bush; Lunch; Marewater; Sallway; Stone Brig; Tickey Hole.

Miss Margaret Lattimer,
Mr Robert Eady, Moulton.

Naseby (near)

Clot Hill; Scrawge or Scrooge Hill.

Newport Pagnell

The Wad.

Northampton

Baulmsholm, a small island in the Nene between the Gas Works and Carlsberg Brewery. Late OE *holm*,

small island; The first element means 'tree'. Mod.
German *baum,* tree; Calvesholm, 'small island with
calves', at the entrance to Becket's Park, formerly
Cow Meadow; Cow lane, road leading to Cow
Meadow, later Swan Street; Danes Camp, local name
for the Iron Age hill-fort at Hunsbury and the green
lane leading to it from east and west; Derngate,
originally the name of a town gate, the first element
being apparently OE *dierne,* hidden; Foot Meadow,
to the south of West Bridge; Gas Meadow, near Gas
Works; Ladybridge; Midsummer Meadow; Millers
Meadow; Newland; Plum Lane, now Park Avenue
North; Seaby's Footpath, now Trinity Avenue;
Gipsy Lane, now Kingsthorpe Grove. The Clay-
banks, hillocks formed when the railway tunnel at
Hunsbury was excavated; The Daisy Field, just past
the Rothersthorpe Road railway bridge; The Dog
Kennels, between Ransome Road and Harding-
stone; The Six Fields, between St James and Far
Cotton.

Piddington

Abbotsford; Awcut, Hall Cut. A footpath to the Hall
runs through the field; The Lusome, apparently
from the growing of lucerne; The Washbrook.

Pury End

The Merrymaking, a green under a tree; The sunken
lanes, sites of earlier village streets.

Pytchley

Brogsdale; Peashill.

Rushden

Packman's Puzzle; Rotten Row.

Scaldwell

Canon Hill, Canon Hill Meadow. Cricksty or stie,
Ston Pikes, Hill Pikes.

Sibbertoft

Banky; Bottom and Top Wrongs; Coombes Mill
Furlong; Cromwell Corner and Meadow. Naseby is
a few miles away; Dumpling; Fennylands;
Follerwell; Middle Mill Furlong; Poor Close;
Pudding bag; Redmill; The Coombes. This field is
left as an SSSI, site of special scientific interest, for the

preservation of wild life and plants; Westlongs; Whitegrass.   *Mr J Hart*, Sibbertoft.

Spratton

Broadmead Balk; Greenwood Balk; Rusick Balk; Brickle Meadow; Bunker's Hill; Foxholes; Hangman's Barn; Landymore, OE *landgemaere*, land-boundary; Lung Stunny, Long Stony, believed to have been the quarry for stone used in the making of the turnpike road from Northampton to Welford; Pitmore Hill; Pon Close; Sykiemore; *Um Clus*, Home Close; Wadells, Woad Hills.
Mr Ray Wykes, Spratton.

Sulby

Big Baxter; Court Green; Rowler; Wicks Hill; Wood Piece.   *Mr R Chance*, Sulby.

Thenford

Astwells; Brickhill Knob; Hayward's Meadow; Houseground; Old Cover; Seedground; The Banky; The Ploughing.
Mr Arthur Seckington, Greatworth.

Towcester

Bathground; Cold Bath; Jetty Close.

Welford

Downton; Little, Mid and Great Hallfields.

Wellingborough

Long Marsh; Kruger's Grave; Radwell; 'ug'ill, Hog Hill; White Horse Yard; White Well.

Weston-by-Weedon Lois

Face Lane; Foxenhill; Great, Little, Middle, Top and Osborn's Wild, rough outlying fields; Gullimer; Gunmer's Hole, a small wood of fir trees; Handpost Ground; Link Piece; Poor's Lot; Rowler; Smithenhill; Sulgrave Ground; Wheatlands; Whitmill Leys. Other forms are Whitemoor, White-male, Perhaps from à lost OE *mealo*, stones, gravel, *PNN*.   *Mr Arthur Seckington*, Greatworth.

Wollaston

Field-names of several centuries can be found in *Wollaston, Portrait of a Village*, David Hall.

Wolverton
> Happy Morn; Pancake Hills, deposits of earth from canal-making.

Wootton
> Blackymore.

Yardley Gobion
> Botany Bay; Little London.

Yardley Hastings
> Cold Oak; Grimpsey Copse; Pinchcut.

> Two very interesting collections come from a few miles west and east of the county borders.

Banbury
> Beargarden; Franklin and Cow Franklin; Drift Way; Gallows Fuz, Furze; Leg-o'-Mutton; Pesthouse; Sanfoin; Salt Way; Turnpike Cottage; Waterloo; Wildmere.
>> *Lt-Col Yates,* Guildford, *Mr A Jones,* Banbury.

Wilstead, near Bedford
> Bermuda; Blackbirds; Brick-kiln Pastures; Charity Field; Cow Hovel; Dane Farm; Driftway; Herds-croft; Jerusalem; Ragged Breeches; Van Diemen's Land; Welshes.
>> *Mr Maurice Boston,* Wilstead, Beds.

THE OLD STREET ROAD AND THE GREEN LANE

Two ancient roads run through Northamptonshire, older than many of its towns and villages.

> 'My grandfather used to call the Watling Street "the old *street* road".' *Mr A Clements,* Harpole.

'*Street*' once meant highway, paved road [Late L *via strata*] and the Strattons and Stratfords were the farms by the road and the fords which had to be crossed.

The other road is harder to find, though the winding Banbury Lane is part of it, and so is the green lane through Hunsbury [Danes] Camp. It continues along the Mere [Mere Way] and the Newport Pagnell road and once was joined by other roads, the *bullock road* up from the Nene Valley and the *dirty road* from Ashton to the south. Spread across the county were other roads and tracks, often called *drift* or *drove,* wide-verged for grazing on the way, green lanes for preference, these being softer to the feet of men and animals, avoiding roads which were turnpiked, because of the tolls which had to be paid.

The main drovers' road of which Banbury Lane, the Mere and the Newport Pagnell road were parts was a route along which sheep, cattle and geese were driven from Wales into the Midlands and thence to London and the south-east coast. Salt from Cheshire was also carried along these ancient trackways, and names such as Drift Way, Green Lane, Welsh Road and Salt Way are found along their routes.

'The idea was to *drift* [drive] them along gently so they arrived in London in good condition.'

Mr Angus Dudley, Clifton Shefford, Bedfordshire.

'An old man's father at Priors' Hardwick used to say that when the drovers got to London End there they used to borrow a bucket to milk the cows. They then gave the milk away. . . . Calves were sometimes carried in sacks on the backs of the cows.'   *The Welsh Road and the Drovers,* John H Drew.

Dusty Hill Road at Brigstock was a drift road and Chase Park Lodge had a noticeboard which read '*Cattle taken in*'. Here, ailing cattle could be rested and tended before resuming their long walk. Inns, one about every four miles on some parts of the road, as well as farms and cottages served the needs of men and animals on their long journey. One woman said she always moved or hid everything she could, and gave the men only '*a stand-up breakfast*'. Others were more accommodating, like Coffee Moll at Padbury in Buckinghamshire, who dispensed coffee and other comforts to the drovers, despite the indignation of the local womenfolk.

Some Welsh farmers bought land in Northamptonshire to save the cost of renting fields, and it is noticeable that there are plenty of Welsh names among the county's farmers. Stock was bought and sold along the way, but the great clearing-house was the cattle-market at Banbury, the largest in Europe. With the coming of the railways, animals arrived and left there by train.

'I remember the old drovers, especially Mr Waters. He and his dog would meet the cattle-trains at the station in the early hours of the morning. The black Irish store-cattle would be unloaded, and Mr Waters would herd them by just walking round and talking to them, and then—truly—he would *lead* them to the fields at the top of our street, the *Causeway*.

At night I have woken to the clop-clop of cattle-hooves and the soft 'Cup, cup' as Mr Waters walked ahead of the cattle, his dog in the rear. *No stick.* I can see the moonlight and starlight on the slate roofs of the houses and on the black backs of the cattle and on the drover's shiny brown leather leggings.

Mrs Sonia Glenister, Australia.

Names and Nicknames

The Rose of Sharon
John the Planter and Half-egg Webb

'Once we were mowing near the bottom of Liza Dodie's garden and she said to us, "Ah, boy, I 'ad five children and I found a name out the Bible for all on 'em. There's Rose, the Rose of Sharon; Solomon in all 'is *glowry*; Joseph in 'is *cooat* o' many colours; Mary who chose the better part, and *Dairvid* who killed Goliath. Ah, boy, an' if I'd 'ad another, I'd a found a name out of the Bible for 'im an' all".'   *Mr Percy Foster,* Pury End.

Many devout parents such as Liza chose Biblical names for the children and Old Testament names were very popular. There are some among the people named in the lively couplets below. All of them lived in Brigstock at the turn of the century.

> Isaac Sturgess has hurt his shins,
> Solomon Rawson burns the skins.
>
> > [He was a mole-catcher]
>
> Mrs Sturgess runs the boys.
> Harry Gadsby sells the toys.
>
> Arthur Freeman sells the bread,
> Mrs Gray is off her head.
>
> Joe East's the town crier,
> Biddy East's an old liar.

Ferdy Johnson grinds the axes,
George Lee Mace collects the taxes.

Eliza Rowe is tall and slender,
Levi Bailey's the britches mender.

> [breeches. He was a tailor]
> *Mr John E Bailey,* Brigstock.

Patience, Mercy, Faith, Hope, Charity and Comfort were quite common, and Temperance Hull signed a receipt at Holcot in 1851.

'Everybody had a nickname years ago. They were real characters in those days.'

This is said so often, and I am sure there is truth in it. In most communities, too, there were several families with the same name, and Christian names could be duplicated.

'There were so many Billinghams that most of them were known by their nicknames. *Dozer* was a shoemender, *Harborough Jack* worked at Market Harborough, *Eli John* kept the Co-op, *Tom Fan* looked like his sister Fan—and he used to go round the villages on his bike, selling yeast. There was *Gawmy* and *Fimmy, Lal* and *Tommy Bunjell.* He was called that because his hair was cut like a *bunjell* [basin]. There was *Blower* Watson, father and son, and *Dar* was the nickname of several of the Labrum family.'

> *Mr Roy Payler,* Kislingbury.

There were no rules, as the last sentence shows. *Lal* is not really a nickname, but like *Hal,* is short for Harry. Sometimes a Harry was called *Herry*—nearer the original Henry. Usually a nickname takes the place of a Christian name, but not always. In Pury End lived *Rebecca Needful,* who had a large family to keep, *Bill Singer,* a shoemaker with a fine singing voice, Liz *Sniffy* and others. '*A staunch Methodist attender*' nicknamed *Faith* died young and his widow was always called *Liz Faith.* Bill Singer's wife was *Mrs Singer.* This was quite common. Wives took their husbands' nicknames with as little concern as they wore the men's old cloth caps to do the housework, protecting their hair from the dust of raking out the ashes and shaking mats. In Little Houghton, Mrs

Caption right: Brigstock in 1905, showing a man at his shop door, a barber's pole, high-wheeled baby-carriage, a horse, several bicycles, several people and a black cat. NL

Gregory Robinson was *Lizzy Grig* and Mrs Jacob Robinson was *Ann Jacup.*

John the Planter was the second Duke of Montague who, between 1720 and 1740, planted avenues of elms radiating out from his home, Boughton House, near Kettering. The fifth Earl Spencer (1835–1910), a leading Liberal politician from the same family as the present Princess of Wales, was always known as *The Red Earl,* because of his luxuriant red beard.

Harry *Bellus* [bellows] was a blacksmith and *Jacky Suet* was a butcher, both in Pury End. These names are understandable, but the reason for others, like *Half-egg Webb,* a Northampton railwayman, is long forgotten. *Cronje, Joubert* and *Kruger,* Boer War leaders, were the nicknames of three brothers from Little Houghton. In the same village lived *Tweddocks,* so-named from his brave attempt to read the sign '*Trespassers will be prosecuted*'. He gave up after the first word, but the name stuck. Some nicknames recur in different places. One of these is *Daddy,* often the nickname of a schoolmaster, as in the skipping rhyme

> Old *Daddy Dixon's* a nice young man,
> He tries to *learn* you all he can . . .

but sometimes used for any older, fatherly man who took an interest in children.

Here then are some Northamptonshire nicknames, most of them from years gone by, but some in use today.

Cogenhoe
> Rossy Becket, Chaddy, Tommy Cocktoe, Bot Drover, Flint, Frick, Pickles, Salt, Scabber.

Croughton
> Fiddler Badby. *The village of Badby is about twelve miles away.* Bagtie.

Duston
> Breakfast, Nink, Rocky, Shoddy.

Earls Barton
> Echo Bond, Brock Nichols.

Easton-on-the-hill
> Dut Hull, Clocker Perkins *[a clock repairer],* Dromy Phillips, Nutty Pinder, Cobber Sharp, Bungy Sower.
> *Mr H Sharp,* Easton-on-the-hill.

Harpole
> Some nicknames arranged by *Mr A W Clements*
> Bolihole, Doubt-it, Darkie *and* Buffer, Nipper, Nart, Nutter, Waxy *and* Scuffer.

Tarty *and* Tant, Tabby *and* Mock, Timber, Tichbourne, Tippy *and* Yok.

Latch, Dates, Chappy *and* Smack, Chink, Tuke *and old* Lack-lack.

Piddle, Poddin, Tarda *and* Titmouse, Major *and* Midgem, Moody *and* Bounce.

Tegga, Eccles, Wibby *and* Wetty, Strut, Goater, Toff, Tiger *and* Toddy.

Inky, Ami *and* Holy Joe, Rogsy, Nutsy *and* Billy Pooh.

Dozer, Gonk, Spindle *and* Bandy, Pincher, Happy, Sardie *and* Sandy.

Helpston

Butty Chambers, Taddy Lilley.

Irthlingborough

Catch-up, *a drover,* Jimmy *[a name for any man in charge of horses],* Davis, Fub and Spider, *his sons,* Gluepot Ette, Daddy Boofar Farrow, Toey Flawn, Hockey, Jeddah Hooton, Narrow Jeyes, Butterfly Loveday, Sugar Parker, Turpin Pinnock, Rags and bones Rathbone, Waxy Spring, Joby Summerfield, Gopher Ward, Scaize Ward, Ranji Wetherington, Hummock White. *Mr Jack Davis,* Northampton.

Kislingbury

Chance-it, Friday Collins *helped in the pub,* 'Erby Dar, *a smallholder, emptied peoples rubbish,* Billy Fiddler, Billy Knocker, Brassy Leeson *kept the pub,* Fan Trunk, Knocker Ward, Spratty Ward.
Mr Roy Payler, Kislingbury.

Little Houghton

Badger, Biff, Bonkin, Holy Hollowell, Jot, Mardy Marshall, Flaggy Peggums, *who made peg-rugs,* Billy Riddle, *the king of the poachers,* Gig Ringrose, Shaddy Shanty, Shy, *who lived in a barn.*
Mrs Loretta Smith, Little Houghton.

Market Harborough

Friday, Fudge, Mossy, Muster.

Milton Malsor

Dither, Trump, Widdle.

Moulton

      Sal Scrat.

Northampton

      Auntie Blick, *a railwayman,* Redrock Brummel, George Pretty, *who was not good-looking,* Hang-it-on-a-meathook, *who had a large nose,* Mantle Jack, Chelsea Morris, Wingy Townsend, What-are-you-laughing-at, Albert. *He had a long face,* Knocker Wolf. Sticky Jane *used to sell home-made toffee,* Lizzie Drip *was 'well-known in Northampton'.* Sheddy Blake, Ticker Blake, Cloggy Elliott, *who had a wooden leg,* Punch Elliott, Docker *or* Dogger Johnson, Waxy Marriott, Friday Pearce—*his name was Ferdinand,* Nutty Phipps, Bungy Powell, Snifty Smith, *the only woman with a nickname here, as far as I know,* Fanny Sutton, *a railwayman,* Plum Webb, Salty Webb, *real name Walter,* Modder Wilson, Nazzer Wright.

Long Buckby

      Freddy Midnight, *a shoemaker. In his youth he was 'one for the girls'.*

Pury End

      Coffee-pot Charlie, Hellfire Jim *and* Steam Ted, *who were a steam-threshing team, the engine's boiler was shaped like a coffee pot.* Cicely Concealer, Till Copper, Essy Dobber, Lapsy Doll, Daddy Fielding, *a schoolmaster,* Jack Flack, Pugh Kite, Lou Lardy, Lovely, *a man.*

              Mr and Mrs Percy Foster, Pury End.

Spratton

      Clonny Blatchell.

Wellingborough

      Charlie- Chuck-chuck-chuck, *who used to walk to Kettering, drive sheep from there to Finedon and walk home to Wellingborough,* Freddy Few, *a very small bandsman, who could hardly see over his instrument. On parade once, he missed a right turn and asked 'Where's the band gone?'* Go-buck, *who sorted through dust-bins.*

JOHN CLARE

He often stands in fond delay
To see the daisy in his way
And wild weeds flowering on the wall
That will his childish sports recall
Of all the joys that came wi spring
From *The Shepherd's Calendar* (1827) May, line 9.

He was born on 13th July 1793, seventeen days after the death of Gilbert White of Selborne, whose mantle must surely have fallen on him. Though the one was an eighteenth century bachelor cleric and scholar, and the other a farm labourer, partly self-taught, struggling to bring up his family in early nineteenth century rural poverty, there is an evident bond between them.

Each loved the world of nature as seen in his own village. Neither ever wanted to live anywhere else. Selborne was and is southern, idyllic, sheltered by the lush green *Hanger*, a wood on a steep hillside. Helpstone, as Clare always spelt it, lies on the border between Northamptonshire and the fens, in the extreme north-east of the county, as it then was. It is now part of Cambridgeshire. Here, from early childhood, Clare wandered to watch with loving eyes as flowers unfolded and birds built their nests. This was his world and he celebrated it in poetry.

Gilbert White's enthusiastic recording of the natural world of

Caption above: Clare's cottage at Helpston.

his Hampshire parish is in a collection of letters to like-minded friends. *The Natural History of Selborne* is the fourth most published book in the English language. Clare fought an unending battle to get his work published, partly because he so desperately needed money, and partly for recognition of the gift he knew he had. Throughout his troubled life, there were few times when poetry did not pour out of him as from a natural spring. Success was fleeting, and despite the help of friends, much of his life was spent in want. A few hundred pounds might well have given him freedom to write as he wished. As it was, his mind broke down under the strains and conflicts of a divided life and he spent twenty-three years in Northampton Asylum, writing moving and beautiful verse almost until his death in 1864.

It is good to remember him in his own county of Northamptonshire, and good to know that he is now recognised for what he is, at his best a nature poet without peer.

John Clare was the son of a thresher, Parker Clare, and his wife Ann. He had a younger sister, Sophie, and their childhood sounded happy enough, to judge from these extracts from his *Autobiography*, unpunctuated, in Clare's usual style.

I had plenty of leisure but it was the leisure of solitude for my sundays were demanded to be spent in the fields at horse or cow tending. . . . I grew so much into the quiet love of nature's preserves that I was never easy but when I was in the fields passing my sabbaths and leisure with the shepherds and herdboys. . . . Ch 1, p 12.

As to my schooling I think never a year passed me till I was 11 or 12 but three months or more at the worst of times was luckily spared for my improvement first with an old woman in the village and latterly with a master at a distance from it . . . every winter night our once unletterd hut was wonderfully changed in its appearance to a schoolroom . . . my mother would often stop her wheel or look off from her work to urge with a smile of the warmest rapture in my father's face her prophecy of my success. . . . (*John Clare*, Eric Robinson and David Powell eds, 1984), Ch 3, p 430.

I went weeding in the spring with old women listening to their songs and stories. Ch 3, p 19.

In this last simple sentence is evidence of the oral tradition at work, one of the strongest influences of Clare's early years. His own father knew more than a hundred songs and ballads, which he would sing by the fireside in the evening. Granny Bains, the village cowherd and weather-prophet, would sing old songs and tell old stories out in the great open fields, and Clare listened with delight.

He also loved the company of gypsies who camped on Langley Bush, and learned from them how to play the fiddle for the tunes which often served for both songs and dances. There was time for play as well, and these three verses from 'Childhood' will sound familiar to anyone who has ever chalked coloured rings on a top or balanced on one aching leg to play hopscotch or watched little children lovingly making 'nests' in the hope that birds will come and live in them.

> We twirled our tops that spun so well
> They scarce could tumble down
> & thought they twirled as well again
> When *riddled* on the crown. . . .   [coloured red]
>
> Hopskotch too a spur of joy
> We thought the task divine
> To hop and kick the stone right out
> & never touch a line
>
> We made birds nests and thought that birds
> Would like them ready made
> & went full twenty times a day
> To see if eggs were laid

When Clare was twelve years old, his father, until then a strong man, proud of his prowess at wrestling, began to suffer from rheumatism, a common ailment at that time in the damp climate of the ill-drained fens. John had to leave school and work to keep the family going. It was the first of many turning-points in his life where duty pulled one way and his own desires another. He had already met Mary Joyce, a farmer's daughter from Glinton, and delighted in her company, though she was only an eight-year-old child. Now he had to put childhood behind him though he was able to attend nightschool to continue the studies he loved.

There followed a period of finding work where he could, here and there in the district, and another, more exciting turning-point—the reading of a fragment of nature poetry in a borrowed book with some parts missing. It was James Thomson's *Winter*, the first of his *Seasons*, and its natural style made an immediate appeal to young Clare. He twice walked to Stamford to buy a copy for himself. The first walk was on a Sunday—he had not realised

The yellowhammer
'Just by the wooden brig a bird flew up'

the shop would be shut. When the book was in his hands, he knew what he must do–he, too must write in this way.

'I usd to drop down behind a hedge bush or dyke & write down my things upon the crown of my hat . . . my heart burnt over the pleasures of solitude and the restless revels of rhyme.' Ch 5, p 32.

He wrote on the edges of newspaper and the coarse blue and brown paper which wrapped his mother's tea and sugar, for a sheet of writing paper cost three farthings. He made ink with a mixture of 'bruised galls, green copper and a piece of stone-blue shaken and soaked in rainwater'. It eventually ate into the paper and made some of his manuscripts unreadable.

He used dialect sparingly, as here in the opening lines of 'The Yellowhammer's Nest'.

> Just by the wooden *brig* a bird flew up
> *Frit* by the cowboy as he scrambled down
> To reach the misty dewberry. . . .

Frit [frightened] is still used, but *brig*, a northern form of bridge, was not used over most of the county. *Childern* was used within living memory.

> The shutter closed the lamp alight
> The faggot chopt and blazing bright
> The shepherd from his labour free
> Dancing his *childern* on his knee.
> > *The Shepherd's Calendar*, January.
> > 'A Cottage Evening' 1. 1-4.

Keck for cow-parsley and *hairiff* for goosegrass are known throughout the county.

> The *haychat* makes her *slighty* bed
> Dead *airiff* stalks and horses' hair

Couch-grass was *twitch* to Clare and still is over most of the county, and we called the poppy *head-ache* when we were children, as Clare did.

There are still country people who know the long-tailed tit as *bumbarrel,* from the shape of its nest, and call the ant *pismire* or *emmet* and the ladybird *cowlady* [Clare's *ladycow*]. Many readers will know that a *pancheon* is a large earthenware bowl with a wide top, used for mixing dough or for wine-making, that *disabill* is a state of untidiness in one's dress [French *déshabillé*], that *puthering* is puffing out smoke. The shepherd was 'smoaking glad his *puthering* pipe'.

I heard an old lady complaining about the *cat-ice* outside her door last winter, and my mother always said that someone with a miserable face looked *like snow in harvest*.

'Began to *learn* a poor lame boy the common rules of arithmetic and find him very apt and willing to learn.' Journal 12th October 1824.

ME *lernen* does indeed mean both learn and teach. Clare was simply carrying on the usage of centuries, though no doubt his publisher and early critics winced at yet another 'provincialism'. Dialect at that time was ignored by most scholars, its linguistic, historical and social lessons as yet unlearned. Clare's use of his native speech was a literary nine days' wonder, soon to be dismissed by the London arbiters of taste.

Some three or four hundred dialect words and phrases may be found in Clare's writing and the words on p 288 are still known in Northamptonshire.

Working, drinking, writing, womanising, sometimes in despair and sometimes with high hopes, Clare grew to manhood. Poverty took its toll. His father was so crippled with rheumatism or arthritis that he could hardly walk, though he still earned a few shillings at roadmending. Clare often felt ill, but he accepted responsibility for the family and found work where he could, even, for a time, in the Militia. England was at war and there were rumours that Napoleon's troops had landed and had reached Northampton. In any case, there was a bounty of two guineas.

Clare was not cut out to be a soldier and his brief military career is chiefly remarkable for his knocking down a corporal, 'a little louse-looking man', who repeatedly made fun of him.

Home, when he returned, was no longer the same. The enclosures seemed a worse threat than Buonaparte. Common land and the old open fields were being sold off and enclosed. Many former tenant-farmers lacked the means to buy, and the loss of grazing rights on the common and the cutting down of woodland where they had gathered fuel was a bitter blow to the poor. This verse from Rev B L Evans' *The Story of Milton Malsor*, p 183 expresses the situation as ordinary people saw it.

> The law locks up the man or woman
> Who steals the goose from off the common,
> But turns the greater villain loose,
> Who steals the common from the goose.

Sometimes the only work Clare could get was the heart-breaking task of making the very fences that were ruining the rural life he knew and loved. He became all the more determined to immortalise in poetry the things that were passing away and to publish them for all the world to read.

A Stamford book-seller became interested enough in the young poet to put him in touch with his cousin, John Taylor, a London publisher. Clare began to hope that his dream might come true.

There were other dreams. Clare had an eye for the girls, as his poems clearly show. This endearing verse is from 'Ballad'.

> Garments light as gales embraces
> That thy lovely shape reveal
> Put thou on thy airy dresses
> Charmer leave thy spinning wheel
> And tend the sheep with me

How unexpected is that last extra line.

> 'My fondness for study began to decline on mixing more with young chaps of loose habits . . . these habits were gotten when the fields were enclosed mixing among a motley set of labourers.' Ch 5, p 34.

There were a number of love affairs and the mystery of his relationship with Mary Joyce. All we really know is that they were childhood friends and that in later life he wrote a great number of poems to her and about her and when his mind became deranged he thought he had married her. She appears to the reader a shadowy figure, unattainable, almost angelic.

But Patty was real. Clare was working as a lime-burner at Bridge Casterton when he met her.

> 'I first saw Patty going across the fields towards her home I was in love at first sight. . . .
>
> Casterton cow-pasture where I used to pass on my visits to Patty was a very favourite spot & I planned & wrote some of my best poems in my first volume among its solitudes. . . . I was then the companion of the evening and very often the morning star.' Ch 8 pp 55 and 56.

Poems Descriptive of Rural Life and Scenery was published in 1820 and was an immediate success. Pastoral themes were fashionable and 'this untaught Northamptonshire hind' as he was called in a [favourable] review in *The New Monthly* had taken the tide at the flood. It would surely lead on to fortune and relieve him of some of his many anxieties. The most immediate of these was that Patty was pregnant. They were married two months later.

Her real name was Martha, and like her Biblical namesake she was a practical country girl and was to prove a good wife and mother in what must have been a very difficult marriage.

It was certainly difficult at first. Clare could not provide a home and Patty had to live for a time with her disapproving parents. Her husband had set foot in a world she could not share. He went to London and met the rich and famous. It was a time of heady delight for the young poet. Such a time was never to come again.

Anna Maria was born on 2nd June 1820. Her parents loved her deeply. The birth of his daughter and the success of his first book sent Clare's spirit's soaring and he worked with great energy to bring out *The Village Minstrel* the next year. Largely autobiographical, it did not sell well. This was one of many anxieties— difficulties with his publisher, the death of a second daughter, worries about his own and his family's health, the unwelcome attentions of some of his many visitors and always the struggle to make ends meet.

The Great North Road was an escape route to London and his literary friends. At home he was apt to turn to the alehouse or to a woman for solace, to be tormented with guilt afterwards. He wrote much of *The Shepherd's Calendar* in sickness and want. It was brought to publication, with many difficulties, in 1827. The fashion for rural poetry had passed. Poet and publisher were at odds with each other. John Taylor was looking for refinements and philosophical meanings which were valueless to Clare, and he, Taylor, took it upon himself to 'slash'—his own word—a good deal of the text, including dialect words, the names of country games which he did not understand and the whole of the July section, which Clare had to rewrite.

A hundred and sixty years later, we see the work as a delightful series of poems and as a valuable social record, a year in the life of an early nineteenth century village in field and at fireside, in the woods and on the green. We see the May games, the gypsies, the Scottish drovers with their herds, harvest and gleaning, November fog and Christmas merriment. Page after page the unpunctuated couplets roll on, and monotony, one's first impression, is forgotten as the people and the scenes appear.

In January

> The shepherd too in great coat wrapt
> And straw bands round his stockings *lapt*
> Wi plodding dog that sheltering steals
> To shun the wind behind his heels

Takes rough and smooth the winter weather
And paces through the snow together.
'A Winter's Day,' lines 49-54.

'Love teazd maidens from their droning wheels' (line 226) steal out to meet their lovers as the March evenings grow lighter, and insects appear.

Blue flyes from straw stacks crawling scarce alive
And bees creep out on slabs before the hive
Stroaking their little legs across their wings
And venturing short flight where the snowdrop hings
Its silver bell. . . .
Lines 235-239.

Sadly, *The Shepherd's Calendar* was a financial failure. There were nerve-wracking delays and frustrations in Clare's dealings with his publisher, especially over payments due to him. The world, it seemed, looked on with indifferent eyes while he struggled for a living and for recognition.

There were good friends who did their best to help and advise, among whom Mrs Emmerson, though over-zealous with literary advice, played a supportive role for many years, especially with much-needed help for the growing family of children.

In the summer of 1831, when Clare was sick in body and mind, Lord Milton offered him a new cottage that was being built, in the village of Northborough, a few miles away. Once again, he had to accept help from his friends as he struggled to pay off his debts and stock his piece of land, at the same time suffering the ignominy of having inaccurate reports about his lack of means published in newspapers.

The move made matters worse. Northborough was a fenland village, without the woods and heathland Clare loved so much. His new home was not part of the village in the same way that his old cottage had been.

From his homesickness and sense of alienation came a wealth of poetry. Here are the opening lines of 'The Flitting', a two hundred and sixteen-line lament.

I've left my own old home of homes
Green fields and every pleasant place
The summer like a stranger comes
I pause and hardly know her face . . .

'Remembrance' is full of field and other local names, some still known in Helpston today—Langley Bush, Eastwell, Lea Close,

The nightingale
'*Up this green woodland ride let's softly rove and list the nightingale . . .*'

Swordy Well, Sneap Green, Cowper Green. The bird poems—
'Autumn Birds', 'Quail's Nest', 'Wild Duck's Nest', 'The School-
boys in the morning soon as drest', 'The Green Woodpecker's
Nest' and others make a collection all on their own. 'Morris
Dancers' has a welcome note of gaiety—

> The children leave their toys to see them play
> And laughing maidens lay their work away.
>
> Lines 5, 6.

The Northborough poems were to be included in a new
collection intended for publication and imaginatively titled *The
Midsummer Cushion.* The name was from 'an old custom among
villagers in summer time to stick a piece of greensward full of field
flowers & place it as an ornament in their cottages which
ornaments are called Midsummer Cushions'.

The book was to be published by subscription, but, once again,
support was lacking and the project had to be shelved.

During the next two years Clare grew worse. He feared for the
health of his children and himself [luckily, Patty kept well] and
was obsessed by thoughts of evil spirits and witchcraft. Though
often unable to leave the cottage or to write more than a few lines
to his friends, he wrote a preface for his new book. Most of the
poems in it were from *The Midsummer Cushion,* but it was
retitled *The Rural Muse,* from the title of Mrs Emmerson's
favourite poem of the collection. It was published in 1835, and
among its eighty-six sonnets and about fifty other poems are lines
of great beauty and maturity. Here are the opening lines of 'The
Nightingale's Nest'.

> Up this green woodland ride lets softly rove
> & list the nightingale—she dwelleth here
> Hush let the wood gate softly clap—for fear
> The noise might drive her from her home of love

How could a mind, seriously disturbed, produce tranquil
thoughts such as these? Only, perhaps, in remembering the peace
of his childhood wanderings, when he was free to steal through
the woods to watch the birds he loved

> Lost in a wildernes of listening leaves

or to lie in a cornfield, watching the comings and goings of
insects,

> Those tiney loiterers on the barleys beard
> & happy units of a numerous herd

Of playfellows the laughing summer brings
Mocking the sunshine on their glittering wings
How merrily they creep and run and flye
No kin they bear to labour's drudgery

                                              'Insects' lines 1-6.

The Rural Muse, though well-reviewed, sold few copies. There was to be no solace for the troubled mind, torn between the knowledge that he was now a master of his craft and wanted nothing more fervently than to go on writing, and the harsh truth that he could not keep his family from want.

Then there was Mary Joyce. She lived only a short distance away and the two may well have met. He addressed poems to her and began to believe that she was his wife. Sometimes his tormented mind caused him to talk in a violent way which must have frightened his wife and children. This was all the sadder because he loved them dearly.

Worse was to come. His dearly-loved mother died just before Christmas. His crippled father came to live with the family and had to watch as Clare grew more withdrawn and deranged. Eighteen months later his friends arranged for him to be taken to a private asylum at High Beech, near Epping Forest.

Dr Matthew Allen gave his patients reasonable freedom, good food and what would now be called occupational therapy. Physically Clare's condition improved, but his mind was not to be healed. He saw himself as a prisoner 'in Allen's madhouse caged and living'. In fact he could wander in the wooded grounds and work in the garden, and he carried on writing, often about Mary Joyce.

Where are my friends and childern Where are they
The childern of two mothers born in joy
One roof has held them—all have been at play
Beneath the pleasure of a mother's eye.

He longed for them all, the two women, the *childern,* his lost home.

It was but one more step to decide to go back to them. He did not know that Mary had died, unmarried, the year he was taken from home.

He met some gypsies in the nearby forest and asked for help. They told him which way to go and would have helped him further if he had been able to pay them. He set off alone to walk more than eighty miles with no money and only a little tobacco in his pocket. His account of his journey is almost unbearable to read.

July 21 . . . I left my lodging (a shed) by the way I got in & thanked God for his kindness in procuring it for . . . any place that gives the weary rest is a blessing . . . a Man passed me on horseback in a slop-frock & said 'here's another of the broken-down haymakers' & threw me a penny to get a half-pint of beer which I picked up and thanked him for & when I got to the Plough I called for a half-pint & drank it & got a rest I recollect at late evening going through Potton in Bedfordshire . . . I went on hobbling with a crippled foot for the gravel had got into my old shoes one of which had now nearly lost the sole . . . I lay down by a shed-side under some elms . . . and tried to sleep but the wind came in between them so cold that I quaked like the ague & quitted the lodging. . . . It now began to grow dark apace & the odd houses on the road began to light up & show the inside tenants' lots very comfortable and my outside lot very uncomfortable and very wretched—still I hobbled forward as well as I could but at last came to the Ram the shutters were not closed and the lighted windows looked very cheering but I had no money . . . so I travelled on . . . I could not sit down or give up but shuffled on. . . . I at length fell in with an odd house all alone by a wood . . . I lay at full length on the stones in the porch—I slept here till daylight & felt very much refreshed. . . . I blest my two wives and both their familys
One night I lay in a dyke bottom from the wind & went to sleep half an hour when I suddenly awoke and found my side wet through from the *sock* [undrained water] in the dyke bottom so I got out and went on. . . . I was very often half asleep as I went on the third day I satisfied my hunger by eating the grass at the roadside which seemed to taste something like bread . . . in fact the meal seemed to do me some good the next and last day. . . . I took to chewing tobacco all day . . . I was completely *foot-foundered* & broken down . . . before I got to Peterborough a man & woman passed me in a cart. . . . I found they were neighbours from Helpstone. . . . I told them I was *knocked up* . . . they clubbed together & threw me fivepence out of the cart I picked it up & called at a small public house near the bridge where I had two half-pints of ale & two pennorth of bread & cheese when I had done I started quite refreshed only my feet were more crippled than ever & I could scarcely make a walk of it over the stones. . . . I reached Werrington where a cart

passed me . . . the woman jumped out & caught fast hold of my hands & wished me to get into the cart but I refused but when I was told it was my second wife Patty I got in & was soon at Northborough but Mary was not there. . . .'

Clare, Patty and the family and old Parker Clare spent five months together until her husband's worsening mental state forced Patty to send for the doctors. They agreed that he was insane. He was admitted to the Northampton General Lunatic Hospital and Asylum on 29th December 1841.

The Asylum, now St Andrew's Hospital, was built in 1836/7 of 'the beautiful white Kingsthorpe stone' and was pleasantly situated on rising ground above the river Nene. It had comfortable rooms, running hot water, baths and showers. Dr Thomas Prichard, the Superintendent, was a liberal and humane man who allowed his patients as much freedom as possible in the spacious grounds. It is well-known that Clare used to walk into town and sit in the portico of All Saints Church, where people would come and talk to him, and he had a number of visitors at the Asylum. One or another of his children made occasional visits and wrote letters, but Patty and he never saw each other again. His father and four of his children died while he was in the Asylum, but he could not remember their deaths. At times he thought he was Byron or Shakespeare.

He remembered his childhood at Helpston, his love for the flowers and fields, and often enquired at length about his old neighbours. The House Steward, WF Knight, took an interest in him and encouraged him to write, which he could do in the privacy of his own room, for Lord Fitzwilliam and the Asylum authorities shared the cost of keeping him as a private patient.

Though the quality of his writing varied, it is surely wonderful that he wrote at all. Some poems of this period are well-known and well-loved—the poignant *I am* [yet what I am, none cares or knows], 'Little Trotty Wagtail' and 'Autumn'. (It begins 'I love the fitfull gusts that shakes/The casement all the day'.)

There are love-poems, not all too serious. 'Come the back way, dear' takes an amused backward glance at some youthful goings-on.

Now Granny's gone to bed steal in the back way
Ye shall be my favoured lad I'll be your lass alway
Come in this happy night for Granny's fast asleep
And I'll put out the light fear some should come to peep.

The hedge-sparrow
'. . . mopes the hedge sparrow with trembling wings . . .'

The chaffinch
'Chaffinch carries the moss in his mouth . . .'
All bird-drawings are by Mrs Elizabeth Davies

'Come Hither' is a moving call to the distressed soul to find peace in rural solitude.

> Come hither ye who thirst
> Pure still the brook flows on. . . .

> Art weary? here's the place
> For weariness to rest
> These flowers are herbs of grace
> To cure the aching breast. . . .

> Poor shipwreck of life, journey hither
> And we'll talk of life's troubles together.

Here is a beautiful unrhymed poem to 'Spring'.

> Pale sunbeams gleam
> That nurtur a few flowers
> *Pile wort* & daisey & a sprig o' green
> On whitethorn bushes
> In the leafstrewn hedge

> These harbingers
> Tell spring is coming fast
> & these the schoolboy marks
> & wastes an hour from school
> *Agen* the old pasture hedge

> Cropping the daisey
> And the *pile wort* flowers
> Pleased with the Spring & all he looks upon
> He opes his spelling book
> And hides her blossoms there

> Shadows fall dark
> Like black in the pale sun
> And lye the bleak day long
> Like black stock under hedges
> & bare wind rocked trees

This verse has short, Anglo-Saxon words, six hard ks and subtle repetitions—*black* and *bleak* and *black* again, *stock* and *rocked,* all softened by the numerous ls. It is dark verse, a memory of clouds and searching wind over the winter-sodden fen. But it is spring and so there is promise.

> Tis chill but pleasant
> In the hedge bottom lined
> With brown seer leaves the last
> Year littered there and left
> Mopes the hedge sparrow

> With trembling wings and cheeps
> Its welcome to pale sunbeams
> Creeping through

The hard ks have gone and the soft ls remain. *Mopes* is a striking word to use in this context and is in a strong position at the beginning of the line.

A more conventional nature-poet of that time might never have thought of using the word, but Clare had watched this humble little bird half-hidden in the ditch. 'Mopes' sounds right.

And so we come to his last poem. It is like an epilogue to the splendid series of bird poems he had written years before, and is simply called 'Birds Nests'.

> 'Tis spring warm glows the south
> Chaffinch carries the moss in his mouth
> To filbert hedges all day long
> And charms the poet with his beautiful song
> The wind blows bleak o'er the sedgy fen
> But warm the sun shines by the little wood
> Where the old cow at her leisure chews her cud

There is this one verse only, irregularly stressed, with a lovely second line. For the last time the old man tells of the fickle spring weather, the nesting birds and the peaceful cow, things he knew and understood and loved. He died on 20 May 1864 and was buried at Helpston as he wished.

The following dialect words used by John Clare are still known in Northampton and the county. Their meanings can be found in the Glossary. Clare's own spellings are used, with the more usual spelling in brackets if necessary. Where a word has more than one meaning in the Glossary, this is indicated by the appropriate number.

agen, airiff [hairiff], bandy, see *bandy-stick, beaver [bever], blather, bob* 2, *bottle, budget, bumbarrel, chelp, childern, chockhole[s], crab, crack up* 2, *crizzle, cuck, eldern, emmet, frail, frit, headache, hurk, keck, land, lap, lauter [lawter, laughter], Lawrence, learn, maul, mizzle, Noah's Ark, pingle, pismire, poddle, puther, rig, roil, sawney, scrat, starnel, swee, thurrow, tong, twitch, waterblob.*

The next group of words used by Clare are still known in the Helpston and Stamford area.

butterbump, the bittern; *chitter*, of a bird, chirp; *clench*, strengthen shoes with rivets; *clodhopper*, the *wheatear; cock's stride*, a short time; *firetail*, the redstart; *gleg*, peep; *hing*, hang; *pad*, path; *pendle*, the upper course in a stonepit; *sen*, self; *sheeptray*, a large hurdle; *sluther*, slide.

A NORTHAMPTONSHIRE GLOSSARY

No word or phrase in this glossary is taken from a book. All, except those I know myself, have been given me by people from Northampton, the county or its borders, many of whom lost no time in giving me expressive examples of how their words were used. These are the sentences in square brackets.

Dialect words make up a significant part of this collection, but there are also a number of ordinary words such as 'come' and 'take' which are used locally in various combinations. 'It *come on* to rain,' as many readers will know, means 'It started to rain,' and '*come back*' is a tanning term, to rehydrate.

'Take' can mean 'grow'—'None of these cuttings has *taken*', or 'ignite'—'The wood's damp and it won't *take*', or add emphasis, in the term 'Take and go'. The sense is 'Make up your mind to go' or *goo,* quite often. In the north of the county 'take' would probably become '*tek*'.

Some words show local pronunciations, an *au* sound in the word 'cost': *peth* and *peck* for 'pith' and 'pick'; *dug* for 'dog', *hug* for 'hog'. Then there are words such as 'abear' and 'abide', both meaning 'tolerate', but seldom heard now and beginning to sound rather archaic. Language is constantly changing as words slip quietly away.

There are lovely flower-names, among them *Mary's taper* and *Candlemass bell* for snowdrop, but none, to my knowledge, for trees. There are many bird-names, as John Clare knew so well, but few for animals. One of these is the well-known *dillin,* smallest pig in the litter, *reckling* in the Stamford area. The standard word 'glean' is replaced by *lease* in the south-west of the county.

Our staple industries of tanning, leather-dressing and making boots and shoes have given us a good number of work-terms, some known in other parts of the country, others that are not to be found in any dictionary, but only in trade-glossaries. I have given many of the words as participles, *drafting, crowing* etc. because that is how they are used. Other work-terms come from brewing, the railways and the cottage craft of lace-making, once widespread in Northampton and the county.

Each word in the glossary was checked in *The Oxford English Dictionary,* complete text, 1979 *(OED)* and *The English Dialect Dictionary (EDD)*. This monumental work was compiled by Dr Joseph Wright after twenty-five years' research, and published in six volumes from 1898 to 1905. The main sources for Northamptonshire were Thomas Sternberg, *The Dialect and Folklore of Northamptonshire,* 1851 *(DFN)* and Anne Elizabeth Baker, *Glossary of Northamptonshire Words and Phrases* 1854 *(GNWP)*. Words recorded in these two dictionaries as known only in Northamptonshire or in a few other countries as well are marked by Nhp. and by Lei., Lin., Bdf. etc.

Between 1948 and 1961 the fieldwork for *The Survey of English Dialects (SED)* was carried out under the direction of Professor Harold Orton of the University of Leeds. Older people in selected, mainly agricultural communities were invited to answer prepared questions concerning their use of words. Northamptonshire villages visited were Warmington, Welford, Little Harrowden, Kislingbury and Sulgrave.

In 1974 *A Word Geography of England,* giving in map form the information collected by *SED* and written in part by Professor Orton, was published. He died on the day of publication.

I am greatly indebted to these two works. Map 25, for example shows the distribution in the county of standard 'slippery' and dialect *slippy*.

The second word is not a sloppy [sorry] pronunciation of the first, but is probably from Low German *slippen* recorded in 1548, while 'slippery' is from OE *slipor*+y. Kislingbury appears to have used standard English, but it was certainly *slippy* in Far Cotton School playground on many a winter's day.

In the glossary, place-names in parentheses show where a word was found. Words with no place-name are in more general use.

All abbreviations will be found in the list on the next page. These include the works of John Clare, where dialect words are so movingly used, and those of another well-loved writer from just over the county border. Flora Thompson's Lark Rise is Juniper Hill, a few miles south of Brackley.

Abbreviations

BOOKS

Can.	Flora Thompson, *Lark Rise to Candleford* (1939)
DFN	Thomas Sternberg *The Dialect and Folk-lore of Northamptonshire* (1851)
EDD	Joseph Wright, ed. *The English Dialect Dictionary,* 6 vols. (1898–1905)
EFDSS	The English Folk Dance and Song Society
GNWP	Anne Elizabeth Baker *Glossary of Northamptonshire Words and Phrases* (1854)
Mid.	John Clare, A Tibble ed and R K R Thornton, assoc ed
Cush	*The Midsummer Cushion.* Most of the poems in *The Rural Muse* (1835) are from this collection, which has Clare's preferred title
NL	Northamptonshire Libraries
NNQ	Rev W D Sweeting, John Taylor and C.Markham, eds. *Northamptonshire Notes and Queries* (1886–90)
OED	*The Oxford English Dictionary,* complete text (1971)
Ox. Auth.	*The Oxford Authors John Clare.* Eric Robinson and David Powell eds. OUP (1984)
PNN	J E B Gover, A Mawer and F M Stenton *The Place-names of Northamptonshire* (1933)
Shep Cal	John Clare, Eric Robinson and Geoffrey Summerfield, eds (1973) *The Shepherd's Calendar* (1827)
Vill Min	*The Village Minstrel* (1821) from J W Tibble and Anne Tibble eds. John Clare *Selected Poems* (1976)

COUNTIES AND REGIONS

Bdf.	Bedfordshire	Oxf.	Oxfordshire
Bck.	Buckinghamshire	War.	Warwickshire
E.An.	East Anglia	Wor.	Worcestershire
Hrf.	Herefordshire	Mid.	Midland
Hunt.	Huntingdonshire	N,S,	north, south,
Lei.	Leicestershire	E,W	east, west
Nhp.	Northamptonshire		

LANGUAGES

Dan.	Danish	Lat.	Latin	OFr.	Old French
Du.	Dutch	ME	Middle English	ON	Old Norse
Fr.	French	Norw.	Norwegian	Scand.	Scandinavian
Ger.	German	OE	Old English	Swed.	Swedish
Icel.	Icelandic				

GENERAL

a.	adjective	chn.	children	ed.	editor/edited
arch.	archaic	coll.	colloquial	et al.	and others
cf.	compare	dial.	dialect	esp.	especially

exc.	except	obs.	obsolete	sing.	singular
fig.	figurative(ly)	orig.	originally	tech.	technical
lit.	literal(ly)	phr.	phrase	tog.	together
MS.	manuscript	pl.	plural	usu.	usually
n.	noun	prob.	probably	vol.	volume
neg.	negative(ly)	pron.	pronounced	WW1	World War 1
nr.	near	qv.	which see	WW2	World War 2

PHOTOGRAPHS

AC — Author's collection   NL — Northamptonshire Libraries
NRO — Northamptonshire Record Office

A Glossary

a have *OED, EDD* [I should a thought you'd a knowed him]. in, into *OED* (Obs.) *EDD* [He cut the loaf a two]. on *OED* (Obs.) *EDD* [She's coming a Sunday]. to *OED* (Obs.) *EDD* [He pushed me a one side].

abear tolerate, usu. neg. *OED, EDD* [I can't abear that colour].

abide tolerate, usu.neg. *OED, EDD* [W.Shakespeare *II Henry IV*, iii,2. 'She would always say she could not abide Master Shallow'] *EDD*.

about ready for, in phr. 'about some teeth' [said of babies]. *OED, Obs. EDD* [His gums are sore—I think he's about some teeth].

about October pregnant, at any time of year. [She looks about October].

above more than, longer than [There's not above ten bobs' worth. Them seeds are bin in above three week].

Acky a greeting, a call in the game I Acky [Acky, tosh (mate)].

act do. *OED* (Obs.) *EDD*. *(Holcot)* [Watcher gunner act?].

adland headland, the strip of land on which the plough turns. *EDD*.

afore before. OED (dial.) *EDD* [She come afore Christmas].

afternoon slow, late. *EDD* [She'll come when she's ready—she's an afternoon customer].

agen against, near. *OED* (dial.) *EDD* [Put your wet clothes agen the fire].

Ah Yes. *EDD* [Ah, I think I can manage that].

all along from the beginning. *EDD* [I knew all along she was up to no good].

all to pieces distracted, despairing. *EDD* [She went all to pieces when he'd gone].

all there of sound mind. *EDD* [She's all there when it comes to money].

aloft in phr '*stitched aloft*', on the surface of the leather, not in a channel [Shoe-making].

– *A Northamptonshire Glossary* –

anew enough. *EDD (Spratton)* [Is there anew on 'em?].
angels and devils the arum lily *(Piddington)*.
apern apron. *OED* (Obs) *(Kettering)*.
apsy abscess. *EDD* [Our boy's got a bad apsy on his neck].
arrant errand. *OED, EDD (Ashton)*, near Roade [There's nobody t'do me arrants now].
arseways obstinate, unwilling [Leave him alone—he's arseways today].
artillery ear deafness caused by gunfire. WW1.
as that. *EDD* [I'll see as she gets the message]. who, which. *EDD* [That's the chap as used to live here. Is this the frock as you made?]. used redundantly *EDD* [I went there a week as last Friday].
as was formerly. *EDD* (colloq) [Nelly Brown as was].
aside at the side of. *OED* (Obs) *EDD* [He gi' me a clip aside the ear].
auction a place or room which is untidy, like an auction room. *EDD* [I've searched all over the auction].
awhile for some time. *OED* (orig a while) *EDD*. Also used redundantly [They won't come home yet awhile].
Ay up Look out. Mind what you're doing.

bab baby. *OED* (earlier and now dial). *EDD* [The bab's just like 'is Dad. *Towneley Mysteries*, c1450, 149. 'Alas my bab, myn innocent'].
back-brook curve of water-bed left when channel is straightened. *(Spratton)*.
backhouse/backus [back hus] 1. back part of house, kitchen, scullery, hence back'us boy, boy who works in the kitchen. *OED backhouse, EDD backus.* 2. bakehouse, a house with an oven, a bakery. *EDD.*
in the back in the kitchen or back part of house.
out the back to the outside lavatory [He's gone out the back].
backen delay, check. *OED* (now rare) *EDD* [She was away from school a long time but it never backened her].
bad abed ill enough to have to stay in bed. *EDD* [I'm bad abed and *wuss* (worse) up].
baffs feet. EDD has *baffles*, Nhp., leggings, gaiters.
bag n. the long-tailed tit, from the shape of its nest. *EDD.*
bagged up with swollen udders, ready to calve. *OED bagged,* pregnant (Obs) *(Spratton)* [The cow's well bagged up].
bagging leather strap of catapult. *(Spratton.)*
'Bags' I claim. (Chn's games) [Bags first go].
bairnt be not, am not. *(Little Houghton.)* [I bairnt gooin' t'the meetin'].
bait enough food for one meal. *(Little Houghton.)* [There's a bait of beans].
bake pudden Yorkshire pudding, often with meat cooked in it.
bake taters potatoes, meat and onions baked in pastry without a top crust.

balt curdle, clot. *OED* 'modern Northampton dial'. *EDD* '*bolter*,
Nhp War Bdf E An' [Mind the custard don't balt. W
Shakespeare, *Macbeth*, IV, i,123. 'For the blood-bolter'd Banquo
smiles upon me'].

bandy-net child's fishing net.

bandy-stick hockey-stick, from bandy, a game similar to hockey.
OED, EDD.

bang throw with force. *EDD* [He banged a snowball at the door].

bang-handed left-handed. *EDD (Pury End)*.

barge brag, boast. *EDD*.

Barnack beauty variety of apple grown at Barnack.

bast inner bark of the lime tree, often cut in strips and plaited to
make baskets. *OED, EDD (Cogenhoe)* ['New bread from the
bast, New shoes from the last'].

bate n. an alkaline solution [Tanning]. v soak hides in this solution.
OED.

bate 1. abate [The rain bates a bit]. 2. force a reduction in price.
OED (Obs) *EDD* [He wanted a pound for it but I bated him
down to fifteen bob].

batten bundle of straw. *OED* (dial) *EDD. (Brixworth)*.

baver light refreshment between meals. OFr. *beivre*, a drinking. Cp
beverage. *OED* (dial) *EDD. (Banbury)*.

bawny sour, sharp to the taste. *(Olney)*.

bazil bark-tanned sheepskin [tanning].

be by. *OED* (dial) *EDD* [I shall be home be dinnertime].

be-all-and-end-all something valued very highly [The house is her
be-all-and-end-all].

beamhouse building housing the tanner's beam, on which hides
are scraped. *OED* [tanning].

bear's ear the plant auricula. *OED, EDD*.

beaumontague a kind of putty used to fill in defects in wood and
cast iron, said to be from name of Fr geologist Elie de
Beaumont (1798–1851) *OED, EDD (Collingtree)*.

before in front of, exposed to. *OED (Collingtree)* [An old lady said
she grew cyclamen from seed, *before* the window].

beggar-lice hurrs or husks of plants, clinging to clothing. *OED.
EDD (Pury End)*.

beggar's lace Torchon lace. [lace-making].

being as, because. *OED* (dial) *EDD* [Being as I knew him I let him
in].

belltinker scolding, punishment. *EDD* [I'd give her belltinker if she
stopped out late].

belver cry loudly, bellow. *EDD. (Spratton.)*

bethink remember, often in past tense and reflexive. *OED* (Obs.)
EDD ['I nearly rang your mother and then I bethought myself
and rang you instead'].

bever 1. see *baver*. 2. shake with cold or fear. *OED* (dial) *EDD.
(Banbury.)*

bibber shake with cold or fear. *EDD. (Harpole.)*

Bill's Mum's 1. over there, usu. of approaching dark clouds. [It looks black over Bill's Mum's]. 2. rhyming slang, usu. said when in a draught [It's a bit cold round Bill's Mum's].

Billy Moonshine small oil-lamp for a child's bedside. *(Pury End.)*

Billy Wind child's name for the wind [Hark at Billy Wind a-blowing].

binge soak a wooden vessel to make it swell and so prevent leaks. *OED* (dial) *EDD* (Nhp) [coopering].

binger sharp frost or keen wind. *EDD.*

binstead bay in a barn for storing or threshing corn. *EDD* (Nhp).

bird of Paradise the plant escholtzia. *(Little Houghton.)*

bisnins first milk from a cow after calving. *OED* beestings. *EDD* ['I used to be sent to fetch the bisnins'].

bivver n. tremor, shiver. v. shiver, shake. *EDD (Banbury).*

blackman household spectre. *OED. EDD.* [Don't goo out there, else the blackman'll get yer].

blackthorn winter cold weather in April, when blackthorn is in blossom. *EDD.*

blare-headed distracted, confused [You kids'll drive me blare-'eaded].

blart talk unwisely, let out a secret. *EDD* [Don't tell 'er—she'll blart it all over the place].

blather n. empty, noisy talk, flattery. *OED* (orig. dial) *EDD* [Take no notice of his blather]. v. talk foolishly, flatter. ON *blathra*, talk nonsense.

blizzy brightly burning fire, bonfire. *EDD* ['Let's have a blizzy'].

blonde made from raw silk. *OED* [lace-making].

Blowbroth Humorous name, esp. for a child. ['Come on, Blowbroth'].

Blüchers Wellingtons, half-boots, after Field-Marshal von Blücher (1742–1819) who fought with Wellington at Waterloo. *OED, EDD* [It's wet underfoot—you'll need your Blüchers on].

blueleg variety of mushroom. *EDD.*

blunt unpolished, said of a playground slide [Are yer got a bit o' candle—the slide's blunt].

board-cut cut out by hand on the *clicker's* board [shoe-trade].

boarding-arm board worn on the arm for graining leather [shoe-trade].

bob jog, knock. *OED, EDD* [He bobbed me arm, Sir].

bobby signalman, earlier called policeman [railways].

bobby-burrs burrs of goosegrass. *(Kettering.)*

bob-hole doorway, alley, small entrance. *EDD* bob=pop, go in and out quickly. *(Stamford)* [I'll just go in this bob-hole].

Bob's-a-dying noise, commotion. *EDD* [They're kickin' up Bob's-a-dyin' next door].

boby half-moon-shaped vessel used for tipping barley into a kiln. *EDD* [malting].

bodge work clumsily or roughly. *OED* (dial), *EDD.*

bogey mucus from the nose.

bogeyman supernatural being. *OED*, and *EDD*, bogy [The bogeyman'll get yer].

boiling enough vegetables to boil for one meal. *OED*, *EDD* [Here's a few carrots−they might make a boilin'].

bolsh sit down heavily, throw oneself down carelessly [Don't bolsh about on the cushions].

bolsher a young fellow, lit. an unfledged bird. *(Piddington.)*

bolshin unfledged bird. *EDD*. *(Spratton, Pury End.)*

bolster stonemason's smoothing tool. *(Helpston.)*

bolt run to seed. *OED*. *EDD* [The lettuce have all bolted in the hot weather].

bolton/bolting bundle or sheaf of straw. *EDD*. *(Moulton.)*

bony-pie pie made with bones with some meat on. *(Tugby, nr. Leicester.)*

bosh water-butt. *(Harpole.)*

bossock fat, heavily-built woman, *EDD*. Hence *bossocking, bossocky*, fat, heavy. *(Long Buckby.)*

bottle bundle of straw for thatching. *OED* (local in use). *(Spratton.)*

bottom-stuff leather cut out for soles, heels, etc. *OED* [shoemaking].

bough-house private house allowed to sell liquor at fair-time and having a bough as a sign. *EDD* (Obs). *(Brigstock.)*

boughten bought, not home-made. *OED* (dial.) *EDD (Brackley)*.

boy male of any age. *OED* (dial) *EDD*.

boy-chap adolescent, young unmarried man. *EDD*.

boykin little boy. *OED*, *EDD*. *(Spratton.)*

brack tear or hole in clothing, always neg. *OED*, *EDD* [Don't throw that coat away−there's not a brack in it.

brackle break, crumple, rub off. *EDD*. *(Spratton)* [The paint brackles off].

Bread and Herring 1. Irish labourer *(Piddington)*. 2. The Stratford-on-Avon and Midland Junction Railway. *(Stoke Bruerne.)*

bread-and-pull-it dry bread *(EDD)*.

break grain characteristic of a hide, tested by folding grain inwards [tanning, shoemaking].

break 1. fail in health. *OED*, *EDD* [Poor old lady−she begins to break]. 2. recall [a dream]. *EDD* [When she said that, it broke my dream].

break over remove flesh from hides *EDD break* of hair or skin of animals, fall off [tanning].

breasting trimming front of heel and waist of shoe. *OED* [shoemaking].

brevit search, rummage. *OED* (dial), *EDD*. *(Long Buckby.)*

brew up graze. *EDD breward*, a crop of grass. *(Tugby, nr. Leicester.)*

brief always in phr. 'I hold no brief for . . .' I have a low opinion of. . . . *OED* 'to hold a brief, to argue for' [I'll dose meself up−I hold no brief for doctors].

bring on tend, encourage to grow. *OED* (Obs) [We bring the plants on in the greenhouse].

britchin breeching, harness passing round hinder parts of horse. *EDD.*

brock badger. A Celtic word, *[broc]*, taken into OE in the same form. *OED, EDD. (Earls Barton, Spratton.)*

browse brushwood, hedge clippings. *OED, EDD. (Spratton.)*

brush trim a hedge by cutting off first-year growth with a sickle. *OED* (local) *EDD (Bugbrooke).*

bruzzened/bruzzy roughened, frizzy. *EDD. (Long Buckby, Rushden.)*

bud small component part of pattern [lace-making].

budget in phr 'empty one's budget', tell the news, have one's say. *OED* (dial), *EDD* [She 's got to empty her budget as soon as she gets in the house].

buff-strap board for sharpening knives. *(Rushden.)* [shoe-making].

bull factory steam-whistle. *OED* (dial) *(Banbury).*

bull-daisy ox-eye daisy. *EDD.*

bulldog pincer for lasting the waist of the shoe. *OED* 'bulldog forceps' [surgery] [hand-sewn shoe-making].

bullies bullace, wild plum. *OED* (Obs) *EDD.*

bumbarrel long-tailed tit, from the shape of its nest. *EDD* [J Clare, *Shep Cal* May, 7-10
        'Bumbarrels twit on bush and tree,
        Scarse bigger than a bumble-bee
        And in a whitethorn's leafy rest
        It builds its curious pudding nest'].

bumfly bouffant, flowing. *(Weedon Lois.)*

bummer 1. foreman *EDD (Cogenhoe). Ask the bummer.* 2. *boaster, foolish talker. EDD.*

bung 1. stop up, close. *OED, EDD* [His eye's all bunged up]. 2. throw with force. *EDD* [He bunged a stone at the cat].

bung-end cul-de-sac. *(Little Houghton.)*

bung-handed left-handed. *(Helpston.)*

bunhouse workhouse ['We shall all end up in the bunhouse'].

bunjell basin. *EDD*(Nhp) *(Kislingbury).*

bunk n a push up, lift. *OED* (chiefly dial). *EDD* ['Give us a bunk up the wall'].

bunking decorative treatment of shoe-bottom [shoe-making].

bunt n. nudge, as a cat gives with its head. v nudge with the head. *OED* (dial) *EDD* [She bunted my hand when I fed her].

bunny-rabbit antirrhinum. *OED* and *EDD* (bunny-mouth).

bup, buppy bread, bread and butter, esp. used when speaking to chn [Eat some bup with it].

burden bundle of straw for thatching. *EDD (Upper Boddington).*

burgoo thick oatmeal porridge. *OED. EDD* (Obs) Nhp Hrt.

burk cuddle a child, gather chickens under the wing. *EDD* (Nhp) *(Milton Malsor, Spratton).*

burnt-to burned slightly in boiling. *EDD. (Little Houghton)* [The custard's burnt-to].

burr sheltered place, leeward side of a hedge. *EDD (Helmdon).*

burrhead pin with a burr for a head, before pins were made with heads. *(Greens Norton)* [lace-making].

burr-hurdle temporary shelter made of hurdles, for sheep and lambs. *(Helmdon.)*

burrow n shelter. a. sheltered. *OED* (dial) *EDD*. OE *beorgan*, protect [Come this side of the wall–it's more burrer here].

butty friend, workmate. *OED, EDD*.

butty-boat canal barge towed by another. *OED, EDD*.

but what except. *OED* (dial, coll) [I can't move but what she follows me].

buzzer a kiss. Cp. Fr. *baiser*, a kiss. *OED* and *EDD* buss.

bwielt boiled. *(Wellingborough)* [Can I have a bwielt egg?].

bwoy boy. One bwoy's a boy [at work]
  Two bwoys is 'alf a boy [because they may waste time],
  Three bwoys is no bwoy at all.   *(Piddington)*

cabbage offcuts of leather. *OED* and *EDD* shreds of cloth.

Ca-ca warning to stop chn touching something dirty.

cack n. excrement. v. void excrement. *OED, EDD*.

cack/cag/caggy-handed left-handed. *EDD*.

cag-mag tough, inferior meat. *OED* (dial) *EDD*. *(Pury End.)*

call slander. *OED* (dial) *EDD* [She called me everything she could lay her tongue to. I know she calls me behind my back].

callybanks ironstone banked up and burned [from calcium].

camp clamp, underground store of vegetables. *OED* (dial) EDD [Store].

candle a drip of mucus from the nose. *OED* (dial) *EDD*.

candleblock tall stool holding a candle and glass flasks to magnify its light. '*Wet the candleblock*'=take drink [lace-making].

Candlemas bell snowdrop, which flowers about the time of Candlemas, 2 February. *EDD (Weedon Lois)*.

cank angle ['You want more cank in it' [the angle of a spade-handle]. **canker** mouth-sore, said to be caused by putting coins or other metal in the mouth. *EDD* [Don't put that penny in your mouth–it'll give you canker].

Cannon game played by throwing a ball at pegs set up against a wall.

card claw, fray by scratching. *EDD* [The cat does card the chairs so].

carnauba hard wax made from leaves of S. American plant [shoe-making].

cart with 'about', trudge about on tiring or unnecessary errands [She's always carting about somewhere].

casioning earning money as best one can, by selling garden produce etc. The sense is of something done from necessity. Cf. 'he had no occasion [need] to do that'. *EDD (Rushden)*.

cast fallen on the back, unable to get up [of an animal]. *OED, EDD (Kettering)* ['If we saw a sheep cast we'd give it a push so it could wobble to its feet again'].

casualty skin skin or hide from a beast which died naturally. *EDD* [tanning].

catch 1. burn slightly when cooked. *EDD* [The milk just caught at the edges]. 2. sew or mend with a few stitches [Just catch it together for me].

catchy changeable [of weather]. *EDD.*

cat-ice very thin ice. *OED, EDD* ['It was all cat-ice on my step.' J Clare, *MS Poems* 'The cat-ice chatters where the schoolboy passed'] *EDD.*

catlick hasty, incomplete wash [Come here—let's give y'a catlick].

Catterns feast of St Catherine, 25 November, kept as a lace-makers' holiday in the north of the county. Cattern-pies, usu. of dough mixed with caraway seeds, were eaten. *EDD.*

cattie/cat and stick game played by hitting a stick into the air with a larger stick. *OED, EDD.*

caulk tread the ground into holes, said of cattle. OFr *cauquer*, Lat. *calcare*, tread. *OED.*

causey raised pavement. 'Causeway' is a later form. *OED, EDD.*

caust cost

cavings chaff, waste from threshing. *OED* (dial) *EDD.*

cedar pencil. *EDD cedar-pencil. (Banbury)* [Where's me bit o'cedar?].

cellar-head space at the top of cellar steps, often shelved and used for storing food. *EDD* ['I hid in the cellar-head when it thundered'].

cess drainage channel at side of line. *OED, EDD* [railways. 'Walk on the cess side'].

chad-pot see *fire-pot. (Greens Norton)* [lace-making].

chain-horse horse helping to pull shaft-horse by means of a chain. *OED, EDD. (Clipston.)*

chamber chamber-pot.

chap husband, sweetheart. *EDD* [My chap's out o' work again].

chap-money commission on a sale. *EDD* (Obs.) *(Banbury).*

Charlie 1. fox *OED.* 2. boar. 3. lump or hump on the back. *EDD.* 3. stupid person [modern] [I felt a proper Charlie].

charm loud chattering noise, of birds *EDD. (Spratton)* [What a charm the children make].

chat small, inferior potato. *OED* (dial) *EDD. (Banbury.)*

chattermagging sound made by a very small child talking to himself. *OED, EDD. (Spratton.)*

chawl chew slowly. *EDD* [The old dog's chawlin' away at a lump o' meat].

chelp n impertinent, argumentative talk ['Less o' yer chelp'] v talk argumentatively. *EDD* 'Produce a chirping sound, as a bird'. J Clare, 'Spring Comes' 1.10 ['The sparrow comes and chelps about the slates'] *Ox Auth.*

cherry-curds first milk from a cow after calving; pudding made from it. *EDD. (Banbury.)*

childer/childern children. *OED* (dial) *EDD. (Ashton, near Roade)* J Clare, *Shep Cal* Jan. 19,20.

> 'The childern cringe away to bed,
> And up the ladder softly tread'].

chimble crumble in small pieces. *EDD* ['I'll just chimble a bit o' cheese f' me supper'].

chin-cough whooping cough, later a cough of any kind, esp of children. *EDD* ['Oo dear, have yer got a chin-cough?'].

chinse work bulrushes into grooves round head of cask to make water-tight. *OED* [coopering].

chit n. small apple, shoot on corn or potatoes v. 1. sprout [1. The taters have chitted]. 2. rub off growing shoots. *OED* (dial) *EDD* [2. We must rub the chits off, else the taters'll wrinkle up].

chitty with small lumps forming, as in milk left standing. *OED*. (obs, rare).

chive knife for cutting a hollow in a stave. *OED* knife [thieves' cant] [coopering].

chockhole game played with marbles rolled into a hole. *OED* (dial) *EDD*. *(Eastcote.)*

chopse talk busily or for a long time. *EDD* Nhp. [The old gals was still chopsin' when I come back].

Christian human being, as opposed to an animal. *OED* (dial.) *EDD* ['Look at him (a dog) sitting in the driver's seat like a Christian'].

Chuck call to hens to come.

chucky child's name for a hen *OED* (N. dial.). *EDD* [You shall have a chucky egg].

chuggard child. *(Earls Barton.)*

churchyarder deep, harsh cough. *EDD* 'graveyard chorus'.

clag muddy, heavy soil *OED* N dial). *EDD*. *(Spratton)* ['Real Northamptonshire clag'].

claim 1. claim acquaintance. [She claimed me, but I didn't know her from Adam]. *EDD* 2. proclaim, in phr. 'claim summer', dress in summer clothes at the first opportunity.

clam clamp, gripped between knees to hold the leather. *OED*. *EDD* [hand-sewn-shoe making].

clape cake with mud. *EDD, claper. (Spratton)* [His boots were claped with mud].

clat cowpat, clod of earth, hence *clat-cold,* cold as a clod. *EDD*.

clay hoof, parts of a cloven hoof. Cp claw. *EDD*.

clean in phr. 'clean dirt' light dust, slight untidiness. *EDD* [It's only clean dirt–I done it properly last week].

clean/cleansing afterbirth of cow or sheep. *EDD*. *(Spratton)* [Has the cleansing come away?].

clearing-up shower last shower before rain ceases. *OED* (1862) [Let's hope it's the clearing-up shower].

clench corn crowfoot. *EDD*. Nhp *(Pury End.)*

click group/club. [We went in a *click* so we had blankets on the bed and coal.] OED, obs. form of clique.

clip n. sharp blow. *OED* (dial.) *EDD* [I'll give you a clip aside the ear]. v strike. *OED* (dial) *EDD* [He clipped me round the ear].

clip up choose sides, call someone out by name. *EDD* Nhp Hunt Suf OE *clypian,* call or name. G Chaucer, *Prologue to the Canterbury Tales,* ['And she was cleped Madame Eglantine'].

clowey state of nausea. *EDD cloy. (Spratton)* ['They're as drunk as clowey'].

clus close, small field. *(Spratton)* ['Um Clus (Home Close)].

coalhod coalscuttle *OED* (dial) *EDD* [Fill me coal'od afore y'goo].

cobhole place too small for effective use. *EDD* [I only had a little cobhole to keep the tools in].

cock 1. heap of corn, beans etc. 2. growing centre of a plant. *(Spratton.)*

cockadoring conceited. *EDD* cockabendy.

cockaroo-stick chn's game played with a ball and a tin of stones.

cockerel young cock. *OED* (arch or dial) *EDD* [We had some hens and a cockerel in the yard].

cock-hen-roost name for carrying a child on the shoulders. *(Spratton, Cogenhoe.)*

Cock Lorell boaster, from *Cock Lorell's Bote*', published by Wynkyn de Worde, about 1510, an imitation of Alex Barclay's *Ship of Fools* (1509). Cock Lorell, a tinker, was captain of a crew of rogues. *(Banbury)* [Take no notice of that Cock Lorell].

cod persuade. *OED* (slang or dial) *EDD*, impose upon. *(Brigstock)* ['He codded me to make some lace-bobbins'].

coddy foreman, man in charge. [You'll have to ask the coddy].

codge, codgel make a rough repair, manage, economise. *EDD (Little Houghton).*

codlins and cream The great hairy willow-herb. *EDD (Collingtree).*

collifoble make pretence, cheat. *EDD (Brigstock).*

collifox make something look right, fake. *EDD.*

colsh fall in, collapse. *OED* (dial.) *EDD.*

comb section of the last, corresponding to the instep [shoe-making].

come form, of butter. *OED, EDD. (Spratton)* ['If the butter wouldn't come, Granny put half-a-crown in'].

come came [Our boy come 'ome last week].

come about happen [I don't know how that come about].

come back rehydrate [tanning].

come by come to possess. *OED, EDD* [How did you come by that book?].

come in be at hand, be useful. *OED, EDD* [Keep it by yer–it'll come in f'summat].

come on 1. make progress, thrive. *EDD* [The bab comes on lovely].

come on 2. start, usu. of rain. *EDD* [It come on to rain just as I got the washing out].

come time when the time comes. *OED* (dial) *EDD* [My chap'll be sixty come time].

come to happen. *EDD* [How did that picture come to be here?].

coom root of barley [come]. *OED* (obs) *EDD* [malting].

cop v. catch, seize. *OED* (dial) *EDD* [Cop hold o' the rope]. n use, in phr. 'not much cop'. *OED* Cp. 'not much capture' [Don't buy them–they're not much cop].

cornbine cornbind, wild convolulus. *OED, EDD.* Cp woodbine.

Cottages game in which three marbles are placed together, with one on top. *(Wellingborough.)*

counter stiffener at heel of shoe. *(Rushden)* [shoe-making].

country region, district. *OED, EDD*. 'to go to the hay country', to travel towards London to work in the hay-harvest. *(Wilstead, nr Bedford.)*

cowflop cowpat. *EDD*.

cowlady ladybird. *OED, EDD*.

coz friend, mate. *OED*. 'abbrev. of cousin, used in familiar address to relatives and in a wider sense'. *(Little Houghton)* ['He calls everybody "coz" '].

crab-ankled lame, having deformed ankles. *(Spratton.)*

crabs 1. crab-apples. *EDD*. 2. Shoes. *EDD crabshulls* [Not worth 'atful o' crabs].

cracknut gate opening into a V-shaped or curved enclosure; kissing-gate. *(Cogenhoe.)*

crackpot n person with crazy ideas. a. crazy *EDD*.

crack up 1. fail in health. 2. boast about, exaggerate [Grandad cracked up last winter. She cracked him up to be worth pots o' money].

cradle-cap patch of scurf on a baby's head.

cratch/scratch rectangular frame, eg manger, pig-killing frame, chicken-run. *OED* (dial) *EDD*. Cp Fr *crèche*, cradle. *(Pury End, Little Houghton)* ['Used as a bier at funerals, with a pole through the handles' *(Tugby, Nr. Leicester)*].

crater creature, drink, esp. whisky. *OED, EDD*. (slang). Cp 'these Thy creatures of bread and wine' from the service of Holy Communion ['I wouldn't mind a drop o' the old crater'].

craunch/scraunch crunch. *OED, EDD* [Don't craunch yer peps like that].

create make a fuss, object strongly. *OED* [Air Mam wun' 'alf create about it].

Creeping Jinny moneywort. *OED* and *EDD* Creeping Jenny.

Creepy-mouse tickling finger-play for a baby. *OED, EDD* [J Carlile, *Fortune-hunters* (1689), p 25. 'Not so old but I can play at Creep-mouse yet. Creep, mouse, creep, catch her'].

creeses water-cress. *OED* (dial) ['Creeses, fresh water-creeses'].

cresset iron fire-basket, used when heating casks to shape them. *OED, EDD*, Lin, Nhp [coopering].

crib untidy room or house. *OED, EDD* (slang). *(Long Buckby.)*

cripple sidings sidings where wagons are repaired [railways].

crizzle roughen on the surface, as water does when beginning to freeze. Cp. 'craze'. *OED* (dial) *EDD*.

croffle hobble, walk with difficulty. *EDD* (Long Buckby).

croodle nestle close, crouch. *OED* (dial) *EDD*. *(Tugby, nr Leicester)* ['Come on, croodle down,' said to hens at night. J Clare, *Vill Min*, 'On the pale traveller's way, Who, croodling, hastens from the storm'].

Crosses chn's truce-term, said while crossing the fingers.

crowing decorative work on shoe-bottom [shoe-making].

crowpickle ground-creeping buttercup. *EDD* buttercup. *(Bozeat.)*

crowstarver boy employed to scare birds from crops. *EDD (Helmdon).*

crowtoe crowfoot or buttercup. *OED, EDD* [J.Milton, *Lycidas* (1645) 143. 'The tufted Crow-toe and pale Gessamine'].

croze tool for making a groove in cask staves. *OED, EDD* Yks Nhp, Oxf [coopering].

cruckle wrinkle or rumple [cloth]. *EDD* [I must iron your shirt–its all cruckled].

crud rubbish. *(Spratton.)* Cf curd.

crumpy crisp, crunchy. *OED* (dial) *EDD. (Burton Latimer)* [He likes his pastry a bit crumpy].

crupper-bone lowest bone of spine. From name of strap passing under horse's tail. *OED* ['My poor crupper-bone aches with standing so long'].

crust dried, of hides. *OED* [tanning].

cub hutch, pen, coop; open-fronted fitment for storing skins. *OED* (dial). *EDD* [shoe-making].

cuck throw, chuck. *EDD. (Pury End)* [J Clare, *MS Poems,* in a poem about the May games at Helpston. 'Where they cuck the ball over till day is nigh gone.'

cuckoo barley late barley, sown after the cuckoo has arrived. *EDD.* 'cuckoo corn'.

cunning able, skilled. This is the orig meaning. *OED* (now arch) *EDD (Weedon Lois)* [He's very cunning at making things from wood].

'Cup, cup' Call to cattle to come. *EDD.*

curlick charlock. *EDD (Helmdon).*

cut canal, artificial watercourse. *EDD* [Mollyblobs grow in the Cut].

cutlan small nail used for heels [shoe-making].

cut-off day day, usu. every five weeks, when lace was measured and cut off, ready for selling [lace-making].

cutting-off laying an egg while cackling loudly [She laughs like an old hen cutting off].

cys cyst [He's got a bad cys on his neck].

dab and sucker lollipop sold with a bag of sherbert. *EDD dab,* sweet.

dab hand expert. *OED. EDD* has *dab,* expert [He's a dab hand at draughts].

dabster 1. expert. 2. someone apt to do a certain thing, in a slightly derogatory sense. *OED* (dial) [She's a dabster at forgetting her key].

dabwash n quick washing by hand. v wash quickly by hand. *OED* (dial) *EDD* [I just had a dabwash this week].

daddler something small of its kind. *OED* farthing, *EDD doddler,* a toddler. (Spratton.)

dado a surprise. *(Spratton)* [That *was* a dado].

daffle handkerchief, rag; earlier, rag for cleaning out oven before baking. *EDD (Pury End)*.

damp drizzle, rain slightly. *EDD* [It just damps a bit].

danny child's word for hand. *EDD* [Go and wash your dannies].

David's sling catapult made with strips of leather. *(Banbury.)*

dawsey sticky, heavy; fig dull-witted. *EDD. (Long Buckby)* [The batter-pudden's all dawsey].

dea/dia drink drink made from the dea-nettle [wild hemp-nettle or bee-nettle]. *EDD (Rushden)*.

dead showing less curvature [shoe-making [design]. 'A dead forme shows less curvature'].

dead-horse money drawn before work is done. 'Work with a dead horse'=do work already paid for. *EDD*.

deadman level of earth higher on one side of a wall than the other. *EDD. (Spratton)* ['The deadman kept the dairy cool'].

deathmonger one who lays out corpses ['Sal Brown was the old deathmonger'].

devil's bread cow-parsley, *keck*.

devil's dancing-hour midnight. *EDD (Eastcote)*.

diabolo game played with a double-headed top spinning on a string held between the hands. *OED*.

diaper baby's napkin. *OED* [Shall I put him a clean diaper on?].

dib dip *OED* (dial) *EDD* [Dib in].

dibby mentally retarded.

dick-pot see *fire-pot*. *EDD* Nhp.

didds teats of animals. *EDD. (Spratton.)*

dilatory lazy, untidy, esp of a woman [She's alwus bin dilat'ry].

dillin smallest or weakest pig in the litter; a small child; something small of its kind. *OED* (dial) *EDD* [Mother brought the dillin up by hand]. [F Thompson, *Can.*, p. 24 'Some men swore by the dilling . . . saying it was little and good and would soon catch up'].

dimmy-simmy/ing affected, languishing. *EDD. (Long Buckby.)*

dimpsey-dawdle simpering, affected person. *EDD dimpsey*, neat, smart.

dinks dress up, adorn oneself; *EDD dink*. walk lightly, self-consciously [You're not dinksin' y'self up in that frock till Sunday. She went dinksin' down the street].

directly in a little while, soon. *EDD* [I'll come directly, when I've done the washing up].

dirty-head yeast left to cover the brew [brewing].

disabil working clothes, untidy wear. *OED* (dial) *EDD*. Fr *en déshabille*, undressed [You must excuse me−I'm all in me disabil. J Clare, *Mid.Cush*. Valentine Eve 73-4. 'Whene'er he caught her in her dissabille/Washing or aught'].

ditched impregnated with dirt. *EDD* [My hands are ditched with weeding the garden].

do at work half-heartedly [You've done it? Done at it more like].

do away with get rid of, kill [We did away with the old table. The poor old gal done away with herself].

dobby-hole/dobs-hole game played with marbles rolled into a hole.

do down 1. cheat. 2. soften in cooking. *EDD* [He done me down right enough. These apples do down lovely].

do in kill. *OED* (slang) [They alwus said he done his wife in].

dod a sweet. *EDD E An (Stamford.)*

doddle n. cigarette end. v pick up cigarette ends [He was doddling along the gutter].

dog it play truant. (Corby, modern.)

dogs metal spikes driven into wood [railways].

doings thing[s] of which one forgets the name [Put the doings on the table].

don hand expert. *EDD* [He's a don hand at whist].

'Done, done' 'Be quiet' ['Have done'], said to noisy chn. *(Irthlingborough).*

done up exhausted. *EDD* [Om done up, walkin' all that way].

donkey cheese poor quality cheese. (WW1).

donkey work hard work, drudgery [She was the one as done all the dunkey work].

dooley milk. Fr *du lait*, of milk (WW1).

dot hit, strike. *OED, EDD* [I'll dot yer eye for yer].

dot and carry one sound made by a lame person walking. *EDD* 'dot and go one'.

dotkin double, *spitten* image [The boy's the dotkin of his father].

doublefold double, twice as much. *OED* (obs) [She loves him doublefold now].

dough v to paw with the front feet, of a cat. *OED* (rare, obs).

dout put out, extinguish. *OED* (dial) *EDD* (do out) [The sun douts the fire].

downgate hole or channel through which molten metal enters mould [iron-founding].

downright tool for shaving a cask [coopering].

drafting pulling uppers into shape over the last [shoe-making].

drag tool for pulling upper leather over last [shoe-making].

drag-rack large hay or corn rake.

drag up bring children up badly. *OED, EDD* [The poor kids was dragged up any'ow].

drawcloth cloth laid on a lace-pillow to take the friction of the bobbins. *(Greens Norton)* [lace-making].

drawter cloth covering upper part of finished lace. *EDD* Nhp [lace-making].

drench warm solution of bran or meal and water [tanning].

dribs and drabs small quantities. *EDD* [He brought his things home by dribs and drabs].

drift drive cattle or sheep. *OED. EDD* has 'drive away'. (Clifton *Shefford, Beds)* [Drift them along gently].

drotchell slovenly woman. *OED drossell. EDD. (Ashton, near Roade)* ['You do look a drotchell this morning'].

drucken sicken, become ill. *EDD drowk,* droop from want of water. *EDD* Nhp Hunt. *(Brafield)* ['That child's druck'nin' fer summat' J Clare, *Vill Min* (1821) line 133. 'Bumble-bees I wandered by, Clinging to the drowking flower'].

duckpuddle very thick mixture ['The soup was like duckpuddle'].

Duckstones game played by throwing stones at a target of larger stones. *OED, EDD.*

dudgy heavy, wet, of land. *(Spratton.) EDD* 'felted, as flannel, or tight, as knitting'.

duff useless. *EDDn* 'a fool'.

duffus dove-house, pigeon-cote. *EDD. (Brington.)*

dug dog. *EDD* ['As cold as a dug's nose'].

dummel slow-witted; sleepy, inactive, of wasps. *OED* (dial) *EDD (Banbury).*

Dutch eye ogling glance, in phr 'to give a Dutch eye'. *(Ashton, near Roade.)*

earthful earthly [I did every earthful thing I could].

eariwig earwig. *EDD.*

eat taste when eaten. *OED. EDD* [The pastry eats nice and short].

eccups hiccups.

eckle hickwall, the green woodpecker. *EDD. (Pury End.)*

edgy nervous, quick to take offence. *EDD* [I feel so edgy today—I could quarrel with the stones in the wall].

egg and bacon birds' foot trefoil, from its yellow and red flowers. *EDD.*

eggler hawker who collects and sells eggs. *OED* (dial.) *EDD. (Wolverton.)* From higgler, pedlar [F Thompson, *Can.* p 91. '. . . the grandfather had followed the old country calling of an eggler'].

eldern elder. *OED, EDD* [J.Clare, *Shep Cal* October 26. 'To press and make their eldernberry wine'].

else otherwise, or. *OED* (Obs) *EDD* [Put your coat on—you'll be cold else. Write it down, else you'll forget].

emery-bat wooden board, covered in emery-paper on one side and leather on reverse, used for sharpening knives [shoe-making].

emmet ant *OED* (dial) *EDD. (Spratton.)*

empt v. empty. *OED* (dial.) *EDD* [Empt the bucket for me].

endless a great deal [I've done endless for her in my time].

entry narrow passage between two houses. *OED* (dial.) *EDD* ['Our cat ran up your entry'—We are related to you].

ep heap. *(Boddington)* ['I've swept the mullocks on to the muck-ep'].

eppern apron. *(Broughton.)*

et eat. *OED* (obs) *EDD* [He'll et anything].

ethering twining pliant-sticks between upright stakes in a hedge. *OED* 'ether, variety of edder'. Obs etc. dial *EDD. (Bozeat.)*

ever such a thing as. *EDD* [Are yer got ever a match on yer?].

ever likely certain, very likely [You're ever likely to feel cold–you don't wear enough clothes].

everlasting all the time. *EDD* [She's everlasting on about moving].

evil very angry or upset. *EDD* [It makes me feel evil when I think what she's done].

Exes Crosses, truce-term in chn's games.

eye-well spring of water believed to cure eye disorders. *(Weston-by-Weedon.)*

face ache tooth-ache.

facen face. *(Spratton.)* Cp *housen,* house [It's cold to my facen].

faddle fuss over trifles. *OED* (dial) *EDD.*

fagging-hook hooked stick for drawing corn towards the reaper. *EDD. (Alderton.)*

faggot annoying, disliked woman; humorous term for a child. *OED* (dial.) *EDD* [She's a miserable old faggot. Hold still, you little faggot].

fake v polish [shoe-making].

fairstitching stitching a sole to the projecting edge of the middle sole [shoe-making].

fall 1. n. woman's veil, used locally of a bride's veil. *OED, EDD* [2. v become pregnant. *EDD.* We were going to move, but then I fell for our Sally].

fallals finery, ornaments. *EDD.*

fallings apples fallen from the tree while small and unripe. *EDD* [You can use up the fallings for cooking].

fan [about] move restlessly in and out or about a room. *EDD* [I wish you'd stop fanning about and sit still].

farden farthing. *OED* (obs and dial) *(Moulton)* ['She'd skin a flint to save a farden'].

farm out clean out. *OED* (dial) *EDD. OE feormian,* clean, purge. *(Wolverton)* [F.Thompson, *Can,* p 80. '. . . Dick used to come sometimes . . . to farm out the pigsties'].

fart [about] occupy oneself with trifles. *EDD* [Whatever are you fartin' about at?].

fathom distance between the arms outstretched sideways, used as a measure of thread. *OED, EDD* [hand-sewn-shoe making].

fatliquor emulsion of various oils used to soften the skin structure [tanning].

feather space between stitch channel and edge of leather. *OED* [shoe-making].

featherfew feverfew, plant of the camomile family 'taken to drive away fever'. *OED, EDD.*

feature resemble in features. *OED* chiefly dial. *EDD.* He features his father.

feelth feel, n *EDD* [I like the feelth of this silk].

feetage measurement of leather by the linear foot [leather-dressing].

fellow n one of a pair. v match up in pairs ['This is the fellow one to it.' Shoe-making].

felt fieldfare, misselthrush or redwing. *EDD*. Often pron. *falt*.

fen-thrush missel-thrush. *OED, EDD*.

fetch 1. cause to come, in phr. 'fetch blood'. *OED* [rare]. [A big boy hit him—look, it's fetched blood.] 2. give. *OED* (coll). I'll fetch you such a thump. 3. draw with difficulty [of breath]. *OED* (rare). [He had to fetch every breath].

fetch out grind ['The clicker's knife is fetched out to the right curve'].

few some, of broth or porridge. *OED* (dial) *EDD* (Wellingborough); a good/nice few=a reasonable quantity. *OED* dial) *EDD* [He likes a few broth for supper. We dug a nice few taters].

fiddler seed-box with handle. As this turns, a bow throws out the seed. *(Spratton.)*

Fig Sunday Palm Sunday. *EDD*.

fillip/fillop quick stinging blow; sudden fall. *EDD (Little Houghton)* [He come such a fillop].

fillyloo uproar. *EDD* [I never heard such a fillyloo].

findings grindery, small shoe-trade goods, welts, heelball, thread etc., found [paid for] by the hand-sewn-shoe maker. *(Rushden.)*

Finedon dried apple apple preserved by slow drying in the oven after each baking [at Finedon].

fine-mouthed fastidious about food. *OED, EDD* [Eat it up and don't be so fine-mouthed].

finicky fussy, fastidious. *OED* (dial) *EDD* [My uncle was very finicky with his food].

fire-foisting huddling over the fire. *(Little Houghton.)*

fire-pot earthenware, brass or iron pot, filled with hot coals or wood-ash, placed near lace-makers' feet in cold weather. *(Greens Norton)* [lace-making].

flack wave to and fro. *ME flacken,* Icel. *flaka,* flap. *EDD* [Wash your hair and flack it about in front of the fire].

flacker piece of card placed in spokes of a bicycle wheel to make a noise. *EDD flacker,* v vibrate.

flag-basket workman's tool basket made of reeds. OED (obs) *EDD. (Spratton.)*

flagging-iron tool for fixing flags (rushes) in the seams of a cask to tighten them. *OED* [coopering].

flam small net used for ferreting. *EDD (Spratton).*

flaming adding colour [leather-dressing].

flash/flask glass globe, filled with water or 'snow-water' (sic), to give extra light from a candle [lace-making].

flig fly. *EDD. (Spratton)* ['Gone flig' [the bird has flown]].

fligger fledgling bird. *EDD. (Spratton.)* Also *flidger (Pury End)* and *fledger EDD. (Banbury.)*

flight chaff, husks, esp of oats. *OED, EDD (Kislingbury)* [An oat-flight].

flimp limp, soft, of material. *EDD. (Long Buckby.)*

flit move house. *OED* (mainly dial). *EDD*.

flittings household effects moved from one house to another *EDD*. *(Earls Barton.)*

flogger tool for beating a cask to dislodge the bung. *OED* [coopering].

flother fly out, of a dress. *EDD*. *(Long Buckby.)*

flummox bewilder. *OED* (prob of dial orig). *EDD* [They all talked at once and flummoxed me].

flurrups water in which meat or fish is boiled, thickened with flour and eaten as broth.

fly take offence quickly. *EDD* [I knew she'd fly if you mentioned the will].

fly-fishing temporary fixing of fish-plates over joints in rails [railways].

Fog Cottages houses built near the track for railway workers, part of whose job was to place detonators [fog-signals] on the line. *(Milton Malsor, Althorp, Gayton)* [railways].

foller fallow. *EDD*. follow [We left the ground dead foller].

fond, joking, foolish. *OED, EDD*. ['He had a fond saying']. *(Draughton)*.

foot/footside straight edge of lace, to be sewn to other material. *(Greens Norton.)*

foreladder frame fixed to the front of a cart to increase capacity. *EDD*. *(Thenford.)*

forket forked stick used to make a catapult.

fornicating fabricating, deceitful. *EDD*. fornicate, 'wheedle, cajole' [The fornicatin' old humbug].

forrest foremost, of a horse in a team. *EDD*. *(Weedon Lois.)*

four o'clocks straps tied below the knees of trousers. *(Harpole.)*

frail flail. *OED* (dial) *EDD (Kislingbury)* [J Clare, *Mid Cush* Signs of Winter, 10.

> '. . . the thresher pale
> Twanks with sharp measured raps
> The weary frail.'

Frank/Old Frank heron, from its cry. *OED* (dial) *EDD*.

frem firm, crisp, of lettuce, rhubarb. *OED* (dial 'juicy, abundant') *EDD* [Pick a lettuce as is nice and frem].

frez frozen [My hands are frez].

frit frightened. *EDD* [That dog frit me. J Clare, *MSPoems*
> 'And larks that fly above the corn,
> Frit by a jilted stone.'
Jilted=flung.

frog-wine well-water.

froxy spirited, of a horse. *EDD* proxy [F Thompson, *Can*, 475. '. . . unless the horse was of the temper called "froxy" '].

fry internal parts of animals, liver, kidneys etc., usu eaten fried. *OED* (dial) *EDD* [We're got pigs' fry for supper].

full of cold having a heavy cold. *EDD* [Air Dad's 'ad t'g' t' work, but e's full of cold].

fur far. *OED* (obs dial) Cf further [How fur is it?].

furr furrow. *EDD. OE furh.*

furrow-horse right-hand horse in a single-furrow plough-team—the horse that walks in the furrow. *EDD.*

furzen furze. gorse. *OED* (dial) *EDD.*

Fusses claim to be first in chn's games. 'Fusses, Secondes, Thirdes'.

fust first ['I'll see'im in'ell fust].

fuzz/fuse v break wind. *EDD* fust, foost.

fuzz n furze, gorse. *EDD* F Thompson, *Can*, 282 ['all common land of turf and fuzz 'twas then'].

gaffle (up) wrap up well. *EDD* 'pad parts of the body, e.g. for cudgel playing.' *(Pury End.)*

gag small portion. *(Brigstock)* [I had a gag o'meat].

gallus rascal, orig. 'one who deserves hanging, "gallows-face".' *EDD.* Also used as mild oath. *EDD* [Them little galluses are bin all over my gardin. What the gallus is that?].

gammy lame. *OED* (dial) *EDD* [He's got a gammy leg].

gannock narrow alley. *EDD* 'narrow passage between *cobs* (islands) in a river'. *(Earls Barton, Bozeat.)*

gansey knitted jumper or cardigan, jersey. *EDD.* Presumably from 'Guernsey', though EDD does not confirm this ['I shall put me gansey on'].

garden-field allotment. *(Kettering.)*

garden-stuff euphemism for 'God' [Good garden-stuff].

gather n infected spot, usu. on hand. v become infected *(EDD)* [He's got a nasty gather on his finger].

gay in good health, usu neg *OED* (dial) *EDD* [I don't feel very gay today].

geared-horse foremost horse of a team. *EDD. (Tugby, nr Leicester.)*

gearing rails fixed to a trailer to increase capacity. *EDD (Spratton).*

gentle v make tractable by gentle handling, tame, used of animals. *OED, EDD* [Just gentle the mare down a bit].

George Horsepool Kettering character remembered for being 'nosy' [Questions, questions, you're as bad as George Horsepool].

get at reach, with no object expressed [Mind out—I can't get at].

get off succeed in making the acquaintance of one of the opposite sex. *OED* [She got off with one of the soldiers].

get on to grumble at, scold [Don't get on to me—I'm sorry].

gilliflower/gilliver/gilly wallflower. O Fr *gilofre. OED* (dial) *EDD.*

gimmer young female sheep. *OED* (dial) *EDD.* Norw and Swed dial *gimber,* 'young ewe'.

gimson n. gimcrack, trifle.

v trifle ingeniously, as opposed to making properly; perform odd jobs. *EDD. (Long Buckby.)*

gin-balls balls of flour mixed with gin, given to calves being carried to market over long distances. *EDD* [J.Donaldson, *General View of the Agriculture of the County of Northampton.* 1794. 51. 'They (calves) are maintained frequently for eight or ten days together on nothing but wheatflour and gin mixed together, which are here called gin-balls'].

ginger careful. *EDD*.
 Cp gingerly [The path was slippy–I had to be a bit ginger].
give/gev gave [She give me two frocks].
give it in decide, come to the conclusion. *OED* (obs) *EDD* 'assert'
 [I couldn't see her so I gev it in she'd gone home].
glarny glass marble, often from a *spruce* [lemonade] bottle.
glaudy having bright sunshine between showers. *EDD* Nhp Bdf.
gleg n and v glance, peep. *EDD (Helpston)* [J Clare, *Vill Min.*
 'Searching with minutest *gleg*.'
gline look furtively, look askance. *EDD* [Did you see her glinin' all
 round?].
glory-hole cupboard or room full of odds and ends or lumber.
 OED (dial) *EDD*.
Go away with you/Get away I don't believe you. *EDD*.
go-by [to give] leave alone. *EDD* [Give housework the go-by for a
 day or two].
go home die [She looks as if she's going home fast].
goings on 1. livelihood [She's got a good goings-on now she's
 married]. 2. commotion [What a goings-on next door].
gobstopper very large sweet which changes colour as it is sucked.
golden/golding corn marigold. *OED* (obs) *EDD*.
goo go [Om gooin' now].
good-living leading a steady, respectable life. *EDD* good-liver [He's
 a good-living boy].
goosegog gooseberry. *OED* widespread, *EDD* [And don't you go
 eating guzgogs].
gorker carrion crow. *OED* gorcrow *(Banbury)*, *EDD* goring-crow.
goss gorse. *OED*. *EDD*. *(Kettering.)*
gossuck gorse-hook, bill-hook for cutting gorse. *EDD*.
grains barley waste from brewing, used as food for pigs. *EDD*.
 (Thenford.)
Grandmother's footsteps game involving creeping up and
 running away.
granny-bonnet/granny-night cap columbine. *EDD*.
grassing sun-bleaching of chamois leather. *OED* [leather dressing].
graveyarder deep, harsh cough. *EDD* 'graveyard chorus'.
Green man, green man, arise game played at haymaking, by
 covering a child with grass, from which he springs up.
gret great, big. *OED* (obs) *EDD*. 'There's a gret dog outside.'
grib squeeze a spot on the skin. *EDD* 'bite'. *(Banbury.)*
grindlestone/grinstone grindstone. *OED* (dial) *EDD*.
grinsard greensward, grassland, grass verge. *EDD* [F Thompson,
 Can, 35 'Their mother would call "Don't go on the road. Keep
 to the grinsard" '].
grinstead grass edge of field. *(Alderton.)*
grip small drainage trench. *OED* (dial) *EDD*. *(Pury End,
 Ravensthorpe.)*
grits groats, crushed barley or wheat ['Blood and fat meat and grits'
 (in the making of pigs' pudding)].

grizzle whine, complain. *OED, EDD.*

ground land, often allotment. *EDD* [He's got a bit o'ground up *Thrupp* Road. (Rothersthorpe Road)].

grounds large upland grazing field; *EDD.* Nhp farm, orig. grazing farm. [Aynho Grounds, *Thrupp* Grounds].

grubber workhouse. *EDD.* grub = work hard and continuously. *(Banbury.)*

grumble ache slightly, of a tooth. *EDD* [My tooth's been grumbling all day].

grummet awkward, bad-tempered person. *(Earls Barton.) OED* (dial) *EDD* 'clumsy awkward youth'.

guide muscle, tendon. *EDD* [He strained one of the guides in his leg].

guinea-pig woodlouse. *EDD.*

gumdragon tragacanth gum, used to smooth sole [shoe-making].

gut-foundered very hungry, starving. *OED* (dial) *EDD (Kettering).*

guttle drink noisily and fast. *OED, EDD. (Earls Barton.)*

gyp pain. *OED* (dial or coll) *EDD gip,* v punish [This tooth does give me gyp].

hackle set in order; work out, come out right. *EDD (Wolverton).*

hag fatigue, tire out. *OED* (dial) *EDD* [You'll hag the poor wench to death].

haggle hack, cut unevenly *OED, EDD.*

hairiff/herriff goosegrass, cleavers *OED, EDD.*

half-and-halfer homosexual man or boy.

half-baked slow-witted, silly. *OED* (dial).

half-larks tricks, shortcomings. *EDD 'half-laugh,* an action done half-heartedly' [Now then, none o' your half-larks].

half-legged [of horses] having less long hair on the legs than shire-horses have.

hand-leather leather protection for the hand. *EDD* [hand-sewn-shoe making].

hand-pat fluent, well-rehearsed. *EDD* [He's got it all off hand-pat].

hand-running one after another, in succession. *OED* (dial) *EDD. (Oundle.)*

hand's turn a small job of work, a little help. *OED* (coll.) *EDD* [There's no one to do a hand's turn for us].

hang-gate gate opening into a V-shaped or curved enclosure, a kissing-gate. *(Cogenhoe.)*

Hanslope curl long curl across the forehead, worn by Hanslope men.

happen of happen on, come across. *(Kettering)* [Om happened of a coat I can give the poor old chap].

harbour keep, give house-room to. *EDD* [Don't harbour these old things].

harden made from hards, the coarser parts of flax and hemp. *OED, EDD. (Pitsford)* ['My grandmother always wore what she called a harden apron to work in'].

hard hat job that of a foreman or someone in authority, who wore a bowler hat ['He had a hard hat job over the Castle.' *(Castle Station)*].

hard on nearly. *EDD. (Harpole)* ['Hard on eighty years'].

hard-sitten having been sat on till nearly ready to hatch. Of eggs. *EDD. (Spratton.)*

hardstick a stick of hard licorice [Hardstick and kali was our Saturday treat].

hardymouse shrew. *EDD.*

harrywig earwig. *EDD.*

hash v. half-dry. (Brigstock.) *EDD hask,* 'of a cough, dry' [The clothes are hashed].

haunch thick slice of bread, half a cottage loaf [What a gret 'aunch].

hawbuck rough ill-mannered man. *OED, EDD. (Barton Seagrave.)*

haychat finch. *(Helpston.) EDD* 'any bird building its nest of hay'.

hazzled dry on the surface, rough, sore, of hands and face. *EDD* [My hands are hazzled with the cold].

head pattern. *(Greens Norton)* [lace-making. 'She used to set me four heads a day, before I could go out to play'].

headache common red poppy. *OED* (local) *EDD* [J Clare, *Prose*, p 27. 'I remember finding some curious flowers . . . one was a yellow headache perennial.'

headside outer edge of length of lace. *(Greens Norton)* [lace-making].

head-sir-rag leader, one in authority. *EDD* [Her brother's head-sir-rag at the works].

hear tell hear. *OED* (dial) *EDD* [I never heard tell of such a thing].

heavens hard heavily, hard, of rain. *EDD* [We can't go yet–it's raining heavens hard].

hedge-backs cuts or swathes of grass nearest the hedge. *(Spratton.)*

hedge-carpenter lit. repairer of hedges and fences; used for a rough carpenter, or one with no workshop, who works by a hedge. *OED, EDD (Litchborough.)*

helt held [I helt on to it as long as I could].

hern hers. Cp. mine. *OED* (arch and dial) *EDD* (south. and midl dial) [That's mine and this is hern].

herne/hernshaw/heronshaw heron. *OED* (arch. or dial.), all forms. *EDD* all forms. herne *(Rushden)*; hernshaw *(Pitsford)*.

herricking wild, rough, of behaviour.

herriff goosegrass. *OED, EDD.*

hezzle v. half-dry, of washing. *EDD. (Helpston)* [The washing's hezzled].

Hi-acky game of hide-and-seek.

hick hitch, hoist. *EDD. (Spratton.)*

hicking-stick stick pushed under heavy sacks to hoist them on to trailer. *(Spratton.)*

hike off take away. *EDD* [Somebody's hiked the spade off].

hilling bed-cover. *OED* dial *EDD. ON hylja,* cover. *(Kislingbury)* ['It's a nice day–we shall have to wash weer [our] 'illin's'].

hinder time delay. *OED* (obs, rare) *EDD* [I know you're in a hurry–I don't want to hinder time].

hisn his. *OED* (south and midl dial) *EDD* [I know that coat's hisn].

hit up ask in an indirect way [She was hitting up to come with us].

hob male ferret. *OED, EDD.*

hob-cutter edge-trimming tool [shoe-making].

hobday operate on a horse to cure a breathing impediment. After Sir F Hobday (1869-1939) ['We declared that the horse had been hobdayed'].

hock and dough pigs hock baked in pastry with potatoes and onions. *(Wellingborough.)*

hockle walk with difficulty, hobble. *EDD.*

hock off drive away *(Spratton.)*

hoddycadoddy/hoddy-doddy snail. *EDD. (Pury End.)*

hodge hedgehog. *(Little Houghton.)*

holler shout loudly, scold. *OED* (dial) *EDD* [My dad'll holler at me].

hollock loaf about noisily. *EDD* [Stop hollocking about and get on with your work].

hollow (of wind). having a low, threatening sound. *OED, EDD* [The wind sounds hollow tonight].

holt hold, in. combinations meaning 'Take hold'. *OED* (dial) [Catch, *cop, cla'* (Wolverton) *scrat (Kettering)* all followed by holt].

home-bringer provider *EDD. (Irthlingborough).*

hommock tread or walk clumsily. *EDD* [Don't 'ommock all over the flower-beds].

homstraps leather straps fastened below the knee. *OE hamm, homm,* angle of the knee.

horse n frame to support a pillow [lace-making]; frame or rack on which skins are hung [leather-dressing].

horsing raising the back part of the upper at the seat, when lasting. *(Rushden.) OED* (obs) *EDD horse,* 'raise or hoist up' [shoe-making].

horse-road roadway for wheeled traffic. *EDD. (Banbury.)*

hot hit (past tense) *EDD* [I hot him where it hurt].

hot-ache pain caused by sudden warmth to very cold hands. *EDD* [She was crying with the hot-ache].

hotch about fidget. *EDD* [Stop hotching about–you'll wear the cushions out].

hotch off drive away. *(Little Houghton.)* Cp *hock off (Spratton)* ['He wouldn't 'otch a poacher off'].

hotch up move up, make room. *EDD* ['Hotch up, will you?'].

house best room, or ground floor room other than the kitchen. *EDD.*

housen 1. house. *EDD. (Spratton.)* 2. houses. *(Earls Barton, Wolverton, Helmdon)* [F Thompson, *Can,* p 18. 'The plural of "house" was not "houses" but "housen" ']!

house-room space or a place in the house, usu used negatively ['I wouldn't give it house-room'].

hovel shed adjoining the house or in the yard; open-fronted shed
for cattle or farm-carts. Fig. dirty place *(Boddington, Brigstock)*.
OED, EDD ['That's where the waggon-hovel stood'. 'What a
hovel they live in'].

hug hog, pig.

hum home. *EDD*.

humpy depressed, *EDD* [I feel 'umpy today].

hunter's moon next full moon after the harvest moon. *OED, EDD*.

hurk shelter made of hurdles and straw to protect lambing sheep.
EDD. (Spratton) ['We make them to lamb the sheep in.' See
lamb v].

hurt take damage. *EDD* 'matter, signify' [Your umbrella won't hurt
in the porch].

hus house, in combinations. *EDD* [Cow-'us, 'en-'us, ale-'us etc].

hutch basket of plaited rushes to hold flask when not in use.
(Greens Norton) [lace-making].

huzzaying noisy singing or shouting in the street. *OED* huzzay.
(Pury End.)

I Am very important person. Exodus iii, 14. 'I Am hath sent me
unto you' [He thinks he's the great I Am].

ikey proud. *EDD* [She's too ikey for me].

image oddity, spectacle. *EDD* [She's making an image of herself,
dressed like that].

iron 1. heated tool for applying wax [shoe-making]; 2. thickness of
bottom leather. One iron = $\frac{1}{48}$ of an inch [shoe-making].

jack n 1. pike. *OED, EDD*. 2. device for holding the last [shoe
making]. 3. frame to hold the *yelms* for the thatcher. *EDD* Nhp
(Spratton) [We caught a jack for our supper].

jack v project. *EDD*.

Jack-at-a-pinch on the spur of the moment [I went out Jack-at-a-
pinch to look for him].

Jack-go-to-bed-at-noon goatsbeard. *OED (Greens Norton)*. *EDD*
'star of Bethlehem'.

Jack-in-the-green boy, covered in a wicker frame hung with
greenery, a performer in the May games. *OED, EDD*.
(Broughton.)

Jack-jump-about ground elder, from its spreading habit. *OED*.
(Bugbrooke.)

jacks game played with five stones. *OED* and *EDD* 'jackstones'.

Jacob's ladder Solomon's seal and other plants with alternate
leaflets or flower stems. *OED, EDD*.

jaconet plain, open-weave cloth, now often rubberised, used for
slipper stiffeners [shoe-making].

jalop/jollop medicine. *OED* (obs) *(Pury End)* ['I used to be sent to
the chemist in Towcester for some jalop'].

janking decorative work on the shoe-bottom [shoe-making].

jaum buttress, jamb. *EDD (Cogenhoe)* ['. . . the jaum on the side of the church'].

jazz plank moving forward and backward [chn's. play apparatus].

jibber chin, underlip. *OED* (dial) *EDD* 'jib' [You're spillin' it down yer jibber].

jigger put out of joint. *EDD (Alderton).*

jill female ferret. *EDD.*

Jill-along-the ground ground ivy. *OED* (dial) *EDD.*

jingle n spangle or bead attached to a bobbin. *EDD* Nhp [lace-making]. v use a jingle-harrow, the blades of which are curved so as to run free of each other. *EDD* jingle-harrow *(Alderton)* ['I was sent to jingle the field'].

jink/s walk quickly and gracefully. *OED, EDD (Rushden).* Cf *dinks.*

Jinny shire horse, large cart horse.

jipper juice, gravy. *OED, EDD.*

jissup gravy. *EDD* 'jessup' ['. . . a bit o' meat and plenty o' jissup'].

jitty narrow pasage between houses. *EDD.*

job poke, jab. *OED, EDD* [He jobbed me in the eye].

Jockey Clubs scented boiled sweets, from the name of a perfume.

Joey rabbit. *(Brigstock.)*

jog small load. *EDD* 'jogget'. *(Spratton)* ['A jog o' wezzels [wurzels]'].

John Blunt blunt in manner, bluntly. *OED* and *EDD* 'a blunt person' [He's a bit John Blunt. She spoke a bit John Blunt].

John Bull petrol-driven rail drill [railways].

John George person with little knowledge of grammar. *(Easton-on-the-hill)* [You'll have to write it for me–I'm a proper John George].

jole knock, strike against. *EDD (Oundle).*

jonnock/s honest, straightforward. *EDD (Harpole)* ['I can't do that–t'aint jonnocks'].

josser fellow, chap. *OED* slang [You hungry-nosed josser].

ju-ju jellied sweet. *OED* 'jujube'.

jummer slow-witted. *EDD 'jummer-head*, stupid person'. *(Earls Barton.)*

jumped-up aspiring above oneself. *OED, EDD* [Some jumped-up kid from the back-streets].

jumper maggot found in cheese. *EDD* [G White, *The Natural Hist of Selborne* (1788–9) p 84. '. . . these eggs produce maggots called jumpers']. 2 bottom-stock press [shoe-making].

(J)Ump-tiddy-ardy game in which one child jumps on the backs of others facing a wall.

June drop fall of small unripe apples in June. *EDD* 'midsummer drop'.

kali sweetened powder to eat or make a drink.

keach dip and take up water, ladle. *OED* (dial obs) *EDD. (Milton Malsor, Pury End)* ['Keach me a drop o' water'].

keacher jug used to ladle water.

keach-hole hole in the bed of a stream, scooped out to collect water. *EDD. (Pury End.)*

keck cow-parsley. *OED* (dial) *EDD. kex/kecks* [J Clare, *Vill Min* 100. 'Half-hid in meadow-sweet and keck's high flowers'].

keckly/kickling unsteady. *EDD kickle,* to upset. Cf cockle [That chair's keckly].

keep grazing land, pasture. *OED, EDD* ['Don't play in the field–it spoils the keep'].

keepered in charge of a keeper [keepered land].

keggy/keggy handed left-handed. *EDD.*

kell caul *OED* (dial) *EDD* ['I feel as if there's a kell over my eye'].

kelter money. *EDD kelt.* Cf. gelt ['He's worth a bit o' kelter'].

keltrement working materials. *EDD 'kelterment',* rubbish ['Put your keltrement on the table'].

kettlin(g)s hot water poured on bread. *EDD 'kettley-broth'. (Kislingbury.)*

kibble walk as if lame. *EDD (Harlestone).*

kick-a-donkey child who kicks.

kicking [about] lying about in disorder. *EDD* [These old clothes have been kicking about for ages].

kid brother or sister [Our kid bosses me about]. *Cf* 'kith and kin'.

kilter [out of] needing adjustment. *EDD 'kelter,* tilt up' [The television's out of kilter].

kimble walk hesitantly, as on ice. *EDD 'kimple,* hesitate at' [I had to go kimbling down the street].

kind soft, having a good 'handle', of leather. *OED* (dial. or technical) *EDD* [shoe-making].

king much better in health, superior. *EDD* [She's a king to what she was. This sofa's a king to the one we used to have].

'Kings' chn's truce term, said while crossing fingers. *EDD.*

kire choir

kiss apply a very light grain [leather-dressing].

kiss-curl small coquettish curl on forehead or side of face.

kit young hare or ferret. *EDD.*

kiver large shallow bowl. *OED* (dial) *EDD.*

K-legged Having one leg turned inwards at the knee.

knave frame for carrying straw up the ladder to a thatcher. Cf 'jack'. *EDD.*

knock about be about, be normally active. *OED* (coll.) *EDD* [Is she still knocking about?].

Knock-down-ginger knocking on doors and running away. *(Spratton.)*

knock off leave off work. *OED, EDD* [Time we knocked off].

knock up exhaust, tire out. *OED.*

knockrowed awkward, obstinate. *EDD* [She's knockrowed if she can't have her own way].

kottled perplexed. *EDD* (obs) Nhp. *(Spratton.)*

lad's love southernwood. *OED* (dial.) *EDD.*

laggy 1. last year's conker, grown hard. 2. Last player in a game. *EDD* 'last of all' ['Tain't fair—he'd got a laggy'].

lamb v tend sheep when lambing. *OED*.

lamb-creep portable wheeled shed in which lambs are fed separately from their mothers. *EDD* 'hole in hurdle to enable lambs to get out'. *(Brixworth.)*

lambing-storm sudden squall of rain or snow in early spring, followed by bright sunshine. *(Little Houghton.)*

lammace(into) strike, attack. *EDD* [You should 'a seen him lammace into our Jack].

land 1. arable division of a furlong in open fields. *OED, EDD*. 2. ridge in a ridge-and-furrow field. *EDD*. 3. part of a field marked out [perhaps only by eye] for ploughing. *EDD*. 4. allotment [I'm going up the land]. 5. ridge of dressed stone.

land-horse left-hand horse of a plough-team, treading on un-ploughed land. *EDD*.

lap wrap. *OED* (dial.) *EDD*. Cp overlap [Lap up well before you go out].

lape hang down, trail on the floor [The bedclothes lape on the floor].

larger seek gifts of money. *(Wilstead, Bedford)* ['To go a-largering'].

larp walk with long, purposeful strides. *EDD lamp. (Rushden.)*

larrup n drink. v eat or drink hungrily [A nice drop o' larrup].

latch-lifter price of a drink, enabling one to lift the latch of the ale-house door. *(Piddington)* [He give me a latch-lifter].

lather ladder. *EDD* [Hold the lather for me].

lattermath aftermath, second crop of hay. *OED* (dial.) *EDD*. *(Weedon Lois.)*

laughter/lawter sitting of eggs, a full clutch. n *OED laughter* (dial) *EDD*. ON *latr*, place where animals lay their young. *(Harpole.)*

laughter v gather up heaped grain. *EDD* [malting].

lavatory basin wash-basin. *OED*. Lat *lavare*, wash.

Lawrence idleness personified. *EDD (Spratton)* ['He's got a Lawrence on his back' J Clare, *Vill Min*. 'The warm sun smiles, And Lawrence wages bids on hill and stiles'. 'wages bids' = 'invites to idleness'].

leaf-lard inner layer of fat of pig or poultry. *OED* leaf-fat (dial.). *EDD* ['At one time you could get leaf-lard from the butcher'].

Leanman third finger.

learn teach *OED* (now vulg) *EDD*. ME *lernen*, learn, teach [He learnt me my trade. A Baker, *GNWP* vol 1 (1854) p 391 '. . . epitaph for a village singing master in the churchyard . . . of Harpole, dated 1729.

> He larned singing far and near
> Full twenty years and more;
> But fatal death hath stopt his breth,
> And he can larne no more'].

lease glean. *OED* (dial) *EDD*. OE *lesan* gather, glean. SW of the county.

leave let. *OED* (arch) *EDD* [Leave go o' me].

leather-eppern leather apron, loose skin on a breast of lamb.

leer sneak about, walk furtively. *OED* (obs) *EDD* [Did you see her leerin' about?].

length slice of bread. *EDD* *(Harpole)*.

let on 1. divulge. *OED* (dial) *EDD* [I never let on as I knew her. as = that]. 2. pretend. *EDD* [He let on as no one had been].

let out scold, swear. *EDD* [Mam let out at me for laughing].

lewbell *lowbell*, express censure by banging tin-cans etc. *OED* (dial) *EDD*. Nhp War Wor.

lew-warm lukewarm. *OED* (dial) *EDD* 'lew' [The water's only lew-warm].

licker puzzle, mystery. *EDD*.

Lickpot forefinger. *EDD*.

lief as lief, rather. *OED, EDD* [I don't like tripe–I'd as lief go without].

ligger liar. *OED* (obs and dial *lig*, lie) *EDD lig*, lie [You little ligger].

limb pull roughly. *OED* and *EDD* 'pull limb from limb' [Don't limb the poor cat about so].

link 1. sausage. *OED* (dial) *EDD*. 2. group of men doing the same term of duty [railways]. fig group of people having something in common ['You're in the same link as Bill–he likes a game of bowls'].

linkman hotel porter. *(Banbury)* ['I should have tripped if the linkman hadn't caught my arm'].

listener wheel-tapper's mate [railways].

Littleman *OED* (obs exc dial) *EDD* the little finger.

little-street-folk people living in the streets of small houses built for railway workers. *(Wolverton.)*

lively handling well, of leather [shoe-making].

lob-dob limpingly [He used to walk lob-dob].

locusts locust beans, fruit of the carob tree, sold in sweet-shops.

London chn's ball game in which a player takes a step 'to London' each time she catches the ball.

longs tops of ridges in a ridge-and-furrow field. *(Market Harborough.)*

long-eared 'uns 'chapel folk'. *(Weedon Lois, Wilstead, Bedford.)*

longlight paraffin oil for lamps. May once have been a trade-name [railways].

Longman middle finger. *EDD*.

long pain, the arthritis.

Long Tom long, four wheeled platform barrow [railways].

luck-money money returned 'for luck' to buyer from seller. *OED. EDD* 'luck-penny'. *(Helmdon.)*

luckybed paving-stone without a crack. [Chn jump over it for luck].

lummox clumsy, unwieldy person. *EDD*.

mackle make a repair or do a job quickly or roughly. *EDD* [Your Dad'll just mackle it up].

madhead reckless person. OED (obs).

maggle tire out, exhaust. *EDD* [I'm maggled to death].

maiden young twig. *EDD (Bugbrooke)* ['I'll tie up the faggot with a maiden'].

make[one] be acceptable, be useful for a short time [My neighbour gave me a dress for the baby. It's not new, but it'll make one].

make words start an argument [Don't make words about it].

malkin scarecrow, *OED* (dial) *EDD (Milton Malsor)*; mop used to clean out an oven, *OED* (obs) *EDD (Helmdon).* effeminate man *(Helmdon).*

manky not good enough, not working properly. *EDD mank,* fail. Fr *manquer,* lack.

manner sort, kind. *OED, EDD* ['She made all manner of excuse'].

mardy bad-tempered. *EDD* spoilt, marred.

mark heed, take notice of ['You mark my words'].

marly 'child's marble', made of marble, not of glass or clay. *OED* (dial) *EDD. (Wellingborough.)*

marnder wander aimlessly. *OED* 'maunder', *EDD* ['. . . marnderin' about as if t'morrer'll do'].

Mary's tapers snowdrops. *(Helmdon.)*

mash infuse tea or malt. *OED* (dial) *EDD* [Give the tea a few minutes to mash].

mastering soaking hides in an infusion of bird-droppings or dog-dung. *EDD* (obs or obsol) [oak-bark tannage].

masterpiece wonder. *EDD* [It's a masterpiece where all that money come from].

match v manage *EDD.*

maudlin poorly, ill. *EDD (Wolverton).*

maul [about] handle, pull about. *EDD* ['If you don't want the goods, don't maul'em about'].

maul (to death) tire, drag down, overheat. *EDD* ['The kids maul her to death.' 'Om mauled to death wi' this coat on'].

maunch munch greedily. *OED* (obs) *EDD.* Cf Fr *manger,* eat [He sat maunching his dinner].

maunge grumble. *EDD* [The ol' gal wus alwus maungin' about summat].

mawkin scarecrow, untidy girl. *OED* (dial) *EDD. (Milton Malsor, Ashton near Roade, Harpole.)*

mawmsey silly, complaining. *EDD. (Little Houghton.)*

mayblob marsh marigold. *(Helpston.)*

mayweed wild camomile. *EDD. (Pury End.)*

meadwort meadowsweet.

medlar apple of any sort. *(Banbury)* [Gi' me one o' they medlars, gal].

meg mark or stake to throw at, in a game. *EDD.*

member person, individual. *OED* (dial) *EDD* [She [mother of a large family] was a busy member].

menfolk men. *OED* (dial) [We shall be done be then [by the time] the menfolk get back].

merry-actors mummers. *(Brigstock.)*

middling not well in health. *OED, EDD* [I felt a bit middlin'. My uncle was pretty middlin'].

migration movement of inferior oil, sulphur etc. to the surface of leather [leather-dressing].

mile-a-minute knotgrass. *(Little Houghton.)*

miller-man personification of sleep, said to throw *sleepy-dust* in children's eyes ['Old miller-man's bin, I see'].

mimmock n. someone fastidious over food. *EDD. mimmocking/y fastidious over food. EDD* [She's such a mimmock. She's so mimmocking/y with her food].

mither worry, bother. Rhyme either. *OED* (dial) *EDD* [Shut up a minute. You mither me].

mizzle 1. rain lightly. *OED* (dial) *EDD* [It's only mizzling a bit]. 2. hurry off. *OED* (slang). *EDD* (dial and slang) [He soon mizzled when we saw him].

mizzy-mozzy perplexed. *OED* and EDD *miz-maze* perplexity *(Spratton)*.

moles *moulds,* the earth, soil. *OED* (dial) *EDD. (Walgrave.)*

mollern *mollhern,* heron, orig the female bird *EDD* (Oxf).

mollin/mullen bridle of a cart-horse. *EDD. mollin* Nhp, *mullen* Nhp et al *(Banbury).*

mollisquash push together, press. *EDD mollicrush* [Get off—you're mollisquashing me].

mollyblob marsh marigold. *EDD.*

mommer confuse, bewilder. *EDD* [Wait a minute—you mommer me. W Shakespeare, *Othello* 111,3,70. 'I wonder in my soul/ What you should ask me, that I should deny/Or stand so mammering on'].

mommy food cooked to a pulp. *EDD* Nhp War Wor [The taters all went to a mommy].

money-spider small spider settling on one's body or clothes, supposed to bring money if twirled three times round the head by its thread. *EDD.*

moodle laze about. *(Ashton, near Roade.)*

mooncalf slow, stupid person. *OED, EDD* [Look at 'im gawpin' about—gret mooncalf].

moondaisy ox-eye daisy. *OED, EDD.*

moonpenny ox-eye daisy. *OED, EDD. (Greens Norton.)*

moor cut shaped strengthener at heel-seam [shoe-making].

Moses - in - the - bulrushes hardy tradescantia. *(Little Houghton.)*

Mossybank ace of spades [Who's got Old Mossybank?].

mothers sediment in vinegar. *OED, mother EDD.*

mothery cloudy, of vinegar. *OED, EDD.*

mouth v scold loudly or rudely. *Th* pron as in *the* [Don't stand mouthing at me].

mow heap of grain, hay or straw. *OED* (dial) *EDD. (Bugbrooke.)* Rhyme 'cow' [The barley-mow].

moz tea [A cup o' moz].

moze smoulder. *EDD. (Ashton near Roade.)* Norw dial *mosen,* warm [The fire was left mozing all night].

mucher someone of consequence, always neg *EDD* [He ain' a mucher].

muckle heap of rubbish or manure. *EDD.*

muckle-bred of mixed breed. *EDD* Nhp 'low-bred' [The sheep are all muckle-bred].

Muckspread month of November. *(Bozeat.)*

muck-sweat heavy perspiration. *EDD* [I was all of a muck-sweat].

muckweed goosefoot. *OED, EDD.*

muggy damp, oppressive, of weather. *OED* (dial) *EDD.*

mulfering/y sultry, close, of weather. *EDD. (Easton-on-the-hill.)*

mullen see *mollin.*

mullock/s rubbish, dirty objects, sickly, worthless food. Hence, *mullocking/y,* dirty, rubbishy. *OED* (dial.) *EDD* [Get rid o' these mullocks. Don't eat them mullocks before y'dinner].

mully child's name for a cow. *OED* (obs exc dial) *EDD mull* [Come and look at the mully-cows].

Nancy Pretty the plant London pride *OED, EDD.*

nanny go at full speed [He was nannying along].

nappa a variety of gloving leather.

nark annoy. *EDD* [I felt so narked with her].

nature strength, essential qualities. *OED* (dial) *EDD* [Nothing grows there–there's no nature in the ground].

naumkeg revolving abrasive tool for cleaning the waists of shoes [shoe-making].

nazzum common sense [It's hard work trying to show him–he's got no nazzum].

neezening birds'-nesting. *EDD. (Spratton)* ['. . . to go neezening'].

Nelson two layers of pastry filled with cake mixture, formerly with stale cake. *EDD* 'sweets' ['We had a Nelson for our dinner'].

nesh tender, feeling the cold. *OED* (dial) *EDD. (Little Houghton.)*

nibby smart, ingenious [That's a nibby little shut-knife].

nice few good number. *EDD* [We've got a nice few plums this year].

nick condition. *EDD* [My old bike's still in good nick].

nit up shaking with cold.

Noah's Ark thin white clouds in the shape of a boat, said to be a sign of rain. *EDD* [J Clare, *Vill Min.* 'By certain signs to judge the weather right, As oft from Noah's Ark great floods descend'].

nobble n small lump, as of coal. *EDD* [Put a nobble on]. v button-hole, engage attention *OED, EDD* [He nobbled me outside the shop].

nobbling small lump of coal. *EDD. (Little Houghton)* [Bring in a shovelful o' nobblings].

no end many. *OED* (coll) [I gave her no end of things].

noggin thick crust of bread. *EDD.*

noggy/nobby as above *(Rushden).*

nointer mischievous youngster. Anointer, one who should be anointed (thrashed). *EDD.*

none (other than) truly, though surprisingly. *OED (arch)* [It was none other than her sister. None the more for. In defiance of. I shall go, none the more for that].

nook bend in a stream, cut off when the watercourse is straightened. Rhyme 'stook'. *(Spratton.)*

noration loud, prolonged talking [an oration]. *EDD (Pury End).*

north eye in phr 'Keep your north eye open,' keep watch. *OED* 'too north', clever. *EDD.*

not hearthed lacking sense. Refers to dough not risen enough [on hearth] *EDD* hearth v bake Nhp.

nowhere near not at all [The coat's nowhere near big enough].

nub/nubby child's name for nose [Let's wipe your nubby].

nuntin[g] too small. *EDD* Nhp E An,Sus [This hat looks nuntin with me new coat].

nurker someone not to be trusted.

ockard awkward, uncertain of temper. *EDD* [She's a bit ockard today].

odd/some odd small amount or number extra. *OED* (dial) *EDD* [He sent fifty-odd sheep to market. We raised thirty pounds odd for Ethiopia. I gave two pounds and some odd].

odds 1. alter, remedy. *OED* (now rare) *EDD* [I shall have to wait–I can't odds it]. 2. in phr 'has the odds', differs. *OED* (dial) *EDD* [Her boy's a good worker–he's got the odds of our Jack].

offal trimmings of raw hides; off-cuts of leather. *OED* (tech and dial) *EDD* [tanning, shoe-making].

offer hold something in place to see if it fits, as in woodworking, picture-framing. *EDD.*

off-hooks out of humour. *OED* (obs) *EDD* [The missis is off hooks with me today].

old in phr 'look old', look askance or knowingly. *EDD* [She knows who I am–she looked old at me when I went in].

old boy baby boy, little boy. *EDD. (Kettering area.)* 'young old boy' *(Brigstock).*

old buck cheek, impudence. *EDD* [Don't give me none o' yer old buck].

old-fashioned quiet in manner, knowing, of a child. *OED* (dial) *EDD* [He's an old fashioned little mite].

Old Harry in phr 'play Old Harry', react strongly, show anger [The boss played Old Harry].

Old man southernwood. *OED, EDD.*

Old Nick the devil. *EDD.*

old soldier in phr 'come the old soldier', try to deceive. *OED* (coll) *EDD* [Don't come the old soldier with me].

old street road Watling Street (A5). Street = highway, paved road.

on 1. of. *OED* (dial) *EDD* [Take one on 'em with you]. 2. acting as leader, chaser, or taking one's turn, in chn's games [Who's on?]. 3. at the point of. *EDD* [It's just on six o'clock].

ondo undo [I can't ondo me shoe-lace].

onempt empty, unload. *OED* (dial) *EDD* [You can onempt the buckets here].

onkers knees. *EDD bunkers.*

ourn ours *OED* (dial) *EDD; my husband EDD. (Eastcote)* [That there dog's ourn. Ourn's comin' 'ome soon].

ours our house. *EDD.*

outdacious audacious. *EDD (Ashton, near Roade.)*

overlayer extension to a waggon to increase capacity. *EDD. (Eastcote.)*

Overs and unders roadside game in the early days of cars, involving guessing the last figure of the registration number. Played by men and boys. *(Cogenhoe.)*

overshot space over which waste water flows from a weir down to the natural course of the river. *EDD* Nhp.

owlers owl-catchers *OED, EDD.* Gloves of thick leather used to protect the hands from thorns.

own acknowledge, recognise. *OED* (dial) *EDD* [He'll pass me in the street and never own me].

pad path, track. *EDD.* Dutch, Low Germ *pad,* path. *(Helpston.)*

paddle small spade-like tool with long handle used for digging up thistles etc. *OED, EDD. (Spratton.)*

pairage number of pairs produced [shoe-making].

pancake flower common mallow, from its flat seed-head. *OED* (dial) *EDD. (Pury End.)*

pancheon large earthenware vessel, wider at the top than the bottom, used for wine-making etc. *OED, EDD.*

parish lantern moon. *OED* (dial and slang) *EDD. (Helmdon.)*

pathfinder a pilot line (trial batch) [shoemaking].

Patsies/Pax chn's truce term. *OED* Pax.

peaky poorly-looking, with pinched features. *OED* (dial) *EDD.*

peck n wooden bucket for holding a peck of corn. *(Banbury.)* v pick, hence peck-axe. *OED* (dial) [The ground's so hard it needs a peck-axe].

Pecks and spans game in which a marble is thrown (*pecked* = pitched *OED* (dial), *EDD*) and a player tries to hit it with another marble, the distance between the two being measured by hand-spans. *EDD.*

peen/pene n sharp or thin end of a hammer-head. *OED* (tech) *EDD.* Norw dial *pen,* pointed part of a hammer. v beat thin with a hammer. *OED* (obs exc dial) *EDD. (Rushden.)*

peg n and v signal. Hence *pegged,* signalled. *EDD* [He's got the peg. [railways] *EDD* vol IV, p 459. Nhp 'The Manchester express was pegged'. *The Daily Mail,* 5 September, 1898'].

peg v spoil the surface of a slide by having a *proud* nail in one's boot. *(Spratton)* [Who's pegged the slide?].

pen and ink sound of footsteps. [She went down the street 'pen and ink, pen and ink' *(Piddington)*].

pendle stratum in a stonepit. *OED* (local term) *EDD* Nhp Shr Glo Oxf Bdf. *(Helpston.)*

pen-feather young quill-feather. *OED, EDD. (Spratton)* [J Clare, *MS Poems*. 'Morning's young dew wets each pin-feathered wing'].

penny-twink candle for chn at night. *(Pury End.)*

pen-thrush missel-thrush. *(Spratton.)*

pep sweet [Give us a pep].

pep peeped. *EDD* [I pep in through the window].

perished/perishing very cold *OED* (chiefly dial) *EDD* [We got perished waiting for the bus. Wrap up – it's perishing outside].

pesthouse building to which smallpox victims were taken to be nursed. *OED.*

peth pith *OED* (dial) *EDD* [These oranges are all peth].

Philip sparrow. *OED* (dial) *EDD.* Chs Nhp [J Skelton, *Poetical Works* (c1529) *A litle boke of Phylyp Sparrowe.*

Phoebe sun. *OED* Phoebus ['Come on, Phoebe'].

piccolo shotgun. *(Spratton)* ['If anyone said "piccolo" you'd know he meant a shotgun'].

pie pit for storing root-crops. *OED* (local) *EDD. (Banbury.)*

pig woodlouse. *EDD (Blakesley.)*

pigeon young girl. *OED* (obs) [What's wrong, my pigeon?].

pigeon pair a son and daughter. *EDD* [Now you've got your pigeon pair].

pightle small field or enclosure, esp near a house; narrow strip of land, running to a point. *OED* (local) *EDD. (Wellingborough.)*

pike n narrow strip of land running to a point. *OED* (dial).
v plough a strip of land to a point; walk, as across a field, at an angle. *OED, EDD* all meanings [He went pikin' off over the field].

pill peel. *OED* (dial) *EDD.*

pin-a-dip child's pastime of inserting a pin between the leaves of a book. If a cut-out picture, a treasure in Victorian and Edwardian days, was revealed, the child had the picture, but if not, forfeited his pin. *EDD pin-a-sight.*

pingle pightle, qv *OED* (local) *EDD.*

pink peer, wink. *OED* (dial) *EDD.* Du *pincken*, shut the eyes.

pinken-eyed John/pinkly John wild pansy. *EDD.*

pinkie fourth finger. *OED, EDD. (Corby.)*

pinny newly-fledged bird. *(Spratton.)*

pin-toed having toes turned inwards.

pip in phr 'got the pip', depression, ill-temper. From pip, a poultry disease *OED*, dyspepsia, or slight cough *EDD*.

pipy having loose fibre rolled in, of leather [shoe-making].

pismire ant. *OED* (dial) *EDD.* ON*maur*, ant, and the urinous smell of an ant-heap. *(Spratton.)*

pisshead dandelion, from its diuretic properties. *(Little Houghton.)*

plater horse-mushroom, 'as big as a plate'. *(Spratton.)*

platter earthenware. *EDD* [The kitchen plates are only platter].

platters broken pieces of earthenware found in the soil, playthings for little girls ['We played with platters on the closet seat'].

pleasure-market street-market. *(Market Harborough)* ['I do not remember the cattle-market in the High Street, only the pleasure-market'].

plenty amply. *EDD* (coll) [That's plenty big enough].

plough name of several cutting and channelling tools [shoe-making]; instrument for turning malt as it dries.

ploughing ploughed land. *(Helmdon)* ['The hunt people called it arable but we always called it the ploughing'].

plough-moll girl who brought out horses ready for ploughing. *(Little Houghton.)*

poach trample soft ground into mud, usu. said of animals' hooves. *OED* (dial) *EDD*. Cp 'poke'. *(Spratton.)*

poacher's stone heavy rounded stone carried by some poachers to throw at a game-keeper if cornered. *(Pytchley.)*

pobs bread and milk. *EDD*.

pods baby's shoes. *EDD (Market Harborough)*.

poddle walk with short, unsteady steps. *EDD*.

polch/polsh poach, take rabbits etc.

pollard spoilt grain used for pig-food. *EDD*. *OED* bran sifted from flour. *(Holcot.)*

polsh search about, rummage. *(Kettering)* ['I call that my polshing drawer'].

Polly-long-frock name for girl wearing a long dress.

pommy food cooked to a pulp. *OED* and *EDD* from 'pomace', apples crushed to a pulp in cider-making.

poor-man's-weather-glass scarlet pimpernel, from its closing its petals before rain. *EDD. (Barton Seagrave.)*

poppy-show sight, spectacle, said disparagingly. From peep-show, a child's plaything, puppet-show. *EDD* [She makes a poppy-show of herself].

positive organ small organ which must be placed on a stand when played. *OED (Grendon)*.

possessioning beating the bounds of a parish. *EDD*. N Cy Nhp.

pottering slow, feeble in movement. *EDD (Ashton near Roade)* [J Clare, *Vill Min* 'With lingering, pott'ring pace And head bleached bare'].

pot-herbs root-vegetables. *EDD* parsley, leeks ['Get the pot-herbs ready for the stew'].

power pour, Rhyme 'grower'. *EDD* [Power us a cup o'tay, gal].

pozzy jam. *OED* WW1 ['There was only one sort of pozzy–plum and apple'].

present immediate. *OED* (obs) ['It would be present death to go out in this weather'].

pretty Rhyme Betty. *EDD (Banbury)* ['Pretty wee mossel [morsel]' said of a baby].

pricker nut-wood peg used in thatching. *EDD.*

prickstitch stitch separator, tool for pressing between stitches [shoe-making].

prong dinner-fork. *OED* (dial) *EDD* [We need two more prongs on the table].

proud projecting, standing out, of objects. *OED* (local or dial) *EDD* [The edge of that joint stands a bit proud].

pruggle stir. *(Wilstead, Bedford)* [J Clare, *Ox Auth*, The Gypsies' Evening Blaze, 1.10. 'With proggling stick she still renews the blaze'].

pudding-bag cul-de-sac. *EDD.*

pudding-bag nest nest of the long-tailed tit. *(Brigstock.)*

puddle tool for spreading clay and straw [thatching].

pudgell puddle. *OED pudge* (dial) *EDD (Yardley Hastings).*

pudluck put-lock, put-log, *OED*, horizontal member of wooden scaffold [railways].

pule fret, whimper. *OED, EDD. (Pury End.)*

pull pull and rub the wool from sheep and lamb skins. *OED* (rare or dial) *EDD* [tanning].

pullover shoe made up to shape as a model [shoe-making].

pun pound, beat down. *OED* (early and dial form of 'pound'). *EDD. (Spratton.)*

pun(about) do trifling tasks fussily, slowly. *EDD* Nhp [Whatever is he punning about at?].

puncheon large cask. *OED* (now rare) [coopering].

punish cause pain, said of the body. *EDD* (coll or dial) [My hip does punish me when I walk].

punt n strong push upwards. [Give us a punt up the wall]. v push upwards, help someone mount a horse, etc. *OED* (orig dial) *EDD.*

pure/puer cleanse and open up hide structure. *OED* [tanning].

purgatory great difficulty. *EDD* 'intense pain' [It's purgatory to try to talk to him today].

puss hare. *OED, EDD.*

put about inconvenience. *EDD* [Will it put you about to fetch the car?].

put in 1. interrupt. *OED* (obs?) [He will keep putting in while we are talking]. 2. gather at a starting-point in a wood, said of the Woodland Pytchley Hunt. *(Brigstock)* ['They'd meet in the village and then put in at Harry's Wood'].

put it past doubt it of [I wouldn't put it past him to deny everything].

puther puff out, of smoke. *OED* (dial) *EDD* [The smoke puthers out from the fire].

Quaits Quoits. *OED* (obs) *EDD. (Harpole.)*

quank subdue, quieten. *EDD. (Weedon Lois.)*

Queenie girls' ball game.
quick n hawthorn left to grow, not layered. *OED* (obs?) *EDD* ['A bit
o' quick in the hedge']. a quick-tempered. *EDD* [He's a bit quick
with the kids].

rack narrow path or animal track through a wood. *OED* (dial) *EDD
(Brigstock)*.
raddle colour red esp. of the face. *OED, EDD* ['The raddled old
harridan'].
rag-and-louse Irish labourer. *(Piddington.)*
rain-beetle shard beetle, said to come out when rain is coming.
EDD.
rake [about] roam, wander. *OED* (dial) *EDD*. ONreika, wander [She
rakes about all over the place].
rammel loose stones, stony soil. *OED* (dial) *EDD.*
ram-sammy boss, man in charge [Ask the ram-sammy].
rand edge, rim. *OED, EDD*. OE *rand*, border, rim [shoe-making].
rape rasp, scrape. fig., scrape a living. *EDD (Kettering)* [She has to
go raping and scraping as best she can].
rapstick wooden board covered with emery board, used for sharpening knives. *EDD. (Rushden)* [shoe-making. Cf. 'rape',
above].
ratty irritable, short-tempered.
reasty stale, of butter, bacon etc. *OED* (dial) *EDD* [There's nothing
but a bit o' reasty bacon].
reaves/reavings raves, framework round cart to increase capacity.
EDD.
recklin[g] smallest pig in a litter. *OED* (dial) *EDD (Stamford).*
redd [up] tidy, clean up. *OED, EDD*. OE *hreddan*, rid.
reddle redden, colour with red ochre or oxide of iron. *OED, EDD* [I
alwus reddle the window-sill].
redicue reticule, small woven basket with lid. *EDD.*
reynard/reynold fox. *OED*. (dial) *EDD* ['The old reynold come
last night'].
rense rinse [Rense everything twice].
ribby poorly made [That's a ribby job].
rick sprain, twist. *OED* (S dial) *EDD* [I ricked me back].
ride up ruck up, cling to the body, of clothes. *OED* '1854*GNWP* p
170. "A badly-made gown rides up more in one place than
another." ' [This frock does ride up so].
rifle board covered with emery board for sharpening knives. *OED*
(dial) [shoe-making].
rig ridge. *OED, EDD. (Tugby, nr. Leicester.)*
rile irritate, annoy. *OED* (dial) *EDD* [He did rile me so].
rilly flat truck for carrying hay. *(Ashton near Roade.)*
rimmer reamer, a hand-tool for enlarging holes.
rine rind. *EDD* [Cut all the rine off the bacon].
ripstitch active, mischievous child [You little ripstitch, you].

road way, manner. *OED* (dial) *EDD* [Don't try and stop me—Om gooin', any road. Get out o' my road. I can't do it this road].

roar weep, not necessarily loudly. *EDD* [She were roarin' her eyes out].

roil frolic roughly. *OED, EDD. (Long Buckby)* ['Roiling and rommacking'].

rommack as above. *OED* (dial) *(Long Buckby)* [J Clare, *MS Poems* 'And yet she's a rommaking, slommaking thing, And as wild as a filly let loose in the spring'].

rooster cock. *OED* (dial) *EDD* ['. . . a few hens and a rooster'].

rootle fidget. *OED* (dial) 'root, grub up the ground with the snout'. *EDD* 'fig turn things over in confusion' [Stop rootling about on that chair].

rough unwell. *OED* (dial) *EDD* [I feel a bit rough today].

rough-rounder shoe making machine. round v = cut.

rough-stuff leather for the bottom parts of shoes, soles, heels etc. Hence *rough-stuff* room, where these components are cut out. *OED* [shoe-making].

roust rouse, disturb. *OED* (dial.) *EDD* ['I'll soon roust 'im out'].

rowler rough ground. *OE ruh hlaw*, rough hill. *(Helmdon.)*

ruddock robin redbreast. *OED* (dial) *EDD. (Litchborough.)*

rumbustical rumbustious, boisterous. *OED* (dial) *EDD.*

run ability of gloving leather to stretch in one direction [leather-dressing].

runner empty waggon next to one with overhanging load [railways].

russets opaque finishes for heels [leather-dressing].

Russian fat grease used on shoemakers' thread [shoe-making].

sad heavy, not well-risen, of dough, cakes. *OED* (dial) *EDD* [The cake's sad in the middle].

sag long, wet grass. *OED* saggy, sedgy, reedy. Obs ex dial. *EDD* sag, name of various species of rushes, reeds and sedges *(Bozeat).*

said told *OED* (dial) [She wouldn't be said].

sale part of woodland divided by ridings to be sold. *EDD* Nhp. *(Rushden.)*

salting-lead lead-lined trough in which pig-meat is preserved in salt and saltpetre. *(Pury End.)*

sam/sammy v half-dry, of skins [tanning].

sandy-grey-russet humorous term for any colour. *OED dandy-go-russet,* faded, rusty colour; *EDD s-g-r,* dirty, ugly colour. Grey-russet, often preceded by 'dandy', coarse grey woollen cloth [What colour is it—sandy-grey-russet?].

sapy saturated, spoilt by water, esp. of lettuce, vegetables. *OED* (obs exc dial) *EDD.*

sarking covering of wood above rafters. *OED, EDD.*

sark-sugged with shirt soaked with wet. *OED sark,* shirt; *EDD. sark* and *sug,* soak. *(Eastcote.)*

sawdle dawdle. *(Long Buckby.)*

sawney silly, stupid, *OED, EDD. (Long Buckby.)*

saw-sharpener great tit-mouse, from its cry. *(Pury End.)*

say in phr. 'have one's say', say what is in one's mind, recount. *OED* (obs exc poet.) *EDD* [There's no stopping her till she's had her say].

scagged tired out, exhausted.

scap-gallus movable bar on frame resembling a gallows, used for jumps in chn's games and village sports. *OED, EDD scape-gallows,* one who has escaped the gallows. *(Everdon.)*

scaut scrape the feet, plough up the ground in trying to stop. *OED* (mod dial) *EDD.*

science walk self-consciously [You should see her sciencing down the street].

scithers scissors. *OED* (dial) *EDD.* Cp scythe ['Gi' me the scithers– I'll soon ondo it'].

scoot creep up behind and surprise, as a joke. *EDD* play about, lark. *(Stamford.)*

scotch sit down on any available seat or ledge. *EDD* n 'prop, support' [I'll just scotch on here].

Scotch cart two-wheeled hand-cart.

scraitch n deep painful scratch; v scratch deeply. *EDD scraze* [Look where I scraitched my leg].

scran-bag bag holding food or food-scraps. *OED* (dial or coll) *EDD.*

scranny distracted. *OED* (dial) *EDD* [You kids'll drive me scranny].

scrat v scratch, lit and fig ['Like an old 'en scrattin' fer daylight']. n someone, usu. a woman, who *scrats* about to save money or time; pacemaker in shoe factory. *OED* (dial Early ME *scratte*) ['She's alwus bin an ol' scrat].

scrat goosegrass. *EDD* Nhp.

scratch see *cratch. EDD.*

scraunch see *craunch. EDD.*

screamer pudding in which currants are so few that 'they have to scream at each other'.

screw barren or consumptive cow. *OED. (Milton Malsor.) EDD screw-meat.*

scribble-lark yellow-hammer, from marks on its eggs. *EDD.*

scriber 1. steel marking tool. 2. worker using this tool [shoe making].

scringe 1. cringe, wince. *OED* (dial) *EDD.* 2. make a grinding sound which sets the teeth on edge. *EDD* ['The doctor squez it [a boil] till I scringed'].

scroffle walk with difficulty. *EDD. (Bugbrooke.)*

scruffy dirty. *OED* 'scurfy', *EDD* [Don't play wi' them scruffy kids].

scrump steal fruit from trees. *EDD* [The boys went scrumping].

scud 1. sudden and short shower ['it come a scud o' rain']. *OED, EDD (Abthorpe).* 2. film left on soaked hides after hair is removed. *OED* 'dirt, refuse' (obs.) *EDD* 'foam, scum'.

scuffle n. mop for cleaning ovens. *EDD (Kislingbury).* n 2. Dutch hoe *OED, EDD.* Dutch *schoffel,* shovel, hoe. v hoe, break up ground. *(Spratton.)*

scummerous ashamed, abased. *(Ashton, near Roade.)*

scutters fast jumps in skipping games. *OED*, (chiefly dial) *EDD*, scutter, scramble, leap.

seat combined bench and seat [hand-sewn-shoe making].

seblet *seedlip*, basket for holding seed to be sown broadcast. *OED* (dial) *EDD. (Spratton.)* Also *sublit, (Alderton)*.

sergeant major's tea with sugar and milk or cream, perhaps with rum. WW1. *OED* ['This is a drop o' sergeant-major's'].

sess pile up hides to drain. *EDD* [tanning].

set n 1. build. *OED* (obs exc dial) *EDD* [He has the same set of the shoulders as his father]. 2. potato or onion used for planting. *OED* 'potato', *EDD* [Potato sets, onion sets].

set v 1. stare at, watch intently. *EDD* [He set me as soon as I went in]. 2. smooth, of hides [tanning]. 3. direct, of the mind. *OED* (rare) *EDD* [Sit down and set your mind to it].

settled a day or more old, of bread [A settled loaf, please].

shackle waste time, idle. *OED* (dial) *EDD*. Hence *shackler*, idle person.

shackles broth, usu. of a poor sort. *EDD* ['I've heard soup in the Navy called some things—"shackles" was the politest'].

shammocks boots and shoes, esp old ones. *EDD (Walgrave)*.

shantry light cart, farmer's market cart. *OED shandry*, dial *EDD shanty. (Newport Pagnell.)*

sharp slippery, said of a playground slide.

sharrig shear-hog, year-old male sheep. *OED* (dial) *EDD*. *(Spratton.)*

shawm walk or climb awkwardly. *EDD* [The children were shawmin' all over the settee].

shed hood of a baby's or doll's pram. *OED* 'covering' Cp. 'shade' [Put the shed up].

shelder shoulder ['It's acrorss my shelders I feel the draught'].

shep sheep. *OED* (obs) *EDD*.

sherbet-dab lollipop with a bag of sherbet in which to dip it.

shewel line of feathers hung in woodland to prevent deer from wandering. *OED* (dial) *EDD. (Rushden.)*

shifter adjustable spanner [railways].

shimrags rags, tatters. *EDD* [The frock's all gone to shrimrags].

ship sheep. OED (dial) *EDD. (Boddington.)*

shittlecock shuttlecock. *EDD*. OE *scytel*, missile, dart.

shommack walk in an ungainly way. *OED shammock*, dial, *EDD*. Hence *shommacky*, ungainly.

shop boot and shoe factory; shed or workplace used by outworkers in the shoe trade. *going up shop* = going to work in a shoe-factory. *going to shop* or *shopping it* = taking work done at home to the factory *(Kettering/Wellingborough area) EDD*. Nhp [We shop it o' Fridays].

shorry short pole or stick used by hedgers to carry faggots, or for walking. *EDD* Cp 'shore up'. *(Piddington.)*

show willing show willingness. *EDD* [I went to the bazaar, just to show willing].

shrammed numbed with cold. *OED* (dial) *EDD*. *(Yardley Hastings.)*

shut fit of a lid on a tin [This tin's got a good shut].

shut-knife pocket-knife, clasp-knife. *EDD*.

shut-knife-carpenter workman whose principal tool is his shut-knife. *EDD (Litchborough)*.

sidder-grinder scissor-grinder, nightjar, from its whirring cry. *EDD*. *(Pury End.)*

sike ditch. *OED, EDD*. OE *sic,* watercourse. *(Brigstock.)*

sing purr, of a cat; bay, of hounds. *EDD*.

sit blow from a certain direction, of the wind. *OED* (fig) [The wind sits in this door].

sit up suffer as a result of something too good too soon. *EDD*. Suffer [We shall sit up for all this mild weather in November].

Sixes ball-game accompanied by six positions of the body.

skave very thin layer of leather pared off. *EDD* Nhp Dan *skave,* scrape. *(Rushden)* ['We put three skaves on it']. Cp *skive*.

skeg n variety of wild plum. *OED* (dial) *EDD*.

skeg n foolish person [suck-egg]. *EDD (Yardley Gobion)*.

skeg v scratch. *OED* (dial) *EDD* 'tear cloth' *(Kislingbury)* [The boys skegged the slide with the iron tips on their boots].

skew-whiff askew, crooked. *EDD* [The tablecloth is all skew-whiff].

skive pare edges of shoe components to prepare for stitching.

skunt asquint.

slathy dirty, muddy. *OED slather,* slide. *EDD slathery* ['Slathy toad,' said to a child who is muddy and wet]. *(Eastcote.)*

sleeper thin gold ear-ring inserted in newly-pierced ears. *EDD*.

sleepers dried mucus on eyelids after sleep. *EDD* [Let's wipe the sleepers away].

sleepy soft inside, of pears. *EDD*.

sleepy-dust dust said to be sprinkled on sleepy chn's eyes by the 'miller-man'. *EDD*.

slicker tool used in 'whitening', shaving off excess grease, together with thin layer of leather [shoe-making].

slipe n slip or strip of land. *OED* (dial) *EDD*.

slipe v creep about, steal away. *EDD*. *(Rushden.)* Hence *slipy,* furtive, shifty.

slippy slippery *OED* (dial) *EDD*. Fig. quick [The path is so slippy. Now then–look slippy].

slon sloe. *OED* (dial) *EDD*. OE *sla,* plur *slan*.

slop-basin bowl put on the table for the dregs of tea-cups. *OED*.

slopper long-handled mop made of strips of sacking for cleaning out the oven before baking. *(Holcot.)*

slotchuck slip about, as a post in too large a hole or feet in large shoes. *EDD slotchut. (Harpole.)*

slummocking/y untidy, slovenly. *OED* (dial) *EDD* [She's so slummocky in the house].

slurrup swallow liquid noisily, slurp. *EDD.*

small-gang mob, set upon, mug. *OED, EDD. (Pury End)* [They small-ganged him in the street].

smawk smear, spread messily. *(Pury End.)*

smell feel. *EDD* [It smells warm in here].

smellsmock wood anemone, ladysmock or sorrel *OED* (dial) *EDD* [J Clare, *Shep Cal* May 131-2. 'And smellsmocks that from view retires, Mid rustling leaves and bowing briers'].

snake metal tube used for pouring liquid into hogsheads in cellar, through opening in kitchen floor. *(Winslow, Bucks)* [brewing at home].

snathe handle of a scythe or thatching tool. *OED* (mostly dial) *EDD. (Tugby, nr. Leicester.)*

snib n bolt of a door. *OED snib* v, bolt, secure. *EDD,* small bolt.

snicket narrow alley. *EDD. (Stamford.)*

snickle small rabbit-snare. *OED* (dial) *EDD. (Pitsford.)*

snift sniff ['We called her Snifty Smith'].

snipe-nosed mean, niggardly. *EDD (Harpole).*

snitch blow across the face. *OED* (obs.) *(Wellingborough School).*

snob shoemaker. *OED* (dial or coll) *EDD.*

snod smooth and tidy. *OED* (Sc and N dial) *EDD.* ON *snothin,* smooth, of hair. *(Kislingbury.)*

snot-ball white berry, species unknown, *EDD* Lin Nhp Som; fruit of yew-tree.

snyvel shrink, shrivel, esp. from cold. *EDD snivel,* Lei Nhp Hnt. *(Long Buckby.)*

so as although [She never comes near us, so as we looked after her all that time].

soldier common red poppy, red campion. *OED* (dial) *EDD.*

sollar sallow, willow. *OED* (dial) *EDD* ['The green sollar'].

soodle saunter, dawdle. *OED* (dial) *EDD. (Rushden.)*

sound long for. *OED* (dial) *EDD.* Cf swoon ['I sound for a bit o'chocolate'].

sourgog gooseberry.

sour grass red sorrel *OED* sorrel. *EDD* [Suck a bit o' sourgrass if you're thirsty].

spadger sparrow. *OED.* (dial or coll) *EDD.*

Spanish Spanish licorice. *EDD* [Spanish and kali's better'n peps].

sparge sprinkle malt with warm water. *OED, EDD* [malting].

spat board for sharpening shoemakers' knives. *OED* flat implement used in ball-games. *EDD* slap, smack.

spike workhouse. *(Helmdon.)*

spitten [image] *exact* [likeness] [He's the spitten image of his dad].

splash 1. trim a hedge at the sides only, using a long-handled *splasher. OED, EDD.*
2. knock down walnuts from the tree with a pole. *EDD (Little Houghton).*

splather-footed having the feet turned outwards. *EDD.*

splay horizontal band used in thatching. *(Spratton.)*

splits mixture of ale and small beer. *(Harpole.)*

spring young tree; young growth in woodland. *OED* (dial) *EDD*. *(Rushden.)*

spue bloom appearing on finished shoes, due to incorrect tanning [shoe-making].

spuntle spoonful, small quantity. *EDD* [I'll have just a spuntle of sugar].

spwile spoil *OED* (dial) ['You'll spwile yer dinner if you eat so many peps'].

squab [out] gape open, squash out. *OED* (dial) *EDD* [These shoes squab out at the sides].

square up make tidy, put to rights. *EDD* [I'll just square up in the kitchen].

squez squeezed [She squez the juice of a lemon].

squib squirt. *EDD* [Squib some soapy water on the roses].

stag n male turkey. v trim a hedge at the sides and across the top. *EDD* . . . at the top. *(Spratton.)*

stalk clog, adhere, of ground. *EDD* Nhp War Glo Oxf.

stale broom-handle. *OED* (dial) *EDD*.

stand 1. pillar-table. *EDD* [This was my grandma's flower-pot stand]. 2. water-butt, barrel. *EDD*. *(Harpole.)*

stand over work long and carefully [I don't stand over the ironing].

stank repair banks of brook or dike, staunch. *OED*. (dial) *EDD*.

stare stand on end, through poor condition, of animals' hair or fur. *EDD* [Its fur was all staring].

starnel starling. *OED* (dial) *EDD*. Also *starbob, stargug* [J Clare, *Shep Cal.* Jan 1.15 'The clouds of starnels dailey fly, Blackening through the evening sky'].

starved very cold. *OED* (rare) *EDD* v suffering with cold ['I got starved waiting for a bus'].

stattie, stattis hiring fair held by statute. *EDD*.

stelch area covered by a thatcher without moving his ladder. *EDD* Nhp War Wor Hrf.

stick it across deceive [He stuck it across me and give me some short].

stick someone out insist against all opposition. *EDD* [She stuck us out he'd gone away].

stick to the ribs be thick and filling, of food [Suet clangers'll stick to your ribs].

wrong end of the stick wrong idea. *EDD*.

in a cleft stick in a difficult position between opposing sides *EDD*.

stick-farmer farmer in a very small way, perhaps renting one field only. *(Cogenhoe)* ['. . . goes out with a dog and a stick looking like a farmer'].

sticking gathering sticks for firewood. *EDD*.

sticking(s) bruised, inferior meat, where the knife was inserted. *OED, EDD*.

stickjaw very chewy toffee.

stine-eye stye on the eye. *OED* (dial) *EDD*.

Stinking Willy ragwort. *OED, EDD. (Brigstock.)*

stitch-bone bone tool for tapping between stitches, to give good appearance [shoe-making].

stockings land reclaimed from woodland. *OED* and *EDD stock,* fell a tree. *(Piddington.)*

stockmanship knowledge of caring for stock animals. *(Tugby, nr Leicester.)*

stocky stubborn, obstinate, often in form *stocky toad. OED* (dial) *EDD (Eastcote).*

stoker fireman on early railways.

stomachful proud, stubborn. *OED* (obs) *EDD* [She's too stomachful to admit she's in the wrong].

'Stone' call from a player reaching an agreed sanctuary or base, chn's games.

stone out mark out a field with stones. *OED* (obs) *EDD. (Rushden.)*

straights shoes made without left and right shaping. *EDD straight-shoon.*

strap draw the last milk from a cow. *OED* (dial.) *EDD (Spratton).*

straw-jack elevator used with a threshing machine. *EDD.*

street highway, paved road. *OED* (obs exc for names) *EDD. (Harpole)* [Watling Street].

strike scrape, smooth. *OED* (obs) *EDD* [tanning].

strit street. *EDD (Pury End).*

stroop/stroup gullet, windpipe. *OED* (dial) *EDD. (Harpole)* [It's stuck in my stroop].

stuff apply grease to tanned hides. *OED.*

stun stone. *EDD* [There was a stunpit there].

sty-baked hot, dirty, a reference to pigs caked with mud or with dry, scurfy skin. *EDD. (Pury End.)*

sugged soaked. *OED* (dial) *EDD. (Eastcote.)*

Sukey tea-kettle, from the name Sukey, a diminutive of Susan. *EDD* [Come on and boil, Sukey].

sulphury sultry, of weather *EDD (Kettering).*

summering early-ripening apple. *OED* (dial) *EDD. (Stamford.)*

summons summon. *OED* (rare) *EDD* [You'll get summonsed if you do that].

swab small sample of leather. *(Rushden)* [shoe-making].

swee sway. *OED* (dial.) *EDD* [J Clare, *Shep Cal* 'Flocking field-fares, speckled like the thrush, Picking the red haw from the sweeing bush'].

sweethearts goosegrass, from its clinging habit. *OED* (dial) *EDD.*

swimmer dumpling. *EDD. (Spratton)* ['Sheep's head and suet swimmers'].

swope sweep *OED* (obs) *EDD. (Greens Norton)* ['Then we swoped in on the boats' [at the Dardanelles]].

swum out flooded. *EDD* [We was swum out after the storm].

tab ear. *EDD* [Let's tuck yer tabs in yer bonnet].

table-run unsorted, of leather bought from the tanner [shoe-making].

tack n. poor quality food. *OED* (dial) *EDD* [I don't want none o' that tack]. v go rotten, of food. *EDD (Earls Barton)* [A tacked orange].

tad matted lump in animal's fur. *EDD*. tat [We shall have to cut out the tads].

tadger ear.

take 1. take root, grow. *OED* (obs) *EDD* [Most of the cuttings have taken]. 2. ignite. *OED* (rare) *EDD*, burn brightly [I can't get the fire to go—the wood won't take]. 3. used as emphasis. *EDD* [Don't just talk about it—take and go].

take-away stomach, appetite. *EDD* [He'll ett all that—he's got a good take-away].

tall [Rhyme shall] tell. *OED,* some very early forms in 'a' [I tall yer—it's too small].

tankeny/tanky small bell, esp. the smallest bell of a peal.

tap thickness of leather. *OED* (dial) *EDD* sole of boot or shoe, metal heel. Hence *tapper,* shoemaker, esp a laster.

tatchy irritable. *OED,* dial from tetchy. *EDD*. *tatchy.*

tater potato. *OED* (dial.) *EDD*.

tatered puzzled, beaten, worn out.

tats walk, outing, said to chn [Shall we go for a tats?].

tay tea. *OED* (dial) *EDD* [A cup o' tay].

tay-kettle-broth water from the kettle poured on bread, or on its own with salt and pepper ['Our breakfast many a day was tay-kettle-broth'].

teer spread messily. *OED* (dial) *EDD*. ME *teeren,* cover or spread with earth [Don't teer your dinner about].

tek take. *EDD*. *(Spratton, Kettering area)* [Tek it with yer].

tell lace-makers' song or rhyme. *OED* (dial). *EDD* Nhp.

tell-clack tale-bearer. *EDD*.

tell off reprimand [I'll soon tell him off if he does that again].

temporary insecure, weak. *EDD* [Be careful of the fence—it's a bit temporary].

thack thatch. *OED* (dial) *EDD*. Hence, *thacker,* thatcher ['They live in the thack' cottage'].

thack-sparrow n. house-sparrow. *EDD*. v kill sparrows which spoil the thatch [Are yer comin' thack-sparrerin'?].

theave young ewe that has not yet borne a lamb. *OED* (local, Mid and south). *EDD*. *(Spratton.)*

they there [Is they any cheese left?].

then the time that, in phr. *by then*. *OED* (dial) *EDD* [I shall be got the dinner be [by] then you get back].

there emphatic or redundant after 'that', 'them'. *OED* (dial or vulg *EDD)* [Give us that there saw. Them there kids are comin' out].

thereabouts reasonably tidy [Just leave it thereabouts].

theirn theirs. *OED* (Mid and south dial) *EDD* [That allotment's theirn].

thin cold, of weather. *EDD* [It's a bit thin this morning].

thing o' purpose tool for the job.

think much begrudge. *EDD* [She thinks much of ev'rything she does for me].

thragged-down cluttered, overfull. *EDD thrag*, throng.

thrail flail. *OED* (obs) *EDD*. *(Kislingbury.)*

thrape beat, flog. *EDD*. *(Spratton.)*

thrash thresh. *OED* ('earlier form') *EDD*. *(Pury End)* ['He worked with the steam-thrasher'].

threaten intend, with no sense of anger. *EDD* ['I threatened to go and see her'].

thribble treble, threefold. *EDD* ['I paid double and thribble that'].

throw-back someone showing the traits of an ancestor. *OED* as verb only ['Our boy's a throw-back. I can see his grandfather in him'].

thrummety frumenty, boiled wheat with sugar and raisins added. *EDD (Little Houghton)*.

thrusher song-thrush. *EDD (Greens Norton)*.

Thumper name for thumb. *EDD*.

thunderbolt belemnite, a fossil. *OED* (local) *EDD*. *(Spratton.)*

thurrow furrow. *EDD*.

tiddle 1. potter, trifle. *OED* (dial) *EDD*. 2. tickle. *OED* (dial) *EDD*. 3. urinate. *EDD*.

tiddy tiny. *EDD* [What a tiddy little dog].

tiffle potter about. *OED* (dial) *EDD* [I tiffle about in the garden].

'Tig' call to pigs. *EDD* Nhp Oxf *Berks* Wil.

'Tiggy' 1. child's name for a pig. 2. child's chasing game. *OED Tig. EDD*.

tiger nuts chewy nuts, edible rhizomes of Cyperus esculentus, sold to chn. *OED*.

tilt movable top or cover on a cart. *OED*, *EDD (Whittlebury)*.

tin-can/kettle see *lewbell*.

ting-tang/tink-tank/tinkler small bell, esp. smallest bell of peal. *EDD (Pury End, Weedon Lois)*.

tingy-mungy poor quality meat. *(Ashton, near Roade.)*

tip-cat game played by hitting a short piece of wood with a stick. *OED*, *EDD*.

tipple fall heavily, of rain; fall, tip, overturn. *OED* (dial) *EDD* [It tippled down last night. The baby tippled off the stool].

tit small, incompetent woman or girl. *OED*, *EDD*. Cp *chit* [She's a poor tit].

titty-bottle 1. baby's feeding-bottle. *EDD*. 2. clover flower, which chn suck because of its sweet taste. 3. cobble-stone set in the ground.

titty-totties/totty-toes trefoil. *(Little Houghton.)*

to 1. into place, not fastened, of a door [Pull the door to]. 2. of [with 'know']. *EDD* [She's lived there forty year, as I know to].

tod fox. *OED* (dial.) *EDD*. *(Rushden.)*

tod pulp, mess, of food. *OED* (Sw dial *todd*, conglomerated mess, esp of wool). *EDD todge. (Pury End.)*

Tom Hackett punishment, beating. *(Rushden)* [He's bin given Tom Hackett].

Tom Hodge thick part of chitterlings. *EDD* ['Tom Hodge and a jug of gravy'].

tong tongue. *EDD* [He stuck his tong out, Miss].

took-to taken by surprise. *OED* (dial) *EDD* [I was took to when she said he'd gone].

tool elderly, feeble person. *OED* (ineffectual person), *EDD* (term of contempt). *(Bugbrooke)* [He's a poor old tool].

top-piece bottom-most layer of heel [shoe-making].

trade emphasis, fuss. *OED* (dial) *EDD* [She makes such a trade of what she does for anybody].

train-oil oil from whale, formerly seal, blubber. *OED, EDD* [tanning].

trammer horse used to draw trams. *OED. (Clipston.)*

translate buy up small lots of second-hand shoes and repair them for re-sale. *OED, EDD.*

travel move or drive animals. *OED, EDD. (Harpole)* ['You couldn't travel the lambs till they got stable'].

tray wash-tub. *OED* (formerly more widely applied to open vessels generally). *EDD.*

trencher wooden plate. *OED* (arch) *EDD.* Hence good trencherman, someone who eats well [Now we'll play 'Spinning the trencher'].

tret treated. *OED* (obs) ['My daughter tret herself to a blouse'].

trig [out] dress smartly, *OED* (dial) *EDD. (Spratton.)*

trills shoes *(Spratton).*

troll trull, woman of loose morals. *EDD* ['She looks like some old troll'].

trough Rhyme loaf. Eat greedily, as a pig at a trough. *OED,* ordinary pron. of trough [He can trough well].

trucks trousers.

trud trod [I trud in a lot o' mud].

tugs chain or iron attached to the hames [harness]. *EDD. (Brixworth.)*

tune n fit of weeping [She had a tune over losing the cat]. v cry, weep. *EDD* W Yks Nhp.

tunk knock, bump. *EDD* Lei Nhp.

tunkey-pig Tonkin pig, small, fat pig. *EDD* ['As fat as a tunkey pig'].

turn repel, of wet. *EDD.* Nhp; curdle, of milk. *EDD* [This old coat will still turn the rain].

turn in begin to form a heart, of cabbage, lettuce. *EDD.*

turnpike sailor tramp. *OED, EDD. (Duston.)*

turnshoe shoe of which the hand-lasted uppers are sewn wrong-side-out and then turned [shoe-making].

tut offence. *EDD* [He took tut when she asked him to wait].

tuzzy-muzzy mossy growth on wild rose. *EDD,* posy.

Twelves game played by throwing ball at wall with the body in twelve different positions to catch it.

twitch couch-grass. *OED, EDD.* OE *cwice.*

twizzle twist, turn. *OED* (dial, coll.) *EDD.*

'T'yer' 'Here's to you,' a greeting. *(Woodford, near Kettering.)*

'ug's pudden hog's pudding, black pudding. *EDD.*

unkid ugly, unpleasant; strange, uncanny. *OED* (dial) *EDD. ME unkid,* not made known [She looks unkid in them clothes. The sky looked dark and unkid].

unmerciful to a great degree, unmercifully. *EDD* excessive, extreme [She wen' on at [scolded] him unmerciful].

unspan unfasten harness. *OED* (rare).

upside up river, of a water-meadow. *(Little Houghton)* ['Take it (a ploughing engine) up the upside'].

us we *OED* (dial) *EDD. (Silverstone)* ['Us was very upset']. me *OED* (dial). *EDD* [Give us a bit o' paper].

vanner horse used for pulling vans. *OED. (Clipston.)*

varges verjuice, juice of crab apples, pressed out and used as vinegar. *OED.*

veal skin of a calf a little older than a milk-fed animal [shoe-making].

vellike very likely [Annie'll vellike come today].

videnar vinegar. *(Brigstock.)*

village man church sexton. *(Harpole.)*

vinegar red sorrel. *(Collingtree.)*

wadge rhyme lodge, a lump of bread with meat, cheese etc. *OED* (dial) *EDD* [He had a gret wadge o' bread and meat].

wadn't wasn't.

wair pond, weir, once meaning pond. *OED, EDD. (Finedon.)*

wale mark of a blow or lash on the flesh. *OED, EDD.* OE *walu,* mark of a blow [The later 'weal' is from a different source. *OED*].

wallop boil fast. *OED* (obs) *EDD.*

wapse wasp. *OED* (obs or dial) *EDD.*

water/blob/blobber/bobble marsh marigold. *OED* (dial) *EDD* water-blob.

weasand throat, windpipe. *OED* (gen dial) *EDD.* OE *waesend,* throat.

weasel accept tips for service [railways].

weather-breeder unseasonably warm day, heralding bad weather. *OED, EDD,* weather-breeding.

wed weed. *OED* (obs) *(Spratton) Poor Law Questionnaire,* Loddington (1834) 'Women work in the hay and harvest, also wed and gather stones from the land. A few make lace.'

weer our. *EDD wor* ['We'll goo when we're had weer dinner'].

weight thickness, of upper leather.

well away happy, engrossed, likely to succeed [He's well away now he's got his own shop].

well-blessed in difficulty, often because of a large family [They're well-blessed with all them mouths to feed].

well-britched well-breeched, having plenty of money. *EDD.*

welt beat, thrash. *OED, EDD* [I had such a welting].

wet-bird chaffinch, said to sing before rain. *EDD* ['It'll rain soon– the wet-bird's singing'].

wet-blue having a bluish tinge, of hides after soaking and liming. Also *in-the-blue* [tanning].

wezzel mangel-wurzel. *(Spratton.)*

whap hit, strike, put down with a bang. *OED* (dial) *EDD* [I'll give that boy such a whapping].

what redundant before 'with', and after 'than'. *OED.* vulg or dial [What with one thing and another. I've got more than what he has].

what for punishment, scolding. *OED* (slang) *EDD* [I soon give 'im what for].

'What then?' said to soothe a baby.

whemble rinse washing. *OED* and *EDD,* whemmle.

whelt wheeled [I whelt me barrer up the 'ill].

whiffet thin, undernourished child. *OED.* an insignificant person. *EDD.* Nhp. *(Long Buckby.)*

while 1. time. *EDD* [Where's he bin all this while?]. 2. until. *OED* (dial.) *EDD* [I shan't see you while Monday].

whim home-made contrivance. *(Spratton)* ['If, say, you made a rabbit-hutch out of bits of wood you'd got in the shed, that'd be a whim'].

whim-wham rattle for scaring birds. *(Pitsford.)*

whitleather white, ie untanned leather, used for hedgers' mittens etc. *OED, EDD* ['As tough as whitleather'].

whitterish faded, washed-out. *OED* (dial) *EDD.* Nhp Hrt.

whittle worry. *EDD.*

whizzle-eyed dazzled by strong patterns. *OED* and *EDD whizzle, whizz. (Rushden)* [That wallpaper'd send me whizzle-eyed].

whosen whose. *OED* (dial) *EDD. (Earls Barton)* [Whosen's that?].

wibble weevil. *OED* (obs) *EDD. (Spratton.)*

wicker v twist, tangle. *EDD* (obs) *(Spratton).*

wicket small window. *OED* obs) *EDD.*

wiggy weak, leggy, of plants. *(Spratton)* ['That's a wiggy lot o' taters y' got there, boy'].

wik week. *(Spratton)* ['When she'd bin gone three wik'].

wild rough, outlying field, let at a cheap rent. *(Thenford.)*

wildfire exact meaning unknown, in phr 'spread like wildfire'. *OED,* destructive agency; *EDD,* inflammable air.

willjew Will-Jill, hermaphrodite. *OED* (dial) *EDD.*

Willy-call-your-father weak tea. *EDD* Billy . . .

window-breaker light mushroom-shaped top, which spun very fast, in game of whips and tops.

winnering machine in phr 'like a winnering machine', very windy and cold. *OED* winnowing ['It's winnering in here'].

winsome happy, joyous. *OED* (dial) *EDD*. *(Pitsford.)*

wish wish bad fortune. *OED* (dial) *EDD* [I wouldn't wish deafness on my worst enemy].

wisht wish [I wisht I could have a toffee apple].

wisket basket with handles, for holding chaff. *OED* (dial) *EDD*. *(Spratton.)*

within inside, indoors. *OED* (dial) *EDD*.

without outside, outdoors. *OED* (dial) *EDD* [G White, *Garden Kalendar* (1751) p 11. 'Sowed nine rows of marrow-fat pease in the plot just without the field garden'].

woods pieces of wood, planks. *EDD* ['I'll just sit on the woods and smoke me pipe'].

word express in words. *OED* (obs). Hence worded, expressed in words. *OED* (rare) [We just don't know how to word it].

work cause to ferment. *OED*. Hence *all of a work*, in a state of fermentation or motion. *EDD* [The yeast's working. My stomach's all of a work].

work-brittle ready to work, often used neg. *EDD* *(Collingtree)* [I don't feel very work-brittle today].

worthy to know able to understand the thoughts and actions of the living, said of the dead. *EDD* able, having knowledge or power [Mother would be pleased to hear you say that, if she's worthy to know].

'Woy up' greeting, often with a sideways nod. *(Wellingborough.)*

wrong strip of land ploughed crookedly, or of an odd shape. *EDD* wrangland.

wunt wont, accustom, get birds or animals used to a new environment. *OED* (arch) *EDD*. *(Harpole)* [J Clare, *Valentine Eve.* 194. Mid Cush 'Dull as a tamed bird wonted to the cage'].

wut walk self-consciously. *(Barton Seagrave)* [She went wutting down the street].

yackle talk on and on. *(Brafield.)*

yaffle green woodpecker, from its cry. *OED* (dial.) *EDD*. *(Pury End.)*

yard garden. *OED* (dial) [Goo down the yard an' fetch me a cabbage as big as your'ead].

Yardley plum large dark plum, the juice of which was used for dyeing. *(Y. Gobion.)*

yark jerk, pull up quickly. *EDD*.

yawn-ups stupid lazy person. *EDD*.

yawp talk noisily, bawl. *OED* (chiefly dial) *EDD*.

yelk yolk of an egg. *OED* (survives locally). *EDD*. OE *geoloca*.

yelm bundle of straw for thatching. *OED* (mod dial) *EDD*. OE *gelm*, bundle. *(Spratton.)*

yep heap *EDD*.

yilt gilt, young sow. *EDD. (Holcot.)*
yimmer/yummer humour. *(Newport Pagnell)* [He's a bad-yummered old So-and-so].
yoe ewe. *EDD. (Brixworth, Holcot)* [J Clare, *Shep Cal* March, 1.185. 'Like the old yoe that wears a tinkling bell'].
young things steers and heifers between about six months and two years. *EDD,* young stock.
yourn yours. *OED* (dial) *EDD.* your husband *EDD.*
yours your house. *EDD.*
yowk yell. *EDD yawk. (Pitsford.)*

Further Reading

My primary source was the spoken word. I used the standard works of reference in the first group and consulted many other books or read them for enjoyment. I hope many readers will do the same.

The Oxford English Dictionary (OUP, 1971), 13 vols, + 4 vols of supplements.
BAKER, A E *Glossary of Northamptonshire Words and Phrases* (Northampton, Abel and Sons and Mark Dorman, 1854).
BREWER, E C (ed) *Brewer's Dictionary of Phrase and Fable,* revised by Evans, IH (Cassell, 1978).
ORTON, H and HALLIDAY, W J (eds) *A Survey of English Dialects* (published for the University of Leeds by E J Arnold and Son Ltd, 1962).
ORTON, H and WRIGHT, N *A Word Geography of England* (Seminar Press, 1974).
STERNBERG, T *The Dialect and Folklore of Northamptonshire* (Northampton, Abel and Sons, G N Wetton, 1851).
WAKELIN, M F *English Dialects, an Introduction* (Athlone Press, University of London, 1977).
WRIGHT, J (ed) *The English Dialect Dictionary* (Henry Frowde, 1898-1905) 6 vols.

FRIENDSHIP-TAYLOR, D E (ed) *Northamptonshire History News,* nos 67-69. (Northampton Museums and Art Gallery, Northampton Borough Council.)
GREENALL, R L *Old Northamptonshire in Photographs* (Northamptonshire Libraries, 1976).
GREENALL, R L *Northamptonshire Life 1914-39* (Northamptonshire Libraries, 1979).
GREENALL, R L *Northamptonshire At War* 1939-45 (Northamptonshire Libraries, 1978).
GREENALL, R L (ed) *Northamptonshire Past and Present* (Northamptonshire Record Society 1980-88), 7 vols.

HOLLOWAY, R *Roland Holloway's Northamptonshire* (Northamptonshire Libraries, 1985).
KING, E (ed) *A Northamptonshire Miscellany* (Northamptonshire Record Society, vol xxi, 1983).
MARKHAM, C A (ed) vol 5 and
SWEETING, REV W D and TAYLOR J (eds) *Northamptonshire Notes and Queries*, vols 1-4 (Northampton Dryden Press, Taylor and Son, 1886-1890).

People at Home

BAILEY, J L H *Finedon, otherwise Thingdon* (SR Publishers, 1975).
BATES, H E *The Vanished World, an Autobiography* (Michael Joseph, 1969).
BATES, H E *Charlotte's Row* (Jonathan Cape, 1953).
The Northampton Cookery Book (compiled by ladies of Doddridge Castle Hill Congregational Chapel, 1908).
PAYNE, R *The Watershed* (Faber and Faber, 1961).
SEABROOK, J *The Unprivileged* (Longman Green and Co Ltd, 1967).

People at Work

COX, A C 'Notes on lace-making in Northampton and county' (MS). Abington Park Museum Library.
FREEMAN, C *Pillow-lace in the East Midlands* (Luton Museum and Art Gallery, 1967).
HANSON, H *Canal People* (David and Charles, 1978).
HATLEY, V A and RAJCZONEK, J *Shoemakers in Northamptonshire, 1762-1911.* Northampton Historical Series no 6 (1971).
LOVELL, A 'Mrs Harrison and the revival of lace-making in Paulerspury, 1878-1910', pp 12-15, *Northamptonshire History News*, no 33, Abington Park Museum Library.
The Manfield Magazine, 1929-30.
THOMSON, R 'Leather manufacture in the post-medieval period, with special reference to Northamptonshire' *Post-Medieval Archaeology 15* (1981).
THORNTON, J H *Textbook of Footwear Manufacture* (Butterworth, 1970).
TONKS, E S *The Ironstone Railways and Tramways of the Midlands* (Locomotive Publishing Co 1959).
WILSON, E *Olney and the Lacemakers.*
WRIGHT, T *The Romance of the Lace-pillow* (Armstrong, 1924).

Country People

EVANS, Rev B L *The Story of Milton Malsor* (Wells, Gardner, Dalton and Co Ltd, 1924).
HALL, D *Wollaston. Portrait of a Village* (The Wollaston Society, 1977).
IRESON, T *Northamptonshire* (Robert Hale and Co, 1964).
MEE, A *Northamptonshire* (Hodder and Stoughton Ltd, 1946).
STURGESS, A *A Northamptonshire Lad* (Northamptonshire Libraries, 1982).

WOOD, G *Lambs' Tails for Breakfast* (Northampton Heart of England Countryside Tours, no date).

Children's Games

OPIE, I and OPIE, P *The Lore and Language of Schoolchildren* (Clarenden Press, 1960).

OPIE, I and OPIE, P *The Puffin Book of Nursery Rhymes* (Puffin, 1963).

OPIE, I and OPIE, P *Children's Games in Street or Playground* (OUP, 1984).

Folksong and Dance

BRIGGS, K M *British Folk Tales and Legends, a Sampler* (Granada Publishing, 1977).

BROADWOOD, L E and FULLER-MAITLAND, J A *English County Songs* (J B Cramer and Co Ltd, no date).

BROADWOOD, L E *English Traditional Songs and Carols* (Educational Products, 1974).

HALLIWELL, J O *Popular Rhymes and Nursery Tales of England* (John Russell Smith, 1849).

HAMER, F *Green Groves* (English Folk Dance and Song Society, 1970).

Seasonal Customs

CHANDLER, K 'An Interim Checklist of Reference to Morris Dancing in Local Newspapers, part 1, 1733-1914'. Monograph.

HELM, A *The English Folk-Play,* part 1 (English Folk Dance and Song Society, Manchester District, 1954).

JUDGE, R *The Jack in the Green: a May-day Custom* (D S Brewer Ltd, 1978).

ROWE, D (foreword) *Comes the Morris Dancer In* (The Morris Ring, 1984).

Places and People

BAKER, G *The History and Antiquities of the County of Northampton* (Nichols and Son, 1822-30).

DONALDSON, J *General View of the Agriculture of the County of Northampton* (Agricultural Survey Report, 1794).

GOVER, J E B, MAWER, A and STENTON, F M *The Place-Names of Northamptonshire* (CUP, 1933).

HOSKINS, W G *Midland England* (B T Batsford, 1948).

HOSKINS, W G *One Man's England* (BBC, 1978).

MARKHAM, C A *The Proverbs of Northamptonshire* (Stanton and Son, 1897).

MORTON, J *The Natural History of Northamptonshire* (Knaplock, 1712).

PAGE, J T 'Notes on Midland Folklore', a collection of newspaper articles, 1897-8, Northampton Central Library.

PALMER, J and PALMER, M *A History of Wellingborough from Roman times to the present day* (Earls Barton, Steeple Press, 1972).

TOWNSEND, D *The Gypsies of Northamptonshire* (J H Waddington, 1877).

WARNER, G T and MARTEN, C H K *The Groundwork of British History* (Blackie Ltd, 1937).

WILLIAMS, J and BAMFORD, H *Northampton – the first 6,000 years* (Northampton Development Corporation, 1979).

John Clare

CLARE, J 'A Collection of Songs, Airs and Dances for the Violin' (1818). Original Manuscripts and Papers of John Clare on micro-film in Northampton Central Library.

DRABBLE, M *A Writer's Britain,* pp 61-65 (Thames and Hudson, 1984).

ROBINSON, M and SUMMERFIELD, G (eds) *The Shepherd's Calendar* (OUP, 1975).

ROBINSON, E and FITTER, R (eds) *John Clare's Birds* (OUP, 1982).

ROBINSON, E and POWELL, D (eds) *John Clare, The Oxford Authors* (OUP, 1984).

STOREY, E *A Right to Song. The Life of John Clare* (Methuen, London Ltd, 1982).

THORNTON, R K R (ed) *The Rural Muse* (Mid Northumberland Arts Group and Carcanet New Press, 1982).

TIBBLE, J W and TIBBLE, A (eds) *The Prose of John Clare* (Routledge and Kegan Paul, 1951).

TIBBLE, J W and TIBBLE, A (eds) *The Letters of John Clare* (Routledge and Kegan Paul, 1951).

TIBBLE, J W and TIBBLE, A (eds) *John Clare, Selected Poems* (Everyman Library 1976).

TIBBLE, A (ed) and THORNTON, R K R (assoc ed) *The Midsummer Cushion* (Mid-Northumberland Arts Group and Carcanet New Press, 1978).

WILSON, J *Green Shadows. The Life of John Clare* (Hodder and Stoughton, 1951).

Other Works of Interest

ANDERSON, P (ed) *Yorkshire at Work* (Yorkshire Dialect Society, 1980).

ASHBY, M K *Joseph Ashby of Tysoe, 1859-1919* (The Merlin Press, 1974).

EVANS, G E *Ask the Fellows who Cut the Hay* (Faber and Faber, 1956).

EVANS, G E *The Pattern under the Plough* (Faber and Faber, 1956).

EVANS, G E *Where Beards Wag All. The Relevance of the Oral Tradition* (Faber and Faber, 1956).

HARMAN, H *Buckinghamshire Dialect* (SR Publications, 1970).

HARRIS, M *Another Kind of Magic* (OUP, 1985).

JAMIESON, I 'Oral History and Libraries, some recent developments' *The Local Studies Librarian,* vol 4, no 2, Winter 1985.

KITCHEN, F *Brother to the Ox* (JM Dent, 1945).

PARKER, R *The Common Stream* (Paladin, 1977).

PHILLIPPS, K C *West Country Words and Ways* (David and Charles, 1976).

THOMPSON, F *Lark Rise to Candleford* (OUP, 1975).

THOMPSON, P and BORNAT, J (eds) and CHAMBERLAIN, M (review ed) 'The Minstrel of Quarry Bank. Reminiscences of George Dunn, 1887-1975), ed Roy Palmer, *Oral History, the Journal of the Oral History Society,* vol 11, no 1, Spring 1983.

WRIGHT, P *Cumbrian Dialect* (Dalesman Books, 1979).

Contributors

Addicott, Mrs D
Adkins, Miss B
Adkins, Mrs D
Adkins, Mr S
Alcock, Mr P

Bailey, Mr J E, Brigstock
Bailey, Mr J L, Finedon
Ball, Mrs M
Ballard, Mr and Mrs D
Bedford, Mrs
Berry, Mrs H
Bicknell, Mr R
Blades, Mrs J
Bodily, Mr R
Boston, Mr M
Boot, Mr
Boyle, Mrs
Broom, Mr A
Brown, Miss C
Brown, Misses F and G
Burt, Mr W

Carpenter, Mrs E
Carpenter, Mrs P
Carr, Miss G
Carter, Mrs O
Chamberlain, Mrs I
Chance, Mr R
Cherry, Mr W
Clark, Mrs R
Clarke, Mrs L
Clarke, Mr T
Clements, Mr A
Cook, Mr V

Cooper, Mr T
Cowper, Mr D
Cox, Mr
Crowson, Mr G
Curtis, Miss J

Davis, Mr J
Dew, Mrs
Drage, Mr E
Dudley, Mr A

Eady, Mr R
Eady, Mrs R
Embrey, Mrs J
Emery, Mrs L
Emmott, Mrs
Evans, Mrs J
Everett, Mrs
Eyles, Mr A

Firth, Mrs L
Flower, Mrs
Fookes, Mr A
Fookes, Mrs F
Fookes, Mr J
Fookes, Mrs M
Foster, Mr P
Foster, Mrs R
Fountaine, Mrs
French, Mr R

Gammage, Mrs E
Garfirth, Mr
George, Mr A
Gibson, Mrs M

Gidley, Mr H
Giles, Mrs
Glanister, Mrs
Glenister, Mrs S
Goff, Mr J
Golby, Mr F
Goodall, Mrs
Goodman, Mrs F
Gray, Mrs
Grimes, Mrs A
Grimes, Mr R

Hamer, Mr F
Hamer, Mrs M
Hancock, Mrs J
Hart, Mr J
Hassett, Mrs J
Haynes, Miss C
Higgs, Mr E
Hill, Mrs R
Hollowell, Mr E
Hollowell, Mrs J
Howlett, Mr C

Jenkinson, Mrs R
Jones, Mr A
Jones, Mr W

Knight, Mr

Lattimer, Miss M
Lay, Mr F
Lewis, Mr B
Lineham, Mrs M
Littlemore, Miss L

Index

Bold page numbers denote illustrations